Arab background series

Editor: N. A. Ziadeh, Emeritus Professor of History
American University of Beirut

Social Life Under the Abbasids

170–289 AH
786–902 AD

Muhammad Manazir Ahsan

Longman London and New York
Librairie du Liban

LONGMAN GROUP LTD
LONDON AND NEW YORK

Associated companies, branches, and representatives throughout the world

First published 1979
ISBN 0 582 78079 9

Ahsan, M M
Social life under the Abbasids.—(Arab background series)
1. Arabia—Social life and customs
I. Title II. Series
953'.02 DS215 78–40802
ISBN 0–582–78079–9

Typeset by CCC and printed and bound at William Clowes & Sons Limited Beccles and London

Contents

Acknowledgements

It is a pleasure to record my sincerest thanks and gratitude to all those who have contributed towards the preparation of the present thesis.

In the first place, with all sincerity and however inadequate the words, I should like to express my deep gratitude to my supervisor, Professor Bernard Lewis, without whose continued encouragement and valuable suggestions all efforts on my part would have proved unfructuous. Throughout my stay in Britain, I found in him a real friend and a sympathetic guide who was a source of great help during all these years, especially in the days of political crisis in my country.

I am also greatly indebted to Mr V. J. Parry of this School for his valuable assistance and suggestions. It is a pity that he did not live long enough to see this work in print.

Thanks are also due to Dr H. Rabie, Dr G. Fehrevari, Dr H. J. Fisher and Dr A. A. Rahmani, who helped me by their valuable suggestions and encouragement.

My thanks are also due to the librarians and staffs of the SOAS, the British Museum Library, the University of London Library, and the Bodleian Library, Oxford, for their willing help in making available books, manuscripts and microfilms.

Finally, I wish to record my thanks and gratitude to the publisher's editorial staff for the skill and care they have taken in the production of this book.

School of Oriental and
African Studies M. M. Ahsan

List of Abbreviations

Sources

Aghānī^{1}	*Kitāb al-Aghānī*, by Abū'l-Faraj al-Iṣfahānī, Bulaq edition
Aghānī^{2}	Ibid. *Dār al-Kutub Miṣriyya* edition
Arab Archery	*A Book on the Excellence of the bow and arrow and the description thereof*, trans. and ed. by N. A. Faris and R. P. Elmer
ʿArīb	*Ṣilat Taʾrīkh al-Ṭabarī*, by ʿArīb
Ashtor, *Prix*	*Histoire des prix et des salaires dans l'Orient mediéval*, by E. Ashtor
Āthār	*Āthār al-Bāqiya*, by Bīrūnī
Azdī, *Ḥikāyāt*	*Ḥikāyāt Abī'l-Qāsim al-Baghdādī*, by Azdī
Bayān	*Al-Bayān wa'l-Tabyīn*, by Jāḥiẓ
Bayzara	*Kitāb al-Bayzara* (attributed to Ḥasan b. al-Ḥusayn)
Buldān	*Kitāb al-Buldān*, by Yaʿqūbī
CONCORDANCE	*Concordance et Indices de la Tradition Musulmane* by A. J. Wensinek and others.
Dhakhāʾir	*Al-Dhakhāʾir wa'l-Tuḥaf*, by Ibn Zubayr
Diyārāt	*Kitāb al-Diyārāt*, by Shābushtī
DOZY, *Dictionnaire*	*Dictionnaire détaillé des noms des vêtements chez les Arabes* by R. P. A. Dozy
DOZY, *Suppl.*	*Supplément aux dictionnaires Arabes* by R. P. A. Dozy
Fakhrī	*Kitāb al-Fakhrī*, by Ibn Ṭiqṭiqa
Fihrist	*Al-Fihrist*, by Ibn Nadīm
Ḥayawān	*Kitāb al-Ḥayawān*, by Jāḥiẓ
Ḥilya	*Ḥilyat al-Fursān fī shiʿār al-shujʿān*, by Ibn Hudhayl
Ibn Ḥawqal	*Al-Masālik wa'l-Mamālik*, by Ibn Ḥawqal
ʿIqd	*Al-ʿIqd al-Farīd*, by Ibn ʿAbd Rabbih
Iʿtibār	*Kitāb al-Iʿtibār*, by Usāma b. Munqidh
Kāmil	*Taʾrīkh al-Kāmil*, by Ibn al-Athīr
Khaṭīb, *Taʾrīkh*	*Taʾrīkh Baghdād*, by al-Khaṭīb al-Baghdādī
Laṭāʾif	*Laṭāʾif al-Maʿārif*, by Thaʿālibī
Manṣūrī fi'l-Bayzara	*Kitāb al-Manṣūrī fi'l-Bayzara*, by Ḥashshāʾ Aḥmad

Maqāmāt	*Maqāmāt al-Ḥamadānī*
Maṣāyid	*Kitāb al-Maṣāyid wa'l-Maṭārid*, by Kushājim
Mercier, *Chasse*	*La Chasse et les sports chez les Arabes*, by L. Mercier
Mez	*Renaissance of Islam*, by Mez; Eng. tr.
Muḥāḍarāt	*Muḥāḍarāt al-Udabā'*, by Rāghib al-Iṣfahānī
Muntaẓam	*Al-Muntaẓam*, by Ibn al-Jawzī
Muq.	*Aḥsan al-Taqāsīm*, by Muqaddasī
Murūj	*Murūj al-Dhahab*, by Mas'ūdī
Nihāya	*Nihāyat al-Rutba fī ṭalab al-ḥisba*, by Shayzarī
Nishwār	*Nishwār al-Muḥāḍara*, by Tanūkhī
Nuwayrī	*Nihāyat al-Arab*, by Nuwayrī
Quṭub al-Surūr	*Quṭub al-Surūr fī awṣāf al-khumūr*, by al-Raqīq al-Nadīm
Rusūm	*Rusūm dār al-khilāfa*, by Hilāl al-Ṣābī
Saracen Archery	*Saracen Archery*, Engl. tr. by Latham and Peterson
Ṣubḥ	*Ṣubḥ al-A'shā*, by Qalqashandī
Ṣūlī	*Akhbār al-Rāḍī wa'l-Muttaqī*, by Ṣūlī
Ṣūlī, *Awrāq*	*Kitāb al-Awrāq*, by Ṣūlī
Ṭabarī	*Ta'rīkh al-Rusul wa'l-Mulūk*, by Ṭabarī
Ṭabīkh	*Kitāb al-Ṭabīkh*, by Baghdādī
Tajārib	*Tajārib al-Umam*, by Miskāwayh
Thimār	*Thimār al-Qulūb*, by Tha'ālibī
Tuḥaf	*Al-Tuḥaf wa'l-Hadāya*, by Khālidiyyān
'Uyūn	*'Uyūn al-Akhbār*, by Ibn Qutayba
Wafayāt	*Wafayāt al-A'yān*, by Ibn Khallikān
Warrāq	*Al-Ṭabīkh wa iṣlāḥ al-aghdhiya al-ma'kūlāt*, by Naṣr b. Sayyār al-Warrāq
Wuṣlā	*Al-Wuṣlā ilā al-ḥabīb fī waṣf al-ṭayyibāt wa'l-ṭīb*, by Ibn al-'Adīm
Ya'qūbī	*Ta'rīkh*, by Ya'qūbī
Yāqūt, *Buldān*	*Mu'jam al-Buldān*, by Yāqūt al-Rūmī

Periodicals

AI	*Ars Islamica*
AESC	*Annales Économiques, Sociétés, Civilisation*
AIEO	*Annales de l'Institut des études Orientales de l'Université d'Alger*
BCA	*Bulletin of the College of Arts* (*Majallat Kulliyat al-Ādāb*, Baghdad)
BSOAS	*Bulletin of the School of Oriental and African Studies*

EHR	*The Economic History Review*
EI[1]	*Encyclopaedia of Islam*, 1st edition
EI[2]	Ibid. 2nd edition
HJ	*Historia Judaica*
IC	*Islamic Culture*
IQ	*Islamic Quarterly*
JAH	*Journal of Asian History*
JAOS	*Journal of the American Oriental Society*
JBBRAS	*Journal of the Bombay Branch of the Royal Asiatic Society*
JASB	*Journal & Proceedings of the Asiatic Society, Bengal*
JEH	*Journal of Economic History*
JESHO	*Journal of the Economic and Social History of the Orient*
JRAS	*Journal of the Royal Asiatic Society*
MGT	*Majalla Ghurfa al-Tijāra*, Baghdad
MMII	*Majallat al-Majmaʿ al-ʿIlmī al-ʿIrāqī*
MW	*The Muslim World*
RAAD	*Majallat al-Majmaʿ al-ʿIlmī al-ʿArabī*
REI	*Revue des Études Islamiques*
RSO	*Rivista degli studi orientali*
SI	*Studia Islamica*
SO	*Studia Orientalia*
ZDMG	*Zeitschrift der Deutschen Morgenländischen Gesellschaft*

Editor's Preface

The Arab World has, for some time, been attracting the attention of a growing public throughout the world. The strategic position of the Arab countries, the oil they produce, their sudden emancipation and emergence as independent states, their revolutions and *coups d'état*, have been the special concern of statesmen, politicians, businessmen, scholars and journalists, and of equal interest to the general public.

An appreciation of the present-day problems of Arab countries and of their immediate neighbours demands a certain knowledge of their geographical and social background; and a knowledge of the main trends of their history—political, cultural and religious—is essential for an understanding of current issues. Arabs had existed long before the advent of Islam in the seventh century AD, but it was with Islam that they became a world power. Arab civilization, which resulted from the contacts the Arabs had with other peoples and cultures, especially after the creation of this world power, and which reached its height in the ninth, tenth and eleventh centuries, was, for a few centuries that followed, the guiding light of a large part of the world. Its rôle cannot, thus, be ignored.

The Arab Background Series provides the English-speaking, educated reader with a series of books which attempt to clarify the historical past of the Arabs and to analyse their present problems. The contributors to the series, who come from many parts of the world, are all specialists in their own fields. This variety of approach and attitude creates for the English-speaking reader a unique picture of the Arab World.

N. A. ZIADEH

Author's Note

Transliteration
The system of transliteration from Arabic is adopted from the *Encyclopaedia of Islam*, Second Edition, with the variations that *dj* is replaced by *j*, and *ḳ* by *q*. Arabic names which have a form generally accepted in English have been used in that form.

Dates
For the sake of conciseness, dates have normally been given in the AH notation; where AD is used, it is marked as such, except where no confusion could possibly arise.

Illustrations
Since hardly any piece of illustration from the third century AH is available, we were obliged to take recourse to paintings of considerably later periods, mainly from the *Maqāmāt al-Ḥarīrī*. Though these pictures have been painted some three or four hundred years later than the period considered by the present study, they represent quite remarkably the social life of the early Abbasid period as well.

The Publishers wish to thank the staff of the Library of the School of Oriental and African Studies, University of London for their kindness and valuable assistance in loaning material for the illustrations used in this book

List of Illustrations

Chapter 1

Survey of the Sources

We have drawn upon a very wide range of source material for the compilation of this work. This diversity of sources has been necessitated by the nature of the topic investigated. The social life of a period is portrayed in the writings of its historians and geographers, its poets and *adīb* (essayists), its writers of proverbs and anecdotes, its lawyers and jurists, its bureaucrats and scribes, its biographers and its natural scientists. We have drawn upon the work of such men and have also incorporated material from manuals on *ḥisba* and culinary art, and from treatises on such matters as hunting, falconry, and *furūsiyya* (chivalry).

An important problem has been the assessment of the comparative reliability of the various sources. Generally speaking, sources on the life of the caliphs, their court and the *ulema* (scholars), tend to be more reliable and better authenticated. The *adab* literature and works describing social practices prevalent among the downtrodden and the middle classes tend to be written with less scruple as regards standards or criteria of historical authenticity, and sometimes with the aim of ridiculing the uncouth manners of the socially inferior groups. However, in the absence of better alternatives such sources have proved invaluable to us in our investigation.

The different types of sources are discussed below in some detail.

Adab literature (Belles-lettres)

Adab literature dealing with general ethics, worldly wisdom and etiquette was brought to Abbasid Iraq mainly by scribes of Persian origin who sought to give moral instruction and lay down rules of conduct for different social groups.[1] The third century AH represents a "Golden Age" of *adab* literature. The most conspicuous place attained in this field was by the encyclopaedic writer Al-Jāḥiẓ, Abū ʿUthmān ʿAmr b. Baḥr al-Baṣrī al-Muʿtazilī (born 160; died 255).[2] He was one of the first Muslim writers to show a great deal of interest in social problems. With his critical power of observation and appreciation he succeeded in recognizing the changes that were taking place in the social fabric of the Abbasids as a result of the active growth of an urban system of life. He was the first Abbasid author to notice the formation and development of a middle class resulting from the economic organization that prevailed in the towns of Abbasid Iraq.[3] The transformation of a semi-agrarian, semi-pastoral economy into a commercial economy was among the most profound changes that occurred during the Abbasid period. Abbasid Iraq represents a dramatic economic metamorphosis for the land of the Tigris and the Euphrates. A number of important urban centres were developed, trade and commerce thrived, new organizations developed such as craft guilds, trader and merchant associations. All this resulted in a fundamental re-orientation of the structure of the economy, with revolutionary effects on social mobility and on the whole fabric of social relationships in general.[4]

In the series of tracts and epistles by Jāḥiẓ, written in a sonorous and witty style of an unequalled linguistic vigour and variety, one would find most of the social changes and tensions of his time. In his prolific writings he makes occasional remarks about the correct language of true beduins and its gradual corruption through the vicinity of towns, about the patois of the lower orders, the cant of pedlars, the argot of beggars, the technical terms of traders and professions,

[1] *EI*², s.v. *Adab* (F. Gabrieli); cf. also Ch. Pellat, *Life and works of Jāḥiẓ*, (English translation by D. M. Hawke, 1969) p. 23

[2] For his life and contributions see Ch. Pellat, op. cit; idem, Djāḥiẓ in *EI*², and the sources quoted there. See also Wadiʿa Taha Najim, "Studies on the writings of Al-Jāḥiẓ", Ph.D. thesis, SOAS, 1958

[3] Duri, *Taʾrīkh al-ʿIrāq al-Iqtiṣādī*, p. 108

[4] Cf. Goitein, *Studies*, pp. 217–241; Lassner, *Topography of Baghdad*, pp. 121–188

and also about mispronunciation and faulty speech on the one hand and euphemism and mannerism on the other. Jāḥiẓ, himself being a man of the third century and not belonging to the court office, offers us reliable and contemporary data on various aspects of social life which have enabled us to undertake the present study. Others have been equally indebted to Jāḥiẓ's work. Ṭāhā Ḥusain, for example, rightly observed that "if one wants to visualize the life of the third century AH one should not look for it in al-Buḥturī, or Abū Tammām, or any other poets, but one will find it in al-Jāḥiẓ."[5]

Born in Basra, Jāḥiẓ spent most of his time in Baghdad and Samarra, without losing contact with his native and favourite town Basra. This is why Basra appears to be the continuous thread running through all his works. Though he adhered to the Muʿtazilī group,[6] he was above mere sectarian prejudice and his writings do not appear to be coloured with factional antagonism. His *Kitāb al-Bayān wa'l-Tabyīn* ("Elegance of expression and clarity of exposition") offers, for example, valuable data on the mode of costume of the people. He declares that every group of people had a specific dress with compulsory headgear, *ʿimāma*: a statement not to be found in such unequivocal terms in other contemporary or nearly contemporary writers.[7] According to his information, *ʿimāma* was the crown of the Arabs, and people from all walks of life habitually wore it on their heads.[8]

His book *Al-Bukhalā'*, written towards the end of his life, which is more imaginative than factual, is a portrait gallery.[9] Supplemented by humorous anecdotes of a piquancy all their own and unique in Arabic literature, the book is designed to demonstrate that Arabs excel in generosity, whereas non-Arabs are inclined to be niggardly. His acute power of observation, his light-hearted scepticism, his comic sense and

---

[5] Ṭāhā Ḥusain, *Ḥadīth al-Arbaʿa*, Cairo, 1948, ii, p. 130

[6] A sect of Islam which required a rational interpretation of all beliefs.

[7] There are, however, some traditions which stress that turbans should form an article of dress of a Muslim. Cf. *Concordance*. s.v. *ʿimāma*; see also, M. Canard, *AIEO*, viii, 200ff. It is only in the seventh century that Ibn Khallikān (d. 681) notes that the Qāḍī Abū Yūsuf was the first man to recommend specific dress for the *ulema* and other officials. Cf. *Wafayāt*, xi, p. 38

[8] Jāḥiẓ, *Bayān*, iii, p. 114

[9] *EI*[2], s.v. *Djāḥiẓ* (Ch. Pellat); idem, *Life and works of Jāḥiẓ*, pp. 25–26

satirical turn of mind fit him admirably to portray human types and society, which he did, generally keeping within the bounds of decency.[10] This book of Jāḥiẓ is a treasure-trove of information on the food and dietary habits of various groups of people living in early Abbasid society. One would not find such details about the food of the common people, table manners and similar information even in the culinary manuals surviving from the Abbasid period. *Al-Bukhalā'* also throws light on costume, house rents and prices of commodities of the third century AH.

His monumental work *Al-Ḥayawān* ("Animals") is not merely a zoological lexicon but a mixture of theology, metaphysics and sociology where one can even find embryonic theories (although it is impossible to say how far they are original) of the evolution of species, of the influence of climate, and of animal psychology. In his own peculiar style, the author takes certain animals and sets out verses, anecdotes and traditions concerning them.[11] Because of the voluminous nature of the work, the book offers us a mass of raw materials on diverse subjects which one has to scrutinize and utilize carefully. *Animals* has offered us a great deal of material on hunting, food, games and sports, and economic matters such as prices. It is not in *Al-Tabaṣṣur bi'l-Tijāra* but in *Al-Ḥayawān* that one would find price quotations of animals and some other commodities. Speaking on pigeons, for example, he reveals that "pigeons have such high intrinsic value and such superiority that a single bird may sell for 500 dinars; no other animal can command such a price, neither the goshawk, the peregrine falcon, the saker, the eagle, the pheasant, the cock, the camel, the ass nor the mule . . . You will find that a young male pigeon of good pedigree will fetch 20 dinars or more, a female 10 dinars or more and an egg 5 dinars."[12] This is but one example of numerous interesting passages contained in *Al-Ḥayawān* by Jāḥiẓ. The prices quoted by Jāḥiẓ may be exaggerated, but we are not in a position to check them as no other source, either contemporary

---

[10] In itself a remarkable feat, given contemporary standards.

[11] *EI*², s.v. *Djāḥiẓ* (Ch. Pellat); idem, *Life and works of Jāḥiẓ*, Eng. Tr. p. 21

[12] *Ḥayawān*, iii, p. 212. The passage is translated in Pellat, *Life and works of Jāḥiẓ*, p. 150

or nearly contemporary, contains such information.[13] In this sense, Jāḥiẓ's information on numerous topics is unique and unchallengeable.

Though the material given by Jāḥiẓ is of high merit, it is not to be taken as infallible. In his rhetorical and humorous style he often fell a victim to exaggeration, and he made some obviously erroneous statements. His remarks on animal psychology[14] and on the specialization of particular trades by certain groups are faulty and should be scrutinized with extreme caution.

The literary *adab* made fashionable by Jāḥiẓ was systematized by a junior contemporary of his, Ibn Qutayba ʿAbd Allāh b. Muslim al-Dīnawarī (died 276), one of the great Sunni polygraphists of this period, being both a theologian and an *adīb*. His *adab* comprises an ethos and a culture in which are united the intellectual currents of Abbasid society of the early third century. It displays an intent to popularize the prevalent social norms and mannerisms among at least a certain literate public.[15] His *adab* has been described as "a kind of humanism",[16] for its egalitarian overtones and its general preoccupation with the problem of introducing the lower social groups into the mysteries of the so-called "higher culture". Unlike Ibn al-Muqaffaʿ and Jāḥiẓ, Ibn Qutayba introduced a prose whose dominant characteristic was ease and facility. His sentences are more simple, short and without artifice. Of his fourteen printed books, *Kitāb ʿUyūn al-Akhbār, Kitāb al-Maysir wa'l-Qidāḥ* and *Kitāb al-Ashriba* are of direct interest for this study. The chapter on food and the detailed information on costume and games in the *ʿUyūn al-Akhbār*—originally a large collection of *adab*—have been extensively used in this study. *Kitāb al-Ashriba*, devoted to fermented drinks, and *Al-Maysir wa'l-Qidāḥ*, a juridico-philological study on games of chance, throw sidelights on various aspects of social life. His other books (e.g., *Kitāb al-Maʿārif*, a

[13] Cf., for example, Ashtor, *Prix*, section, "Animal Prices"

[14] For example, that animals could be hunted by music: *Ḥayawān*, vi, pp. 471–72. On this point see below, Chapter 5, *Hunting*

[15] *Fihrist*, p. 121; Khaṭīb, *Ta'rīkh*, x, p. 170; Yāqūt, *Irshād*, i, p. 161f.; cf. also, *EI*[2], s.vv. *Ibn Ḳutayba* (G. Lecomte), *ʿArabiyya* (H. A. R. Gibb), *ʿIrāḳ* (Ch. Pellat)

[16] *EI*[2], s.v. *Ibn Ḳutayba* (G. Lecomte)

historical manual with encyclopaedic appendices on very varied subjects, *Adab al-Kātib, Kitāb al-Shi'r wa'l-Shu'arā'*) have also occasionally been consulted.

An Andalusian writer and poet who was born, lived and died at Cordova, Ibn 'Abd Rabbih (born 246, died 328),[17] astonishingly provided a great deal of material on contemporary Abbasid society. His monumental work on *adab* entitled *Al-'Iqd al-Farīd*, "The Unique Necklace", is apparently based on data drawn from the works of Jāḥiẓ, Ibn Qutayba, and others who had assembled the elements of Arab culture. The *'Iqd* is a sort of encyclopaedia of knowledge and general culture. The 6th, 7th, 22nd, 23rd, 24th and 25th chapters deal respectively with religious knowledge and the principles of good conduct (*adab*), with proverbs, the nature of man and of animals, food and drink, and diverse anecdotes; they are directly related to our study. A basic characteristic of this encyclopaedic work is that, apart from a portion of the *urjuza*, it contains very little of Andalusian origin, and aims at presenting the social and cultural practices of Abbasid Iraq to an Andalusian audience.[18]

In his anthology of verse and prose entitled *Kitāb al-Muwashshā*, the well-known litterateur Abū Ṭayyab Muḥammad b. Isḥāq, known as Al-Washshā' (died 325),[19] gives us a vivid description of a social group known as *Ẓurafā'*: people of elegant and sophisticated taste. In his typical style, Washshā' enumerates the habits of elegant people in matters of their dress, food, drink, table manners and social conduct. While concentrating on the traditions relating to the dandies of Baghdad, he occasionally mentions as a contrast the common people and their behaviour in society. Under such headings as food and dress of the elegant, he explicitly distinguishes between the tastes of the common people on the one hand and of the élite on the other. Washshā' is, therefore,

---

[17] See for his biography and literary appreciation, *EI*², s.v. *Ibn 'Abd Rabbih* (C. Brockelmann) and the sources quoted there, in particular the introductory note given by the editor of *Al-'Iqd al-Farīd*

[18] *EI*², s.v. *Ibn 'Abd Rabbih* (C. Brockelmann)

[19] *Irshād*, vi, pp. 277f.; Khaṭīb, *Ta'rīkh*, i, p. 253; *GAL*, i, p. 124; *Suppl.* i, p. 189; cf. also *EI*², s.v. *'Irāḳ* (Ch. Pellat); *EI*¹, s.v. *al-Washshā'* (C. Brockelmann); F. Rosenthal, *Humour in early Islam*, p. 71, n. 1.; *SI*, xi, pp. 39ff.

an indispensable source for the Baghdādī society of the late third and early fourth century AH.

The fourth-century bellettrist (*adīb*), a great admirer and imitator of Jāḥiẓ, Abū Ḥayyān al-Tawḥīdī (died 414) was a capable recorder of contemporary intellectual life, with an interest in social affairs.[20] Though Al-Tawḥīdī does not belong to our period of study, his information on food and labouring classes contained especially in his masterpiece *Kitāb al-Imtā' wa'l-Mu'ānasa* is of great value. The material derived from this book shows that the food habits of the people living in the fourth century underwent almost no change from the third century onward. His *Kitāb al-Baṣā'ir wa'l-Dhakhā'ir* contains invaluable material on the economic and social status of the lower professional groups such as cuppers, building workers, sailors, *ṭufayliyūn* (parasites who lived largely by attending functions to which they had not been invited).

The versatile genius Al-Tha'ālibī (350 to 429) though not an *adab* writer in the strict sense, was a writer with wide interests in cultural and social problems.[21] His encyclopaedic work *Laṭā'if al-Ma'ārif* is in fact a mine of information on diverse topics, among which social topics are prominent. The excellent English translation of the book by Professor C. E. Bosworth has increased the value of the book in many ways. Materials contained in his other books will be discussed in other groups of work.

Another powerful writer, with a style equalling that of Ibn Qutayba and indeed of Jāḥiẓ, was the fifth-century writer Al-Rāghib al-Iṣfahānī (died about 502).[22] His popular book *Muḥāḍarāt al-udabā' wa muḥāwarāt al-shu'arā' wa al-bulaghā'*, as is evident from the title, is a collection of miscellaneous topics drawn from Arab poetry and history, politics and rhetoric, anthologies and collections of anecdotes, and popular ethics. Though written in the late fifth century,

---

[20] For a study on Tawḥīdī, see *EI*², s.v. *Abū Ḥayyān al-Tawḥīdī* (S. M. Stern) and the sources listed there; see also *EI*², s.vv. *'Arabiyya* (by H. A. R. Gibb), and *'Irāḳ* (by Ch. Pellat)

[21] On Tha'ālibī, see *EI*², s.vv. *'Arabiyya* (H. A. R. Gibb); *'Irāḳ* (Ch. Pellat); *EI*¹, s.v. Tha'ālibī (C. Brockelmann); cf. also, Professor Bosworth's long introductory note in *Latā'if's* English translation

[22] *EI*², s.v. *Al-Rāghib al-Iṣbahānī* (C. Brockelmann)

the *Muḥāḍarāt al-Udabā'* contains sufficient information on the social life of the early Abbasid period. It gives considerable detail of the social life of the lower professions, and supplies information on social and economic developments that had occurred in Abbasid Iraq since the days of Jāḥiẓ.

The work of scholars from Jāḥiẓ to Rāghib al-Iṣfahānī provides us with an opportunity to study the evolution of Abbasid culture over a period of 300 years. Perhaps no other mediaeval civilization can be studied over such a long span of time, as large gaps separate the findings of the scholars whose work has reached us.

Anecdotal and narrative literature

Though anecdotes and stories are contained in almost every writing of bellettrists, some writers have devoted special attention to producing anecdotal literature, a literature not merely entertaining but incorporating a portrayal of society and civilization. In the course of our discussion on Jāḥiẓ we have already mentioned his *Kitāb al-Bukhalā'*. Here we may introduce the anecdotal and narrative writings of Abu'l-Faraj al-Iṣfahānī, Tanūkhī, Azdī, *Ḥamadānī*, Ibn al-Jawzī and Khaṭīb al-Baghdādī.

The Arab historian, litterateur and poet Abu'l-Faraj al-Iṣfahānī's (born 284, died after 360) voluminous compilation entitled *Kitāb al-Aghānī* (Book of Songs) is an indispensable source for the social history of the early Abbasid period.[23] An estimate of Iṣfahānī's talents and of his writings, by his junior contemporary Al-Tanūkhī, would not be without interest here. "I never found," he says, "a person knowing by heart such a quantity as he did of poems, songs, historical accounts, anecdotes of ancient times, authentic narratives and genealogies; besides which he possessed information on other sciences, such as philosophy, grammar, story-telling, biography and the history of Muslim conquests; he was acquainted with the branches of knowledge requisite for a boon-

[23] *EI²*, s.v. *Abu'l-Faradj al-Iṣbahānī* (M. Nallino); see in particular Nabih Akil's thesis on the social life of the Umayyads in the light of *Aghānī*; cf. also *EI²*, s.vv. *'Arabiyya* (H. A. R. Gibb) and *'Iraḳ* (Ch. Pellat)

companion, such as falconry, farriery, the preparation of beverages, a smattering of medicine and astrology."[24]

It must be remembered however that Iṣfahānī lived a life worthy of any wooer of Bacchus and worshipper of Venus. He was an admirer of song, of the cup and the dance. He has even acknowledged his preference for "young boys".[25] From the religious point of view he was a pro-Shī'ite. In order to accept or reject a statement from the *Aghānī*, one should look into its sources, a perusal of which would reveal that the author used three different sources of information: oral narrations, written books, and written narratives. As the *Kitāb al-Aghānī* is not a religious study, there is no reason why it should not be given its proper place among writings on social history. If one excludes minor discrepancies, contradictions and historical faults, Iṣfahānī's *Kitāb al-Aghānī*, comprising 21 volumes, stands as an important source for a graphic picture of Arab civilization from its very first days down to the end of the third century. Since Iṣfahānī was a nearly contemporary author, his information on the third century is more reliable and less defective from the point of view of the sources. His materials on the gay life at the caliphal court, especially of Hārūn al-Rashīd, where convivial parties with caliphs, high officials, boon-companions, poets, singers and dancers dominated the scene, would seem far from erroneous. Apart from the material on literary criticism, Arabic music and songs, and the court life of the Umayyads and early Abbasids, the *Aghānī* contains much scattered information of great value on such subjects as food, clothing, sports, festivities, houses and furniture, business and commerce. Indeed the *Book of Songs* is sometimes so detailed in its information on social aspects that it is possible to write some of the chapters of early Muslim social history based mainly on the material to be found in this voluminous book of Iṣfahānī.[26] A few examples of such interesting material

---

[24] *Wafayāt*, ii, p. 250; to this the high regard shown by the following scholars should be added: Tha'ālibī, *Yatīma*, iii, p. 109; *Irshād*, v, p. 152; Khaṭīb, *Ta'rīkh*, xi, p. 400

[25] *Irshād*, v, pp. 158–9, 167

[26] See, for example, the Ph.D. thesis of Nabih Akil on Umayyad social life, entitled "Studies in the social history of the Umayyad period as revealed in the *Kitāb al-Aghānī*", SOAS, 1960

will perhaps be of interest here. An anecdote, relating to the late second century, mentions that a well-dressed man requires three items of clothing to walk outdoors: the *durrāʿa* as the top-coat; the *jubba* as the middle garment; and the *qamīṣ* as the undergarment which touches the skin.[27] In another anecdote, belonging to the third century, Iṣfahānī describes the difference between a *qamīṣ* and a *qabā'* by saying that when a man tears his *qamīṣ* from the opening below the neck (the *jayb*) to the foot, it becomes a *qabā'*.[28]

Another of Iṣfahānī's books, written on the tragic history of the ʿAlīds and entitled *Maqātil al-Ṭālibīn*, is not related to our study and therefore has not been used extensively.

Al-Tanūkhī, Al-Muḥassin b. ʿAlī b. Muḥammad (327 to 384), a *qāḍī* by profession and a courtier of Muhallabī and ʿAḍud al-Dawla,[29] was the author of some brilliant works containing material for the social history of the second half of the third and the first half of the fourth century. His monumental book *Nishwār al-Muḥāḍara* (originally contained in 10 volumes, but surviving only in three volumes) is a portrayal of the social life of the Iraqi people.

His *Nishwār*, like two other books, *Al-Mustajād min faʿlāt al-ajwād* and *Al-Faraj baʿd al-shidda*, is, in the form of entertaining stories, rich in detailed information on food, costume, prices of commodities, estates, games and sports, feasts and festivities, the gay life of the caliphal court, and the social position of various groups of people living in Abbasid society. He seems to be more cautious in accepting narrators than his teacher Abu'l-Faraj al-Iṣfahānī, and more comprehensive than his other teacher, Ṣūlī. Apart from personal experiences, Tanūkhī derived his materials from oral traditions, from his father and learned scholars and savants (*mashā'ikh*, *ʿulamā'* and *udabā'*), from literary sources, and a great deal from secretaries and judges.[30] His choice of sources and his citing of a full chain of transmitters lend weight and credence to his writings.

[27] *Aghānī*[1], xxi, p. 150

[28] Ibid, vii, p. 134. And see below, Chapter 2, *Costume*, pp. 36–7, 41

[29] *EI*[1], s.v. *Al-Tanūkhī* (R. Paret); *EI*[2], s.v. *ʿIrāḳ* (Ch. Pellat); Margoliouth, *The Table Talk of a Mesopotamian Judge*, Preface, pp. v–vii. Cf. also Badrī Fahd, *Al-Qāḍī al-Tanūkhī wa Kitāb al-Nishwār*, Baghdad, 1966, p. 7ff.

[30] See the preface of the *Nishwār*

Being inspired by Jāḥiẓ, the fourth-century prose-writer Muḥammad b. Aḥmad Abū'l-Muṭahhar al-Azdī created a new genre in the field of prose by delineating in his *Ḥikāyāt Abī'l-Qāsim al-Baghdādī* a satirical but realistic picture of life and manners in Baghdad.[31] For our study of the social life of the early Abbasid period, Azdī offers us a good deal of material on the food, drink and furniture of the Baghdādī and Iṣfahānī houses. It corroborates the data given by Washshā' on the refined culture of Baghdad and contains a volume of additional information not available in other sources.[32]

Another specimen of anecdotal literature, somewhat different from other narrative literature but forming a part of social history, is the *Maqāmāt* of the Arabo-Persian writer Badī' al-Zamān al-Ḥamadānī[33] (358 to 398). The theme of the *Maqāmāt* or "seances" of Ḥamadānī, like that of Ḥarīrī, is, as seen by Professor Gibb, "firmly rooted in the common life of the Islamic city, and portrays its manners and its humours so realistically as to constitute one of the most precious social documents of the Islamic Middle Ages."[34] Since Ḥarīrī (died 516) is a very late source, we have tried to draw some material from Ḥamadānī, who is nearly contemporary with our period. Ḥamadānī's *Maqāma Maḍīriyya* and *Maqāma Baghdādiyya* are of special interest for our study as they reveal fascinating information on food, food shops, houses, and other fields of social interest.

The anecdotal and humorous writings of the Sunnī Ḥanbalite Ibn al-Jawzī[35] (died 597) and those of al-Khaṭīb al-Baghdādī[36] (died 463), though belonging to the later Abbasid

---

[31] *EI*², s.vv. *Abu'l-Ḳāsim* (J. Horovitz); *Ḥikāya, 'Irāk* (Ch. Pellat)

[32] Cf., for example, the information on the Abbādānī mats which could be folded like cloth: Azdī, *Ḥikāyāt*, p. 36

[33] On Ḥamadānī, see *EI*², s.vv. *al-Ḥamadhānī* (R. Blachère); *Ḥikāya* and *al-'Irāḳ* (Ch. Pellat); see also, W. Prendergast, *The Maqāmāt of Badī' al-Zamān*, Madras–London, 1915; on the historical authenticity of the *Maqāmāt*, see Māzin Mubārak, in *RAAD*, 43–45 (1968–70) in six series, "*Mujtama' al-Ḥamadhānī fī khilāl . . .*"

[34] *EI*², s.v. *'Arabiyya* (H. A. R. Gibb)

[35] *EI*², s.v. *Ibn al-Djawzī* (H. Laoust) and the extensive bibliography quoted there

[36] On Khaṭīb Baghdādī see *EI*¹, s.v. (W. Marçais); cf. also Muniruddin Ahmad, *Muslim Education and the scholars' social status up to the 5th century Muslim era in the light of Ta'rīkh Baghdād.*; also, J. Lassner, *The Topography of Baghdad*; and Maleeḥa Raḥmatullāh, *The women of Baghdad in the*

period, are veritable repositories of all sorts of interesting information on diverse aspects of social life. Ibn al-Jawzī's *Akhbār al-Ḥumaqā wa'l-Mughaffalīn, Akhbār al-Ẓirāf, Kitāb al-Adhkiyā', Dhamm al-Hawā, Talbīs Iblīs* all deal with the social life of the Abbasid period until the end of the twelfth century AD. These writings also present some valuable economic data not to be found in other sources. Khaṭīb Baghdādī's *Kitāb al-Bukhalā'* (no equal with Jāḥiẓ's *Bukhalā'* either in style or in content) and *Al-Taṭfīl* contain a number of interesting tales of social life, ranging from the rise of Islam to his own period, the eleventh century AD. Unlike Ibn al-Jawzī's writings, Baghdādī's monographs are not comprehensive, and are limited to two groups of people: the misers and the *ṭufayliyūn* (parasites).

The collections of *Thousand and one Nights* are fictitious, and contain very little historical authenticity. For these reasons we have avoided utilizing materials buried in these fairy tales.

Collections of proverbs

The Arabic proverbs, excelling in wisdom, wit and acute observation, couched in comparatively easy language and clad in similes of general human character, are treasures for contemporary classical society, and some are of particular importance because they are confined to certain localities, social groups and communities.[37] The topic of the present-day Arabic proverb as a testimony to the social history of the Middle East has been vividly discussed by Professor Goitein in one of his masterly essays; the topic also reveals the importance of the classical Arabic proverbs for mediaeval Muslim social history.[38]

Al-Maydānī's (died 518) comprehensive collection of proverbs *Amthāl al-'Arab*, Al-Ṭālaqānī's (c. 421) *Risāla al-*

9–10th centuries as revealed in the History of Baghdad of al-Khaṭīb, Baghdad, 1963

[37] *EI*[1], s.v. *Mathāl* (C. Brockelmann); Goitein, *Studies*, pp. 361–379. Cf. also, M. A. J. Begg, *The social history of the labouring classes in 'Iraq under the 'Abbasids*, Ph.D. thesis, Cambridge, 1971, Chap. *Survey of the Sources*, section, "Proverbs and proverbial phrases"

[38] Goitein, *Studies*, pp. 361–379

Amthāl al-Baghdādiyya allatī tajrī bain al-ʿĀmma, and Thaʿālibī's *Thimār al-Qulūb* and *Tamthīl al-Muḥāḍara*, on the collections of proverbs, maxims and dicta, and the chapters on proverbs contained in *adab* literature (e.g., Ibn Qutayba's *ʿUyūn*; Ibn ʿAbd Rabbih's *ʿIqd*) together with De Goeje's lists of the proverbs occurring in the *Taʾrīkh* of Ṭabarī, *Kitāb al-Aghānī* of Iṣfahānī and other classical texts, are mines of information on social, cultural and political events of the period concerned. Quotation of only a few such proverbs would suffice to prove this fact. "Heavier than the rent of the house" (*Athqal min kirāʾ al-dār*) recorded by Ṭālaqānī,[39] reveals that the housing problem in Abbasid society was acute and that the rent was exorbitant, a fact corroborated by the statements of the third, fourth, and fifth-century writers.[40] Though the phrase does not explain the period in question, it can be applied on the basis of other corroborative evidence from the third to the fifth centuries alike. "Apples of Syria", "Figs of Ḥulwān", "Mulḥam of Khurāsān", "Melons of Khwārazm"[41] not only express the proverbial speciality of a particular locality but also explain the excessive demands for these commodities everywhere, with the refinement of taste and culture of Abbasid society. "Gluttony diminishes wisdom" (*Al-biṭna tudhhab al-fiṭna*),[42] and "A table without vegetables is like an old man devoid of wisdom" (*Al-māʾida bilā baql ka-shaykh bilā ʿaql*)[43] are indicative of the awareness of dietetics and the evil effects of gluttony, and of the importance of vegetables in the daily diet of the people. These examples make it clear that the proverbial sayings constitute important source material for the study of the social life of the Abbasids.

Poetical literature

That the poetry is the *dīwān* (register) of the Arabs does not hold good for the Abbasid period. From the third century

---

[39] Ṭālaqānī, *Amthāl*, p. 7, No. 77

[40] See below, Chapter Four, *Housing*

[41] *Laṭāʾif*, pp. 156, 183, 237, 238; *Thimār*, pp. 531, 536

[42] Jāḥiẓ, *Bayān*, ii, p. 81; Ibn Qutayba, *ʿUyūn*, iii, p. 219

[43] Rāghib, *Muḥāḍarāt*, ii, p. 612. According to Thaʿālibī (*Thimār*, p. 609) vegetables are the "Ornaments of the table" (*Ḥilyat al-khiwān*).

onward poetry was displaced from its former social function by the new prose literature.[44] Nevertheless, the *dīwāns* of the third and fourth-century poets preserve many interesting traits of social history in an indirect form.[45] The witty and humorous verses of Abū Dulāma, a court jester in the palaces of Saffāḥ, Manṣūr and Mahdī (died 160 or 170)[46] contained in *Aghānī*, Ṭabarī, Masʿūdī and other writers are interesting and useful. It is to him that we owe, among other things, the knowledge of the introduction of the tall head-gear and other official marks introduced by the Caliph Manṣūr.[47]

The *dīwān* of Abū Nuwās (died in Baghdad between 198 and 200) contains for the first time in Arabic literature, together with panegyric poems, acrimonious satirical poems, funeral odes and drinking songs, a special chapter containing hunting poems (*ṭardiyyāt*). The so-called *zuhdiyāt* (ascetic) poems of Abu'l-ʿAtāhiya (died 213), written in lucid and simple style,[48] also throw some light on contemporary society. The collection of verses of Buḥturī (died 284), Ibn al-Rūmī (died 283), the Abbasid prince Ibn al-Muʿtazz (died 296), and the encyclopaedic writer Kushājim (died 360), all throw some light on contemporary social life from different angles.

Historical literature

The contemporary historian Ibn Jarīr al-Ṭabarī (died 310) is an eye-witness of the events occurring during the latter half of the third century. Since his main interest was to record "the History of the Prophets and Kings", one would not expect a great deal of material on the social aspects of life. Except for some passing remarks and incidental records of topics of social interest, it contains almost nothing on the social history of the early Abbasid period. Nevertheless he records the court life with comparative detail and gives some economic data

44 *EI*², s.v. *ʿArabiyya* (H. A. R. Gibb)

45 Cf. B. Lewis, "Sources for the Economic History of the Middle East", in *Studies in the Economic History* . . ., p. 92

46 *EI*², s.v. *Abū Dulāma* (J. Horovitz)

47 See, for example, *Aghānī*,² x, p. 236

48 For the life and literary assessment of Abu'l-ʿAtāhiya, see M. A. A. el-Kafrawy, "A Critical study of the poetry of Abu'l-ʿAtāhiya", Ph.D. thesis, SOAS, 1951–52

and some fragmentary information on social groups such as *fityān, ʿayyār, shuṭṭār.* On the life of the *dhimmīs* (non-Muslims), however, he has much to say, especially in respect of their dress, mounts and festivities[49]—material conspicuously missing from other contemporary and nearly contemporary sources.

His junior contemporary, a brilliant historian and a capable geographer, Masʿūdī (died 345 or 346), shows great interest in social life and records a volume of unique informative material in his *Murūj al-dhahab wa maʿādin al-jawhar.* Though he is not an eye-witness of the events of the third century, his narratives on the whole would seem credible and trustworthy. The details he gives, though in an indirect form, on the costume of the various groups of people, on the food habits of the rich and poor alike, on the pastimes of the caliphs, wazirs and high dignitaries, and on such other interesting topics, give him a unique place among Abbasid historians. To list but a few instances of his unique information would suffice here to prove his keen interest in social life. Speaking about the times of Mutawakkil, he reveals that the Caliph favoured a special type of fabric known as *mulḥam*; people imitated him widely, with the result that the fabric itself came to be known as "*thiyāb al-Mutawakkiliya*". He adds that this fabric was popular among the masses even during his own time (*c.* 332).[50] Speaking about the same Caliph he further notes that Mutawakkil introduced a new type of building style: the Hira style, which was largely followed.[51] Writing on costumes, he once remarked that the sleeve of the *qamīṣ* became so wide that it measured three spans (*ashbār*),[52] whereas the tall caps (*ṭawīla, danniyya*) of the qāḍīs became so popular among the masses that the Caliph Mustaʿīn had to issue orders confining their use to the qāḍī.[53] Speaking on the game of *shaṭranj* he remarks that a new type of play was introduced towards the end of the third century, which went by the name of *al-Jawāriḥiyya.*[54] The detailed description of the special gathering held at the bidding of the Caliph Mustakfī to discuss the favourite food of the period, and the

---

[49] Ṭabarī, iii, pp. 1389–90
[50] *Murūj*, vii, p. 190
[51] Ibid, vii, pp. 192–93
[52] Ibid, vii, p. 402
[53] Ibid, vii, p. 402
[54] Ibid, viii, p. 314

recording of poems on the topics of choice food,[55] otherwise found only partially in the *dīwāns* of the poets, make his writings all the more valuable and useful. Judging from all this, his minor faults, such as contradictory statements (cf. the report on the origin of *nard*[56]), are overshadowed by his invaluable, informative and unique materials on social history. For all these reasons, to call him a social historian would perhaps not be an overestimation.

The contemporary geographer and historian Yaʿqūbī (died 284) in his *History*, and Balādhurī (died 279) in his *Futūḥ al-Buldān* give no more than some random information about the social life of the early Abbasid period. Among the later historians, Ibn al-Athīr (died 630) and Ibn al-Jawzī (died 597) provide some socio-historical data about Abbasid Iraq. The surviving parts of Ibn al-Jawzī's *Muntaẓam*, comprising historical events of Baghdad and obituaries from 257 to 574, are richer as a source of information on social matters than the *Kāmil* of Ibn al-Athīr, written in the style of Ṭabarī.

Of much value and interest are contemporary local histories written by Ibn Abī Ṭāhir Ṭayfūr, and by Azdī. Ibn Abī Ṭāhir Ṭayfūr, the Baghdādī litterateur and historian (born in 204 in a family of Persian origin and died in 280) is the author of the famous *History of Baghdad* up to the reign of Muhtadī. Unfortunately his work is not extant except for the sixth section, dealing with the caliphate of Ma'mūn.[57] Though the work, as F. Rosenthal observes, "is a pioneering and highly successful effort in the field of political local historiography leaning heavily towards literary and cultural matters,"[58] it also throws many sidelights on the social life of the period concerned.

The *Ta'rīkh al-Mawṣil* of Abū Zakariyyā al-Azdī (died 334), "a highly creditable achievement of early Muslim historiography",[59] is, like his contemporary Masʿūdī's writings, a mine of information on various aspects of social interest not confined to Mawṣil but extending to Baghdad and other important Abbasid cities.

---

[55] Ibid, viii, pp. 392–406
[56] Ibid, i, pp. 157–58
[57] *EI*², s.v. *Ibn Abī Ṭāhir Ṭayfūr* (F. Rosenthal)
[58] Ibid.
[59] Ibid, s.v. *Al-Azdī* (F. Rosenthal)

Bureaucratic writings

The officials and the *kuttāb* (secretaries) in the Baghdādī court produced from the beginning of the 4th century onward a new type of historical writing[60] which may be called "secretarial historiography". Since these writers maintained close links with bureaucratic personnel, had easy access to the official documents and possessed intimate knowledge of the court gossip and the happenings of the inner circles, their treatises abound in interesting materials on statecraft and civil administration, and indirectly on various aspects of social life. Their information, especially the economic data on the salaries of the various officials, the annual budget of the caliphal court and the like, are quite reliable and of particular use for our present study.

A nearly contemporary member of the bureaucracy, Jahshiyārī (died 331), in his biographical type of chronicle *Kitāb al-Wuzarā' wa'l-Kuttāb*, tracing the history of the secretaries of state and the wazirs until 296, preserves some incidental but valuable data on social and economic life of the early Abbasid period. It is from him, for example, that we come to know about the court holidays of the early Abbasid caliphs.[61] However, the history of the secretaries is extant only up to Ma'mūn's time.[62]

The *kātib* (secretary) and *nadīm* (intimate companion) of the caliphs and the contemporary of Jahshiyārī was Abū Bakr b. Yaḥyā al-Ṣūlī (died 335 or 336).[63] His *Kitāb al-Awrāq* deals with various social aspects and is rich in poetic citations. His other book, dealing with the history of the Caliphs Rāḍī and Muttaqī, is of very little importance for our study except for some cursory remarks incidentally related to earlier periods.

An important fifth-century "secretarial historian" was Abu'l-Ḥusain Hilāl b. Muḥassin al-Ṣābī (died 448),[64] an officer in the Chancellery (*Dīwān al-Inshā'*). His *Rusūm dār al-khilāfa*, in which he quotes extensively from the personal

[60] *EI*[1], *Suppl.* s.v. *Ta'rīkh*, (H. A. R. Gibb)

[61] *Wuzarā'*, p. 166

[62] *EI*[2], s.v. *Al-Djahshiyārī* (D. Sourdel and the bibliography noted there)

[63] Mas'ūdī, *Tanbīh*, pp. 345, 352; Khaṭīb, *Ta'rīkh*, iii, pp. 427–32; *Irshād*, vii, pp. 36–37 etc.; see also *EI*[1], s.v. *Al-Ṣūlī* (I. Kratschkovsky)

[64] On Ṣābī, see *EI*[1], s.v. *Al-Ṣābī* (F. Krenkow) and the detailed bibliography listed there

experiences of his grandfather, a member of the bureaucracy, is of great significance to the study of this work. Among other matters, it throws some light on the feasts and festivals of the Abbasid court and on the official costume worn by the caliphs in their processions. Another of his books, entitled *Kitāb al-Wuzarā'*, the extant part of which is devoted to the early fourth-century wazirs ʿAlī b. ʿĪsā and Ibn al-Furāt, is a fund of economic and social data. In many respects he is unique in his information and supplements the data of Jahshiyārī and Ṣūlī.

Biographical literature

The biographical and encyclopaedic writings devoted to the life and works of individual authors throw many sidelights on the social affairs generally connected with an individual's life. The *Fihrist*, a biblio-biographical writing of Ibn Nadīm (died 385), the *Ta'rīkh Baghdād* of the Khaṭīb Baghdādī (died 463), the *Wafayāt al-Aʿyān* of Ibn Khallikān (died 681), the *Ta'rīkh al-Ḥukamā'* of Qifṭī (died 646), the *ʿUyūn al-Anbā'* of Ibn Abī ʿUṣaybiʿa (590–668), and the *Irshād al-Arīb* of Yāqūt (died 626) offer, within the framework of an individual's biography, a great deal of direct and indirect information on various aspects of social life. Though these writings were not compiled in the period with which our present study is concerned, yet their discussions on the lives of individuals belonging to the third century AH, with occasional references to social practices, are on the whole reliable and useful. These sources generally confirm the materials found in historical or *adab* literature, and at times furnish much additional and unique information which enhances the value of the biographical literature as source material for social history.[65]

Geographical and topographical literature

A great deal of material on socio-economic history can be had from the writings of the geographers and travellers of the

[65] B. Lewis, "Sources for the economic history . . ." in *Studies in the Economic History of the Middle East*, ed. M. A. Cook, London, 1970, pp. 91–92. Cf. also, H. A. R. Gibb, *Islamic biographical literature*, in B. Lewis and P. M. Holt, *Historians of the Middle East*, London, 1962, pp. 54–58

third and fourth centuries AH.[66] The *Kitāb al-Buldān* of Yaʿqūbī (284) is a primary source for the topography of Samarra, its buildings, markets and economic life. Though all the works edited and published by De Goeje in the *BCA* series contain various material on matters of social interest, the works of the fourth-century geographers, Ibn Ḥawqal (died 367) and Muqaddasī (died 355), entitled *Al-Masālik* or *Ṣūrat al-Arḍ*, and *Aḥsan al-Taqāsīm*, are of particular interest for our study of society. Both Ibn Ḥawqal and Muqaddasī drew upon the experiences of preceding geographers as well as on their own observation and study. They opened up a new vista in geographical writing and widened its scope to such an extent that now it included a variety of subjects ranging from physical features of the *iqlīm* (region) to mines, languages and races of peoples, customs and habits, religion and sects, character, weights and measures, and the territorial divisions, routes and distances.[67] The writings of these two authors have furnished us with detailed material on the production and trade of various lands, prices of the commodities, regional differences in the habits of food and clothing, housing and other interesting topics.

Of no less value is the encyclopaedic work of Yāqūt al-Rūmī (died 626) entitled *Muʿjam al-Buldān*. His geographical dictionary, although it dates from the late Abbasid period, is a repository of historical, economic, social, geographical and topographical material, and as such can be used to substantiate or supplement the material found in the earlier sources.

The topographical treatise of Ibn Mihmandār (*c.* third century) entitled *Faḍā'il Baghdād*, and the *Manāqib Baghdād* attributed to Ibn al-Jawzī (died 597) furnish data on the foundation of Baghdad, its population, a census on the basis of the number of baths in Baghdad, and other economic details. The material of Ibn Mihmandār on public baths and their personnel has been incorporated in the writings of the

---

66 *EI*², s.v. *Djughrāfiyā* (S. Maqbul Ahmad)

67 *EI*², s.vv. *Djughrāfiyā* (S. Maqbul Ahmad); *Ibn Ḥawḳal* (A. Miquel); cf. also Y. Kračkovskiy, *Arabskaya geografičekaya literatura* (vol. iv of his collected works) Moscow–Leningrad, 1957 Ar. tr. (chap. i–xvi published so far) by S. D. ʿUthmān Hāshim, Cairo, 1963; A. Miquel, *La géographie humaine du monde musulman jusqu'au milieu du xi. s.*, 1967

authors of the later Abbasid period (e.g., Ṣābī's *Rusūm*, and Tanūkhī's *Nishwār*).[68]

Ḥisba manuals

Ḥisba manuals written for the guidance of the *muḥtasib* (market inspector; the municipal officer) contain a wealth of information for our study. These manuals abound with insights into the economic and social life of the various groups of people.[69] The Zaidī manual of *ḥisba*[70] of the third century is interesting in the sense that it mentions various topics of social interest in a direct or indirect form. To this the *Aḥkām al-Sūq* of Yaḥyā b. ʿUmar of Cordova (third century) could be added for comparative study and be supplemented by Al-Shayzarī's (died 589) *Niḥāyat al-rutba fī ṭalab al-ḥisba* and Ibn al-Ukhuwwa's (died 729) *Maʿālim al-Qurba.* The material in these monographs is theoretical in nature, yet its importance for social history cannot be underestimated.

Juristic literature

Juridical writings such as the *Kitāb al-Kharāj* of Abū Yūsuf (died 182), Qudāma b. Jaʿfar (died 238 or 337) and Yaḥyā b. Adam, and the *Kitāb Sharḥ Adab al-Qāḍī li'l-Khaṣṣāf* by Ibn Māza[71] (died 536) contain useful insights into prevalent social practices, and as such are indispensable for a comparative study of the theory and practice of social norms and behaviour.

Biographies of the judges

The biographical studies of the judges compiled in narrative style by the contemporary Qāḍī Wakīʿ (died 306) in his *Akhbār al-Quḍāt,* and by the Qāḍī al-Kindī (died 350) in his *al-Wulāt wa'l-Quḍāt,* contain a number of instances of practical demonstration of the theoretical juridical literature.

---

68 See, *Rusūm,* p. 19f.; *Nishwār,* i, p. 193

69 *EI*², s.v. *Ḥisba*; Serjeant, *Islamic Textiles, AI,* ix, p. 54; cf. also, Begg, op. cit. "Survey of the Sources", section, "*Ḥisba* Manuals"

70 Edited by R. B. Serjeant, in *RSO,* 28 (1953), pp. 1–34

71 The monograph has been edited by M. I. H. I. Surty for a Ph.D. thesis, SOAS, 1972

Special mention has been made of the status of the qāḍī in Islam, their robes, their emoluments, and their private life. Both Wakīʿ and Kindī offer us a great deal of direct and indirect information on social and religious status of different groups of people. For example, Wakīʿ records that according to the Qāḍī Shurayḥ the *shahāda* of the pigeon trainer and the *ḥammāmī* was not accepted in the court,[72] a point indicative of the lower legal status of these professions in society.

Ḥiyal literature

Ḥiyal literature, according to Schacht, is "one of our most important sources for the knowledge of the legal practice of the Muslims in the middle ages".[73] The books on *ḥiyal* written by Shaybānī (died 189) and Khaṣṣāf (died 261) which have survived and have been edited are contemporary documents of direct and great value for our study of social history. They show how people, from almost all walks of life, tried to find out, within the limits of the *sharīʿa*, certain devices (*ḥiyal*) to solve their complicated problems in social, economic and other spheres of life. A typical example can be seen in a *ḥīla*, recorded by Shaybānī, that if a man vows not to wear an *izār*, and afterwards he wears a *ridā*ʾ in the fashion of the *izār*, he would not be a *ḥānith* (sinner)[74]—indicating that the *ridā*ʾ could also be used as an *izār*.

Culinary manuals

The manuals of culinary art, though directly related to cuisine, embrace a great deal of material on social topics related to food, such as table manners, diet and dietetics, drinks and the like. The earliest surviving treatise on cuisine is that of Al-Warrāq (a writer of the early fourth century) entitled *Kitāb al-Ṭabīkh wa Iṣlāḥ al-aghdhiya al-maʾkūlāt*,[75] a book of prime importance for our study. The *Kitāb*

---

[72] Wakīʿ, *Akhbār al-Quḍāt*, ii, p. 308

[73] *EI*², s.v. *Ḥiyal* (J. Schacht)

[74] *Makhārij fī'l-Ḥiyal*, p. 64

[75] The unique manuscript is lodged at the Bodleian Library, Oxford (No. Hunt, 187)

al-Wuṣlā ila'l-Ḥabīb by Ibn ʿAdīm (died 660),[76] and the *Kitāb al-Ṭabīkh* of ʿAbd al-Karīm al-Baghdādī (died 637) are also useful supplementary evidence. Of almost equal importance are the books entitled *Fawā'id al-Mawā'id*[77] and *Risāla Ādāb al-Mu'ākala*, of Ibn al-Jazzār (died 679) and of Muḥammad al-Ghazzī (died 984) respectively, enumerating various do's and don'ts of wining and dining.

Treatises on falconry and the chase

Though a number of treatises exclusively devoted to the art of hunting with animals were written in the early Abbasid period, very few of them have survived. Written primarily on the art of training predatory animals, their species, their diseases, etcetera, and interspersed with poetic citations from contemporary poets, they are a good source of information on many social aspects.

The earliest surviving works on hunting are those written by a writer of many-sided interest, Kushājim (died AD 961 or 971). His first tract on falconry, entitled *Kitāb al-Bayzara*, exists in manuscript form,[78] of which a few extracts were published in *JASB* in 1907. It is the basic work on falconry and the art of the chase, and has been much exploited by later writers. His second book, entitled *Kitāb al-Maṣāyid wa'l-Maṭārid*, is in fact a complete monograph on the art of venery and falconry. It also gives great attention to *adab*, and supplies us with a lot of valuable information otherwise not found in *adab* literature or in historical writings. Kushājim's writings, like other Arab works of chase and hunt, suffer from certain naive and fabulous beliefs which originated in part in the imagination of the Greeks and came to the Arabs through Arabic translations (e.g., Aristotle's "History of the Animals").

A contemporary of Kushājim, belonging to the court of the Fatimid Caliph ʿAzīz Bi'-llāh (AD 975–96), devoted a treatise, *Al-Bayzara*, to this Caliph, which possesses rich materials on the nature of predatory birds and beasts, on the long experience of the anonymous author and that of the specialists

---

[76] Br. Mus. Ms. No. Or. 6388; also SOAS, Ms. No. 90913

[77] Br. Mus. Ms. No. Or. 6388

[78] A transcribed copy of the original Gotha manuscript is in SOAS, Ms. No. 2091

in hawking. The book is excellent for the history of hunting of the Fatimid period, but is of little use for our study except in corroborating some data derived from Abbasid writers.

Apart from these three nearly contemporary works, the "hawking-sport memoirs" of the illustrious Syrian hunter-knight of the sixth century, Usāma b. Munqidh (died AD 1188), in his *Kitāb al-I'tibār*; the work of the Mamluk Muḥammad al-Manglī, entitled *Kitāb Uns al-malā' bi waḥsh al-falā'*, written in AD 1371; and the *Kitāb al-Manṣūrī fi'l-Bayzara* of an uncertain date; all help in supplementing, elucidating and corroborating materials to be found in the writings of the early Abbasid authors such as Kushājim. These writings contain a number of long quotations from the writers of the Abbasid period otherwise lost to the world (cf., for example, many excerpts in *Al-Manṣūrī fi'l-Bayzara* from an unknown author called Al-Mutawakkilī, perhaps the falconer of the Caliph Mutawakkil), and thus help in creating a bridge over the gap created by the loss of these valuable books.

Of considerable use and value are the materials found in the zoological writings of the contemporary author Jāḥiẓ (died 255), *Kitāb al-Ḥayawān*; of the seventh-century naturalist Qazwīnī's (599–682) *Kitāb 'Ajā'ib al-Makhlūqāt*; and of the eighth-century author Damīrī's (742–807) *Kitāb Ḥayāt al-Ḥayawān.* All of them tend to give materials on diverse aspects of social life, whether directly or indirectly. The last-named author also has an unusually interesting chapter on the Muslim table games *Shaṭranj* and *Nard.*

Writings on *furūsiyya* and horsemanship

The *furūsiyya* literature surviving from the Abbasid period is of great help for our study of social life. Some of it is devoted to equitation, hippology, farriery, archery and similar subjects. The *Kitāb al-Khayl* of Aṣma'ī[79] (died 213) and *Kitāb Asmā' al-khayl al-'Arab wa fursānihim* of Ibn al-Kalbī and Ibn al-'Arabī (died 207 and 231)[80] are treatises of philological erudition, but the *Kitāb Ḥilyat al-fursān wa shi'ār al-shuj'ān*[81]

[79] Edited by Haffner, Vienna, 1875
[80] Ed. by G. Levi Della Vida, Leiden, 1928
[81] Ed. and translated into French by L. Mercier, Paris, 1924

of the Andalusian Ibn Hudhayl of the eighth century; *Kitāb al-Waḍīḥ fī maʿrifat ʿilm al-ramy* (Br. Mus. Or. 9454) of Waḍīḥ al-Ṭabarī (AD 1295); *Kitāb Nihāyat al-sūl waʾl-umniyya fī taʿlīm aʿmāl al-Furūsiyya* of b. ʿĪsā al-Aqsarāʾī (died AD 1384?);[82] *Kitāb al-Qaws waʾl-sahm* (Br. Mus. Or. 3134); *Kitāb al-Bayṭara* (Br. Mus. Or. 1523); *Risāla fiʾl-rimāya* (SOAS, Ms. 46339) of anonymous authors; *Kitāb Ghunyat al-Ṭullāb fī maʿrifat al-ramy biʾl-nushshāb* by Taybughāʾ al-Baklāmishī al-Yūnānī[83] (ca. AD 1368); and *Kitāb al-Furūsiyya* of Ibn Qayyim al-Jawziyya (691–751) are important sources for materials on games and sports of Islamic periods in general and of the Mamluk period in particular. These treatises, most of them far removed in time from the third century AH, provide much useful data on the early Abbasid period as they derived information from earlier books of such nature available to them but no longer extant.

Archaeological studies

The archaeological evidence is a vital complement to the literary sources. The voluminous works of Creswell and Herzfeld on Baghdad and Samarra, the recent excavation reports on Sīrāf by David Whitehouse,[84] the publication of the Iraqi Government department of antiquities entitled *Ḥafriyāt Sāmarrāʾ* (Excavations at Samarra AD 1936–39), and similar other findings not only enable us to collate the reports of historians and geographers but sometimes furnish additional information on municipal and public houses, sanitation, baths, ceramics, and a host of other topics related to the social life in the early Abbasid period.

Numismatic sources

The surviving dinars and dirhams of the early Abbasid period provide documentary evidence for social history. Like miniature paintings, numismatic sources, especially those

[82] Critical edition by A. L. S. M. Lutful Huq for Ph.D. thesis, SOAS, 1956

[83] Translated into English by J. D. Latham and W. F. Paterson, entitled "Saracen Archery", London, 1970

[84] See *Irān*, 1968–1970

with figures, offer us visual aids, giving us, among other things, an opportunity of seeing the costume of the caliphs, which can be identified through the help of literary sources. The coins adorned with the portraits of the Caliphs Mutawakkil and Muqtadir are of particular interest. The reconstruction of Mutawakkil's portrait on the basis of the debased dirham seems to be faulty, as our literary sources do not mention any headgear similar to that shown on the head of Mutawakkil.

Inscriptions

Inscriptions, surviving on the pious foundations, various mosques, tombs and marble slabs, now dispersed in many museums, are of particular interest for the social and economic historian. According to Professor Lewis the inscriptions on metrological objects (weights, coin-weights, measure-stamps, vessel-stamps, tokens) and trade-marks or certificates on manufactured articles, especially textiles and metalworks, are also of interest.[85] It is known through inscriptions, for example, that the Caliph Hārūn al-Rashīd built a cistern at Ramla in Palestine in 172.[86]

Dhimmī sources

The chronicles and other literature of the *dhimmī* populations under Muslim rule are useful for our study of social history. As Professor Lewis observes, the non-Muslim communities living within the Muslim world, by virtue of their coherence and institutional structure, often enjoyed a continuity lacking in the larger and more fragmented Muslim society, and were thus able to accumulate and preserve records over long periods of time.[87]

Both ʿAmr b. Matti and Mārī b. Sulaymān, in their biographical books entitled *Akhbār faṭāriqat kursiʾl-Mashriq*,

---

[85] B. Lewis, "Sources . . .", in *Studies in the Economic History of the Middle East*, ed. by M. A. Cook, London, 1970, p. 86

[86] Creswell, *Early Muslim Architecture*, ii, pp. 161–64; for one of the earliest *waqf* inscriptions see M. Sharon, *A waqf inscription from Ramlah, Arabica*, xiii, 1966, pp. 77–84

[87] B. Lewis, "Sources . . .", pp. 79–80, 91

have preserved in detail, though in a critical tone, th regulations issued by the Caliph Mutawakkil pertaining the distinctive dress, mounts and dwellings of the *dhimmīs*. A certain points they add information on Ṭabarī's statemen on the regulations.[88] Mārī b. Sulaymān also informs us th the Caliph Hārūn, who had once imposed the wearing distinctive dress (*ghiyār*) on the Christians, allowed them wear costumes of their choice at the indirect request of th Caliph's private physician, Jibrīl b. Bakhtīshū'[89]—a point n to be found in Ṭabarī and other Muslim writers.

Other *dhimmī* authors, either contemporary such as Den of Tell-Mahré (*c.* third century),[90] or late such as Yaḥyā Sa'īd (died 458), Michael the Syrian (died AD 1199), B Hebraeus (died 685), Benjamin of Tudela (*c.* twelfth centu AD), and others make sporadic allusions to various soci aspects of the Abbasid period. Besides furnishing materia on the life of the non-Muslims, these authors have incorpo ated in their writings, within their limited scope, som interesting information on Muslim economic, social an political history.

Miscellaneous sources

The heresiographical writings such as *Al-Farq bain al-firaq* Baghdādī (died 429) and *Al-Milal* of Shahrastānī (died 548 the pseudo-philosophical "Epistles" of Ikhwān al-Ṣafā (ten century AD onward); the *ansāb* literature of Sam'ānī (die 562) and Balādhurī (*c.* 893); the mystic literature such *Kashf al-Maḥjūb* of Hujwīrī (died between 465 and 469); th lexicographical writings such as *Mukhaṣṣaṣ* of Ibn Sīda (die 458), *Kitāb al-Mu'arrab* of Jawālīqī (466–539), *Lisān* of Ib Manẓūr (died 711), all supply us with fragments of inform tion and cross references which are, at times, as necessary other literary sources to construct a composite picture Abbasid social life.

[88] 'Amr b. Matti, *Akhbār faṭāriqat kursi'l-mashriq*, ed. by Gesmon Rome, 1896, p. 71; Mārī b. Sulaymān, *Akhbār faṭāriqat kursi'l-Mashriq*, e by Gesmondi, Rome, 1899, p. 79; cf. also Ṭabarī, iii, pp. 1389–90

[89] Mārī, op. cit., p. 73

[90] See C. Cahen, "Fiscalité, propriété, antagonismes sociaux en Haut Mésopotamie au temps des premiers 'Abbasides, d'après Denys de Te Mahré", in *Arabica*, i, 1954, pp. 136–52

The *Āthār al-Bāqiya* of Bīrūnī (died after 442) offers us valuable materials on the origin and development of festivals and festivities of different religions, and the *Mafātīḥ al-ʿUlūm* of Khwārizmī (died 387) provides definitions of technical and scientific terms such as the terminologies relating to a study of numismatics, administration, weights and measures, food, and the like. Shābushtī's (died 399) *Kitāb al-Diyārāt* is very rich in materials useful for social history. Among other things, it describes the festivals of the Eastern Christians and the role of the impious Muslims who frequented the monasteries in quest of pleasure and sin. Ibn Zubayr's (*c.* fifth century) *Al-Dhakhā'ir wa'l-Tuḥaf* is really a treasure of varied information concerned with the court life, such as the festivities and the gifts of the court, the annual budget of the early Abbasid caliphs, the lists of articles left by the caliphs and wazirs, and the like.

Secondary sources

The secondary sources are, at times, very important and of great assistance for our present study, not because of the information they supply, but for their analysis and criticism of the primary sources. A number of orientalists have examined various aspects of social history of the Muslims in the mediaeval period. The economic historian E. Ashtor, in his *Histoire des prix et des salaires dans l'Orient mediéval*, and *A Social and Economic History of the Near East in the Middle Ages*, as well as in articles published in various journals, has very ably dealt with the cost of living and the earnings of various social groups in the early Abbasid period. Though Ashtor's study deals at greater length and more comprehensively with the economic life of the late and post-Abbasid period, his critical approach and his valuable information on the early Abbasid period is no less important. F. Viré's articles in the EI^2 on hunting animals and sporting birds (e.g., *bayzara, fahd, ibn ʿirs, ḥamām*) provide very useful material. The author, intimately familiar with Muslim natural history, critically examines the information often intermingled by Muslim writers with their personal prejudices and with naive remarks on animal psychology inspired mainly by Greek sources. F. Viré is, therefore, very helpful in the understanding of various hunting terminologies current in the mediaeval period but rarely used in modern Arabic. M. Rodinson in his article *Ghidhā'* in the *EI*^{2} has collected useful information on the food habits of mediaeval Muslim society. His writings may, with benefit, be supplemented by those of scholars such as E. Ashtor, M. Canard and Ḥ. Zayyāt. Other authors who have dealt with social history, either directly or indirectly, such as Dozy, L. Mercier, R. Levy, B. Lewis, C. E. Bosworth, F. Rosenthal, R. B. Serjeant, Dūrī, and M. Jawād, have also been of great help in solving problems related to various aspects of mediaeval social history.

Observations on the sources

The sources portraying life in early Abbasid society are not without defects. Sources such as anecdotes and stories contain exaggeration and inventions; *ḥisba* manuals and juridical writings are theoretical and seem divorced from reality; and the works on *adab* embody elegance and rhetoric rather than a factual picture of social behaviour and cultural developments. Nevertheless, they cannot be brushed aside as untrue and ignored in any serious study of Iraqi social life. Indeed they are indispensable for a clear picture of mediaeval society. The late and sometimes post-Abbasid sources also are important for their rich references and citations from earlier sources. Thus, for instance, works such as *Al-Manṣūrī fi'l-Bayzara* preserve lengthy excerpts from earlier works now no longer available.[91] These fill in the lacunae when other sources are sparse, and provide detail and precision or offer possibilities for a critical study when contemporary sources are copious. Since mediaeval Muslim society was more or less traditional and conservative, sources nearly contemporary or of a slightly later period may justifiably be relied upon, especially when contemporary evidence is absent or scant. It is with this end in view that we have supplemented, corroborated and sometimes derived materials from the sources not belonging to our period of study.

---

[91] See above, p. 23

Chapter 2

Costume

The sartorial concept in Islam is more functional than formal. It also reflects social status, work, sex and even religious and ethnic affiliation. Some articles of wear represented an official mark and symbol. References available in our sources relate more to the sartorial fashions and habits of the court and the important functionaries than to social habits in general.

The general picture emerging from Arabic sources reveals that the various ethnic and social groups in the Abbasid period wore their own distinctive dress. They also used to wear different dress for festive and ceremonial occasions and seasons.[1] On the formal plane one finds that the various state functionaries, such as the qāḍīs, the deputy qāḍīs, the *kuttāb*, the *kuttāb al-jund* (military secretaries), all had different ceremonial dress.[2]

The costumes worn by the people of different social groups, in this period, can be divided into three broad divisions: head-gear, articles of dress for the body, and foot-wear. It is to be noted that most of the costumes were common to all sections of the people, but varied in colour, design, and quality of fabric.[3]

[1] Jāḥiẓ, *Bayān*, iii, pp. 114–15; *Murūj*, vii, p. 124, viii, pp. 14, 181; *Aghānī*[2], i, p. 49, v, pp. 317, 407–8; *Muḥāḍarāt*, iv, p. 373; Ibn al-Jawzī, *Ẓirāf*, pp. 85–86

[2] Ibid, *Bayān*, iii, p. 114. Ibn Khallikān tells us that differences in dress for different functionaries were first introduced by the qāḍī Abū Yūsuf (d. 182). Cf. *Wafayāt*, xi, p. 38

[3] Describing Arab costume, Ibn Manẓūr, the famous Arab lexicographer, treated it in two broad divisions: (i) garments which are cut and sewn, like the *qamīṣ, jubba, sirwāl*; (ii) garments which are not cut and sewn, like the *ridā', izār, miṭraf*. Cf. *Lisān*, s.v. *qaṭa'*. Dozy, in his dictionary of Arab

Headgear

Caps and turbans formed the main headgear of the people from all walks of life.

During the time of the Umayyads and even earlier, an ordinary and short *qalansuwa*, probably shaped like a skull-cap or a fez and made of fur or cloth,[4] was in vogue; a turban was generally wrapped around it. During the Abbasid period a tall cap, probably made of silk and known as *qalansuwa ṭawīla*, became a popular article of wear.[5] It is reported that the Caliph Manṣūr, perhaps in imitation of the Persian head-gear, introduced the practice of wearing this tall *qalansuwa*, which resembled the long tapering wine-jar known as *dann*.[6] This assumption is further supported by the pictorial representation of the Persian kings with tall caps on their heads.[7] It appears to have been cone-shaped, though it could also be in the form of a truncated cone. The tall shape of the *ṭawīla* was maintained by means of an internal frame-work of wood or reeds (*Tudʿam bi-ʿīdān min dākhilihā*).[8] On account of its extraordinary height and its popularity it was frequently known by the adjective *ṭawīla*, without the noun *qalansuwa*.[9] According to Masʿūdī, Hārūn al-Rashīd did not like the

---

costume, has fully described the dress worn by the Arabs at different periods, but his book seems to have a bias towards the usages of the western rather than of the eastern Islamic world; cf. the omission of a word like *miṭraf* from his dictionary as well as from his Supplement. Dozy, indeed, is of no great help in determining the fashion of some of the Baghdādī costumes. Nevertheless, his dictionary is an indispensable work for students of the history of Arab dress.

4 Ibn Saʿd, *Ṭabaqāt*, vi, p. 196; *Aghānī*[1], xv, p. 71; *Muḥāḍarāt*, iv, p. 366

5 *Aghānī*[2], x. p. 236; Ṭabarī, iii, p. 1328; Azdī, *Taʾrīkh al-Mawṣil*, p. 216 Ḥuṣrī, *Jamʿ al-Jawāhir fiʾl-mulaḥ waʾl-nawādir*, p. 106

6 *Aghānī*[2], x, p. 236; Shābushtī, *Diyārāt*, p. 188. Referring to it, Abuʾl-Faraj al-Isfahānī quotes the following two verses, which satirize the introduction of the fashion into society; cf. Aghānī[2], x, p. 236. (*Kunnā nurjī min imām ziyādatan fa-jāda biṭūl fazādahū fiʾl-qalānis; tarāhā ʿalā hām al-rijāl ka-annahā dinān yahūd jullilat biʾl-barānis*) "We expected an increase (of favour) from the *Imām*, but he showed benevolence by an increase in the height of *qalansuwa*; you see them reposing on men's skulls as if they were Jewish wine-jars wrapped in burnous-cloaks."

7 Jalīl Ḍiyāpūr, *Pūshāk ba-Āstāni Īrāniān*, Pls. 151, 162, 176

8 *Aghānī*[2], x, p. 236; Azdī, op. cit., p. 216; Balkhī, *Kitāb al-Badʾ waʾl Taʾrīkh*, p. 91

9 Dozy, *Supplement*, s.v. *ṭawīla*

general use of the *qalansuwa ṭawīla.*[10] Muʿtaṣim, however, is reported to have re-introduced and popularized it once again.[11] His fashion of wearing this tall headgear, and also of using muslin for his clothes, was so widely imitated in society that the fashion itself came to be known as *Muʿtaṣimiyāt.*[12] Although the tall cap (*danniyya*) was to become a characteristic head-dress of the qāḍī (a fact evident from Shābushtī's story of Saʿd b. Ibrāhīm and ʿUbāda,[13] and also from Dozy's definition of *danniyya*),[14] its use seems not to have been confined to any particular group, until the Caliph Mustaʿīn limited its use to the qāḍī only.[15] The tall caps of the Abbasid period, although designed as *ṭawīla* and *danniyya*, were also known merely by the adjectives *Ruṣāfiyya* and *Dawraqiyya.*[16] The *Ruṣāfiyya* derived its name from a suburb probably in Baghdad and was a favourite headgear of the caliphs, princes and wealthy people.[17]

It is worth mentioning here that the Abbasids wore turbans on all caps, perhaps in response to the Prophetic tradition that "the difference between a Muslim and an infidel is the wearing of a turban on the cap."[18]

The second popular head-dress of the period under discussion was the *ʿimāma* or turban. From the caliphs down to the *ʿāmma*, which included even the thieves and the rogues,

---

[10] *Murūj*, viii, p. 302

[11] Ibid, viii, p. 302

[12] Ibid, viii, p. 302

[13] *Diyārāt*, p. 188; these two persons lived in the time of the Caliph Mutawakkil; the former was a secretary and the latter was a *mukhannath.* Saʿd b. Ibrāhīm's remark (*Yakūn mukhannaṭh bilā baghghāʾ mithl qāḍī bilā danniyya*) "a *mukhannath* without whore is like a qāḍī without *danniyya*", indicates that as whoredom was indispensable for the *mukhannath*, so the *danniyya* was essential for the qāḍīs. For more details on the qāḍī's head-gear, see *Danniyyat al-qāḍī fi'l-ʿaṣr al-ʿAbbāsī*, Mikhael ʿAwwād, in *al-Risāla* (Cairo), x (1942); nos. 485–96, pp. 979–81; 1006–7

[14] Dozy, *Dictionnaire*, p. 185

[15] *Murūj*, vii, p. 402. The tall cap (*danniyya*) of the qāḍī sometimes became so long and limp that a litigant called it a top-boot (*khuff*). Cf. Kindī, *Wulāt*, p. 589f.

[16] *Tajārib*, iii, pp. 152–3; Ṣābī, *Rusūm*, p. 81; *Nishwār*, viii, p. 12; Khaṭīb, *Taʾrīkh*, iv, p. 6. Cf. also Badrī, *ʿAmma*, p. 13

[17] Yāqūt, *Buldān*, ii, pp. 783–4; Serjeant, *Islamic Textiles*, Chap. II, p. 84

[18] *Concordance*, s.v. *ʿimāma*; see also the verse quoted earlier in connection with the tall cap, p. 30, n. 6

all had an *ʿimāma* suited to their position.[19] *ʿImāma* was a length of cloth wound round the head, sometimes as far down as the ears,[20] and even the cheeks,[21] one end of it being hung between the shoulders. This tail, or hanging portion of the cloth, was called *ʿadhaba*. An *ʿimāma* without an *ʿadhaba* was considered a *bidʿa*. There was no fixed rule with regard to the length of this turban cloth and that of the *ʿadhaba*. The former depended on individual taste, and the more ostentatious a man was, the greater was the length of his turban cloth.[22] The length of the *ʿadhaba* was usually four fingers.[23]

The wearing of the *ʿimāma*, when out of doors, was considered indispensable for males except on occasions of pilgrimage[24] or of condolence.[25] While in their offices, government personnel, following the official colour of the Abbasids, had to wear black turbans and were not allowed to take them off, even for a respite. Anyone found not strictly observing this official etiquette was subjected to humiliation and even to corporal punishment. Hilāl al-Ṣābī (359–448 AH), in his *Rusūm*, relates some interesting anecdotes about such punishments.[26]

According to Abu'l-Faraj al-Iṣfahānī and Iḥn al-Jawzī the *ʿimāma* was the main distinctive dress of a man.[27] To put off the *ʿimāma* in an assembly was a kind of punishment.[28] In the language of Abu'l-Aswad al-Du'alī the *ʿimāma* was "a shield on the battlefield, a net in the summer; a *dithār* or outer garment in the winter, and an honour in the assembly, a protector in vicissitudes, and an increase in the stature of a man".[29] It also served the purpose of a purse[30] and was sometimes used to hide the identity of a man when he was in

---

19 Jāḥiẓ, *Bayān*, iii, p. 114

20 Ibid.; *Bukhalā'*, p. 310

21 Ṭabarī, iii, p. 761

22 Muq. p. 129

23 *EI*[1], s.v. *Turban* (B. Walter)

24 Ibn al-Jawzī, *Talbīs*; cf. also the books of *Fiqh*, Chap. *Manāsik al-Ḥajj*

25 *Aghānī*[2], x, p. 190

26 Ṣābī, *Rusūm*, pp. 77, 96, 72

27 *Aghānī*[1], xv, p. 71; Ibn al-Jawzī, *Mudhash*, p. 169; cf. also, Kattānī, *Diʿāma li-maʿrifat aḥkām sunnat al-ʿimāma*, p. 43

28 *Muntaẓam*, x, p. 89

29 Jāḥiẓ, *Bayān*, iii, p. 100; *Muḥāḍarāt*, iv, p. 371

30 Nishwār, in *RAAD*, xii, p. 693; Dozy, *Dictionnaire*, p. 236

a disadvantageous position.[31] Needless to say, people in all walks of life must have striven to enhance the quality of such an important article of wear. They not only chose fine stuff for it, but also adorned it sometimes with gold and costly materials. We are told that the turban presented to Mukhāriq, the singer, by the Caliph Amīn was so heavily woven with gold that "it dazzled the eyes."[32] From Masʿūdī's *Murūj* it can be seen that the *ghuzāt* had a special type of turban known as *ʿamāʾim al-ghuzāt*.[33] Although our sources do not give any specific information about it, it must have been a part of uniform or a distinctive turban by which the *ghāzīs*, the frontier warriors who made *jihād* against the infidel,[34] could be distinguished from the regular soldiers of the Caliph.[35] Another kind of *ʿimāma* known as *ʿAmāʾim al Muṣmata*, i.e., a turban made of a cloth of a single colour, was, according to Ṣābī, a special article of headgear reserved for high-ranking officials and commanders,[36] whereas the intimate companions (*nadīm*) of the caliphs wore mostly the *ʿamāʾim al-washī al-mudhahhaba*, turbans of gold-figured silk.[37] From Ṣābī it is also known that the descendants of Anṣār (*awlād al-Anṣār*) wore a special yellow turban in the earlier centuries of the Muslim era. The practice, however, ceased from the fifth century AH onward.[38] Wealthy people had a number of turbans which they wore on different occasions,[39] while the poor used the scrap of cloth as their *ʿimāma*.[40] Some of the ṣufis and the peasants in general used for their *ʿimāma* dyed *fūṭ*,[41] a kind of coarse silk which is said to have been imported from India.[42]

---

31 *Murūj*, vi, p. 478; *Aghānī*², v, p. 218; *Nishwār*, ii, in *RAAD* xvii, p. 521

32 *Aghānī*¹, xxi, p. 239

33 *Murūj*, vii, p. 135

34 *EI*², s.v. Ghāzī (I. Melikoff)

35 Badrī, *ʿImāma*, pp. 14–15; The Caliph Hārūn al-Rashīd is believed to have worn a *qalansuwa*, inscribed with the words "*ghāz ḥājj*" when he invaded Greek territory in the year 190/805. (Cf. Ṭabarī, iii, p. 709 seq.)

36 *Rusūm*, p. 96

37 Ibid, p. 96. *Washī* is a kind of silk material made in different colours, and sometimes threaded with gold. (Cf. Dozy, *Suppl.* s.v.)

38 *Rusūm*, p. 41

39 *Dhakhāʾir*, pp. 229–30; Ibn ʿImad, *Shadharāt al-Dhahab* (Cairo, 1350–1), iv, p. 101

40 Ibn al-Jawzī, *Talbīs*, p. 198

41 Sharīshī, *Sharḥ Maqamāt al-Ḥarīrī*, iii, p. 30; *Fakhrī*, 228

42 *Lisān, Tāj* and *Mukhaṣṣaṣ*, sv. *Fūṭ*. Cf. also Badrī, *ʿĀmma*, p. 145

Articles of dress for the body

As has been mentioned above, the costume of the people in Abbasid society varied according to the social group, ethnic affiliations, occasions and seasons. According to Jāḥiẓ the costume of the Arabs was known by the name of *shiʿār*: clothes worn next to the bare body, and of *dithār*: clothes worn outside the *shiʿār*.[43] The shirt and the trousers are *shiʿār* and the other garments are *dithār*.[44] The general articles of wear, other than the headgear and the footwear, were the *izār* (waist wrapper), the *ridā*ʾ (mantle), the *jubba* (long garment), the *qamīṣ* (shirt), the *durrāʿa* (a long coat of wool open in front), the *miṭraf* (a square wrap with ornamental borders); the *ghilāla* (chemise), the *sirwāl* (drawers), the *ṣudra* (waist-coat), the *ṭaylasān* (a robe with hood), the *qabā*ʾ (a loose outer garment), the ʿ*abā*ʾ (a simple outer garment).

Izār

The *izār*, an unsewn close-fitting garment wrapped round the waist and legs and extending upwards as far as the navel, which it might cover or not, and downwards as far as the middle of the leg or beyond, was a characteristic dress of the Arabs.[45] During the Abbasid period this term was also applied to an outer wrap used by both males and females.[46] Women used it for outdoor wear. Ṭabarī records the flight of women found in the street without an *izār* at the time of raids carried out on private houses, when Muʿtamid returned to Baghdad from Samarraʾ.[47] Muṣṭafā Jawād, in his article *Azyā*ʾ *al-ʿArab al-shaʿbiyya*, further informs us that women covered their heads with their *izār*.[48] To make it firm on their

[43] *Tāj* (attributed to Jāḥiẓ), p. 154

[44] Ibid., p. 154

[45] Dozy, *Dictionnaire*, pp. 24–26; Ibn Saʿd, *Ṭabaqāt*, ii, pp. 153–54; *Muḥāḍarāt*; iv, p. 373; Ṣāliḥ Aḥmad, *Al-Albisa al-ʿarabiyya fī qarn al-awwal al-hijrī*, in *MMII*, 1966, pp. 47–49

[46] Levy's statement that, during the Abbasid period, it was "an outer-wrap worn exclusively by women" is misleading (cf. Levy, "Notes on Costume", *JRAS*, 1935, p. 321). The reference in Khaṭīb al-Baghdādī to the appearance of a *muḥaddith* (early 10th century AD) in a *majlis* without an *izār* indicates that the use of this garment was not confined to women. (Cf. Khaṭīb, *Taʾrīkh*, i, p. 374; cf. also Azdī, *Taʾrīkh al-Mawṣil*, p. 261 for a reference of this kind)

[47] Ṭabarī, iii, p. 2122

[48] M. Jawād, *Majalla al-Turāth al-Shaʿbī*, Baghdad, viii (1964), p. 6

heads they sometimes fastened it with a cincture (*zunnār*) and a silk thread. Mutayyam, a slave-girl of the court of Ma'mūn and Muʿtaṣim is said to have invented this fashion,[49] which was widely followed by women of her own and also of later times. During the period of our study this *izār* was considered to be an essential part of a gentleman's dress.[50] This is why Khaṭīb Baghdādī records with surprise that the *muḥaddith* Muḥammad b. Aḥmad al-Sadūsī was found in an assembly without an *izār*.[51] During the time of the Caliph Hārūn al-Rashīd the *izār* underwent a certain modification when he introduced a special wide-bordered and profusely decorated *izār*, known after him as *Izār Rashīdiyya*.[52]

Miʾzar

The *miʾzar* was a smaller type of *izār*, generally unsewn, which was wrapped round the waist and covered the legs down to the knees.[53] It was an important article of wear of the common people. The *miʾzar* or the loin-cloth was regarded as essential for entering a bath.[54] According to Ibn al-Ukhuwwa, the bath-keeper should supply the bather with a large *miʾzar* which could properly cover the portion from the navel to the knees.[55] The *miʾzar* could also be used as a *ridāʾ* or mantle.[56] According to Ibn Ḥawqal the people of Khūzistān and Sind, because of the hot climate of these regions, habitually wore *izār* and *miʾzar*.[57] A person not wearing a *miʾzar* might be regarded as an uncultured man. The phrase used by Tawḥīdī, "*Yā qamīṣan bilā miʾzar*" (O one wearing a shirt without a *miʾzar*), for an uncultured man shows the degree of importance attached to the *miʾzar*, especially by men of refined taste.[58]

---

[49] *Aghānī*², vii, p. 302; L. A. Mayer, *Mamluk Costume*, p. 71

[50] Azdī, *Ḥikāyāt Abīʾl-Qāsim*, p. 85

[51] Khaṭīb, *Taʾrīkh*, i, p. 374

[52] *Aghānī*², v. p. 224; Ṭabarī, iii, p. 753

[53] Dozy, *Dictionnaire*, s.v. *miʾzar*; Ibn al-Ukhuwwa, *Maʿālim al-Qurba*, p. 156

[54] Serjeant, *A Zaidi manual of hisba of the 3rd century H. RSO*, 28 (1953), p. 27; Ibn Abī Zaid, *Risāla*, Ms. 1193, fol. 747, quoted by Dozy, *Dictionnaire*, s.v. (Persian trans. Husain ʿAlī, Tehran, p. 37)

[55] Ibn al-Ukhuwwa, op. cit., p. 156

[56] Dozy, op. cit., s.v. *miʾzar*

[57] Ibn Hawqal, pp. 174, 228

[58] Tawḥīdī, *Imtāʿ*, ii, p. 59

Ridā'

The *ridā'* was a cloak worn over the shoulder, covering the *qamīṣ*.[59] It might also be put over the head for protection against the weather or to take the place of a *qināʿ* (veil) to cover the face.[60] The Abbasid caliphs, like the Umayyads, were very fond of the *ridā'* and used it through most of the year.[61] Like the *izār*, the *ridā'* was also a common article of wear amongst men and women.[62] Washshā' speaks of a girl who wore a *ridā'* embroidered all over with a pattern of circles like eyes (*muʿaiyyan*) and adorned with a *ṭirāz* border.[63] A popular *ridā'* known as *ridā' Rashīdī* (perhaps after the fashion of the Caliph Hārūn al-Rashīd) was, as Serjeant suggests, often embroidered with *ṭirāz* inscriptions.[64]

Qamīṣ

The *qamīṣ* seems to have been a kind of shirt with a round hole for the neck and without an opening in the front.[65] A vertical round collar in the shirt was introduced by the Barmakid wazir Jaʿfar b. Yaḥyā, a change which is said to have been widely accepted in society.[66] Fashion varied as to length of a shirt; a full length was popular in the Umayyad period, but it went out of favour under the early Abbasids, when it was felt that no garment should be so long as to cover the heels.[67] During the period of Mustaʿīn, the *qamīṣ* for men acquired wide sleeves.[68] From a statement of Masʿūdī in his *Murūj al-Dhahab* we learn that the width of a sleeve was three spans (*shibr*).[69] It seems that a wide sleeve was regarded as an essential for a well-dressed person. A narrow sleeve reflected

---

59 *ʿUyūn*, i, p. 301; Ibn Saʿd, *Ṭabaqāt*, vii, p. 133; Ṣāliḥ Aḥmad op. cit., p. 47

60 *Murūj*, vi, p. 328; Ṭabarī, i, p. 2736. The *ridā'* could also be used as an *izār*. Cf. Shaybānī, *Makhārij fi'l-ḥiyal*, p. 64

61 *Tāj* (attributed to Jāḥiẓ), p. 154

62 Levy, *Notes on Costume*, *JRAS*, 1935, p. 321

63 *Muwashshā*, p. 252

64 Serjeant, *Islamic Textiles*, Chap. xxii, p. 67

65 *Aghānī*[1], xiv, p. 3. The poet Farazdaq is reported to have worn a *qamīṣ* with an opening cut in front reaching to the navel. Cf. ibid., ix, p. 40

66 Jāḥiẓ, *Bayān*, iii, p. 356

67 *ʿUyūn*, i, p. 298; iii, p. 238; Ibn al-Jawzī, *Talbīs*, pp. 206, 218

68 *Murūj*, vii, p. 402

69 Ibid, vii, p. 402

either lesser affluence or miserliness on the part of the wearer.[70]

The wide sleeves of the *qamīṣ* were used as pockets. The word *jaib*,[71] in the meaning of pocket, was indeed not unknown at this time, but it is clear from the sources that the sleeves of the *qamīṣ* were often used as a receptacle for documents, money and other important items.[72] It seems probable that the word *jaib* indicated a pocket in the sleeve and not elsewhere in the shirt. The available evidence does not suffice to show whether there were pockets elsewhere in the *qamīṣ*. The sleeves, in time, appear to have become even more wide and capacious.[73] Ordinary people carried coins in them.[74] Sometimes a book or a casket was also kept there.[75] A tailor might keep a pair of shears in his sleeve.[76] We are also told that, when ʿAlī b. ʿĪsā, the celebrated wazir of Muqtadir, was arrested in 316, he had with him a copy of the Qur'ān and a pair of scissors in his sleeve-pocket.[77] Students, teachers, *ʿulamā'*, secretaries and *udabā'* used to place therein their slates, tablets, inkpots, books and official documents.[78] Magicians and conjurors concealed in them their tricks and items of magic.[79] There is even one mention of a snake carried in a sleeve.[80]

---

[70] Ṭabarī, iii, p. 298

[71] ʿUlayya, the sister of Hārūn, is reported to have once composed this verse which indicates the use of the word *jaib* in the sense of "pocket":

Khaba'tu fī shiʿrī ism alladhī aradtuhū kal-khab' fi'l-jaib.

"I have concealed in my poem the name of one whom I wanted; like the concealing of something in the pocket (*jaib*)" (cf. *Aghānī*[2], x, p. 166). Badīʿ al-Zamān al-Hamadānī has recorded in one of his *risāla* the sentence "*Qalīl fi'l-jaib khair min kathīr fi'l-ghaib*" (A bird in the hand is better than two in the wilderness), which also indicates that the word was known at that time. (Cf. Ḥamadānī, *Rasā'il*, p. 43.) *Aghānī* also mentions a singer who put his hand in his *jaib* and brought out a playing instrument (cf. xi[1], p. 21).

[72] *Diyārāt*, pp. 151, 158; Jāḥiẓ, *Bukhalā'*, p. 108

[73] *Aghānī*[2], x, p. 109; Jāḥiẓ, *Bukhalā'*, p. 117

[74] Yāqūt, Irshād, i, p. 254; Ibn al-Jawzī, *Ẓirāf*, p. 81

[75] Irshād, vi, p. 56; Ibn Abī ʿUsaybiʿa, *ʿUyūn al-Anbā'*, i, p. 141

[76] *Murūj*, vi, p. 345

[77] *Tajārib*, i, p. 185

[78] Jahshiyārī, *Wuzarā'*, p. 228; Ḥ. Zayyāt, *Azyat al-akmān*, in Mashriq, 1947, p. 472

[79] H. Zayyāt, op. cit., p. 474; Ibn al-Jawzī, *Adhkiyā'*, p. 106

[80] Shābushtī, *Diyārāt*, p. 11

In addition, sleeves could be used as a kerchief to wipe away tears or to clean the face; to hide the face from other people and even, at need, to blot the ink from writing-paper.[81]

As the power of the Abbasids declined, so the width of the *qamīṣ* sleeve and also of the turban increased in size, a development not without irony. Things came to such a point that a man with a tall cap, a turban over-elaborate, or sleeves too wide was regarded as on the verge of ruin.[82]

The Abbasid caliphs appear to have been fond of the *qamīṣ* made of *Dabīqī*,[83] a cloth produced in Dabīq, between Farama and Tinnis in Egypt.[84] The Dabīqī cloth seems to have been a favourite article of wear among the Abbasid caliphs, their wazirs, and the governmental élite. Abu'l-Faraj al-Iṣfahānī informs us that Isḥāq al-Mawṣilī, a well-known singer who was a favourite of Ma'mūn and Muʿtaṣim, found the latter wearing a Dabīqī shirt (*qamīṣ*) which looked as if it had been cut out of the planet Venus[85] (*Ka-annamā qudda min jirm al-Zuhra*). According to Masʿūdī, Muʿtaḍid (279–89 AH) asked his *khazzān* (wardrobe keeper) to choose the best of Sūs and Dabīqī material and to set them aside for his personal use.[86] Hilāl al-Ṣābī, referring to the time when ʿAlī b. ʿĪsā was wazir, mentions a precious red Dabīqī shirt.[87] From Tanūkhī we come to know another use to which Dabīqī was put: we are told that Muqtadir's mother used to wear sandals covered with Dabīqī cloth.[88] The same source informs us that a certain man of Anbar possessed a large number of clothes, his Dabīqī shirts being kept in boxes separate from the ones containing the other clothes.[89]

The Abbasid caliphs were ostentatious in the wearing of

---

[81] *Murūj*, vii, p. 110; *Aghānī*², x, p. 61; H. Zayyāt, op. cit., p. 470

[82] Rāghib, *Muḥāḍarāt*, iv, p. 371

[83] Yāqūt, *Buldān*, ii, p. 548

[84] Dabaqa is one of the villages of Egypt near Tinnis (a port in lower Egypt frequented by ships from Syria and from the Maghrib). It was from Dabaqa that the material called Dabīqī came, a material described in the sources as unparalleled in its excellence. Cf. Yāqūt, *Buldān*, ii, p. 548; *Dhakhā'ir*, pp. 299–30; Mez, p. 460; *EI*², s.v. *Dabīḳ*

[85] Aghānī², v, p. 345

[86] *Murūj*, viii, p. 115

[87] Ṣābī, *Wuzarā'*, p. 327

[88] *Nishwār*, viii, p. 143

[89] Ibid., viii, pp. 190–91

the *qamīṣ*. Unless it was made of precious and rare material, they seldom used a *qamīṣ* more than once.[90]

Durrāʿa

A loose outer garment with sleeves, slit in front, known as *durrāʿa*,[91] seems to have been generally donned by the Abbasid caliphs when going out of their palaces.[92] It was often made of wool and was thickly embroidered.[93] Its colour varied.[94] From a passage in Ṭabarī it would seem that the *durrāʿa* was sometimes worn by the caliphs at their installations.[95] The Abbasid caliphs favoured a *durrāʿa* made of *dībāj*[96] (brocade) and employed it for personal as well as for ceremonial robes (*khilʿa*) offered to dignitaries and officials who were high in their esteeem. Masʿūdī records that in 223 AH Afshīn received a *durrāʿa* of brocade embroidered with red gold, the front of the robe being studded with rubies and pearls.[97]

The chief part of the wazir's costume was a special *durrāʿa*[98] with buttons and loops and with an opening below the neck.[99] With it went a belt called *wishāḥ* (a broad belt of leather studded with jewels)[100] and a sword which in the language of Jāḥiẓ was "dignified".[101] Under Mutawakkil the wearing of the *durrāʿa* became obligatory for all persons (except the qāḍīs) who wished to have audience with the Caliph.[102] During the fourth century the officials and secretaries in

[90] *Tāj* (attributed to Jāḥiẓ), p. 154

[91] According to the *Tāj al-ʿUrūs* it was a *jubba* with a slit front. (Cf. s.v. *Dirʿ*)

[92] *Murūj*, vii, p. 134; Ṭabarī, iii, p. 1368

[93] The Caliph Muʿtaṣim is said to have worn a white woollen *durrāʿa* when he set out on his campaign against ʿAmūra (Amorium) in 224 AH. Cf. *Murūj*, vii, p. 134

[94] *Murūj*, vii, pp. 135, 270; Ṭabarī, iii, p. 1368

[95] Muḥammad b. Wāthiq was invested by the Turks with a black *durrāʿa* and a *Ruṣāfī qalansuwa*. Cf. Ṭabarī, iii, p. 1368

[96] *Dībāj* is a cloth whose warp and woof are of silk. Cf. Serjeant, *Islamic Textiles*, Chap. iv, p. 72, n.

[97] *Murūj*, vii, pp. 127–28

[98] *Aghānī*[1], xx, i, p. 49; *Nishwār*, i, p. 29; Mez, pp. 84, 89, 389

[99] Dozy, *Dictionnaire*, p. 45

[100] Ibid., p. 429

[101] Jāḥiẓ, *Bayān*, iii, p. 118

[102] *Nishwār*, in *RAAD*, i–ii (1930), p. 9

Shīrāz and Western Persia in general wore *durrāʿa* and commanded great prestige.[103] The secretaries in Baghdad also used *durrāʿa*, and according to Miskāwayh the Barīdī *kuttāb* (secretaries) were called *Aṣḥāb Darārīʿ*.[104]

Jubba

The *jubba*, which was often used in place of the *durrāʿa*, was a long outer garment with an open front and wide sleeves. Like the *ridā'*, it was also used by the caliphs in all seasons.[105] The *jubba* was often used with the *qamīṣ*, *izār* and *ridā'*, though sometimes a *jubba* alone could be worn without adding other garments.[106] The Abbasid caliphs seem to have been fond of sartorial display, using for the *jubba* silk and other rich materials woven with gold thread. Amīn is said to have offered a *jubba* of gold-figured silk to the singer Mukhāriq. He soon regretted that he had given such a precious garment to a singer, and spoiled it by throwing a piece of meat at it. The material was so fine that it could not be cleaned by the washers and bleachers of Baghdad.[107]

Miṭraf

The *miṭraf*, a garment made of silk and richly embroidered, was a large piece of cloth, sometimes so large as to enfold the whole body of the wearer.[108] According to Thaʿālibī and Ibn Manẓūr, the *miṭraf*-cloak was something like a wrapper (*kisā'*, *ridā'*) with the two borders embroidered.[109] It was generally worn by rich people and by high dignitaries.[110] People wishing to call on high ranking officials as a rule donned the *miṭraf*.[111] Rāghib mentions the words of a certain Ḥabīb b.

---

103 Muq. *Aḥsan al-Taqāsīm*, p. 440

104 *Tajārib*, i, p. 375

105 *Tāj* (attr. to Jāḥiẓ), p. 154

106 Ibn Saʿd, *Ṭabaqāt*, v, p. 215; Ṣāliḥ Aḥmad, op. cit., p. 59

107 Ṭabarī, iii, p. 968; *Aghānī*[1], xxi, pp. 239–40

108 Levy, *Notes on Costume, JRAS*, 1935, pp. 322-23; Ibn Abī ʿUṣaybiʿa, *ʿUyun al-Anbā'*, i, p. 139

109 Thaʿālibī, *Fiqh al-Lugha*, p. 246; *Lisān*, s.v. *miṭraf*

110 Levy, op. cit., pp. 322–23; Ṣāliḥ Aḥmad, op. cit., p. 62

111 *ʿUyūn*, i, p. 297; cf. also *Aghānī*[1], xiii, p. 132, who notes that care was taken to remove the *miṭraf* (a voluminous and expensive garment), when going to the water-closet.

Thābit: "I would be delighted to be respected in a *khamīṣa*[112] rather than despised in a *miṭraf*":[113] a statement which suggests that the wearing of the *miṭraf* without proper cause was regarded as a mark of ostentation. Abu'l-ʿAbbās al-Saffāḥ seems to have been fond of the *miṭraf*-robe made of *khazz* silk, whereas people of elegant taste are reported to have preferred cotton to other materials for their *miṭraf*-cloaks.[114]

Ghilāla

The *ghilāla* (chemise) was a garment worn next to the body[115] beneath other clothes. The name is also given to a chemise worn beneath a coat of mail.[116] It seems to have been used by men and women alike, and was considered to be an indoor costume. Dozy describes it as a very light and transparent robe.[117] Slave-girls and singers of our period wore it in their homes.[118] Their *ghilāla* may have been fairly long, as they wore it sometimes without a *sirwāl*.[119] The Caliph Hārūn al-Rashīd is said to have worn a *ghilāla raqīqa* during the summer season.[120]

Qabā'

The *qabā'* was a kind of sleeved, close-fitting coat resembling the *qaftān*, generally reaching the middle of the calf, divided down the front and made to overlap over the chest.[121] It was regarded as a characteristic dress of the Turks.[122] Like the *durrāʿa*, the *qabā'* also seems to have been an official dress of

---

[112] It was a long coarse stuff which could be used as a blanket (cf. *Aghānī*[1], xix, p. 131). According to the *Tāj* it is a black square blanket having two borders. A blanket having no borders cannot be called a *khamīṣa*. Cf. *Tāj*, iv, p. 390; Dozy, *Dictionnaire*, pp. 170–75

[113] *Muḥāḍarāt*, iv, p. 367

[114] Washshā', p. 180; Serjeant, *Islamic Textiles*, Chap. ii, p. 69

[115] *Lisān*, s.v.

[116] Dozy, *Dictionnaire*, pp. 319–23

[117] Dozy, *Dictionnaire*, p. 322

[118] *Diyārāt*, pp. 138–39; Ṭabarī, iii, p. 753

[119] *Diyārāt*, pp. 138–39; *Quṭub al-Surūr*, p. 78

[120] Ṭabarī, iii, p. 753

[121] Dozy, *Dictionnaire*, pp. 352–362; Levy, op. cit., p. 324; Tritton, in *JRAS*, 1927, p. 480. From a passage of the *Aghānī*[1] (vii, p. 134) it appears that when a man tears his *qamīṣ* from the opening below the neck (the *jaib*) to the foot it becomes a *qabā'*.

[122] Rāghib, *Muhāḍarāt*, iv, p. 373; Ibn al-Jawzī, *Ẓirāf*, p. 132

the wazirs. This is evident from the fact that ʿAbd al-Mālik b. Zayyāt accepted the post of wazir on condition that he would be obliged to wear neither the *qabā'* nor the *durrāʿa*.[123] Miskāwayh notes that the wazir Abu'l-Faḍl received, at the time of his appointment, a *qabā'* together with a sword and a belt, both of which were adorned with gold.[124] The *qabā'* and the *minṭaq* (belt) are also reported to have been the dress of young boys.[125] It is said that Zubayda, the consort of the Caliph Hārūn al-Rashīd, wishing to draw the attention of her son, Amīn, to her *jawārī* (slave-girls), ordered the girls to don the *qabā'*, the *minṭaq* and the *ʿimāma*—a report which throws a little light on the attire of boys.[126] Shābushtī notes that Amīn, when he was Caliph, bade his favourite slave girl, ʿArīb, to wear the *qabā'* and the *minṭaq* in his presence.[127]

Ṭaylasān

The *ṭaylasān* was a piece of material worn over the shoulders and hanging down from them like a hood thrown back.[128] It might be long enough to cover the head, the shoulders and the back in the manner of a *ridā'*.[129] The *ṭaylasān* was a

[123] *Aghānī*[1], xx, p. 49
[124] *Tajārib*, i, p. 241
[125] *Aghānī*[2], x, pp. 111–12; *Diyārāt*, pp. 155, 165; Ṭabarī iii, pp. 543–44
[126] *Murūj*, viii, pp. 299–300
[127] *Diyārāt*, p. 165
[128] Dozy, *Dictionnaire*, s.v. Lane, *Arabian Nights*, ii, p. 512, thinks it to be similar in origin to the academic hood and scarf worn in the Europe of his own time.
[129] Yāqūt, *Irshād*, i, p. 373. Cf. also the illustration which G. Demombynes published in *REI*, 1939, p. 424; also the illustration of the *Maqāmāt al-Ḥarīrī*, published by O. Grabar, in "The Islamic City", pl. no. 7. Yāqūt and Abu'l-Faraj al-Isfahānī record that in the reign of the Caliph Amīn, the Qāḍī Khulayjī, when his *qalansuwa* was removed in a mosque, covered his head with his *ṭaylasān* (cf. *Irshād*, i, p. 373; *Aghānī*[1], x, p. 123). Dozy describes this robe as a certain article of apparel worn by the *ʿajam* (i.e., non-Arabs), round in form and black in colour, its warp and woof being of wool (cf. *Dictionnaire*, pp. 278–90). He notes also that because it was thrown over the shoulder it was sometimes called *ṭaraḥa* (cf. Ibid., pp. 254–57; 278). Levy suggests that this word has been derived from the Persian *talishan*, which itself comes perhaps from the Hebrew *tallith* "the cloak of honour, the scholar's or officer's distinction". (Cf. *Notes on Costume, JRAS*, 1935, p. 334, n. 5). Ibn Qayyim al-Jawziyya describes it as an article of wear characteristic of the Jews (see *Aḥkām ahl al-dhimma*, ii, pp. 752–53).

special garb of the *qāḍī* and the *faqīh.*[130] The qāḍī Abū Yūsuf is reported to have made the wearing of the *ṭaylasān* compulsory for the qāḍīs.[131] Although it was the insignia of the qāḍīs and the lawyers, it was also in use amongst the common people.[132] Even an ordinary clerk in the imperial palace of Baghdad could wear it.[133] Nevertheless, the qāḍīs and their *aṣḥāb*, from their wearing of this article, were often given the special designation of *arbāb al-ṭayālisa.*[134] Shābushtī records that a certain ʿAbbās of Basra wore a *ṭaylasān* resembling the costume of the qāḍīs (*yatashabbahu bi'l-quḍāt).*[135] Moreover, Isḥāq al-Mawṣilī is said to have appeared at the court of Ma'mūn wearing a *ṭaylasān*, a piece of apparel "similar to the costume of the qāḍīs" (*mithl ziyy al-fuqahā'*).[136]

Shamla

The *shamla* was a garment of the kind called *kisā'*, a robe, smaller than the *qaṭīfa*, which a person wrapped around himself.[137] It might be a small *kisā'* which one wrapped in the manner of the *izār* (waist-wrapper).[138] Muṣṭafā Jawād, quoting from Abū Manṣūr al-Azharī, states that the *milḥafa* was known to the Arabs as a wrapper (*mi'zar*) made of wool or hair. When its two ends were adorned, it became a *mashmala* which could also be used as a blanket.[139] The *shamla* seems to have been in frequent use amongst the poor. It was, to all appearance, a dress indicative of poverty and austerity. The *shamla* could be both voluminous and short. It is reported by *Aghānī* that the poet Abu'l-ʿAtāhiya once wore

---

130 *Aghānī*², v, p. 390; vi, p. 291; *Irshād*, v, p. 261; Mez, p. 389

131 Ibid., v, p. 390; Ibn Khallikān (de Slane), iv, p. 273; xi, p. 38; Ibn Abī ʿUsaybiʿa, *ʿUyūn al-Anbā'*, ii, p. 4. The importance of this insignia (*ṭaylasān*) was so great that the usher refused to introduce the qāḍī ʿAbd al-Raḥmān b. Mushhir to the Caliph Hārūn in the gathering of the judges, unless the qāḍī put on his official gown (*ṭaylasān*) (cf. *Wafayāt*, xi, p. 44).

132 *Diyārāt*, p. 297; Azdī, *Ḥikāyāt*, pp. 5–6

133 Ṭabarī, iii, p. 627

134 Levy, *Notes on Costume, JRAS*, 1935, p. 335

135 *Diyārāt*, p. 297

136 *Aghānī*², v, p. 390

137 *Qaṭifa* was an outer garment made of material which had *khaml*, i.e., a nap or pile (cf. *Lisān*, s.v.).

138 Ibid., s.v.

139 M. Jawād, *Azyat al-ʿArab*, in *M. Turāth al-Shaʿbī*, 1964, p. 9

a small *shamla* which, if he covered his head, exposed his legs and if he covered his legs, exposed his head.[140] This small *shamla* was also known as *falawt.*[141]

Kisā'

Among the dress of the common people, especially of the beduin, we also find mention of the *kisā'*, which was used as a blanket and as a wrapper.[142] It was generally made of wool and worn in the cold season.[143] Jāḥiẓ wore one such *kisā'* before winter had really come and was admonished by a miser to change it for a *jubba mahshuwwa* (a quilted *jubba*), as the wind might harm the *kisā'* irremediably. Like the *barnakān*, a long outer garment large enough to enfold the whole of the body, the *kisā'* was worn by men and women alike.[144]

'Abā'

The *'abā'* seems to have been a dress common to men and women, worn among the Arabs both in pre-Islamic and in Islamic times.[145] According to the *Lisān*, the *'abā'* is a costume similar to the *kisā'*.[146] Dozy defines it as a robe resembling a mantle, short and open in front, with no sleeves, but having two holes for the arms to pass through. This *'abā'* was a characteristic dress of the beduins, generally made out of coarse cloth or sometimes of wool in different colours.[147] The *'abā'*, when worn in the large towns, underwent a considerable change, being often fashioned from fine and expensive material. The Baghdadis, as a summer dress, wore an *'abā'* of thin cloth. Baghdādī women, however, often wore an *izār* instead of an *'abā'*.[148] One beduin, who possessed only a solitary *'abā'*, regretted his inability to go to the mosque for

---

140 *Aghānī*², iv, p. 83
141 Ibid¹, xv, p. 309; cf. also, M. Jawād, op. cit., p. 9
142 *'Uyūn*, iii, p. 300
143 Jāḥiẓ, *Bukhalā'*, p. 52
144 Ibid., p. 52
145 M. Jawād, op. cit., p. 11
146 *Lisān*, s.v. *'abā'*
147 Dozy, *Dictionnaire*, pp. 200–2
148 M. Jawād, op. cit., p. 15

prayer, reciting the following verses:

> *"Fa-in uksinī rabbī qamīṣan wa-jubbatan uṣalli wa-aʿbudhu ilā ākhir al-dahr*
> *wa-in lā yakun illā baqāyā ʿabāʾ mukharraqa mālī ʿalā ʿal-bard min ṣabr."*

"If the Lord grants me a *qamīṣ* and a *jubba,* I will pray and worship Him till the end of time; were it not for this torn *ʿabāʾ*, all that remains to me, I should not be able to endure the cold."[149]

Sirwāl

The *sirwāl* (plural *sarāwīl*), trousers or drawers, is a word probably of Persian origin.[150] This garment was "worn next the bare body under the other garments".[151] When Amīn was arrested and brought to prison by Ṭāhir, he was found to be wearing a *sirwāl.*[152] Similarly, Mutawakkil wore a *sirwāl* at the time of his installation as caliph by the Turks.[153] Like the *izār*, the *sirwāl* was also commonly used by men and women in the society. For women it was wide and capacious. Ḥamadānī informs us of a woman who made her *sirwāl* from a piece of material twenty *dhirāʿ* long.[154] The *dhirāʿ* seems to have been introduced by the Caliph Ma'mūn for the measurement of the cloth known as *dhirāʿ al-sawād.* It was the official Abbasid measure of twenty-four fingers (*iṣbāʿ*).[155]

The *sirwāl* was supported by a special girdle which was tied round the body, called *tikka* (plural *tikak*). Although the *tikka* was covered by the other garments and could not be seen, it was the object of luxurious decoration.[156] It was usually made of ibrisim silk.[157] The special *tikka* (trouser-cord) produced in Armenia was regarded as the best.[158] The

---

149 *Muḥāḍarāt*, iv, p. 368

150 See the pictorial representations of the costume of the Persian kings in Jalīl Ḍiyāpūr, *Pushāk ba-āstāni Irāniān.*

151 *EI*[1], s.v. *sirwāl* (B. Walter)

152 Ṭabarī, iii, p. 922

153 Ibid., iii, p. 1368

154 Ḥamadānī, *Maqāmāt*, p. 120

155 *Murūj*, i, p. 183; cf. also Serjeant, *Islamic Textiles*, Chap. ii, pp. 69–70; also *EI*[2], s.v. *Dhirāʿ* (W. Hinz)

156 *EI*[1], s.v. *sirwāl.* (B. Walter)

157 Dozy, *Dictionnaire*, pp. 95–9

158 *Tabaṣṣur bi'l-Tijāra*, pp. 336–7; *Laṭā'if*, p. 236

elegant wore trouser-bands of ibrisim silk and *khazz* silk. They also used woven girdles (*tikak*) of brocade or of twisted sharrāb-cloth made from ibrisim silk (*sharrābāt al-ibrisim al-maftūla*).[159]

Tubbān

The *tubbān* was a short *sirwāl* which covered the *ʿawra*, the lower portions of the body from the navel to the knees.[160] Attendants at the public baths wore the *tubbān* habitually. It was also worn at times of hunting, because it allowed the huntsmen ample freedom of movement. According to Samʿānī the *tubbān* was worn by fishmongers and sailors who were the inland river transport workers.[161]

Ṣudra

The *ṣudra* was a waistcoat which appears to have been a special dress used in playing outdoor games.[162] The Caliph Muʿtaṣim is reported to have refused to allow his partner Isḥāq b. Ibrāhīm to play polo with him, unless he donned a *ṣudra*.[163] It is also probable that the *ṣudra* could be worn as an undergarment with other clothes.

Mandīl

The *mandīl* (kerchief, towel) was an article of common use. People of all walks of life made use of it. It was of two types, one large and one small.[164] The small one was used for wiping tears and cleaning the nose and the mouth.[165] The extravagant wazir Ibn al-Furāt was in the habit of using more than ten *mandīl* (kerchiefs) a day. Whenever he sniffed at one, he threw it aside and took another.[166] The small *mandīl* was also used at dinners and at drinking parties.[167] The large *mandīl* was sometimes wound around the head in the absence of an

---

159 *Muwahshā*, p. 186

160 Ibn Sida, *Mukhaṣṣaṣ*, i, Chap. iv, p. 83; Dozy, op. cit, s.v.

161 Samʿānī, *Ansāb*, (Hyderabad ed.) iii, p. 13

162 Ṭabarī, iii, pp. 1326–7; Dozy, *Dictionnaire*, s.vv. *ṣudra, ṣadariyya*

163 Ṭabarī, iii, pp. 1326–7

164 *Dhakhā'ir*, pp. 75, 104, 215, 218, 229; Muq. p. 367; F. Rosenthal, *Four Essays . . .*, p. 73

165 Ibid., p. 259; *Aghānī*², x, p. 191

166 Ibid., p. 230

167 Ṣābī, *Wuzarā'*, p. 261; cf.; also, F. Rosenthal, op. cit., 76

'imāma;[168] ordinary people used it also as a shopping bag; lovers sent *manādīl al-kabīr* as presents to each other with beautiful verses written in gold, and perfumed.[169] At need the large *mandīl* could be worn as a wrapper (*izār*).[170]

Footwear

There were several types of footwear used at this period. They were known as the *khuff, na'l, tamashshuk, madās*. They also used stockings known as the *jurāb, mūzaj, ra'n*, etcetera.

Khuff

The *khuff* seems to have been a kind of top-boot made of leather. The Abbasid caliphs often used to line their *khuff* with sable (*sammūr*), marten (*fanak*), and other types of animal fur.[171] The fur of the *sammūr* (sable) was regarded by Damīrī as excellent for its softness, lightness, warmth and beauty.[172] The *khuff*-boot was sometimes used as a pocket for books, documents and other articles.[173] While mentioning the numerous furred boots of the Caliph Hārūn al-Rashīd, the Qāḍī Rashīd b. Zubayr in his *al-Dhakhā'ir wa'l-Tuḥaf* says "*Fī kull khuff minhā sikkīn wa mandīl*" (each boot had a knife and a kerchief in it).[174] That boots were used as repositories for some articles is also mentioned in the *Maqāmāt* of Ḥamadānī, where the author states that his hero Al-Iskandarānī stabbed his foe with a knife which he kept concealed in his *khuff*.[175] The *khuff*-boots were quite long and covered both the ankle and a portion of the leg. The *khuff* which did not cover the ankle and the shank is mentioned by the sources with a special adjective: *ajzam: maqṭū' al-Sāq*, a boot having no legging.[176] On account of the length, the

[168] *Murūj*, vii, p. 398
[169] *Muwashshā*, pp. 262–4
[170] Ṭabarī, iii, p. 623; *Manāqib Baghdād*, p. 31
[171] *Dhakhā'ir*, p. 218
[172] *Ḥayawān*, s.v. *sammūr*
[173] *Murūj*, vii, p. 240; *Irshād*, vi, p. 56; *Maṣāyid*, pp. 167–8; *Wafayāt*, xi, p. 68; Jah. *Wuzarā'*, 188; Ṣābī, *Rusūm*, 66–7
[174] *Dhakhā'ir*, p. 218
[175] *Maqāmāt*, p. 41
[176] *Aghānī*², xiii, p. 180; *'Uyūn*, iii, p. 238

upper end of the *khuff* was sometimes folded downward.[177] The *khuff* might also be provided with laces.[178]

Naʿl

The *naʿl* (plural *niʿāl*) was an ordinary sandal having thongs (*shirāk*).[179] It was generally made of leather, though linings of cloth could also be used.[180] Amongst the sandals in use at this time there is mention of the *niʿāl Sindiyya*, described by Jāḥiẓ as a very thick and heavy kind of footwear characteristic of the Magians and producing a particular sound in walking.[181] It is interesting to note that in his *Rasāʾil*, Jāḥiẓ has discussed the reasons for the origin and development of the use of these sandals in Abbasid society.[182] In his book on Misers (*Al-Bukhalāʾ*) he criticizes the niggardliness of a wealthy man called Asad b. Jānī who used to walk through the streets with his shoes in his hand, sometimes wearing broken-heeled sandals throughout the day.[183] It is reported that the poet Abu'l-ʿAtāhiya once presented to the Caliph Ma'mūn among other things a pair of *sabatiya* sandals,[184] a type of footwear which, since it was presented to a caliph, may well have been expensive and made of fine leather.

---

177 Levy, *Notes on Costume*, JRAS, 1935, p. 327

178 L. A. Mayer, *Mamluk Costume*, p. 35

179 Jāḥiẓ, *Bayān*, iii, p. 121; Khālidiyyān, *Tuḥaf*, p. 27; *ʿUyūn*, iii, p. 39; *ʿIqd*, vi, p. 283; cf. also Dozy, op. cit. s.v.

180 *Nishwār*, viii, 143; *Bayān*, iii, p. 121

181 *Bukhalāʾ*, pp. 91–2

182 Speaking about this sandal, Jāḥiẓ states that "there is divergence of opinion amongst us about the origin of the *Sindiyya niʿāl*. Some say that the author of the *Kitāb al-Bāh* was dreadfully short but very anxious to impress women, and therefore had the idea of wearing sandals like this in order to increase his stature by the thickness of their soles. In time it came to be supposed by the ignorant that they were merely decorative, or had some advantage or comfort in walking. Others say that they were designed to give protection against scorpions by night and mud by day, but that with the passage of time their origin was forgotten. Certainly they are thick enough to allow one to walk through almost any mire, and a scorpion's sting will not penetrate their sole. Others again say: on the contrary, they were adopted by Indian rulers because of the noise they make, so that their tapping might give their wives and free or slave women advance warning of their approach when they were busy about some task; the tapping became the signal of their arrival and their request for admission." Cf. *Tarbīʿ*, pp. 157–8; *Rasāʾil*, ed. Sandūbī, p. 230; also, Ch. Pellat, *Life and Works of Jāḥiẓ*, Eng. Tr. by D. M. Hawke, p. 128

183 Jāḥiẓ, *Bukhalāʾ*, pp. 91–2

184 Ibid., *Bayān*, iii, p. 121; Khālidiyyān, *Tuḥaf*, p. 27

Madās

The *madās* seems to have been a light sandal, used as indoor footwear and also carried to the *ḥammām* (baths). Dozy thinks that it was often embroidered and used both by men and women.[185] Ibn al-Jawzī observes that a certain Muḥammad Sakara entered a *ḥammām* with *madās* on his feet, but when he came out he lost them. He then returned home bare-footed and composed these clever verses:

> "*Ilaika adhumm ḥammām ibn Mūsā* *wa-in fāqa al-Munā ṭīban wa-ḥarrā*
> *Takātharat al-luṣūṣ ʿalaihi ḥattā* *layuḥfā man yātīh wa yuʿrā*
> *Wa-lam afqad bihī thawban wa-lākin* *dakhaltu Muḥammadān wa-kharajtu Bishrā*"

"To you (my friend) I condemn the bath of Ibn Mūsā, even though its fragrance and heat are beyond expectations; the number of thieves has increased in it to such an extent that visitors are left bare-footed and naked; although I did not lose any clothes there, I entered it as Muḥammad and came out as Bishr." The allusion is to the famous bare-footed Ṣūfī Bishr al-Ḥāfī (died 227 AH).[186]

Tamashshuk

Most probably people of lesser means and also the slaves wore a kind of sandal known as *tamashshuk*. It was light and helped its wearer to walk quickly. Tanūkhī records the story of a man wearing *khuff* boots who, finding himself unable to keep pace with his companion, borrowed a pair of *tamashshuk* from his slave and walked quickly.[187] It is possible that there were different kinds of *tamashshuk*. Ibn Abī ʿUṣaybiʿa tells us that a certain Ibn Ṣalāh ordered from a shoe-maker a pair of *tamashshuk* described specifically in our sources as "Baghdādī".[188]

---

185 Dozy, *Dictionnaire*, s.v. *madās*

186 Ibn al-Jawzī, *Ẓirāf*, p. 83

187 *Nishwār*, ii, in *RAAD*, xvii, p. 521

188 Ibn Abī ʿUṣaybiʿa, *ʿUyūn al-Anbā*ʾ, ii, p. 164. Ṣābī (*Rusūm*, 75, 92) mentions a special type of shoes known as *lālaka* which were worn by the caliphs and dignitaries. The word has not received attention from the lexicographers. The *lawlak* was perhaps some type of boot which resembled the *khuff* (cf. Badrī, *ʿĀmma*, 159). From Ibn al-Jawzī (*Dhamm al-Hawa*, p. 89) it appears that the *lawlak* (or *lālaka, lālaja*) was footwear common to both men and women. It was also provided with laces (*Rusūm*, p. 92).

Jurāb

The *jurāb* or *jawrab* (socks) were worn beneath the usual forms of footwear: *khuff* (boot), *niʿāl* (sandals) or *ahdhiya* (shoes).[189] Much attention was paid to the cleanliness of the *jurāb*. Thaʿālibī criticizes people who did not take good care of their socks and wore them unwashed and emitting a bad odour.[190] The *jurāb* was also called *mūzaj*—an arabicized word from the Persian *mūza*.[191] One wazīr, Fatḥ b. Khāqān, raised to that office in the time of Mutawakkil, used to wear fairly long *mūzaj* (socks). He used the *mūzaj* as a pocket for the book which he read, while going to make his ablutions.[192]

Ra'n

Sometimes with the *khuff*, people used to wear a special type of legging called *ra'n*,[193] presumably worn in cold weather.[194] According to the *Tāj al-ʿArūs* and the *Muḥīṭ al-Muḥīṭ* the *ra'n* is an article of wear longer than the *khuff*, but, unlike the *jurāb*, without a foot.[195] Lane observes that *ra'n* is a Persian word taken over into Arabic.[196] The *ra'n* has also been described as a piece of cloth made like the *khuff*, stuffed with cotton, and worn beneath the top-boot to ward off the cold.[197]

It will be interesting to quote here a passage from *Washshā'* regarding the shoes, boots, and socks of men of elegant taste. According to him, such men "use Zanjiyya (Negro) shoes and thick Kanbātī[198] shoes, furred shoes from the Yemen, also

---

[189] *ʿUyūn*, i, p. 299; *Dhakhā'ir*, p. 218

[190] *Thimār*, p. 486; cf. also, Ṭalaqānī, *Amthāl*, p. 8 (n. 100)

[191] Dozy, *Dictionnaire*, s.v. *mūzaj*

[192] *Fakhrī*, p. 4

[193] Figurative representations in L. A. Mayer's book clearly show a number of leggings worn on the *khuff*-boot (cf. *Mamluk Costume*, pl. 11).

[194] *Diyārāt*, pp. 138–9; Bayhaqī, *Maḥāsin*, p. 128; *Walīma ibn Wāsāma*, in *RAAD*, x (1930), pp. 641–719

[195] *Tāj*, ix, p. 223; *Muḥīṭ*, i, p. 846

[196] Lane, *Lexicon*, s.v. *ra'n*

[197] Ibid.

[198] Kanbātī shoes were brought from Cambay in India. Muqaddasī while speaking of Sind says "and from Manṣūra were brought fine Kanbātī shoes" (cf. p. 481). Manṣūra was the capital of Sind, which was conquered by Muḥammad b. Qāsim, a nephew of Ḥajjāj, in 92/711 (cf. Lane-Poole, *Mohammadan Dynasties*, p. 283). Azdī (*Ḥikāyāt*, p. 41) regards the Kanbātī shoes as fine and smooth. For more details on Kanbātī shoes see Dozy, *Suppl.* ii, p. 491; Aḥmad Taymūr, in *RAAD*, iii (1923), p. 77

Fig. 1. *A Khil'a* (*Robe of Honour*), with inscription of Baha al-Dawla

Fig. 2. *A Qāḍī in Session*. Illustration showing a *Qāḍī* with some of his litigants. The *Qāḍī* is wearing the *Ṭaylasān* robe and is seated on a dias.

Fig. 3. A Cooking Scene showing the oven, cooking utensils, and in the background the slaughtering of an animal.

fine and light shoes of the *mukhattam* type: of checked leather. The black kind can be worn with red laces [or thongs], and the yellow [kind] with black laces. These men wear Hāshimī boots and the split shoes of the officials, [also shoes made of] firm leather and of heavy black leather, with stockings of *khazz*-silk [or of] goat-hair (*mirʿizzī*) and silk. They dislike the red style of boots and black leather [boots] called *dārish*."[199]

The official colour and the ceremonial robes of the caliphs.

On ceremonial occasions the caliph sometimes wore the sacred mantle (*burda*) of the Prophet[200] with a girdle and sword.[201] Black, during the reign of Manṣūr, had become the colour prescribed for the officials serving the Abbasid regime.[202] The caliphs themselves wore black on occasions of state. Muʿtaṣim wore a vest of figured silk when he went out to play polo.[203]

Black remained in fashion until Ma'mūn, seeking at that time (201 AH) to secure the succession to the throne of an ʿAlid prince, ʿAlī al-Riḍā', ordered that green should become the official colour.[204] This change was of brief duration, black coming once more into favour after the death of ʿAlī al-Riḍā' in 203 AH. Black continued now to be the colour held in esteem. Muʿtaḍid, when he went into a battle wearing a yellow *qabā'* (an outer garment with full-length sleeves), found himself exposed to ridicule.[205]

Servants at the court of Baghdad as a rule had to wear black, and "to wear black" was a sign that a man was in the

---

[199] *Muwashshā*, p. 180; Serjeant, op. cit., Appendix i, 78

[200] M. Canard, *Cambridge Medieval History* (new edition), iv, pt. i, p. 700. *Burda* is a kind of striped garment generally used, of the fabric of the Yemen. From the fact that it could be worn by the successive caliphs it appears to have been a sleeveless cloak or shawl. Cf. Lane, *Lexicon*, s.v. *Burd*; Dozy, *Dictionnaire*, s.v. *Burda*; for details on the *burda* of the Prophet see *Ṣubh*, iii, p. 273

[201] *Aghānī*², x, p. 236; Ṣābī, *Rusūm*, pp. 90–1

[202] Ibid., x, 236

[203] Ṭabarī, iii, pp. 1326–7

[204] Ibid., iii, p. 1012; Azdī, *Ta'rīkh al-Mawṣil*, pp. 342, 352

[205] *Nishwār*, viii, p. 277

service of the caliph. Persons disliking this usage sometimes left the imperial service and even departed from the capital. Ibn al-Athīr tells us that Ḥāmid b. ʿAbbās,[206] to avoid the wearing of "the black", left Baghdad in disgust.[207] A qāḍī who refused to wear black is reported to have been threatened and warned that his failure to adhere to the custom would be interpreted as a sign of adherence to the Umayyad cause.[208]

The *burda*, the *qaḍīb* (staff) and the sword seem to have been the royal insignia of the Abbasid caliphs.[209] Ṭabarī tells us that Amīn, as a sign of his submission, sent the *ridā'*,[210] with a sword and a staff, to Ṭāhir b. Ḥusayn, victorious in his siege of Baghdad in 198 AH.[211] Though it was one of the royal insignia, the *burda* was not always worn by the caliphs at their installation. The Turkish soldiers invested Muḥammad b. Wāthiq with a black *durrāʿa* and a Ruṣāfī *qalansuwa*, but, finding him unworthy to be a caliph, transferred the tall *qalansuwa* to Mutawakkil. This *qalansuwa* with a turban formed the only mark of sovereignty.[212]

The Abbasid caliphs and affluent members of Abbasid society seem to have been much given to fine fabric, silken garments and material woven with gold thread. *Washī* (figured stuff) and *washī muthaqqal* (*washī* heavily adorned with gold) were much favoured by the caliphs.[213] *Washī*, produced in Alexandria, Kufa and the Yemen, was highly prized.[214] The Caliph Hārūn al-Rashīd was so fond of *washī*

---

206 Ḥāmid b. ʿAbbās (223–311) was an able financier who later became the wazīr of the Caliphs Muʿtamid and Muqtadir. For details see *EI*[1], s.v. *Ḥāmid b. ʿAbbās*

207 *Kāmil*, viii, p. 101

208 Kindī, *Wulāt*, p. 469

209 *Murūj*, vi, p. 482, vii, pp. 294, 364, 366, viii, p. 351; Ṭabarī iii, p. 771; Azdī, *Ta'rīkh al-Mawṣil*, p. 331; *Laṭā'if*, p. 131

210 Ṭabarī would seem to use the word *ridā'* with the same sense as *burda*. The event has been recorded by Masʿūdī and Ibn al-Athīr with the word *burda* (cf. Ṭabarī, iii, p. 928; *Murūj*, vi, p. 482; *Kāmil*, vi, pp. 198–9).

211 Ṭabarī, iii, p. 928

212 Ibid., iii, p. 1368

213 *Diyārāt*, p. 169; *Tajārib*, v, p. 85; *Aghānī*[1], xxi, p. 239

214 *Murūj*, v, p. 400; *Aghānī*[2], v, p. 318; Suyūṭī, *Ḥusn al-Muḥādara*, ii, p. 193; Serjeant, *Islamic Textiles*, Chap. xiii–iv; pp. 79–101; ix, p. 70. On reciting two verses of Ishāq al-Mawṣilī, Aṣmaʿī is reported to have said, "This is *washī al-Iskandarānī* and this is *dibāj al-khusruwānī*" (cf. *Aghānī*[2], v, p. 318). Fine texture of Yamanite *washī* was sometimes compared to the

that he used to have his *durrāʿa*, *ʿimāma*, *izār* and other garments made from this material.[215] In Muḥarram 175 AH, when he came to the Khuld palace, after his marriage with Zubayda, he bestowed on various people *al-washī al-mansūja*, *washī* woven, it would seem, with gold.[216] He also offered to the ladies of the Banū Hāshim, gifts of *washī muthaqqal*.[217] At the time of his death he left a large number of garments made from *washī* embroidered with gold: 4,000 garments according to Ibn Zubayr.[218] Ibn Zubayr mentions the following garments left by the Caliph in the royal wardrobe.[219]

Four thousand *jubba* of variegated silk said by Ghazūlī to have been woven with gold;
Four thousand *jubba* of *khazz* silk lined with the fur of the sable, the marten and other animals;
Ten thousand *qamīṣ* and *ghilāla* (shirts and chemises);
Ten thousand *qaftān* (a kind of robe resembling the *qabā*');
Two thousand *sirwāl* (trousers) of different materials;
Four thousand *ʿimāma* (turbans);
One thousand *ridā*' (wrappers) of different stuffs;
One thousand *ṭaylasān* (robes furnished with a hood);
Five thousand *mandīl* (handkerchiefs) of different materials;
One thousand *minṭaq* (girdles), which Ghazūlī described as studded with gold;
Four thousand pairs of *khuff* boots, most of them lined with the fur of the marten, sable and other animals;
Four thousand pairs of *jawrab* (stockings).

Hārūn's wife Zubayda was also extravagant in her dress. Her robes made of *washī* material were so expensive that a single one of them cost her fifty thousand dinars.[220] The

skin of the beautiful girls. Suyūṭī quotes:

"She is like the figured cloth of the Yemen, which the merchants brought from Ṣanʿā'" (cf. *Mustaẓraf*, pp. 42–3).

[215] *Aghānī*², v, p. 218

[216] *Diyārāt*, p. 157

[217] Ibid., p. 157

[218] *Dhakhā'ir*, p. 214

[219] Ibid., pp. 214–18. Another list, differing somewhat in points of details, can be found in Ghazūlī's *Maṭāliʿ*.

[220] *Murūj*, viii, p. 298. The report seems exaggerated and the figure 50,000 dinars seems incredible.

Caliphs Amīn and Mutawakkil are also said to have liked *washī* cloth.[221] The Caliph Mutawakkil is said to have introduced a new kind of material called *thiyāb al-mulḥama*, a cloth with a warp of silk, but a weft of some other stuff.[222] He preferred it to all other materials, and this fashion was followed by all the members of his household and spread among the people. Everyone wished to imitate the Caliph, with the result that the *thiyāb al-mulḥama* rose to a high price, the manufacture of it being increased to meet the fashion and satisfy the taste of the Caliph and his subjects.[223] Masʿūdī tells us that some of this material was still being made even in his own time (332 AH) and was known as *thiyāb al-Mutawakkiliyya*, a cloth of very beautiful weave and excellent colour.[224] It is noted that Mutawakkil, when he was at the Burj palace in 239 AH, donned a robe of gold-embroidered *washī* and ordered that no one should be allowed to call on him unless wearing *washī* or *dībājī* (brocade) garments.[225] The annual expenditure of this Caliph on clothes is said to have reached three hundred thousand dinars.[226]

The Abbasid caliphs and their high dignitaries often received valuable robes from foreign rulers. Ṭabarī records that in 190 AH the Byzantine emperor sent a present of one hundred robes of *dībāj* and two hundred of *buzyūn* material (brocade) to the Caliph Hārūn al-Rashīd.[227] In 293 AH the Frankish queen Bertha, the daughter of Lothair, sent a present to the Caliph Muktafī Bi'-llāh, which included twenty robes woven with gold.[228]

The Caliph Ma'mūn is reported to have sent a number of gifts to princes in India. Amongst the gifts were five different kinds of robe (*kiswa*). Of each kind the Caliph sent 100 items: of "*biyāḍ Miṣr*" (Egyptian white),[229] of *khazz* silk from Sūs, of

---

221 *Aghānī*[1], xxi, p. 239; *Diyārāt*, p. 15

222 Dozy, *Supplement*, ii, p. 522

223 *Murūj*, vii, p. 190

224 Ibid., vii, p. 190

225 *Diyārāt*, p. 161

226 *Dhakhā'ir*, p. 219

227 Ṭabarī, iii, p. 711

228 *Dhakhā'ir*, pp. 48–9. On the Frankish Queen (*Malaka Ifranja*) see M. Ḥamidullāh, *Journal Pakistan Historical Society*, 1953, pp. 272–300; cf. also, *EI*[2], s.v. *Ifrandj*

229 Possibly it meant white uncoloured linen, as it was the true Egyptian style and was compared, as the current saying went, with "the membrane round an egg" (cf. Mez, p. 460).

washī material from the Yemen and Alexandria, of Khurāsānī *mulḥam*, and of Khurāsānī *dībāj* (brocade).[230] In 282 AH ʿAmr b. Layth al-Ṣaffār is said to have sent to the Caliph Muʿtaḍid gifts which included one thousand robes of Rūmī *dībāj* and twelve pairs of sandals (*niʿāl*) studded with silver.[231] In the same year the Caliph Muʿtaḍid also presented to ʿAmr b. Layth al-Ṣaffār two hundred *badana* robes[232] and a *tāj*[233] which cost him thirteen thousand dinars.[234]

Distinctive costumes of some social groups

As has been mentioned above, the government functionaries generally wore their official distinctive robes. For example, the qāḍī wore the *danniyya* (tall cap) and the *ṭaylasān*, the wazirs and the secretaries (*kuttāb*) wore the *durrāʿa*, etc.[235] According to Jāḥiẓ, for a *khaṭīb* the *ʿimāma* and the *mikhṣara* (staff) were indispensable. Sometimes, however, he wore the *izār* instead of the *sirwāl*, when dressed for the *khuṭba*.[236] Jāḥiẓ also tells us that the poets wore *washī*,[237] *muqaṭṭaʿa*[238] and *ridāʾ* (of black), and were fond of wearing clothes of bright colour.[239] Singers, in general, wore fashionable and bright hues.[240] Isḥāq al-Mawṣilī is reported to have possessed *durrāʿa*, *qabāʾ* and other garments made from *khazz* silk and

---

230 *Dhakhāʾir*, p. 27

231 Ibid., p. 43

232 According to Serjeant, *Islamic Textiles*, xiii–xiv, 105, the *badana* was a garment made especially for the caliphs. Mez, on the evidence of Maqrīzī and Ibn Duqmāq, notes that *badana* was a special manufacture of the Tinnisians, woven in the shape of a garment, so that it had not to be cut and no stitching was required. Being a caliphal robe it contained no more than two ounces of linen, all the rest being gold; its value was 1,000 dinars (cf. Mez, p. 460).

233 *Tāj* literally means crown, but here perhaps turban.

234 *Dhakhāʾir*, p. 45

235 See above, pp. 34, 43; Ṣābī (*Rusūm*, p. 91) notes that the *danniyya* was abandoned towards the end of the 4th/10th century from the official marks of the qāḍīs.

236 Jāḥiẓ, *Bayān*, iii, p. 92

237 *Washī*: here a robe of *washī* cloth i.e., a figured material

238 *Muqaṭṭaʿa*: a long robe fashioned like the *jubba* and made of *khazz* silk (cf. *Lisān*, s.v. *qaṭaʿ*)

239 Jāḥiẓ, *Bayān*, iii, p. 115; Ḥamadānī, *Maqāmāt*, p. 84

240 *Aghānī*², v, p. 317

mulḥam material.[241] Ordinary singers, of course, could not afford such costly robes, and had therefore to be content with the less pretentious *qamīṣ*, *izār*, and other garments in common use.

Dress for convivial parties

At the convivial parties known as *majlis al-sharāb* a special dress called *thiyāb al-munādama* was worn. This dress consisted of a fine *ghilāla* (chemise), a bright *mulā'a*[242] and a *qamīṣ* (shirt) made of silk.[243] Failure to don the *thiyāb al-munādama* at these *majālis* was looked at askance. *Aghānī* tells us that a certain ʿAbd al-Mālik, through a mistake of the *ḥājib* (chamberlain), entered a *majlis al-sharāb*, arranged by the wazir Jaʿfar b. Yaḥyā, without wearing the prescribed dress. All the participants were puzzled to find a man with a *qalansuwa* and a *ṭaylasān* present at the *majlis*. He was persuaded to don the *thiyāb al-munādama* forthwith.[244] According to Ṣābī the robes of honour for the *nadīms* (*khilaʿ al-munādama*) consisted of the following items: *ʿimāma washī mudhahhaba*,[245] *ghilāla* (chemise), *mubaṭṭana*,[246] *durrāʿa dabīqiyya*,[247] and other gifts and perfumes.[248]

Dress of the elegant people *(Ẓurafā')*

Though the people of sophisticated and refined tastes did not form a distinctive social group in the real sense of the term, they received special treatment by mediaeval authors who

241 *Diyārāt*, pp. 42–4

242 The *mulā'a* would seem to have been a garment made from two pieces of cloth sewn together to form a robe. It should be contrasted with the *rīṭa*, a robe fashioned out of a single piece of cloth. The *mulā'a* was, in general, yellow in colour. Cf. Ibn Saʿd, *Ṭabaqāt*, vi; p. 197 "*mulā'a ṣafrā'*"; also, *Lisān*, s.v., and in addition Lane, *Lexicon*, s.v. *mulā'a*

243 *Aghānī*², v, pp. 407–8; *Quṭub al-Surūr*, p. 15; *Muwashshā*, p. 179; Azdī, *Ta'rīkh al-Mawṣil*, pp. 262–3

244 *Aghānī*², v, p. 408; Azdī, op. cit., pp. 262–3

245 Turbans of variegated silk woven with gold or embroidered with heavy gold. On *ʿimāma* see above, pp. 31–3

246 On *mubaṭṭana*, see Dozy, s.v.; also, Serjeant, op. cit., Index

247 The *durrāʿa* made out of the Dabīqī stuff. On the *durrāʿa* and the Dabīqī stuff see above, pp. 39, 38

248 *Rusūm*, p. 96

wrote books on their social lives and described their modes of dress, food, etcetera, in detail.[249] The nearly contemporary author Washshā' (died 325 AH) is perhaps the most copious in providing details of the costumes these people generally wore, a description which also throws some light on the specialities of different lands in the manufacture of textiles and garments.

According to Washshā' these people wore fine chemises (*ghilāla*) and thick shirts (*qamīṣ*) of excellent kinds of linen, soft and pure of colours, such as Dabīqī and Jannābī (from Jannāba in Fārs), linings (*mubaṭṭanāt*) of *tākhtanj* and raw stuffs (*khāmāt*), *durrā'as* of Dārābjird and Alexandria, garments made out of *mulḥam*, *khazz* silk and Khurāsānī materials with linings of soft Kūhī stuff, *izārs* of thin linen, bordered gowns (*ridā'*) from Aden, *ṭaylasān*-hoods of Nīshāpur *mulḥam* and Dabīqī of one colour, *jubbas* (gowns) of Nishapur, other stuffs with *ṭirāẓ* inscriptions,[250] Sa'dī figured *washī*-stuffs, Kufan *khazz* silk, *miṭraf*-cloaks of Sūs, robes of Fārs, and the like.[251] They used trouser-bands (*tikka*) of *ibrisim* silk and *khazz* silk, and cotton *miṭraf*-cloaks of figured Armenian stuffs.[252]

The elegant, noble and educated men did not wear soiled clothing with clothing which had been washed, nor garments which had been washed with new garments, nor linen with cotton, nor cotton with Kūhī[253] material. The best taste advocated the wearing of clothes which suited one another in gradual range of colour, and materials which had something in common and did not clash.[254]

According to a passage of the *Ḥikāyāt Abi'l-Qāsim* of Azdī, the wealthy people and the men of refined taste wore garments

---

[249] Cf. M. Ghazi, "un groupe social: 'les raffinés' (*Zurafā'*)", *SI*, xi (1959), pp. 39–71

[250] On the *Tirāẓ* see below, pp. 68–70

[251] *Muwashshā*, pp. 178–9. The passage has been translated into English by Serjeant in *Islamic Textiles*, Appendix I, p. 78 and by Carl Johan Lamm in "Cotton in the Medieval Textiles of the Near East", Paris, 1937, pp. 182–3

[252] *Muwashshā*, p. 180

[253] On the material called Kūhī cf. Serjeant, *Islamic Textiles* Chap. ix, 119, referring to Ṭabarī, ii, p. 1636 (*wa'l-dībāj al-Marwī wa'l-Qūhī*), and also to Ṭabarī, iii, 949 (*Abha wa-anqa min al-Qūhiyya al-judud*), passages which perhaps indicate a kind of brocaded cloth.

[254] *Muwashshā*, p. 179

of reddish Dabīqī, of Qīrāṭī Zuhayrī (perhaps a stuff with patterns embroidered all over in the shape of the coins called *qīrāṭ*, a fraction of a dinar, and manufactured in the Zuhairiyya Quarter of Baghdad) and of reddish woven stuff. They also wore the *ridā'* of Aden, garments of *qaṣab*-linen, of figured material of brocade with woven gold and decorated with beautiful designs.[255]

It is to be noted that the accounts of Ziryāb in Spain give a good indication of Baghdadi standards of elegance. According to Maqqarī, Ziryāb introduced a change of clothing according to the different seasons of the year. For spring he suggested wearing the *jubba* of coloured silk or *mulḥam* material, and the *durrā'a* having no linings, and made of light materials. For summer and autumn he introduced light clothes such as were found in Marv, and thickly lined and wadded clothes to be worn in the morning when the cold began to be sharp. On the approach of winter, warmer clothing of different colours was suggested, lined whenever the weather required it, with various kinds of fur.[256]

Dress of the sufis

The sufis (ascetic mystics) of our period wore woollen garments and patched robes.[257] Striped clothes and garments having different colours were also sometimes worn by them.[258] The most conspicuous items of dress, which set them apart from other people, were the *jubba* of wool[259] and the *khirqa*, a garment made of materials in two or three different colours stitched together.[260] It was also used as a robe of investiture, which sufi novices received from their *shaikhs*.[261] The sufis also sometimes wore the *ridā'*, the *ṭaylasān*, the *qamīṣ* and the *izār*, often bearing a few patches.[262]

255 Azdī, *Ḥikāyāt*, p. 35f

256 Maqqarī, *Nafkh al-Ṭīb*, Beirut, 1968, iii, p. 128

257 Ibn al-Jawzī, *Talbīs*, pp. 181, 183, 188

258 Ibid., pp. 180, 186, 198

259 Ibid. Cf. also Ḥarīrī, *Maqāmāt*, ed. Steingass, p. 405: "He wore the wool and became a leader of the rows (of people at prayer) and a well-known mystic."

260 Ibid., *Talbīs*, p. 198. The *Ansārs* of Mahdī in the Sudan also used the patched garments.

261 Ibid., pp. 186–7

262 Ibid., pp. 216–19; *Ẓirāf*, pp. 6–7

There were some sufis who piled patch on patch until the garment became abnormally thick. It is reported that once the sleeve of such a patched garment weighed eleven ratls.[263] Such heavily patched garments were known as *al-kabl.*[264] Ibn al-Jawzī informs us that some of the sufis of later Abbasid times used to take new materials of various colours, cut a piece out of each, and stitch the pieces together most elegantly. Others donned clothes of fine material and fine Byzantine head-wear[265] without embroidery; the shirt and the head-dress thus worn might have cost five times as much as a similar article in silk.[266]

Dress of the soldiers

It appears that regulations defining the dress to be worn by officers and soldiers of the caliph's army were laid down and maintained. Uniforms for soldiers are not heard of until the formations of the standing bodyguards of Turkish mercenaries during the time of the Caliph Muʿtaṣim.[267] Masʿūdī notes that the Caliph dressed them in magnificent costumes which distinguished them from the rest of the army.[268] The various divisions of troops had different distinguishing signs. Thus the *abnā'*[269] wore turbans and garments with a

[263] Ibid., p. 186. For equivalent weights, v. p. 138 below

[264] *Kabl* literally means chain or fetters; since the garment was heavily patched and became abnormally thick, it was perhaps satirically called *al-kabl* (a garment as fetters for the wearer).

[265] *Talbīs*, pp. 189–99 "*ʿimāma al-Rūmiyya*", perhaps from the material of Byzantine textiles

[266] Ibid., pp. 189–99

[267] Qalqashandī, *Ṣubḥ*, iii, 272; *Eclipse*, iii, p. 152

[268] *Tanbīh*, p. 356

[269] *Abnā* 'was a term applied in the early Abbasid period to the members of the Abbasid house, and by extension to the Khurāsānī and other *Mawālī* who entered its services and became adoptive members of it (cf. *EI*², s.v. *Abnā'*). The first generation of the Khurāsānians, who took pride in their decisive role in bringing about the Abbasid revolution, were reverentially called *abnā' al-dawla* or *abnā al-da'wa,* the Sons of the Revolution. They were frequently referred to simply as the *abnā'*. They were deeply involved in the commercial life of Baghdad and utilized their prestige to increase their wealth and power. (Cf. M. A. Shaban, *Islamic History A New Interpretation, 2,* pp. 30, 37–46.) According to Sāleḥ el-Alī, most of the commanders of the *Abnā'* were Arabs. They were probably the descendants

border.[270] The standard-bearers of the *abnā'* used to wear coats of mail. The Khurāsānī soldiers wore a special epaulette called *bāzbakand* or *bāzfakand*.[271] The high ranking commanders used to wear coats of mail.[272] Mas'ūdī notes that it was only Bughā al-Kabīr, one of the Turkish commanders in Mu'taṣim's army, who "never donned any dress made of iron".[273] There is also mention of soldiers wearing tunics of royal satin (*aṭlas*), with close-fitting caps and hoods pointed at the top.[274] Among other dress of the soldiers, *sirwāl* has been particularly mentioned, which in winter was lined with the fur of various animals.[275]

Some indirect information about the uniform of the military commanders can be gleaned from the *khil'a* (robes of honour) they frequently received from the caliphs. According to Hilāl al-Ṣābī, the Abbasid caliphs offered their military commanders the following articles as the *khil'a*: a black turban of one colour (*'imāma muṣmata sawdā'*); a robe (*sawād*) of a single colour having a collar and a lining; a similar robe without the collar; red *khazz* silk of Sūs, gold-figured silk (*washī mudhahhab*) and *mulḥam* stuff or single-coloured stuff of *Khazz*; Dabīqī *qabā'* and a sword with a red sheath studded with silver; mounts with saddles. The commanders who distinguished themselves in battles received, in addition, a collar (*ṭawq*), two bracelets (*siwārayn*), a sword and a girdle (*minṭaq*). The collar and the bracelet were often studded with jewels.[276] Afshīn, the military commander of Mu'taṣim, Badr, the commander of Mu'taḍid, Mu'nis, the commander of

of the army levied by the Arabs on the local cities and provinces of Khurāsān and Central Asia (cf. *The Islamic City*, p. 98). The *Abnā'*, according to Ṭabarī, were about 20,000 fighters who fought in many battles, and sided with Amīn in his struggle with Ma'mūn (cf. Ṭab. iii, pp. 828, 840). They spoke Arabic and some of them were poets (Ṭab. iii, pp. 833, 936). For their various names see Ṭab. iii, pp. 499, 849, 825, 830

270 Jāḥiẓ, *Rasā'il*, i. p. 19 (Eng. Tr. *JRAS*, 1915, 651–2)

271 The word *Bāzbakand* or *bāzfakand*, *bāzīkand* means "epaulette", though the origin and sense of the term seem to be hitherto without an adequate explanation. The word seems a Persian Arabicized one from *bāz*, hawk and *bagand*, nest (cf. ibid., i, p. 19; *Bayān*, iii, p. 115).

272 *Murūj*, viii, p. 47; Balādhurī, *Futūḥ*, p. 318; 'Arīb, p. 12

273 *Murūj*, vii, p. 361

274 *Tajārib*, i, p. 54

275 Ṭabarī, iii, p. 1731

276 *Rusūm*, pp. 93–4

Muqtadir, and others received these robes of honour and distinction.[277]

Dress of the *dhimmī*

Dhimmī were required to wear particular forms of dress. According to the Shāfiʿī *madhhab* the *dhimmī* had to wear a cap, a girdle round the waist, while he was at the *ḥammām*, a boss (*khātam*) of copper or lead around his neck. No *dhimmī* was to wear a turban or a long coat; *dhimmī* women had to wear girdles under or over the skirt and also one shoe of black and one of white.[278] In his *Kitāb al-Kharāj* Abū Yūsuf mentions a number of regulations which affected the non-Muslims in respect of their dress, of their mount, and of their general attire. *Dhimmī* should wear "the *zunnār*[279] round their waist resembling a thick cord which each of them would wear as a belt, their *qalansuwa* should be quilted, and on their saddles they should put pommels of wood, as large as pomegranates, and not pommels made from precious metal. They should also twist the straps of their shoes and should not (in general) imitate the fashion of the Muslims. Their women should be forbidden to wear leather sandals in riding. The *qalansuwa* of the fire-worshippers, however, should be long and quilted."[280]

In 191 AH Hārūn al-Rashīd, according to Ṭabarī, issued an ordinance for the *dhimmī* living in Baghdad to the effect that they should distinguish themselves from the Muslims in their dress and in their mounts.[281] Ṭabarī, however, gives no

[277] Ibid., p. 94. The victorious Muwaffaq was decorated by Muʿtazz with a diadem and a double *wishāḥ* (a broad belt of leather adorned with jewels) as Afshīn before him had been for his success against Bābak (cf. *Murūj*, vii, pp. 369; 132f).

[278] Ishbihī, *Mustaṭraf*, i, p. 106; Shayzarī, *Nihāyat al-Rutba*, p. 106; Ibn al-Ukhuwwa, *Maʿālim al-Qurba*, pp. 40–1; cf. also Tritton, *Islam and the Protected Religions*, in *JRAS*, 1927, pp. 479–84

[279] Cf. A. S. Tritton, op. cit., p. 482: "The word is Greek, came into Arabic through Aramaic, and came into popular favour only gradually. Finally it was so identified with the non-Muslims that in modern Arabic the Jew's lovelocks—the corners of the head which he is forbidden to shave—are called *zunnār*."

[280] *Kharāj*, p. 72; cf. also, I. Lichtenstadter, *The distinctive dress of non-Muslims*, in *Historia Judaica*, 1943, p. 42

[281] Ṭabarī, iii, p. 712; Azdī, *Taʾrīkh al-Mawṣil*, p. 311

details about this decree of Hārūn al-Rashīd. According to Mārī b. Sulaymān, the Caliph was persuaded by his private physician, Jibra'īl b. Bakhtīshū', to reconsider the ordinance. The Caliph acceding to the request of the physician allowed the non-Muslims to wear costumes of their choice.[282] Ṭabarī and other *dhimmī* authors offer a full account of the similar ordinance which the Caliph Mutawakkil issued in 235 AH. According to this ordinance Christians and *ahl al-dhimma* had to wear honey-coloured hoods (*ṭaylasān*), the *zunnār* or girdle, and also two buttons on their caps, the caps differing in colour from those worn by the Muslims. Their slaves should wear two patches on the outer garment. The patches should be yellow and four fingers square. If a *dhimmī* wore a turban, it was to be yellow. Their women, while visiting outdoors, had to wear a yellow wrapper (*izār*) and their servants had to wear the *zunnār* and not the *minṭaq*.[283] In the year 239 AH Mutawakkil imposed some new regulations and ordered the Christians to wear *durrā'a* and *qabā'* (tunics) with two yellow *dhirā'* (sleeves ?),[284] and forbade them to ride horses.[285]

One of the distinctive garments which the *dhimmī* had to wear was the *ghiyār*.[286] The word *ghiyār* is Arabic, and means distinction or cognizance.[287] Perlmann explains it, in relation to dress, as a robe of distinction imposed on the *dhimmī*, or as a piece of cloth having a patch of stipulated colour placed on the shoulder.[288] In his *Aḥkām Ahl al-dhimma* Ibn Qayyim al-Jawziyya has given us his legal opinion regarding the dress of

282 Mārī b. Sulaymān, *Akhbār faṭāriqat kursī'l-Mashriq*, p. 73

283 Ṭabarī, iii, pp. 1389–90; Mārī, op. cit, p. 79; 'Amr b. Matti, *Akhbār faṭāriqa kursī al-Mashriq*, p. 71. The *minṭaq* was a kind of girdle or waist-belt, fastened around the waist with a buckle or clasp. It was worn by both men and women. Women of means sometimes adorned their *minṭaq* with plates of silver or gold, and with jewels also (cf. Dozy, *Dictionnaire*, p. 420).

284 *Dhirā'*, meaning forearm or arm, but perhaps to be construed in the sense of sleeve

285 Ṭabarī, iii, p. 1419

286 *EI*², s.v. *Ghiyār* (M. Perlmann); Mārī, op. cit., pp. 114, 115; Matti, op. cit., p. 71; Serjeant, "A Zaidī manual of *ḥisba* of the 3rd century H", *RSO*, 28 (1953), p. 29; *Nihāya*, pp. 106, 124

287 Ibid., *EI*², s.v. *Ghiyār*., 'Amr b. Mattī notes that the *ghiyār* indicated distinctive colour: blue for the Christians and black for the Jews (cf. op. cit., p. 71).

288 *EI*², s.v. *Ghiyār*

the *dhimmī.* He says that the non-Muslims should not wear the *ʿimāma* or the *lāṭiya* (a close fitting cap).[289] Their shoes and sandals should be different from those of the Muslims. They should not wear the *ridāʾ*, because this was the characteristic dress of the Arabs. They could wear the *ṭaylasān*, because this was a traditional costume of the Jews. *Dhimmī* should not carry swords; their women should wear one red shoe, when visiting outdoors. In order that their status should be visible to all, the *ahl al-dhimma* ought to wear ash-coloured (*ramādī*), yellow or blue dress, since Muslims, in general, did not use garments of these hues.[290]

Regional and ethnic differences in dress

It will be of some interest to examine the differences of dress worn by the people of various classes in different regions. The main source of information on this point is the eye-witness reports of the geographers and travellers who travelled over long distances in the east and the west and recorded their experiences in the form of excellent treatises. Both Ibn Ḥawqal and Muqaddisī (also pronounced Maqdisī), were keen observers of social life. They recorded the picturesque life of the common people in the second half of the fourth century AH. The accounts of these geographers, though representative of the fourth century, throw some light on the practices of the third century, as the Muslim community in the mediaeval period was mostly conservative and rather unwilling to accept changes in its social life and general attire.

Speaking about the dress worn in Iraq, Muqaddasī notes that the people there are fond of sartorial fashions.[291] According to Ibn Ḥawqal and Muqaddasī the use of the *ṭaylasān* (a robe with hood), the *qamīṣ*, long turbans, linen stuff (*shurūb*) and sandals was widespread among the Iraqis.[292] They seldom cut their *ṭaylasān* in a round form

---

[289] Ibn Qayyim al-Jawziyya, *Aḥkām ahl al-dhimma*, ii, p. 738. It was regarded as the favourite headgear of the Prophet Muḥammad.

[290] Ibid., *Aḥkām*, ii, pp. 735–44

[291] Muq. p. 129

[292] Ibid., p. 129; Ibn Ḥawqal, p. 174

(*muqawwar*).[293] The merchants (*tujjār*) wore the *qamīṣ* and the *ridā'*,[294] whereas the preachers (*khuṭabā'*) donned the *qabā'* and the *minṭaq* (girdle).[295]

In the Arabian Peninsula, Muqaddasī notes that most of the people wore the *izār* without the *qamīṣ*. In some places the *izār* was the only garment with which they covered their body.[296] They used cotton for their clothing and took sandals as their footwear.[297]

The Syrians had a decent taste in the choice of their dress. People from all walks of life, whether educated or ignorant, wore the *ridā'*; they used the *khuff*-boot in winter and sandals in summer. They did not wear *ṭaylasān* in round shapes. The *durrā'a* was a costume worn exclusively by the villagers and by the secretaries. In some villages of Syria people wore only a single *kisā'* without a *sirwāl*.[298]

According to Ibn Ḥawqal, the people of Khūzistān mostly wore such costumes as were worn by the Iraqis: the *qamīṣ*, the *ṭaylasān*, and the *'imāma*. Among the old people the *izār* and the *mi'zar* were also common.[299] Muqaddasī notes that the *ṭaylasān* was worn mostly by the élite (*wajīh*), and the other people generally used the square *ridā'*, the *mandīl* (perhaps in the form of a wrapper) and the *fūṭa* (wrappers). The *khaṭīb* in Khūzistān, following the Iraqi fashion, wore the *qabā'* and the *minṭaq*.[300]

The dress of the people of Fārs (Iran) presented a variety of forms. The sulṭān donned the *qabā'* and the *durrā'a*, the latter being loose with a wide collar and with an opening like the *durrā'a* of the secretaries. They used tall caps under their turbans, girdles round their waist, and top-boots of short length on their feet. The judges wore the extraordinary tall caps such as the *danniyya*, the *ṭaylasān*, the *qamīṣ* and the *jubba*. The judges did not wear the *durrā'a*, the split boots, nor caps which covered the ears. The secretaries wore costumes similar to the dresses used by the secretaries of Iraq, the *durrā'a*. They did not use the *qabā'* and the *ṭaylasān*. Other local residents used the *ṭaylasān*, the *ridā'*, the *kisā'*, the *qamīṣ*, the *jubba*, the *mubaṭṭana*, the unsplit *khuff*, turbans,

---

293 Muq. p. 129
294 Ibn Ḥawqal, p. 232
295 Muq. p. 129
296 Ibid., pp. 99–100
297 Ibid., pp. 95–6
298 Ibid., p. 183
299 Ibn Ḥawqal, p. 174
300 Muq. p. 416

and other costumes of *khazz* silk worn in Iraq.[301] Muqaddasī notes that the people of Fārs adhered to the "Abbasid black" and the use of the *ṭaylasān* was so common among the masses that its wearer lost all prestige. He also notes that in Shīrāz those wearing the *ṭaylasān* received no respect from the masses; on the contrary those who wore the *durrāʿa* commanded greater respect and prestige.[302] In this connection he also notes his own experience that when he went to have an audience with the wazir wearing the *ṭaylasān*, he was refused permission to enter the house; but next time, when he donned the *durrāʿa*, he was welcomed.[303]

Like the Syrians the people of Kirmān showed elegance in their dress.[304] The textile industry of Kirmān was highly specialized and, according to Ibn Ḥawqal, fine qualities of *ṭaylasān* were exported to Iraq, Egypt, and Khurāsān, and were liked by the caliphs and the dignitaries.[305] The general customs (*rusūm*) of the people of Kirmān resembled those of the people of Fārs.[306]

The people of Daylam, Ṭabaristān, Ray and Sijistān wore costumes similar to the costume of the Iraqi peoples.[307] In Jurjān the *ṭaylasān* was not an article in common use.[308]

The mode of the costume of Khurāsān, Marv and Nīshāpūr differed from that of other regions. The *khaṭīb* did not wear the *qabā'* or the *ridā'*; they wore, instead, the *durrāʿa*. The use of the *khuff* in these regions was common both in summer and in winter; hence, sandals were rarely seen on their feet.[309] In big cities such as Nīshāpūr the *faqīh* and the *kabīr* (dignitaries) wore the *ṭaylasān*. In winter they put their *ṭaylasān* over the turban and then wore a *durrāʿa* over it, the lower portion of the *ṭaylasān* being thrown back over the shoulder on the *durrāʿa*.[310] In Transoxiana, the *ṭaylasān* was the special costume of the dignitaries; other people wore the *qabā'* which was open in front. In Marv, some ulema put their *ṭaylasān* on only one shoulder. It was the custom there that

---

301 Ibn Ḥawqal, pp. 205–6
302 Muq. pp. 7, 440
303 Ibid., p. 7
304 Ibid., p. 469
305 Ibn Ḥawqal, p. 223
306 Muq. p. 469
307 Ibn Ḥawqal, pp. 270, 302
308 Muq. p. 368
309 Ibid., p. 327
310 Ibid., p. 328

whenever a *faqīh* was promoted or given an honour, he was asked to don the *ṭaylasān.*[311]

Dress of women

Although *Aghānī* informs us that the dress of women differed from that of men only in the omission of the turban, Washshā', in his *Kitāb al-Muwashshā*, states that it differed both in kind and in colour from that of men. The Arabic words "*fa-jamaʿtu ʿalayya thiyābī*" (I put on my dress), if spoken by a male, meant an *izār*, a *ridā'*, an *ʿimāma*, a *durrāʿa*, and a *khimār*;[312] and if spoken by a female, referred to a *dirʿ*,[313] a *milḥafa*[314] and a *khimār.*[315]

According to Washshā' elegant women of this period wore neither the trouser-cord (*tikka*), unless it was made of ibrisim silk, nor any garment sprinkled or perfumed (*marshūsh* or *muṭayyab*), nor one of a single colour, nor any garment of white linen except that which is coloured by nature or dyed according to its kind, or altered from being exclusively the garb of men with some kind of musk or perfume of sandalwood, so that the scent made a different kind of dress, since the wearing of white was a man's prerogative.[316] The *ghilāla dukhāniyya* (smoke-coloured chemise), the *ridā' Rashīdiyya* (the Rashīdī cloak, perhaps from Rosetta), the *ardiya Ṭabariyya* (the Ṭabarī cloaks), the *ḥarīr muʿayyan* (silk embroidered with round circles), the *miqnaʿ Nīshābūrī* (the Nīshāpūrī veils), the *izār al-mulḥam al-Khurāsānī* (the *izārs* of Khurāsānī *mulḥam*)—these were some of the dresses worn especially by ladies of elegant taste.[317] Zubayda, the cousin-

---

311 Ibid., p. 328

312 The *khimār* was a head-cover or veil with which women covered their head and face (cf. Dozy, *Dictionnaire*, s.v. *khimār*).

313 *Dirʿ*: a women's garment, either a *qamīṣ* (shirt) or a robe to be worn over the *qamīṣ*, made from wool; or else a tunic something like the *durrāʿa* (cf. Lane, s.v. *dirʿ*)

314 The *milḥafa* was an outer garment worn usually in cold weather. All garments which one wraps around oneself can be described as *liḥāf* or *milḥafa*. To the Arabs the *liḥāf* was the "*mulā'a al-sumuṭ*" (a kind of cloth used to cover tables). When the *liḥāf* was lined with some other material or with fur, it became a *milḥafa* (cf. *Lisān*, s.v. *laḥaf*).

315 *Lisān*, ix, p. 405

316 *Muwashshā*, pp. 184–5

317 *Muwashshā*, p. 184

wife of the Caliph Hārūn al-Rashīd, is said to have set the fashion for the smart set and was the first to ornament her shoes with precious stones.[318] Similarly, the princess ʿUlayya, the daughter of Mahdī, devised a fillet set with jewels.[319]

The distinctive feature of women's dress lay in the variety of colour and multiplicity of decoration.[320] Widows and scabby women with skin disease (*muqarraʿāt*)[321] wore indigo or black.[322] Dancers and singers and Nabaṭī[323] women used garments dyed red, green or rose colour.[324] *Aghānī* tells us that a certain Abū Isḥāq found the singing girls of Hārūn al-Rashīd wearing bright rose coloured *qamīṣ*, *sirwāl* and *qināʿ*, so that it looked as if "a hyacinth had been placed upon a rose".[325] One difference between the dress of the well-to-do and the less well-to-do was that the former never used a garment which was dyed a second time, while the latter did.[326]

As to their head-dress, the women of our period used the *khimār* (head-cover) and the *miqnaʿ* or *niqāb* (veil), the latter being generally worn when going out.[327] For the decoration of the head, women used to wear the *ʿiṣāba*. According to Dozy the *ʿiṣāba* was something like a piece of wide lace tied round the head. It was richly embroidered and decked with jacinth and pearls by wealthy women.[328] Ladies of elegant taste also used the *wiqāya*, a band to hold the hair in place,

318 *Murūj*, viii, pp. 298–9

319 *Aghānī*², x, p. 162

320 Miskāwayh, *Tahdhīb*, p. 49; Suyūṭī, *Mustaẓraf*, p. 66

321 The word *muqarraʿāt* is difficult to interpret in a precise sense. The dictionaries (*lisān*, s.v. *qarʿ*) give to this term the meaning of "women suffering from skin disease"; Serjeant, however, translates this word as "women in trouble" (cf. *Islamic textiles*, Appendix, I, p. 79).

322 *Muwashshā*, p. 185

323 On the term "Nabati" cf. *EI*¹, s.v. Nabatean, where the word is given the following definition: in the Muslim era the Arabs used it to denote, in Syria and Iraq, people who were neither shepherds nor soldiers. It was also applied with a somewhat contemptuous connotation to the Aramaic-speaking peasants.

324 *Muwashshā*, p. 185

325 *Aghānī*², v. p. 299

326 *Muwashshā*, p. 185

327 *Aghānī*², iii, pp. 45–6; Ṭabarī, iii, p. 1084; *Quṭub al-Surūr*, pp. 163–4; Khaṭīb, *Taʾrīkh*, ii, p. 319

328 Dozy, *Dictionnaire*, pp. 301–3; *ʿIqd*, iv, p. 370f.; *ʿIṣāba*, when used of a man, had the sense of a turban (cf. *Aghānī*², v, p. 317).

which was ornamented and sometimes adorned with *ṭirāz*[329] inscriptions.[330] Such ladies decorated the sleeves of their *qamīṣ* too, with *ṭirāz* bands and other luxurious embroideries.[331] From the writings of Washshā', it is known that the slave-girls of the well-to-do people sometimes used *qalansuwa* as their headgear, profusely decorated with *ṭirāz* inscriptions and ornamented.[332]

Among the dresses that women used as *shiʿār*[333] were the *itb*, the *ṣidār*, the *shawdhar*, the *qarqur*, and the *qarqal*. All these words designated sleeveless blouses and chemises similar in shape, but different in sartorial fashion.[334].

The ladies of Baghdad wore special shoes called *khifāf zanāniya*. They preferred *mushaʿara* (furred shoes) from Kanbay for winter wear, and the split type (*maksūr*) and the Edessa (Rahāwī) shoes for summer use.[335] Muqtadir's mother is reported to have been in the habit of using luxurious sandals of Dabīqī stuff[336] studded with precious materials.[337]

Ṭirāz inscriptions

A student of Abbasid sartorial fashions often comes across the word *ṭirāz*: an inscription on a dress. A. Grohmann, in his article "Ṭirāz" in *EI*[1], and R. B. Serjeant, in his work on Islamic Textiles, have discussed at length the origin of the word and the introduction of the practice into the Muslim world.[338] According to them, *ṭirāz* is a word of Persian origin taken into Arabic. It would seem that the *ṭirāz* was first introduced into Muslim practice during the time of the Umayyad Caliph Marwān II (139–45 AH).[339] The demand of the caliphs for fine fabrics, not only for their own use but also

329 On the *Ṭirāz* see below.
330 *Muwashshā*, pp. 257–8, 259
331 Ibid., p. 242
332 Ibid., p. 256ff.
333 On the *shiʿār* see above, p. 34
334 Dozy, *Dictionnaire*, pp. 21–3, 245–6; Badrī, *ʿĀmma*, pp. 162–3
335 *Muwashshā*, p. 186
336 On the Dabīqī stuff see above, p. 38
337 *Nishwār*, viii, p. 143
338 *EI*[1], s.v. *Ṭirāz* (A. Grohmann); Serjeant, *Islamic Textiles*, Chap. i, pp. 60–8
339 Serjeant, op. cit. pp. 66–7

for robes of honour, for gifts, for the covering of the Kaʿba, for banners and for military uniforms, was so great that a *dār al-ṭirāz* was established to meet this need.[340] *Ṭirāz* textiles bearing decorative inscriptions were produced in two types of workshop: the public establishment (*al-ṭirāz al-ʿāmma*) and the private or royal establishment (*al-ṭirāz al-khāṣṣa*). The former was owned by merchants (*bazzāzūn*) who sold their goods publicly or exported them to other countries, while the latter, situated within the royal palace, was devoted to the making of cloth for the caliphs' household, for robes of honour and the like.[341] The Abbasid caliphs had indeed several *ṭirāz* factories located in cities important for their production of clothes, cities such as Baghdad, Samarra, Khurāsān, and Dabīq.[342]

Fragments of costumes surviving from our period are to be found in various museums of the world. These fragments demonstrate the fact that the inscriptions are in Kufic script, a type of square angular writing. The fragments, in general, bear the "*basmala*" followed by the name of the caliph, his personal title (*laqab*) and also various benedictory phrases. The date and place of manufacture are also usually mentioned there.[343] The earlier textile inscriptions, of the second to the fifth centuries, tended to be simple and precise, whereas the later ones, from the fifth century onward, became more elaborate and, as it were, debased in character.[344]

For the decoration of the *ṭirāzī* garments, three methods were adopted: tapestry, embroidery, and painting or printing. Tapestry was woven directly onto the ground material at the time of its manufacture. It was a ribbed cloth technique, using wefts of more than one colour. Embroidery, as the word implies, was applied to a previously woven ground material. Needles were used for stitching. When gold thread was used, it was sewn lightly at short intervals to the surface of the cloth

---

340 Serjeant, op. cit., Chap. I, pp. 60–8; *EI*[1], s.v. *Ṭirāz* (A. Grohmann); cf. also, *Encyclopaedia of Social Sciences*, s.v. *Industrial Art*

341 Serjeant, op. cit., Chap. xiii–xiv, p. 97; N. P. Britton, *A Study of some early Islamic Textiles in the Museum of Fine Arts*, Boston, 1938, pp. 18–20

342 Serjeant, op. cit., Chap. II, pp. 69–84; cf. also, E. Kühnel, *Catalogue of dated Ṭirāz fabrics*, p. 6ff.

343 Serjeant, *Islamic Textiles*, Chap. ii, p. 72; cf. also *Early Islamic Textiles in the Museum of Boston*, pp. 17–20

344 Britton, op. cit., pp. 17–18; E. Kühnel, op. cit. Pls. II–XXI

with a fine silk thread, as the clumsy but fragile gold thread could not pass easily through the ground cloth. In painting and printing the brush or stylus and the block or stencil respectively seem to have been used by the people concerned with the production of *ṭirāz* material.[345]

Prices of garments

On the prices of costumes worn by Muslims in different periods Ashtor has quoted some evidence, and has tried to estimate the cost of clothing in relation to other essentials of life.[346] His evidence on the third century is, however, not copious, and therefore needs more careful investigation.

A comparative study of the prices of the second and third centuries, recorded in literary sources, shows that in the third century prices rose, and it was almost impossible for the poor people to have more than one or two pieces of clothing in their wardrobes. The wealthy people who could spend a lot of money on luxuries bought and had their garments tailored at very high and sometimes exorbitant prices.

According to Abū Ṭālib al-Makkī (died AD 977) the pious Muslims and sufis in the earlier centuries of Islam did not spend more than 7 to 8 dirhams[347] on clothing; the Companions of the Prophet and their Successors spent about 20 to 30 dirhams. The theologians sometimes declined to wear clothes which cost more than 40 dirhams, and others allowed themselves to wear clothes of up to 100 dirhams only.[348]

We will now discuss the prices of the major items of clothing.

---

345 Ibid., pp. 21–3

346 Ashtor, *Prix*, pp. 52–5; idem, "Essai sur les prix et les salaires dans l'empire califien", *RSO*, 36 (1961), pp. 19–69

347 The dinar was the gold unit of currency in early Islam; its weight was approximately 4·25 grammes. The coin is still used in some Middle Eastern countries. The dirham was the silver unit of currency from the rise of Islam to the Mongol period (thirteenth–fourteenth centuries AD). Its weight varied from 2·91 to 2·95 grammes. During the third century AH, the dinar was worth from 15 to 20 dirhams; one dirham was worth six dānaqs.

348 *Madkhal*, i, p. 132; ii, p. 238f.; *Qūt al-Qūlūb*, ii, p. 183; cf. also Ashtor, *Prix*, p. 53

Qamīṣ

In 204 AH at Mawṣil, one *qamīṣ* of standard quality cost about 2 dinars.[349] In the fourth century one ordinary Saqlāṭānī *qamīṣ* cost 5 dinars.[350] At the same period we hear of a Dabīqī shirt worn by an ostentatious *qāḍī* which cost him 200 dinars.[351] The shirt might have been embroidered with costly materials, otherwise 200 dinars for a shirt is incredibly high. This is why the wazir ʿAlī b. ʿĪsā ridiculed the *qāḍī* for such extravagance and told him that his own *qamīṣ* and the *durrāʿa* did not cost more than 20 dinars.[352] From Masʿūdī we learn that in the third century the cost of the tailoring of a *qamīṣ* was 2 dirhams.[353]

Izār

In the second century 6½ dirhams were paid in Basra for an *izār*.[354] An anecdote, probably from the third century, recorded by Ibn al-Jawzī, shows that a woman bought an *izār* for 22 dirhams.[355] In Mawṣil, probably in the middle of the second century, the price of an *izār* varied between 6 and 18 dirhams.[356] The *izār* which was imported from far-off lands, and worn by the wealthy and men of elegant taste, might have been more costly.

Kisā'

During the period of Ma'mūn a *kisā'* could be bought for two dirhams.[357] The *kisā'* imported from places known for their textile industry was highly priced. Jāḥiẓ notes that a Ṭabarī *kisā'* cost 400 dirhams, whereas one brought from Qumis cost 100 dirhams.[358] *Aghānī* also notes that a price of 400 dirhams was paid for a *kisā'* of *khazz* silk.[359] The *kisā'* made of silk and other fine fabrics cost 500–700 dirhams.[360] According to

[349] Azdī, *Ta'rīkh al-Mawṣil*, p. 355
[350] *Tajārib*, iii, p. 67; cf. also, Ashtor, *Prix*, p. 55
[351] *Nishwār*, i, p. 29; Ṣābī, *Wuzarā'*, pp. 353–54
[352] Ibid.
[353] *Murūj*, vi, p. 344
[354] *ʿUyūn*, i, p. 251
[355] *Ḥumaqā*, p. 65
[356] Azdī, *Ta'rīkh al-Mawṣil*, p. 237; cf. also Begg, op. cit., s.v.
[357] Ibn Ṭayfūr, *Baghdād*, p. 24
[358] *Ḥayawān*, iii, p. 27; Ibn al-Jawzī, *Ẓirāf*, p. 187
[359] *Aghānī*, iii, p. 25
[360] Ibn Saʿd, *Ṭabaqāt*, v, p. 96; iii, p. 40; v, p. 561

Ibn Ḥawqal the *kisā'* made in Susanjird (in Fārs) was sold at the highest prices, such as 100 dinars.[361]

Ridā'

The *ridā'*, a robe which resembled the *kisā'*, was sold probably at the same price as the *kisā'*. According to one report the *ridā'* made in Aden was sold at 2,000 dirhams.[362] This *ridā'* might have been of wool and richly embroidered. Ibn ʿAbbās, according to Ibn Qutayba, wore a *ridā'* of 1,000 dirhams, which was made perhaps in Aden and was richly embroidered.[363]

Durrāʿa and *Ṭaylasān*

There is very little material on the prices of the costumes worn by the wazirs and the judges, such as the *durrāʿa*, the *qabā'*, and the *ṭaylasān*. The cost of such clothes must have been dependent on the material used. We have already seen that the *durrāʿa* and the *qamīṣ* which the wazir ʿAlī b. ʿĪsā—a wazir well-known for his frugal household—donned, cost him 20 dinars altogether.[364] Thus the *durrāʿa* might have cost him 10 to 15 dinars. About the price of the *ṭaylasān* we have one report dating from the first half of the second century. A Basran *Muḥaddith* is said to have purchased a *ṭaylasān* for 400 dirhams.[365] The *ṭaylasān* and other excellent robes manufactured in Bamm (in the province of Kirmān) were of very high quality. They were exported to Khurāsān, Iraq, and Egypt, and fetched about 30 dinars. The garment had a durability similar to that of the clothes of Aden and Sanʿā', the cheapest of which lasted for five to twenty years.[366] Similarly the Wīdhārī garments (from Wīdhār, a place in Samarqand) were much prized and were exported to many countries. Of Wīdhārī garments Ibn Ḥawqal noted that they were woven of cotton employed raw without being cut. They were of a colour approaching yellow saffron, soft and light to

---

361 Ibn Ḥawqal, p. 212

362 *Aghānī*[1], xviii, p. 89

363 *ʿUyūn*, i, p. 298

364 *Nishwār*, i, pp. 29–30

365 Ibn Saʿd, *Ṭabaqāt*, vii, p. 153; cf. also, Ashtor, *Prix*, p. 54

366 Ibn Ḥawqal, p. 223; cf. also, Idrīsī, *Geographie*, trans. by P. A. Jaubert, Paris, 1836–40, i, p. 423

the touch, but nevertheless very thick, excellent in their wearing qualities, and durable. He further noted that there was not a prince, wazir, or qāḍī in the whole of Khurasan who did not wear one Wīdhārī garment in winter over his clothes. Such Wīdhārī robes varied in price from 2 to 20 dinars.[367]

Sirwāl

The price of trousers (*sirwāl*) has not been recorded in available sources. Like other garments it depended on the quality and quantity of the fabric. Since the *sirwāl* for women were wide and capacious, they might have cost more than those worn by men. Ibn Zubayr, speaking about the costume of the wazir Ibn al-Furāt, notes that each *sirwāl* cost him 30 dinars.[368] The trouser-band (*tikka*) was sold in various colours and at varying prices. It was usually made of ibrisim silk and was sometimes luxuriously decorated. The best quality of *tikka* brought from Armenia was sold, so Tanūkhī informs us, at a price of one dinar each.[369] Some of these trouser-bands, according to Ibn Ḥawqal, fetched even 10 dinars.[370]

ʿImāma, mandīl

During Ma'mūn's reign 18 dirhams are recorded as the price of a turban.[371] One *mandīl*, at the beginning of the 2nd century, was sold at 2 dirhams.[372] From an anecdote in Jahshiyārī's *Wuzarā'* it appears that a Ṭabarī *mandīl* was worth 12 dirhams.[373] Qumis was well-known for its excellent *mandīls*, both large and small, made of fine cotton and often embroidered. The large *mandīl*, according to Maqdisī, might have fetched two thousand dirhams.[374]

---

[367] Ibid., Ibn Ḥawqal, p. 403; Idrīsī, op. cit., ii, p. 201

[368] *Dhakhā'ir*, pp. 229–30

[369] *Nishwār*, viii, p. 125

[370] Ibn Ḥawqal, p. 264; cf. also, Mez, p. 464

[371] Ashtor, *Prix*, p. 53, quoting from "Lost fragments of *Kitāb al-wuzarā' wa'l-kuttāb*", by Jahshiyārī, ed. M. ʿAwād, Beirut, 1965, p. 32

[372] Khaṭīb, *Ta'rīkh*, ii, p. 48

[373] *Wuzarā'*, p. 184

[374] Muq. p. 367. See for some other quotations, F. Rosenthal, *Four Essays*, pp. 75–6

Footwear

The prices of footwear are sparingly mentioned in our sources. The famous sufi Bishr al-Ḥāfī (died 227 AH) is said to have spent two dāniq for his sandals (*naʿl*),[375] an exceptionally low price, which cannot be taken as representative of the prices of the third century. The top-boots (*khuff*) and other varieties of sandals which were often imported from India, Kufa and other places may have been very costly. A papyrus record shows that a pair of the *naʿl Sindiyya* with laces, made in Tinnis, cost about 4 dirhams.[376]

Fabric

Garments made out of the Dabīqī stuff were a common sight in the wardrobes of the wealthy people. The Dabīqī stuff was highly priced. In one report (311 AH) we find the lowest price of a red Dabīqī stuff (*al-shuqqa al-Dabīqiyya-al-shuqayriyya*) to be 70 dinars.[377] The wazir Ibn al-Furāt, who was fond of sartorial display, donned the *ṭaylasān, kisāʾ*, and *ʿimāma*, all made out of fine Dabīqī stuff, which cost him 70 dinars each.[378] Similarly the *washī* stuff used generally by the caliphal household and wealthy people cost a lot of money. The famous physician of Mutawakkil, Bakhtīshūʿ, wore a *jubba* of *washī* which cost him 1,000 dinars.[379] The pieces of *washī* bought for the mother of Hārūn cost 5,000 dinars each.[380] They were certainly decorated with gold or other precious jewels, otherwise 5,000 dinars would seem an exaggerated figure. Ṣābī records a price of 200 dinars for a *dībājī* robe (*thawb*) presented to the Caliph Ṭāʾīʿ in 367 AH.[381]

---

375 *Wafayāt*, i, p. 112; cf. also, Samʿānī, *Ansāb*, iv, p. 27

376 A. Grohmann, *From the world of Arabic Papyri*, Cairo, 1952, p. 152; cf. also, Ashtor, *RSO*, 1961, p. 46

377 ʿArīb, p. 116

378 *Dhakhāʾir*, pp. 229–30

379 Qifṭī, p. 102; Ashtor, *Prix*, pp. 54–5

380 *Murūj*, viii, p. 298. There is also one report, perhaps exaggerated, showing that an excellent robe made out of the best available *washī* stuff in the Baghdad market, for the Caliph Wāthiq, cost 6,000 dinars. (Cf. Khālidiyyān, *Tuḥaf*, pp. 114–15; Ḥuṣrī, *Jamʿ al-Jawāhir*, pp. 200–1.) According to Jāḥiẓ the *washī* woven with gold was sold for 1,000 dinars in Baghdad (*Tabaṣṣur biʾl-Tijāra*, p. 26).

381 *Rusūm*, pp. 100–1

Fur

In winter, garments were often lined with some kind of fur, which was generally expensive. The skins of foxes and marten were often used for lining. According to Masʿūdī foxfur was sold at 100 dinars per piece.[382] In the *Tabaṣṣur bi'l-tijāra* we find a list of furs exported from various lands sold in the Baghdad markets.[383] Ibn Zubayr records that the sons of the caliphs Ma'mūn and Muhtadī possessed robes lined with fox fur, white and black, each costing five hundred dinars.[384]

The *Khilʿa* robe

The *khilʿa* (robes of honour) usually offered to dignitaries and high-ranking officials in the early Abbasid period came in three price ranges. The first grade was of robes worth 300 dinars, the second grade of 100 dinars and the third grade of 30 dinars.[385] The *khilʿa* generally consisted of a set of clothes: an *ʿimāma*, a *qamīṣ*, a *sirwāl*, a *ṭaylasān*, a *qabā'* or a *durrāʿa*.[386] Sometimes a single garment could also be given as *khilʿa*.[387]

---

[382] *Murūj*, ii, pp. 14–15; cf. also, *EI*[2], s.v. *Farw*

[383] *Tabaṣṣur* ... (attributed to Jāḥiẓ), ed. Hasan H. ʿAbd al-Wahhāb, *RAAD*, 1932, p. 335f; see also, *EI*[2], s.v. *Farw*

[384] *Dhakhā'ir*, p. 196

[385] Ṣābī, *Rusūm*, pp. 98–9

[386] Ibid, pp. 93–9

[387] *Murūj*, vii, pp. 127–8

Chapter 3

Food

Under the Abbasids there was a keen interest in the art of cooking, an interest strong enough to produce a number of manuals on this art. In the course of time, cooking became a special subject of study and a number of people wrote treatises on it.[1] Unfortunately, few of the books written by these scholars seem to have survived.[2] Thus far it has been possible to trace only three works on the subject:[3] one by Abū

[1] For example: Ḥārith b. Bushkhiz (*c.* third century), Ibrāhīm b. al-Mahdī (d. 224), Yūḥannā b. Māsawayh (d. 243), Ibrāhīm b. al-ʿAbbās al-Ṣūlī (d. 243), ʿAlī b. Yaḥyā al-Munajjim (d. about 257), Aḥmad b. al-Ṭayyib al-Sarakhsī (a contemporary of the Caliph Muʿtaḍid), Aḥmad b. Jaʿfar Jaḥẓa (d. 325), Abū Bakr Muḥammad b. Ẓakariyyā al-Rāzī (d. 313), Makhbara (a grammarian at the court of Muʿtaḍiḍ), Ḥunayn b. Isḥāq (d. 260), Ibn Manduwayh al-Iṣfahānī (d. 372), Miskāwayh (d. 420), Aḥmad b. Ismāʿīl Naṭṭāha al-Anbārī (d. 291), ʿUbayd Allāh b. Aḥmad b. Abī Ṭāhir (d. after the reign of Muqtadir, AD 908–932), Ibn Khurdādhbih (d. 300), Yaḥyā b. Abī Manṣūr al-Mawṣilī (a contemporary of the Caliph Ma'mūn), Ibn al-Shāh al-Ẓāhirī (d. fourth century ?), Dāwūd b. ʿAlī (d. 270), Ibn Dāyā (d. about 340) and a host of others contributed to this science (cf. *Fihrist*, pp. 180, 210, 213, 218, 304, 440; Qifṭī, *Ḥukamā'*, pp. 173, 438; *Murūj*, viii, p. 332; *Irshād* ii, p. 160; cf. also M. Rodinson, in *REI*, 1949, pp. 100–2; Ḥ. Zayyāt, in *Mashriq*, 1947, pp. 16–17; Mez, p. 396; Badrī, *ʿĀmma*, p. 96). The great historian Masʿūdī (d. 346) tells us that he himself wrote a manual of cooking, in which he discussed, among other things, the kinds and quantities of spices required for various types of dishes (cf. *Murūj*, viii, pp. 103–4). See, on some writers of a later period, Ḥabīb Zayyāt, in *Mashriq*, 1947, pp. 17–18; cf. also M. Rodinson, *Cuisine*, in *REI*, 1949, p. 102ff.

[2] See, M. Rodinson, *Cuisine*, in *REI*, 1949, p. 100f; H. Zayyāt *Ṭabākha*, in *Mashriq*, 1947, p. 16ff.

[3] Ḥabīb Zayyāt notes that another three manuscripts, two by anonymous authors and the third by a certain Jamāl al-Dīn Yūsuf al-Dimashqī (d. 909 AH), exist in some Egyptian libraries. The work of Dimashqī was published by him in *Mashriq*, 1937, pp. 370–6 (cf. *Mashriq*, 1947, pp. 17–18).

Muḥammad al-Muẓaffar b. Naṣr b. Sayyār al-Warrāq (died early fourth century), the second by Muḥammad b. al-Ḥasan b. Muḥammad b. ʿAbd al-Karīm al-Kātib al-Baghdādī (died 637 AH)[4] and the third by Kamāl al-Dīn b. al-ʿAdīm (died 660 AH). The work of Warrāq, entitled *Kitāb al-Ṭabīkh wa Iṣlāḥ al-aghdhiyat al-ma'kūlāt*, exists in manuscript.[5] This discusses not only matters of cuisine but also the beneficial and harmful properties of various foods. Written presumably some time in the late third or the early fourth century,[6] during the period with which our work is mainly concerned, and by a writer who had access to the actual recipe-books of the Abbasid caliphs of that time, the text is of great interest to us.[7]

Of the other two works, entitled *Kitāb al-Ṭabīkh* and *Al-Wuṣlā ila'l-ḥabīb fī waṣf al-ṭayyibāt wa'l-ṭīb*, the second is in manuscript form,[8] while the former has already been published and translated.[9] Though written at a considerably later period, during the thirteenth century of the Christian era, these books throw much light on the cooking of the classical dishes.[10] The culinary terms used in these two books

[4] The book was written in 623 (cf. *Ṭabīkh*, Introduction).

[5] The manuscript is unique and is preserved in the Bodleian Library, Oxford, Hunt, No. 187.

[6] This is evident from the fact that the last caliph to be mentioned by the author in this book is Muktafī, who reigned from 289 to 295. He has also mentioned some of the poets who flourished during the end of the third and the beginning of the fourth centuries. Arberry, however, suggests that Warrāq belonged to the fourth century (cf. *A Baghdad Cookery Book*, p. 10, n. 5).

[7] The text of this manuscript has been briefly discussed by Ḥabīb Zayyāt in *Mashriq*, 1947, pp. 18–26 and by M. Rodinson, in *REI*, 1949, p. 104

[8] A copy of this manuscript can be seen in the British Museum, Or. 6388 and in the SOAS Library, No. 90913. The book has been analysed and translated into French, in abridged form, by M. Rodinson, in *REI*, 1949, p. 117ff.

[9] The book *al-Ṭabīkh* was edited by Dr. Daoud Chelebi and published at Mosul in 1934. It has been translated into English by A. J. Arberry under the title, "A Baghdad Cookery Book". Chelebi's information that the manuscript of the *Kitāb al-Ṭabīkh* is unique is wrong. There is an excellent copy of this manuscript in the British Museum (Or. 5099), a manuscript which, at some points, contains additional information (cf. for example, the addition of fols. 7–8 in the introductory chapter, where instructions on cooking are set forth).

[10] Baghdādī, in his *Kitāb al-Ṭabīkh*, notes (p. 6) that he came across several books composed on the culinary art and rejected some recipes, as they did not correspond to the usual food habits of the Baghdādīs.

are almost identical with those employed in the work of Warrāq, from which it can be assumed that the dishes of this period had not undergone much change.

In addition to these sources, devoted exclusively to the culinary art, books such as Ibn Qutayba's *ʿUyūn al-Akhbār*, Ibn ʿAbd Rabbih's *ʿIqd al-Farīd*, Ibn Jazala's *Minhāj al-Bayān fīmā yastaʿmiluhū'l-insān*,[11] Rāghib's *Muḥāḍarāt al-Udabā'*, Ibn Sīda's *Mukhaṣṣaṣ* and also a *Risāla fi'l-sukkar*,[12] contain chapters and occasional remarks on food and eating. Books on *ḥisba* also supply us with some material on the subject.

Meat and meat dishes

Meat was one of the staple foods of the affluent class. Chickens were recommended by mediaeval physicians[13] and widely used in the daily diet of the wealthy. They were used in various kinds of dishes known by different names relating to the use of specific ingredients or to particular methods of cooking.

The breeding of chickens appears to have been common amongst the people living in the countryside. Even town dwellers kept chickens in their homes as a source of eggs and meat.[14] In Baghdad, there were several markets (such as *sūq al-ṭuyūr*) where chickens were one of the main articles of sale.[15]

Of the four types of chicken mentioned by Jāḥiẓ, the *faraj al-Kaskariyya* was highly prized.[16] Kaskar, according to Thaʿālibī, was a village of the Sawād situated between the Euphrates and the Tigris. The Kaskarī chicken, being fat and good to taste, sometimes became "as heavy as a goat or

[11] The book is in manuscript. There is a copy in the British Museum, No. 5934

[12] See Cairo Cat vi, p. 148

[13] See Ashtor, in *AESC*, iv (1968), p. 1022 and in *JAH*, iv (1970), p. 4, who quotes Rāzī, Ibn Jazla, Moses Maimonides and Ibn Jumaʿī.

[14] Jāḥiẓ, *Ḥayawān*, ii, p. 357; iii, p. 170; *Aghānī*[1], iii, p. 31

[15] Cf., for example, the origin of the name *Nahr al-dajāj* in Baghdad

[16] *Ḥayawān*, ii, p. 248. Whether or not there were poultry farms in the country-side for the supply of chicken and eggs to the markets is not known. Egypt was noted for its artificial poultry farming, especially for the ingenious incubators (cf. *Ḥayawān*, ii, p. 333; also Mez, p. 457).

sheep".[17] An Indian species of chicken (*Dajāj al-Hindī*) was also much esteemed for eating.[18] Castrated cocks were thought to taste better than uncastrated ones.[19] Chickens, ducks and francolins, according to Jāḥiẓ, were slaughtered in the evening and were left overnight macerated perhaps in curd.[20]

A special feature of Abbasid cooking was the use of seasoning freely with plain dishes as well as with fried and dry food (the latter of the sweet rather than the sour variety), but sparingly with sour dishes providing their own broth. Meat was cleansed thoroughly of blood, dirt, ganglions, veins and membranes, washed in warm water and salt and fried lightly in oil (*taʿrīq*), before boiling and cooking. *Taʿrīq*, frying the meat gently, until the juice of the meat exuded like perspiration, tended perhaps to remove the unpleasant smell of meat so common in hot countries.[21] In order to have the meat cooked quickly, borax (*bawraq*), wax (*shamaʿ*) or melon (*baṭṭīkh*) were thrown into the saucepan.[22] In chicken dishes dry coriander was used but seldom onion or garlic.[23]

The chicken dishes were varied in number and nature: *ḥāmiḍa, maṣūṣ, mamqūr, muṭajjan, maqlū, isfīdbāj, khashkhashiya, fālūdhajiyya* and *ḥalawiyya.* One had to boil the chicken first, cut it into pieces, fry them lightly in fresh sesame oil and add the seasonings.

For the *ḥāmiḍa* (sour) dishes, a preparation of sumach juice or pomegranate seeds, or lemon juice or grape juice, or even vinegar was added. For the *maṣūṣ* (macerated chicken) the meat was cooked after maceration in a seasoning of vinegar, celery and saffron. For the *mamqūr*, fried meat was thrown into boiling water after mixing with vinegar and *murrī* (brine) in equal parts. For the *muṭajjan* (fried chicken) the meat was

---

[17] *Thimār*, p. 426; Yāqūt, *Buldān*, s.v. *Kaskar*; *Aghānī*², xi, p. 336; Azdī, *Ḥikāyāt*, p. 39

[18] Ibn Jazla, *Minhāj al-Bayān*, Br. Mus. Ms. No. 5934, fol. 91a; Azdī, *Ḥikāyāt*, p. 39; Baghdādī, *Bukhalā'*, p. 144; *Thimār*, pp. 533, 615; *Laṭā'if*, p. 214

[19] Jāhiẓ, *Ḥayawān*, ii, p. 248

[20] Ibid., i, p. 299

[21] *Ṭabīkh*, pp. 8–9, Eng. Tr. pp. 13–14; cf. also ibid., in MS. Br. Mus. (Or. 5099), fol. 7

[22] Ibid., (Or. 5099), fol. 8b

[23] Ibid., *Ṭabīkh*, pp. 50–51

fried until it turned brown, and was served with lemon juice squeezed over it. For *maqlū* (roast or baked chicken) the fried meat was mixed with a little hot water and was garnished with poached eggs. For *isfīdbāj*, the chicken was boiled with mastic, cinnamon and salt, then some ground almonds (small and sweet) mixed with water and a handful of peeled and soaked chick-peas and a ring of dill were added, after which the dish was garnished with poached eggs. For *khashkhashiyya* and *fālūdhajiyya*, a more elaborate method of cooking was adopted: the meat was fried lightly, then it was thrown into boiling water, mixed with spices, flavouring, sugar and poppy flour, and was left on a slow fire to settle. For the *ḥalawiyya*, the usual spices were used, with sweet almonds, raisins, and special types of cakes called *mubahthara* and *quraḍiya*.[24]

Among other domestic animals the meat of which was used in various dishes, hot and cold, sour and sweet, were goats, lambs, sheep, camels and cows. Mutton was always regarded as important in the daily diet of the people. Syria had an abundant supply of sheep, and in the fourth century the flocks of sheep were so numerous in some areas that they were exported to other regions.[25] *Aghānī* mentions Basra as being famous for its fattened sheep, especially pastured for the sacrifice at the *ʿĪd al-Aḍḥā*.[26] The preference given to mutton corresponds to the precepts of Abbasid physicians. According to Rāzī all kinds of meat except mutton contained some degree of harmful property.[27] Ibn Jazla went further and is said to have recommended that one should not eat a great deal of meat, even that of a sheep.[28] Beef was regarded as an inferior meat and was said by some physicians to be possessed of harmful properties.[29] Isḥāq al-Isrāʾīlī, the famous physician of the third century, strongly advised against eating beef, as it was "dry" and likely to adversely affect health.[30]

---

[24] Cf. Warrāq, fols. 45ff.; *Ṭabikh*, pp. 50–51; *Wuṣlā*, Br. Mus. MS. 6388, fol. 30ff.

[25] Muq. p. 180; cf. also E. Ashtor, in *JAH*, 1970, p. 3

[26] *Aghānī*[1], iii, p. 62

[27] *Kitāb al-Hāwī*, as cited by E. Ashtor, in *AESC*, 1968, p. 1022

[28] *Minhāj al-Bayān*, cited by Ashtor, op. cit.

[29] Cf. the references in E. Ashtor, in *AESC*, 1968, p. 1022

[30] *K. al-Adwiya al-mufrada wa'l-aghdhiya*, Hebrew Tr. of the Paris Ms, 1128, fol. 22a, cited by E. Ashtor, in *AESC*, 1968, p. 1022, n. 9.; cf. also Mez, p. 456

This belief perhaps explains why Ibn Rusta recounts with surprise (*c.* 300 AH) that the inhabitants of the Yemen preferred beef to mutton.[31] Young cows and calves were, nevertheless, not disliked as food.[32] The Nabatean inhabitants of Iraq, famous for their raising of cattle, were often ridiculed as "cow-knights".[33] The buffalo attested in Iraq before 2500 BC was perhaps reintroduced from Sind by the Arabs. Buffaloes made their appearance in the marshlands of Iraq during the Umayyad period. This animal is said to have surpassed in number the oxen of Iraq during the fourth century.[34] Buffaloes, effectively employed by the government to drive off lions in the region of the north Syrian frontier, were not slaughtered for meat in that area.[35]

Various dishes were prepared with the meat of these animals, cooked with broth or fried and eaten hot or cold. It will suffice here to mention, as illustrative examples, some of the special meat dishes in frequent use amongst the rich.

Bazmāward

One important and popular dish was *bazmāward.* The name *bazmāward* is a Persian compound word deriving from *bazm*, "feast", and *āward,* "brought". The main ingredients of the dish were roasted meat and the core of good white bread. In its preparation the hot roast, which had been allowed to cool, was sprayed with a little rose-water, and leaves of mint, vinegar, salted lemon and walnuts were added also. The roast, chopped up and moistened in vinegar, was now stuffed with soft white bread and left in the oven for an hour. Finally, at the time of its serving on the table, the strips of meat were placed one on top of the other and covered with a layer of fresh mint.[36] *Bazmāward* was a favourite dish among men of

[31] Ibn Rusta, *Aʿlāq*, p. 112; cf. also, Mez, p. 456

[32] *Minhāj al-Bayān*, Br. Mus. MS, No. 5934, fol. 183b

[33] Mez, p. 455

[34] See, for example, A. F. E. Zeuner, *History of domesticated animals*, 1963; Mez, p. 455. On the pastures of Kaskar, buffaloes, oxen and goats were fattened (cf. Le Strange, *Eastern Caliphate*, p. 43).

[35] Jāḥiẓ, *Ḥayawān*, vii, p. 131ff.; Nuwayrī, *Nihāya*, x. p. 124; Mez, p. 456. The horns of the buffalo were sometimes furnished with a sharp, pointed cover (cf. Nuwayrī, x, 124).

[36] Warrāq, fol. 35; *Ṭabīkh*, p. 59, Eng. Tr. p. 41

elegant taste in Baghdad.[37] The names "*luqma al-qāḍī*" (judge's mouthful), "*luqma al-Khalīfa*" (caliph's mouthful) and "*narjis al-mā'ida*" (narcissus of the table) given to *bazmāward* indicate clearly the esteem and the demand for this dish in high society.[38]

It is rather surprising to note that the wazir Faḍl b. Yaḥyā was especially fond of *bazmāward* prepared with hornets (*zanbūr*, plural *zanābīr*), a dish which the people of the wazir's native land, Khurāsān, could perhaps not imagine except with a mixed feeling of incredulity and indignation.[39] That hornets were included and eaten in such an important dish is not corroborated in other sources. It is Jāḥiẓ alone who makes mention of these insects, and states that the wazir was so fond of them that he engaged some of his servants in the task of collecting them regularly.[40]

Maḍīra

The word *maḍīra* is derived from *maḍīr*, meaning curd, and meant meat cooked with curd. The meat was cut into medium-sized pieces, including the tail. If chicken were used, they were divided into quarters. The meat was placed in a saucepan with a little salt, covered with water and boiled. When the meat was almost cooked, large peeled onions and Nabatean leeks, washed in salt and water and then dried, were put into the pot. Dry coriander, cumin, mastic, and fine ground cinnamon were added. When cooked, the meat was transferred to a bowl, and curdled milk was poured into the saucepan, with lemon and fresh mint, and was boiled and stirred. The meat and the spices were put into the liquid when the boiling subsided, the saucepan was covered and the dish was left to settle.[41] *Maḍīra* was much favoured in Baghdad, and Badīʿ al-Zamān al-Ḥamadānī wrote a *maqāma* entitled *Al-maqāma al-maḍīriyya*.[42] A story recorded by

---

37 Washshā', *Muwashshā*, p. 191

38 *Shifā' al-Ghalīl*, p. 98; *Muḥāḍarāt*, ii, p. 612; cf. also Munajjid, *Bain al-Khulafā'*, p. 79

39 Jāḥiẓ, *Ḥayawān*, iv, pp. 44–5

40 Ibid., iv, p. 45

41 Cf. Warrāq, fol. 69; *Ṭabīkh*, p. 23; Prendergast, English translation of the *Maqāmāt* of Ḥamadānī, p. 88, n. 2

42 *Maqāmāt*, pp. 109–23

Fig. 4. A Banquet in the House of a Merchant. The illustration shows eight people busy eating and serving.

بُطَانٌ كَانِعَالٌ مَا بِهِ فَلْبَهُ وَالْجَعَاظِ الأَجْنَ وَقِيلَ الْمُنْتَحَطَ عِنْدَ الطَّعْ
وَالسَّنَاطِيرُ وَالْعَاظِلُ وَالْعِلْظَمُ وَالبَظْرُ بَغْدُ وَالإِنْعَاظُ
نَاطِينَ جَمْعُ سَنْظِيرٍ وَهُوَ الشَّيُّ الْخَلْنِ وَالْعَنَاظِلُ لِلأَنُمِ الْجَرَادُ وَالْكِلاَبُ
السِّفَادُ وَالْعِظَّمُ الْخَظِيِّ هَ

Fig. 5. Use of Khaysh Punka. Illustration showing a teacher lecturing some young
students and the attendant pulling the *punka* for cooling the classroom.

Tanūkhī in his *Nishwār* makes it clear that a dining table without *maḍīra* was considered to be "a desert".[43] Extolling a dish of *maḍīra*, one poet declares:[44]

> *Maḍīra* on the festive tray
> Is like the moon in full array,
> Upon the board it gleams in light
> Like sunshine banishing the night.
> 'Tis as delicious as 'tis good—
> A very miracle of food.

Sikbāj

Sikbāj, a word indicative of a Persian origin (probably from *sirka*, vinegar), was cooked with fat meat, carrots or egg-plants, almonds, currants, dried figs, a mixture of date-juice and vinegar, and the usual spices. The meat was boiled in water with fresh coriander, cinnamon bark, and salt. The froth and the fresh coriander were skimmed off, and dry coriander, onions, Syrian leeks, carrots, or egg-plant, already skinned and half stewed, were thrown in. When these were almost cooked, a mixture of date juice and wine vinegar was added and the whole was boiled for an hour. A little of the broth was taken and mixed with saffron, and was replaced, with peeled sweet almonds, raisins, currants, and dried figs added. Rosewater was sprinkled on the dish before it was served, to add fragrance.[45]

Sikbāj was regarded as a dish appropriate for all seasons and for all conditions. Whether it was winter or summer, during travel or in residence, people always wished to see this dish on their table.[46] That is why it was also given such names as *mukhkh al-aṭʿima* (marrow or essence of food), *sayyid al-maraq* (chief of broth).[47]

Isfidbāj

Isfidbāj, a Persian compound word, with the sense literally of "white gruel", was named after its main ingredients: almond

---

[43] *Nishwār*, i, p. 63

[44] *Murūj*, viii, p. 403 (passage translated into English by Professor Arberry in "A Baghdad Cookery Book", p. 8)

[45] Cf. Warrāq, fol. 75f; *Ṭabīkh*, pp. 9–10; Jāḥiẓ, *Bukhalā'*, p. 110; Azdī, *Ḥikāyāt*, p. 40; *Minhāj al-Bayān*, Br. Mus. Ms. No. 5934, fol. 123

[46] Munajjid, *Khulafā'*, p. 79

[47] *Thimār*, p. 490; cf. also Munajjid, *Khulafā'*, p. 79

milk and meat. *Isfidbāj* was cooked in a more or less similar manner as described above for *sikbāj*, with the exception that here almond milk was used for making the broth, and the whole was garnished with poached eggs. Sometimes, cabobs of red minced meat with spices, and a quartered, washed chicken would also be put in before the almond milk was added.[48]

Dīkbarīka[49]

This dish was prepared with meat cut into medium-sized pieces and left in the saucepan, a little salt being thrown in with a handful of peeled chick-peas, dry and green coriander, sliced onions and leeks. Covered with water, the meat was boiled and the froth removed. Now, with the addition of wine-vinegar and *murrī*,[50] and also a little fine-ground pepper, the meat was boiled and cooked until the flavour was distinct. Some people sweetened the dish with a little sugar.[51]

There were some notable sour meat dishes cooked more or less in a similar fashion, but given different names, mainly after their respective souring and distinguishing ingredients: *sumāqiyya* (sumaq juice), *līmūniyya* (lemon), *rummāniyya* (*rummān*, pomegranates), *ḥiṣrimiyya* (*ḥiṣrim*, unripe grapes), *tuffāḥiyya* (*tuffāḥ*, apples), *rībāsiyya* (*rībās*, red currants), *nāranjiyya* (*nāranj*, oranges).[52]

Fish and fish dishes

Like meat, fish appears to have been an important item of food in the time of the Abbasids. The fish of the river Tigris were highly prized, because of its sweet water.[53] For a similar

---

48 Warrāq, fol. 88; *Ṭabīkh*, pp. 9–10; Warrāq (fol. 88f) mentioned two types of *isfidbāj* called *ṣafadiyāt* and *mukhaḍḍarāt*.

49 This word has been vocalized as *dīkbarīka*. Dr Chelebi maintains that the word is derived from the Syrian *Dīka Barīka*: holy chicken; whereas Professor Arberry considers it unlikely and maintains that the word comes from the Persian *Deg bar ek*: pot on the ember (cf. *Ṭabīkh*, p. 12, n. 1; Arberry, *A Baghdad Cookery Book*, 15, n. 3).

50 For *murrī*, see later on in this chapter, p. 105

51 *Ṭabīkh*, p. 12 (Eng. Tr. p. 15); Warrāq, fol. 84

52 On the preparation of all these dishes see *Ṭabīkh*, pp. 15–21. Eng. Tr. by Arberry, pp. 17–21

53 Warrāq, fol. 21a; cf. also Anonymous, *al-Manṣūrī fi'l-bayzara*, in *Mashriq*, 1968, p. 213

reason the fish of the Euphrates seem to have been esteemed more highly than the fish of the Nile.[54] Large fish, as a rule, were more popular than small ones.[55] Such large fishes as the *ushbūr*, *juwāf* and *barastūj* (species *qawāṭi*ʿ, migratory in their habits) came mainly from the sea and from the great rivers.[56] Among the fish caught mainly in rivers and canals were the *shabbūṭ*[57], *bunnī*, *hāzibā*', *jarīth* and *shalūq*.[58] Of all these, the *shabbūṭ* would seem to have been the most prized under the Abbasids.[59]

There is mention also of a fish called *ṭirrīkh*, which was caught in Lake Van (Arjīsh) in Armenia.[60] Maqdisī notes that there were twenty-four kinds of fish to be found in the Tigris near Basra.[61] Like the chicken and the goat of Kaskar, *samak Kaskarī* (fish from Kaskar) was also highly esteemed.[62] Whether a fishery existed at Kaskar is not known. However, the chief fish, caught in great numbers from the canals of Kaskar, was the *shabbūṭ*, which was often salted and exported.

The boatmen (*mallāḥūn*) and the divers (*ghawwāṣūn*) delighted in eating sea and river creatures such as *ḥalazūn* (snail), *rūbiyān* (lobster?) and *ṣadaf* (conch).[63] The common people did not disdain to eat crabs (*surṭān*). Some of them ate crabs regularly;[64] others took them merely to increase their sexual power (*shahwa*).[65]

---

[54] Ibid., fol. 21a; *al-Manṣūrī fi'l-bayzara*, p. 213

[55] For a description of fishing see Chapter Five, *Hunting*, below, pp. 232–3

[56] Jāḥiẓ, *Ḥayawān*, iii, pp. 259–60

[57] "The name *shabbūṭ*", states Professor Arberry, "has puzzled the lexicographers, who variously described it as chad, carp and turbot" (cf. *A Baghdad Cookery Book*, p. 42, n. 5).

[58] Khawārizmī, *Mafātīḥ al-ʿUlūm*, pp. 101; Jāḥiẓ, *Ḥayawān*, i, pp. 107, 149–51; Azdī, *Ḥikāyāt*, p. 39; Warrāq, fol. 21f.; *Minhāj al-Bayān*, Br., Mus. Ms. 5934, fol. 125b. *ʿUyūn*, iii, p. 297

[59] Ibid., *Ḥayawān*, i, pp. 233–4; *Bukhalā*', p. 88; *Ḥikāyāt*, p. 39; Khālidiyyān, *Tuḥaf*, p. 119; *ʿUyūn*, iii, p. 297

[60] *Ḥikāyāt*, p. 39; Shayzarī, *Nihāyat al-Rutba*, p. 33, Mez, p. 436 (Ar. Tr. ii, p. 306); Arberry, *A Baghdad Cookery Book*, p. 43, n. 5; cf. also Le Strange, *Eastern Caliphate*, pp. 124, 183, 184

[61] Muq. p. 131

[62] Jāḥiz, *Ḥayawān*, iii, p. 295; *Thimār*, p. 424; Le Strange, op. cit., p. 43

[63] *Mafātīḥ al-ʿUlūm*, p. 101

[64] Jāḥiẓ, *Ḥayawān*, iv, p. 45; vi, p. 84

[65] Ibid., v, p. 406

From a passage in the *Ḥayawān* of Jāḥiẓ, it would seem that the Christians living under Abbasid rule took fish as their main food.[66] This fact would help to explain why they monopolized fish supplies in the market.[67] Jāḥiẓ criticizes the Christians of Baghdad for frequenting the fish markets and causing fish to become dear by their excessive demands, especially on Fridays, Sundays, Mondays and Wednesdays. Hence the Muslims were obliged to come to the fish markets on Saturdays, Tuesdays and Thursdays, as only on these days did the demand and the price remain low.[68]

The celebrated epicure, Ibrāhīm b. al-Mahdī (162–224) is said by Masʿūdī to have been delighted by dishes made from fish tongues.[69]

Fish was cooked both fresh and salted; hence the method of cooking varied. Some dishes could be prepared either with fresh or with salted fish. The most important amongst them was *samak mashwī*, or roast fish. This was prepared from fresh fish, from which the skin had been scraped off. The fish was split open, washed thoroughly, dried, and smeared inside and out with sesame oil and saffron mixed with rosewater. A paste was then made of a quantity of ground sumach, half the quantity of dry ground thyme, a quarter of the quantity of skinned and chopped garlic, and walnuts to half of the total weight, with a little ground coriander, cumin, cinnamon, mastic, fresh sesame oil, and salt. This mixture was stuffed into the fish, which was then tied with strong cotton, placed on a new roasting-spit, put into the oven over a slow fire, covered and left to cook well.[70]

Among other fish dishes, both fresh and salted, mention can be made of *samak maqlū* (fried fish), *samak mamqūr* (soused fish), *samak maqlū bi-khall wa-rashī* (fish fried with vinegar and sesame oil) and *ṭirrīkh muḥassā* (soup made with *ṭirrīkh* fish).[71]

The common people, unable to buy large fish and costly

66 Ibid., iv, p. 431ff.
67 Jāḥiẓ, *Bukhalā'*, pp. 431–2
68 Ibid., iv, pp. 431–2
69 *Murūj*, vi, pp. 349–50
70 Cf. *Ṭabīkh*, p. 60; Warrāq, fol. 33
71 *Ṭabīkh*, pp. 62–4 (Eng. trans. pp. 42–4). On the preparation of all these dishes, see ibid., pp. 62–4; cf. also Khawārizmī, op. cit., p. 101

seasonings, contented themselves with small fish, preparing them only with salt and with cheap ingredients. Such ordinary dishes were known as *rubaythā'*, *ṣaḥnā*, (or *shaḥnā'*), *ṣayr*, *sumaykiyāt*,[72] dishes which were seldom touched by people of elegant taste.[73]

Bread

Bread varied in its materials and its shape, and was therefore known by different names. It was made of millet, rice, barley, or wheat.[74] Bread made of wheat was considered to be the best of all. The predominance of wheat bread was a striking feature of the diet of the Orientals, as compared with that of the Westerners in the Middle Ages.[75] Iraq was essentially a wheat-growing land;[76] in some regions so much was grown that great quantities could be exported. Bread made of wheat, barley or dates was the favourite food of South Arabia, even in the pre-Islamic period.[77] Wheat, during the Abbasid period, was everywhere a commodity traded on a large scale.[78] Mediaeval Muslim physicians, whose precepts influenced the dietary customs of the people to a great extent, warmly recommended wheaten bread and urged people to abstain from others.[79]

Flour-grinding, a task done by women in the country districts, was often carried out in towns by mills which sold

---

[72] *Mafātīḥ al-ʿUlūm*, p. 101; cf. also Azdī, *Ḥikāyāt*, p. 39; these dishes were, as it would seem, known after particular fishes.

[73] *Muwashshā*, p. 192

[74] Jāḥiẓ, *Bukhalā'*, pp. 102, 108, 117; *Minhāj al-Bayān*, Br. Mus. MS. 5934, fols. 81–2

[75] E. Ashtor, "The diet of salaried classes in the medieval Near East", in *JAH*, iv (1970), p. 3; idem, in *AESC*, 1968, 1019f.

[76] Mez, p. 430; Ashtor, *A Social and Economic History of the Near East in the Middle Ages*, London, 1976, pp. 41–2

[77] *EI²*, s.v. *Ghidhā'*, (M. Rodinson)

[78] Ibid., s.v. *Ghidhā'*. E. Ashtor, quoting from Ṭarṭūsī (*Sirāj al-mulūk*, p. 243), notes that before the Muslim conquest of Iraq, the people of Iraq had only one type of bread, known as "Isphahan" (cf. *AESC*, 1968, p. 1019).

[79] Rāzī, *al-Ḥāwī fi'l-ṭibb* (Hyderabad, 1955–62), i, pp. 62, 84; Hibatallāh b. Jumaʿī, *Kitāb al-Irshād li maṣāliḥ al-anfus wa'l-ajsād*, MS. Paris 2963, fol. 49b, as cited by E. Ashtor, in *JAS*, 1970, p. 3, n. 12

flour ready prepared.[80] People in the towns kneaded dough at home and brought it to the owner of the bakehouse (*farrān*).[81]

Wheat bread existed in two main varieties called *al-khubz al-ḥuwwārā* and *al-khubz al-khashkār*. The former was made of white flour finely ground and sieved, while the latter was prepared from coarse, unhusked flour.[82] People of elegant taste preferred the white bread because of its fine quality and softness.[83] A special kind of borax (*bawraq*), used by bakers for glazing bread, was exported at this time from Lake Van in Armenia.[84] It was known as *bawraq al-khubz*: bread borax.[85]

Bread was made in a number of shapes. It was sometimes prepared in the form of a mountain-top, or as waffles and flat loaves stuffed with honey, sugar, almonds and mastic.[86] These loaves were often known by the name of their inventor or of the person for whom they were first made.[87] Sometimes the bakers made thin bread so skilfully that it might almost be taken for a fine cloth. Abu'l-Faraj al-Iṣfahānī affirms that the poet Nāhiḍ b. Thauma al-Kilābī once attended a wedding banquet, held in a village near Aleppo, where he was served, among other dishes, with a kind of fine thin bread. He took it for a fine piece of cloth and wanted to ask the host to favour him with some of these pieces, so that he might make a shirt out of them. When the party sat before the dining table, he was taken aback to see that people were eating them. Now, he realized that it was nothing but bread.[88] Ḥamadānī also

---

[80] *EI*², s.v. *Ghidhā'*, (M. Rodinson). On the mills of the Abbasid period, see Mez, pp. 466–7

[81] Ibid., s.v. *Ghidhā'*; Shayzarī, *Nihāya*, p. 24

[82] Ḥabashī, *Baraka*, p. 237; cf. also, Badrī, *'Āmma*, pp. 125–6. Ibn Jazla mentions other varieties of bread, such as ***khubz maghsūl*** (bread made of soft, stale bread washed in hot water), ***khubz samīdh*** (bread of semolina); ***khubz fātir*** (pancake), ***khubz ṭabūn*** (bread baked in a *ṭabūn*, a small jar-shaped oven, sunk in the ground and open on top). Cf. *Minhāj al-bayān*, fols. 81–2b

[83] *Muwashshā*, p. 191

[84] Mez, p. 438. Some manuals of *ḥisba* discouraged its use on grounds of health (cf. Shayzarī, *Nihāya*, p. 23).

[85] Ibid.

[86] Warrāq, fols. 24b–26a

[87] Ibid., fols. 24b–26a

[88] *Aghānī*², xiii, p. 179; cf. also Ibn Qutayba, *'Uyūn*, iii, pp. 236–7; *'Iqd*, iii, pp. 486–7

mentions thin, wide bread, baked in an oven (*tannūr*), and called "*awrāq al-riqāq*" (the leaves of flat bread).[89] Thin bread was often known as *riqāq*, without the addition of the noun *khubz*.[90]

The recipe books at our disposal give the names and ingredients of various types of bread eaten with meat dishes or with cheese and olive oil. Some of these were also taken with sweet dishes. Among such dishes, mention can be made of *khushnānaj*,[91] *muṭbaq*,[92] *akrās mukallala*,[93] *khubz al-abāzīr*,[94] and *jardhaq*.[95]

From our sources it appears that bread made of barley, *dhurra*, or other cereals was consumed at times of great distress, when warfare or insufficient production cut off the supply, and at all other times only by the poor and the ascetics.[96] *Khubz al-aruzz*, bread made from rice-flour,

---

[89] *Maqāmāt*, p. 65; see also, for *khubz al-riqāq*, Jāḥiẓ, *Bukhalā'*, p. 65. The word *riqāq* has also been vocalized as *ruqāq*.

[90] Ibid., *Bukhalā'*, pp. 47, 49; Ṭabarī, iii, p. 584; Jahshiyārī, *Wuzarā'*, pp. 119–20; *Fakhrī*, p. 259. Thin bread was, most probably, made with white and husked flour (*ḥuwwārā*).

[91] *Khushknānaj* (cf. Persian *khushk* + *nān*, meaning dry bread) was made of fine white flour, three oqiya of sesame oil being mixed with every ratl of flour and the whole kneaded into a firm paste. It was then left to rise and shaped thereafter into long loaves. A suitable amount of ground almonds and scented sugar, mixed with rose water, was put into the middle of such a loaf. It was then pressed together and baked in the oven (cf. *Ṭabīkh*, p. 78; *Minhāj*, fol. 68a).

[92] *Muṭbaq* (i.e., "enveloped"). A dough was made with fresh sesame oil (three oqiya of oil to one ratl of flour) and shaped into loaves in a mould. Now, a small portion of plain *ḥalwā* (a paste of various sweetening ingredients) was placed between each pair of loaves and the whole then baked in the oven (cf. *Ṭabīkh*, pp. 78–9, Eng. trans. p. 51).

[93] *Akrās Mukallala* (i.e., "crowned loaves") were made of a dough left to rise, with the addition of a paste of ground pistachios, syrup and scent. The loaves, after baking, were dipped into dissolved, scented sugar (cf. *Ṭabīkh*, p. 79, Eng. trans. p. 52).

[94] *Khubz al-Abāzīr* (i.e., "seasoned bread") was prepared with dry dates, shelled sesame, roasted poppies, rose-water, and almonds or pistachios. For the cooking process see *Ṭabīkh*, p. 79; cf. also Ḥ. Zayyāt, *Khizānat al-Sharqiyya*, pp. 380–1

[95] A kind of thick, coarse bread used mainly by the common people. Cf. Jāḥiẓ, *Bukhalā'*, pp. 20, 48, 50, 66, 83, 95, 267; also *Rasā'il*, i, p. 387; ii, p. 367

[96] *Kāmil*, viii, pp. 285, 293, 311; Nāṣir Khusraw, p. 35; Sibṭ Ibn al-Jawzī, *Mir'at al-zamān*, ed. Jewett, p. 367; Abū Shāma, *Dhail 'alā al-rawḍatain* (Damascus, 1948), p. 178. Cf. also E. Ashtor, "The diet of salaried classes in

appears to have been an important item of food for the common people. In Baghdad there were several mills where the Baghdādīs obtained their rice already ground.[97] Rice and rice-bread must have been cheap, since people of lesser means often took *khubz al-aruzz.*[98] The people of Khūzistān and Ṭabaristān ate it through most of the year.[99] People of Basra also ate it regularly.[100] At the beginning of the fourth century there lived in Basra a baker-poet who acquired the title of *Al-khubzāruzzī* (baker of rice-bread).[101] Rice-bread is mentioned by Jāḥiẓ as the food of some misers, which they even presented to their guests.[102]

Rice

Rice, apart from its use in the preparation of *khubz al-aruzz*, does not seem to have been a principal food in the time of the Abbasids. It was, however, employed in the preparation of various sweet dishes.[103] Rice with fine sugar, milk or butter was indicative of a rich diet. We are told that Ibn al-Jaṣṣāṣ, the ṣūfī, could not refrain from tears when he heard of a sweet dish prepared with cooked rice, covered with ghee and fine sugar.[104] On the authority of Aṣmaʿī (died 828 AD) Ibn Qutayba relates that white rice with melted butter and white

the medieval Near East", in *JAH*, iv (1970), p. 3; idem, *A Social and Economic History* . . ., p. 43

97 Ḥ. Zayyāt, *Khizānat al-Sharqiyya*, pp. 378–88, quoting from Br. Mus. MS. No. Or. 51, fol. 2a

98 See, for example, various stories, quoted by Ḥabīb Zayyāt in the *Khizānat al-Sharqiyya*, from Jāḥiẓ, Ibn Baṭūṭa and Ibn Qutayba. Cf. also, *EI*², s.v. *Ghidhā*' (M. Rodinson)

99 Iṣṭakhrī, p. 212; Ibn Ḥawqal, p. 173

100 Yāqūt, s.v. *Baṣra.* Ibn Qutayba, in the third century, mentions Basra to be the paradise of the poor, as a young unmarried man could live there on two dirhams a month, feeding himself with rice-bread and salted fish (cf. *ʿUyūn*, i, p. 221).

101 *Irshād* vii, pp. 206–7; the poet's actual name was Abu'l-Qāsim Naṣr. Cf. also Ḥ. Zayyāt, *Khizānat al-Sharqiyyā* pp. 379–80; *Muntaẓam*, vi, p. 329; and, in addition, M. Canard, "Le Riz dans le proche orient aux premiers siècles de l'Islam", *Arabica*, vi (1959), p. 125

102 Jāḥiẓ, *Bukhalā*', ed. Van Vloten, p. 101f; 129

103 M. Canard, *Le riz*, in *Arabica*, vi (1959), pp. 113–31; cf. also *EI*², s.v. *Ghidhā*' (M. Rodinson); see also Jāḥiẓ, *Bukhalā*', p. 117; Ashtor, *A Social and Economic History* . . ., p. 43

104 Tawḥīdī, *Imtā*ʿ, iii, p. 77

sugar "is not the food of the people of this world"[105] (*laisa min ṭaʿām ahl al-dunyā*). According to Warrāq, rice was eaten either with milk, clarified butter, or sugar.[106]

From time immemorial rice had been a popular foodstuff in Lower Mesopotamia.[107] According to Ibn Ḥawqal the Ḥamdānīds introduced rice in the middle of the fourth century in Upper Mesopotamia, and his contemporary Maqdisī mentions the important rice plantations in Palestine and in some provinces of Egypt at about the same period.[108] Our sources make it clear that there was a considerable increase in rice plantations during the early Abbasid period. Rice became, of course, almost a luxury in the regions where it was not extensively grown.[109] The people of the marsh areas in Māzendran depended on rice for their food.[110]

The culinary manuals contain numerous recipes of rice dishes which were considered delicious.[111] The Caliph Hādī, it is said, favoured the rice dish (*aruzza*),[112] and Yaʿqūb b. Layth al-Ṣaffār is said to have taken a rice dish (*aruzza*) daily at his table.[113] One of the few dishes prepared with rice and used as a popular food was *aruzz mufalfal*: peppered rice. It was cooked with fat meat and the usual spices: salt, coriander, cumin, cinammon-bark, mastic and saffron.[114]

---

105 *ʿUyūn*, iii, p. 200; cf. also, E. Ashtor, in *AESC*, 1968, p. 1019

106 Warrāq, fol. 23a

107 E. Ashtor, in *JAH*, iv (1970), p. 2

108 Ibn Ḥawqal, p. 213; Maqdisī, pp. 162, 180, 201, 203, 208; see also E. Ashtor, in *JAH*, 1970, p. 2 and in *AESC*, 1968, 1018

109 M. Canard, *Le riz*, in *Arabica*, vi (1959), pp. 113–31; *EI*², s.v. *Ghidhā*'

110 Ibn Ḥawqal, p. 272; cf. also, Mez, p. 431

111 Warrāq, *Ṭabīkh*, svv.; cf. also Ḥ. Zayyāt, *Mashriq*, 1937, 371ff.

112 Bayhaqī, *Maḥāsin*, p. 591

113 *Murūj*, viii, p. 54. Extolling the dish of *aruzza*, the poet Muḥammad b. al-Wazīr (known as the Ḥāfiẓ of Damascus) says:

"Its brilliance dazzles the beholding eye
As if the moon ere even shone in sky;
While sugar sprinkled upon every side
Flashes and gleams, like light personified."

Cf. *Murūj*, viii, p. 401; translated into English by A. J. Arberry, in *A Baghdad Cookery Book*, p. 7

114 *Ṭabīkh*, pp. 27–8; K. al-Ṭabākha, ed. by Ḥ. Zayyāt in the *Khizānat al-Sharqiyya*, p. 373; cf. also, M. Canard, in *Arabica*, vi (1959), p. 127f. Following Lane, Canard observes that *aruzz mufalfal* was equivalent to the Turkish "Pilaw" (cf. Ibid., *Arabica*, p. 127).

Another plain rice dish was known as *bhatta*.[115] The word *bhatta* is a Persian loan-word from the Sanskrit *bhāt*, boiled rice.[116] *Bhatta* was also cooked with fat meat and seasoning. It was coloured with saffron and sweetened with syrup or sugar.[117]

Rice was also eaten with fresh milk.[118] A sufi declared that rice with milk is the most delicious of dishes.[119]

Vegetables

A variety of vegetables were eaten in Abbasid times. We have already quoted the sayings: "A table without vegetables is like an old man devoid of wisdom," and "Vegetables are the ornament of the dining table."[120] Several places in Iraq and Syria were noted for their production of fruits and vegetables. Kufa, Basra and Damascus occupied a prominent place among the vegetable-growing areas.[121] Among the more popular vegetables can be mentioned the following.

Bāqillā' (Beans)

Of all the vegetables, *bāqillā'* seems to have been the favourite of rich and poor alike.[122] Beans were eaten parched or roasted and often used in the meat dishes. Green beans could be peeled and boiled in water and salt and served with a little sesame oil or walnut oil. Some people soaked bread crumbs in *bāqillā'* water, the resulting liquid being a kind of *tharīd*[123] called *tharīd al-bāqillā'*.[124]

---

115 Jāḥiẓ, *Bukhalā'*, p. 115; cf. also M. Canard, op. cit., p. 126

116 Khawārizmī, *Mafātīḥ al-'Ulūm*, p. 101; *Mukhaṣṣaṣ*, i, Chapter, v, p. 3; cf. also Arberry, *A Baghdad Cookery Book*, p. 26, n. 3

117 *Ṭabīkh*, pp. 31–2; *Mukhaṣṣaṣ*, i, Chap. v, p. 3; cf. also, M. Canard, op. cit., p. 126

118 Azdī, *Ḥikāyāt*, p. 39

119 Tha'ālibī, *Khāṣṣ*, p. 44

120 See p. 13

121 Ibid., *Laṭā'if*, pp. 187, 237; Muq. p. 181; Ṣābī, *Rusūm*, 18

122 *Nishwār*, i, pp. 14–15; *Laṭā'if*, pp. 187, 237

123 *Tharīd* was a popular food of the Arabs. It was a sort of pudding made of bread-crumbs soaked in broth, served with meat (cf. *Ṭabīkh*, p. 34; *EI*^{2}, s.v. *Ghidhā'*).

124 Tha'ālibī, *Khāṣṣ*, p. 46; cf. also, Badrī, *'Āmma*, p. 112. For the cooking method of *tharīd al-bāqillā'*, see, Warrāq, fol. 61

A dish called *mā' al-bāqillā'* (bean soup) was prepared with beans. It was cooked with meat, beans and common spices and was eaten with lemon or with ground sumach sprinkled over the dish.[125] It is reported that ʿAbdallāh Abu'l-Qāsim al-Jurjānī (died 368 AH), a well-known *muḥaddith*, used to give a certain man one dānaq per month to provide him with *bāqillā'*, in the soup (*mā'*) of which he soaked his bread crumbs.[126]

The common demand for *bāqillā'* is evident from the report of Isḥāq b. Ibrāhīm al-Maṣʿabī, who was *Ṣāḥib al-shurṭa* at Baghdad during the time of Ma'mūm, Muʿtaṣim, Wāthiq and Mutawakkil. In that report we are told that the money earned daily from the sale of cooked *bāqillā'* in one quarter of Baghdad amounted to sixteen thousand dinars.[127] Though the markets of Jurjān had an abundant supply of vegetables, notably *bāqillā'*,[128] the best quality of beans, according to Thaʿālibī, was to be found only in Kufa.[129]

Bādhinjān (Egg-plant)

The egg-plant was eaten in several ways. It was cooked with meat dishes, made into relish (*ṣabāgh*), or eaten alone as a vegetable dish. Some important meat dishes cooked with egg-plants were *sikbāj*,[130] *ḥiṣrimiyya*,[131] and *madfūna*.[132] *Bādhinjān mukhallal* (egg-plant in vinegar), *bādhinjān muḥassa* (egg-plant soup); *bādhinjān bi-laban* (egg-plant with milk)[133] were but a few of the sauces and relishes made with egg-plant. Ḥamadānī in his *Maqāmāt* mentions *bādhinjān muqlā* (fried

[125] *Ṭabīkh*, p. 34

[126] Khaṭīb, *Ta'rīkh*, ix, p. 407

[127] Ṣābī, *Rusūm*, pp. 18–19; Ibn Mihmandār, *Faḍā'il Baghdād*, p. 19. The amount in dinars seems incredible; 16,000 dirhams might be a right figure.

[128] *Laṭā'if*, p. 187

[129] Ibid., p. 237

[130] See, for its method of preparation, above, p. 83

[131] A sour meat dish cooked with unripe grapes, see above, p. 84

[132] *Madfūna*, literally buried, so called because the dish was prepared with large egg-plants stuffed with minced meat, and usual spices (cf. *Ṭabīkh*, p. 42)

[133] Azdī, *Ḥikāyāt*, p. 38. For the preparation of all these items see *Ṭabīkh*, p. 65f. (Eng. Tr. pp. 44–5)

egg-plant) as one of the important courses in a feast.[134] The Caliph Wāthiq was reportedly so fond of egg-plant that he took forty at a time.[135] Its popularity among the masses, according to Rāghib, was such that a public denunciation of egg-plants was sure to bring the offender into trouble.[136] *Bādhinjān* was not a costly vegetable in Baghdad even in the 4th century, when a hundred egg-plants were sold at the price of one dānaq only.[137] This price perhaps represents a period of abundant supply.

Jazar (Carrots)

Like egg-plants, carrots were mainly used as an ingredient in the meat dishes. A special dish called *khabīṣ al-jazar* was prepared with this vegetable.[138] Boiled carrots were also taken with vinegar, olive, and *murrī*.[139] Men of elegant taste in general disliked carrots and would not even touch them, not to speak of eating them.[140] Unlike *bādhinjān*, *jazar* was found only in a particular season, probably in winter.[141]

Kurrāth (Leeks)

Leeks were found in two varieties: *kurrāth shāmī* and *kurrāth nabaṭī*.[142] The Syrian leeks resembled large onions, whereas the Nabatean ones looked like garlic.[143] The *kurrāth*, a popular complementary food of the poor, was mainly added by the well-to-do to various meat dishes. Poor people ate leeks with bread of barley,[144] whereas the affluent sometimes took it as the *nuql*.[145] The Prophet reportedly disliked the coming

---

[134] *Maqāmāt*, p. 133; Ibn al-Jawzī (*Muntaẓam*, vi, p. 5) mentions *bādhinjān mashwī*, which seems to be the same as the *bādhinjān muqlā*

[135] *'Iqd*, vi, p. 300

[136] *Muḥāḍarāt*, ii, p. 617

[137] Baghdādī, *Taṭfīl*, p. 79

[138] Carrots were peeled and boiled, the hard core removed, and then they were brayed in a mortar. Then sesame-oil was boiled and mixed with flour and carrots. Finally a syrup was poured on the mixture, which was then removed from the fire (cf. *Ṭabīkh*, p. 74 Eng. Tr. by Arberry, p. 49).

[139] Jāḥiẓ, *Bukhalā'*, p. 110; for *murrī* see below, p. 105

[140] *Muwashshā*, p. 194

[141] Jaḥiẓ, *Bukhalā'*, p. 110; cf. also, *Ṭabīkh*, p. 9

[142] *Ṭabīkh*, pp. 9–18

[143] Ibid., p. 18, n. 1, quoting from Dāwūd Anṭākī

[144] *Murūj*, vi, p. 228; cf. also *Fakhrī*, p. 243

[145] *Muwashshā*, p. 193; for *nuql* see below, p. 112

to the mosque of a person immediately after eating leeks.[146] Due to its obnoxious odour, people of elegant taste avoided it as *nuql*.[147]

Qarʿ (Gourd)

Like other vegetables, the gourd was used as an ingredient in various dishes,[148] and also in preparing a special dish called *khabīs al-qarʿ* (gourd *khabīṣ*).[149] Sometimes relishes were prepared with it, called *qarʿ bi-laban* (gourd with milk).[150] Jāḥiẓ tells us that the *qarʿ* was available in the markets almost throughout the year.[151]

Baṣal (Onion)

Onion was an ingredient of all the meat dishes. It was peeled and cut into pieces and added with other ingredients.[152] Sometimes sliced raw onion was also placed on cooked meat dishes. Men of refined taste, however, disliked raw onion on their table, mainly because of its odour[153] and the Prophet's censure of leeks also applied to onions.[154]

Onions were abundantly produced in Sicily.[155] Ibn Ḥawqal in the middle of the fourth century found onions to be one of the main foods of the Sicilians. They used raw onions in large quantities, and the dietary effect was visible in their manners and behaviour. Ibn Ḥawqal was very critical of them, and wrote a lot of abuse about their character and intelligence only because they used raw onions profusely in their meals.[156]

Thawm (Garlic)

Like onions, garlic also formed one of the main ingredients of the Abbasid meat dishes. People of elegant taste sometimes

---

146 *Concordance*, s.v. cf. also, *EI*², s.v. *Ghidhā'*

147 *Muwashshā*, p. 194; cf. also, M. Ghazi, *Les Raffinés in SI.* xi (1959), p. 61

148 Jāḥiẓ, *Bukhalā'*, p. 110; cf. also, *'Uyūn*, iii, p. 289

149 For cooking instructions see *Ṭabīkh*, p. 74

150 For cooking method, see ibid., p. 67

151 Jāḥiẓ, *Bukhalā'*, p. 110

152 Ibid., p. 110; *Ṭabīkh*, p. 9ff.

153 *Muwashshā*, p. 193

154 *Concordance*, s.v.; cf. also *EI*², s.v. *Ghidhā'*

155 Ibn Ḥawqal, p. 86

156 Ibid., pp. 86–7

called it the "amber of the saucepan",[157] while physicians regarded it as an antidote to poisons.[158] In chicken dishes, as a rule, onion and garlic were avoided.[159]

Naʿnaʿ (Mint)

Among the *buqūl* (herbs), mint occupied a prominent place. There was hardly a dish wherein mint, either fresh or dried, was not used. The culinary treatises advised placing layers of fresh mint over prepared dishes, for its sweet flavour was very stimulating for the appetite. It was mainly because of this quality that the *ẓurafā'* (men of elegant taste) always favoured mint on their dining tables.[160]

Hilyawn (Asparagus)

Asparagus was such a favourite vegetable that poetry was written about it. In the gastronomical sessions of the Caliph Mustakfī, where the courtiers vied with each other in describing various kinds of food in poetry, asparagus also formed the theme of a poem.[161] Washshā' notes that the men of elegant taste avoided asparagus because of its innate cooling effects.[162] Damascus was famous for the production of this vegetable,[163] and it was from here that the Caliph Muʿtaṣim used to receive *hilyawn* regularly through his private post (*barīd*).[164] Ziryāb, the arbiter of fashion at Cordova, is said to have introduced *hilyawn*, which soon became popular in Spanish society.[165]

Other Vegetables

Among other vegetables, mention may be made of radish (*fujal*), cress (*ḥurf*), melilot (*ḥandaqūq*), tarragon (*ṭarkhūn*), cucumber (*qiththā'*), chicory (*hindibā'*), beet (*silq*), turnip (*saljam*), chick-peas (*ḥimmaṣ*), spinach (*isfānākh*), and lettuce

---

157 Qāḍī Jurjānī, *Muntakhab*, p. 135

158 Ibn al-Bayṭār, *Durra*, p. 190

159 *Ṭabīkh*, p. 51

160 *Muwashshā*, p. 193

161 *Murūj*, viii, pp. 399–400

162 *Muwashshā*, p. 194; Jāḥiẓ, *Bukhalā'*, p. 134; *Muntaẓam*, vi, p. 5

163 Muq. p. 181

164 Sābī, *Rusūm*, p. 18. For the methods of transportation and preservation see below, pp. 113–17, also *Muqtaṭaf*, 1943, pp. 170–1

165 Maqqarī, ii, pp. 87–8 (Beirut (1968), iii, 127)

(*khass*).[166] These were either cooked or eaten fresh as salad, or as *nuql*. People of refined taste, however, disliked many of these vegetables, as some of them caused colds and others left a colouring on teeth and gums.[167]

Milk and milk products

Milk (*laban*), which was the most important beduin drink,[168] was at this period not regarded as an important food. It was used in preparing dishes of bread, rice or meat, among which were *maḍīra*[169] and *labaniyya*.[170] Some relishes (*ṣibāgh*), such as *bādhinjān bi-laban* (egg-plant with milk) and *qarʿ bi-laban* (gourd with milk), were also prepared with milk.[171] Milk with dates also formed an important item of food of the Abbasids.[172] Sometimes people used milk as *idām* (condiment) with bread.[173] Professor Goitein in his *Mediterranean Society* observes that there is no equivalent term in English for *idām*, which means "that which is taken together with bread". In Arabic *adam* and in Hebrew *lippet* mean "taking something as food additional to bread".[174]

Milk of cows, goats, sheep or camels was generally used. Hārūn al-Rashīd is reported to have liked gazelle milk. In 198 AH, when the governor of Basra presented gazelle milk and butter on the caliphal dining table, the Caliph Hārūn was highly delighted.[175] His wazir, Faḍl, also reportedly liked gazelle milk.[176]

Milk products were: *saman* (clarified butter) which was

---

166 *Muwashshā*, pp. 193–4; *Ṭabīkh*, pp. 28, 30, 32f.; Azdī, *Ḥikāyāt*, p. 42; *Nishwar*, i, p. 65

167 *Muwashshā*, pp. 193–4. For a discussion on the beneficial and the harmful properties of these vegetables see *ʿUyūn*, iii, pp. 383–92

168 *Murūj*, vi, p. 229; cf. also *EI*², s.v. *Ghidhā*' (M. Rodinson)

169 For the description of *maḍīra*, see above, p. 82

170 *Labaniyya*, literally "milk dish", was made with meat, sour milk, leeks, egg-plants and the usual spices (cf. *Ṭabīkh*, 24).

171 *Ṭabīkh*, p. 67 (Eng. Tr. by Arberry, p. 45); for the preparation of all these relishes, see ibid., p. 67 (Eng. Tr. p. 45)

172 Jāḥiẓ, *Bukhalā*', pp. 64, 67; Khālidiyyān, *Tuḥaf*, p. 112

173 Ibid., *Bukhalā*', p. 186

174 *Mediterranean Society*, ii, p. 126

175 *Dhakhā'ir*, pp. 97–8; Ghazūlī, *Maṭāliʿ*, ii, p. 59

176 Khālidiyyān, *Tuḥaf*, p. 112

used for cooking;[177] *zubad*, (butter), which was, at times, used as *idām*;[178] *jubn*, cheese of an unknown sort which was often taken with bread;[179] and *aqiṭ* (sour milk cheese).[180] Butter and cheese of Dīnawar (a district of the province of Media) are reported to have been of superior quality.[181] One of the specialities of Khawārazm was a buttermilk cheese called *raḥqīn*.[182] Ibn Ḥawqal mentions that Daylam produced an excellent kind of cheese which was exported to various places. The inhabitants of Daylam took milk as one of their main items of food, and they prepared a delicious confection known as *māyastanj*.[183]

In our treatises of cooking there is mention of *al-laban al-fārsī*[184] (literally, Persian milk), a word not explained by the lexicographers. Dā'ūd Chelebī and Professor Arberry, however, are of the opinion that the word evidently meant "curdled milk".[185] *Al-laban al-fārsī*, it would seem, was used in preparing all types of milk dishes.[186] Apart from this, *shīrāz* (dried curds), *al-laban al-māst* (coagulated milk) and *al-laban al-ḥāmiḍ* (sour milk) were also used in preparing some dishes, especially relishes.[187] *Liba'*, or "beestings", was often taken with dates.[188] Butter and dates suggested a rich diet.[189]

Sweet dishes

The people of Abbasid society were addicted to sweet dishes, especially after their principal meals. We are not sure of the authenticity of the report, but it was and still is current among the Muslims that "a sweet dish after the principal meal is *sunna*". This practice was not confined to the affluent houses. Even people of lesser means who could not afford to prepare

[177] Jāḥiẓ, *Bukhalā'*, pp. 44, 47; Tawḥīdī, *Imtā'*, iii, p. 77
[178] Jāḥiẓ, *Bukhalā'*, p. 163
[179] Ibid., pp. 20, 119, 186
[180] Ibid., p. 111; *Minhāj al-Bayān*, Br. Mus. MS. 5934, fol. 32a
[181] Khālidiyyān, *Tuḥaf*, p. 119; Azdī, *Ḥikāyāt*, p. 38
[182] *Laṭā'if*, p. 226
[183] Ibn Ḥawqal, p. 267
[184] *Ṭabīkh*, p. 23ff.
[185] Ibid., p. 23, n. 2; Arberry, *A Baghdad Cookery Book*, p. 22, n. 1
[186] *Ṭabīkh*, pp. 23–6 (Eng. Tr. pp. 21–3)
[187] Ibid., p. 67 (Eng. Tr. p. 45)
[188] Jāḥiẓ, *Bukhalā'*, pp. 67, 111, 163; Khālidiyyān, *Tuḥaf*, p. 112; cf. also, Ibn Sīda, *Mukhaṣṣaṣ*, i, Chap. v, p. 40
[189] *Muḥāḍarāt*, ii, p. 621

such dishes contented themselves with some such sweet as candy, molasses, treacle, oilcake, or dates.[190]

Sweet dishes taken at the table of the well-to-do people were of a large variety and, in the language of Shayzarī, "these were innumerable."[191] Of the "innumerable" the following dishes were commonly used.

Fālūdhaj

Originally a Persian dish, *fālūdhaj* made its appearance in Arabia in the pre-Islamic period. ʿAbd Allāh b. Judʿān is reported to have introduced it into Mecca to cater for the needs of the pilgrims.[192] It was prepared with ground almonds, sugar, rose-water and other ingredients.[193]

Its importance can be seen from the fact that the host who presented *fālūdhaj* to the guests was regarded as "a man of refined taste and culture".[194] That is why it was also given the name of "*abū maḍā*" "the father of sagacity".[195] Extolling a dish of *fālūdhaj*, one humorist remarked: "had Moses come to Pharaoh with *fālūdhaj*, he would have accepted Moses' mission, but, alas, he came to Pharaoh with the stick."[196]

Lawzīnaj

Lawzīnaj ("confection of almonds") was made of brayed almonds, bread crumbs, syrup of rose-water, and sugar and sesame oil.[197] Because of its rich ingredients and delicious taste this confection was called "the Chief Justice of the sweets" (*qāḍī quḍāt al-ḥalawāt*).[198] Ḥamadānī describes *lawzīnaj* as "the easiest to swallow and the quickest to penetrate through the veins".[199] *Lawzīnaj* made overnight

---

190 *Nishwār*, ii, in *RAAD*, xvii (1942), p. 151; Khaṭīb, *Taʾrīkh*, vii, p. 215; xiv, p. 395; Warrāq, fol. 31b; Shayzarī, *Nihāyat al-Rutba*, p. 40

191 *Nihāyat*, p. 40

192 Ibn Ḥawqal, *Ṣūrat al-Arḍ* (1938 ed.) p. 28; cf. also *EI*², s.v. *Ghidhāʾ*, (M. Rodinson) who quotes from Alūsī, *Bulūgh*², i, 381

193 Warrāq, fol. 13a; see also Baghdādī, *Ṭabīkh*, p. 80, where the composition of this pastry is fully described.

194 Khaṭīb, *Taʾrīkh*, v, p. 147

195 Qāḍī Jurjānī, *Muntakhab*, p. 95

196 Ibn al-Jawzī, *Ẓirāf*, p. 40; cf. also *Muḥāḍarāt*, ii, p. 619

197 Baghdādī, *Ṭabīkh*, p. 80; Ḥamadānī, *Maqāmāt*, p. 68; cf. also *Murūj*, viii, p. 240

198 *Muḥāḍarāt*, ii, p. 619

199 *Maqāmāt*, p. 66

was considered to be better in taste than that produced on the same day.[200]

Zalābiya

This was a tart filled with almonds and sugar and flavoured with rose-water, musk, or camphor. It was baked in moulds of various shapes.[201] Azdī has mentioned a kind of *zalābiya* known as *Qāhiriyya* (probably after the Caliph Qāhir), which was soaked in almond oil.[202]

Ṣābūniyya

Ṣābūniyya (from *ṣābūn*, soap, because it was moulded into shapes like soap[203]) was prepared with dissolved sugar and ground almonds. When thoroughly cooked it was ladled out onto a plate, stretched flat and sprinkled with fine ground scented sugar.[204]

Khabīṣ

Khabīṣ was a kind of jelly[205] which had several varieties, such as *khabīṣ al-qar'*, *khabīṣ al-zujar*, and *khabīṣ al-lawz*. These were prepared with a quarter of a ratl of sesame oil boiled in a tinned copper dish, over which half a ratl of crumbled pith of white loaf was sprinkled, little by little, stirring over a low fire. Pure ground and sifted sugar was added and stirred, leaving it moist. It was then served with sugar sprinkled on it. Some people used fresh milk instead of sesame oil.[206]

Ingredients for sweetening

Among the ingredients used for sweetening at this time, sugar (*sukkar*), honey (*'asal*, *shahd*), treacle (*dibs*), syrup (*julāb*) were prominent.[207] Sugar, originally a product of India, reached

---

200 Ibid., p. 66

201 Azdī, *Ḥikāyāt*, note given by Mez, p. 144f. cf. also Levy's Glossary in Ibn al-Ukhuwwa's *Ma'ālim al-Qurba*, s.v.; also Shayzarī, *Nihāya*, p. 40

202 Azdī, *Ḥikāyāt*, p. 41

203 *Nihāya*, p. 40; cf. also Badrī, *'Āmma*, p. 129

204 Baghdādī, *Ṭabīkh*, p. 80; *Nihāya*, p. 40; Ibn al-Ukhuwwa, *Ma'ālim al-Qurba*, p. 113

205 Dozy, *Suppl.* s.v. *khabīṣ*

206 Baghdādī, *Ṭabīkh*, p. 74; Shayzarī, *Nihāya*, p. 40

207 Jāḥiẓ, *Bukhalā'*, pp. 26, 110, 272; *Ṭabīkh*, p. 9

Persia shortly before the Muslim conquest; thence it was exported to the entire Mediterranean world.[208] It was mostly used by the moneyed people, but its use among the less affluent, though not frequent, was not rare.[209] As honey, the universal sweetening agent, was generally less expensive, the poor used it in place of sugar. A treacle of grapes, carobs and other fruits, called *dibs*, was in particular very popular in poor households.[210] Arrājān (in Fārs) was famous for a kind of *dibs* made from raisins.[211]

Sugar-cane was the chief product of Makrān, and it was from here that special white sugar, known to the Arabs as *al-Fānīdh* (from the Persian *pānīd*), was brought.[212] From the revenue lists of the Abbasids, quoted by Jahshiyārī, it is known that Sijistān, a place also noted for white sugar, sent 20,000 ratls of *fānīdh* sugar every year, as part of their *kharāj*, to the Caliph Hārūn al-Rashīd.[213] Kuhistān, in the district of Jundishāpūr, was also known for sugar-cane, and possessed a flourishing sugar industry.[214] Sugar-cane grew in almost all parts, and Maqdisī states that in the fourth century Khūzistān alone supplied sugar to Persia, Mesopotamia, and Arabia.[215] The district of Sūs in Khūzistān was particularly noted for its refined quality of sugar.[216] In Mesopotamia, the neighbourhood of Basra was also famous for its sugar industry.[217] In Syria in the fourth century, sugar-cane was grown on the coast of the Mediterranean and in Palestine.[218] The table sugar brought from the Yemen was often made from honey, and was packed by a special process. It was dried in the sun,

---

[208] N. Dear, *The History of Sugar*, London, 1949, i, pp. 68ff., 74ff., quoted by M. Rodinson, in *EI*², s.v. *Ghidhā'*; cf. also *EI*¹, s.v. *Sukkar* (J. Ruska); also *JESHO*, vii (1964) pp. 57–72

[209] *EI*², s.v. *Ghidhā'* (M. Rodinson)

[210] Ibid.; cf. also E. Ashtor, in *AESC*, 1968, p. 1024

[211] Le Strange, *Eastern Caliphate*, p. 294

[212] Ibid., p. 239; cf. also *Laṭā'if*, p. 237, who mentions Maskān as *fānīdh* producing land, which in fact adjoined Makrān (modern Baluchistan). Cf. Yāqūt, *Buldān*, v, p. 42; see also the Eng. Tr. of the *Laṭa'if*, by C. E. Bosworth, 146, n. 178

[213] Jahshiyārī, *Wuzarā'*, p. 283

[214] Muq. p. 408

[215] Ibid., p. 461; cf. also Le Strange, *Eastern Caliphate*, p. 246

[216] Baghdādī, *Bukhalā'*, p. 104

[217] Mez, p. 435; cf. also, E. Ashtor, in *JAH*, iv (1970), p. 5

[218] E. Ashtor, *JAH*, 1970, p. 5, quoting from Muq. pp. 162, 180

stuffed in osier-rods, and then kept for a few days in cold storage until it hardened. The openings of the rods were sealed with gypsum. At the time of its use the rods were broken and the sugar was cut with a knife onto a dish or a loaf of bread. This sugar was mainly exported to Mesopotamia and Mecca.[219]

Sugar-cane and sugar of Ahwāz were also proverbial.[220] It was Ahwāz which supplied Iraq with most of its sugar and sent to the caliphs 50,000 ratls per annum in addition to the land tax (*kharāj*).[221] A physician living in the fourth century, Abū ʿAbdallāh Muḥammad b. Aḥmad al-Tamīmī, noted that the white sugar was in great demand in Iraq. It was called *al-qand* in Iraq and *al-Ahwāzī* in Syria.[222]

People chewed sugar-cane for its sweet juice and used the remains as fuel.[223] The best sugar was the transparent kind called *Ṭabarzad*.[224] Sometimes dates (*tamr*) could also be used for sweetening.[225]

Honey from Armenia was regarded as one of the best kinds.[226] Nevertheless, the honey of Iṣfahān remained unequalled,[227] and according to Ibn Rusta, the caliphal court consumed none but the pure white honey of Iṣfahān.[228] Together with the *kharāj*, 20,000 ratls of honey and 20,000 ratls of wax used to be taken from Iṣfahān each year to the seat of the central government.[229] Similarly, in the days of the Caliph Hārūn al-Rashīd, Hamadhān, Mosul and Takrit each sent 20,000 ratls of Arwand and white honey every year as

---

219 Mez, p. 435, quoting from Hamadānī, ed. D. H. Muller, p. 198

220 *Laṭā'if*, pp. 174, 183, 237; *Thimār*, p. 536

221 Ibid., *Laṭā'if*, p. 174; *Thimār*, p. 537, where 30,000 ratls have been mentioned. Cf. also Ibn al-Faqīh, pp. 253–5; Jahshiyārī, *Wuzarā'*, p. 282; *Tijāra* (attributed to Jāḥiẓ), p. 41

222 *Kitāb al-Murshid ilā jawāhir al-aghdhiya*, Paris, MS. No. 2870, fol. 10b, cited by E. Ashtor, in *AESC*, 1968, p. 1023, note, 11

223 Jāḥiẓ, *Bukhalā'*, p. 23

224 *Murūj*, vi, 227; Azdī, *Ḥikāyāt*, 41; *Tajārib*, iii, 194; Bayhaqī, *Maḥāsin*, pp. 594, 605; cf. also Lane, s.v. *Ṭabarzad*

225 Jāḥiẓ, *Bukhalā'*, p. 361

226 Khālidiyyān, *Tuḥaf*, p. 119; cf. also, Le Strange, *Eastern Caliphate*, p. 93

227 *Laṭā'if*, pp. 181, 237

228 *Aʿlāq*, p. 157

229 *Laṭā'if*, p. 182; *Thimār*, p. 538; Jahshiyārī, *Wuzarā'*, p. 285

part of their *kharāj*, to Baghdad.[230] In the same period, Babr and Taylasan paid part of their *kharāj* in the form of 30 *ziq* (containers) of honey.[231]

Abāzīr, Tawābil (Spices)

Spices were commonly used in food. The rich families rarely used a dish that was not flavoured with some sort of spice.[232] The use of spices, it would seem, was primarily for flavouring and taste.[233] It is also likely that they were used to remove the odour of meat or fish, which soon went bad in a hot country. The insufficient means of preservation of meat therefore compelled people to have recourse to spices, which were used to an inordinate extent, perhaps, to disguise the taste of incipient decomposition. Moreover, spices were also needed to remedy the tastelessness of the salted and dried meat (*qadīd*) commonly used in this period. Yet another reason was that in hot regions like that of Baghdad, people's eating habits were so conditioned that without spicy flavour they lost all appetite for food.

The following spices were used in cooking: coriander (*kasfara*), especially freshly gathered, green or dry; cumin (*kammūn*); caraway (*karawāya*); cinnamon (*dār-ṣīnī*), especially where the bark was thick and luxuriant, strong-scented and burning to the tongue; mastic (*muṣṭakā*) especially the kind with large, bright grains, and free of dust and dirt; pepper (*fulful*) fresh, large-grained and not old; ginger (*zanjabīl*); clove (*qaranful*); thyme (*ṣaʿtar*); *anjidhān*, a kind of leaf used for flavouring; sticks of dill (*ṭāqāt shibitt*).[234]

These spices were brought from distant lands, especially from China, India and Southern Arabia. The lightness of their weight and the high profits they fetched justified the

---

230 Jahshiyārī, *Wuzarā'*, p. 285

231 S. A. El-Ali, "A new version of Ibn al-Muṭarrif's list of revenues in the early times of Hārūn al-Rashid", in *JESHO* 1971, p. 309

232 See, for example, *Ṭabīkh*, p. 9ff.

233 Ibid., p. 8, n. 1

234 Warrāq, fol. 14b; *Ṭabīkh*, pp. 8, 11, 28, 31; Azdī, *Ḥikāyāt*, p. 39ff.; *Minhāj al-Bayān*, Br. Mus. Ms. (5934), fol. 34b; cf. also Badrī, *ʿĀmma*, pp. 122–3

long and difficult journeys.[235] Some countries sent spices to Baghdad as part of their *kharāj*. We are told that Kirmān supplied Baghdad with one hundred ratl of *kammūn* seeds as a part of the *kharāj*.[236]

The utmost care was taken in cleaning spices and grinding them fine. They were either ground in a mill or pounded in a copper mortar.[237] Spice-pounding was done by women at home.[238] In some dishes, however, spices were also used without grinding or pounding.[239]

Salt in cooking, an adage said, was as necessary as grammar in speech (*al-milḥ fi'l-ṭa'ām ka'l-naḥw fi'l-kalām*). During the Abbasid period two kinds of salt were used: the ordinary common salt, and the Andarānī salt, the latter variety being the more prized.[240] "Milḥ Andarānī" was brought from the rocks of Andarān, a place near Nīshāpūr.[241] Ibn Bayṭār compares its brightness with crystal (*ballūr*),[242] while Azdī calls it "polished silver" (*al-fiḍḍa al-masbūka*).[243] The culinary manuals preferred Andarānī salt for all varieties of cooking. In its absence, the manuals recommended pure white salt free from dust and particles of stone.[244]

Flavouring

In addition to spices, some flavourings were also used to make the food dainty and delicious. Rose-water (*mā' al-ward*) and saffron (*za'farān*) seem to have been commonly used in the houses of the well-to-do.[245] The rose-water of Fārs (more precisely Jūr, one of the towns of Fārs) and the saffron of

---

235 *Tijāra* (attr. to Jāḥiẓ), p. 34; Tha'ālibī, *Laṭā'if*, p. 215; *Thimār*, p. 533; cf. also, *EI*² s.v. *Ghidhā'* (M. Rodinson)

236 Jahshiyārī, *Wuzarā'*, p. 283; also some unspecified quantity of cloves (cf. ibid., 283)

237 *Ṭabīkh*, p. 8

238 Ḥamadānī, *Maqāmāt*, p. 111; cf. also, Mez, p. 363

239 *Ṭabīkh*, p. 9ff.

240 Ibid., pp. 7–8; Azdī, *Ḥikāyāt*, p. 39

241 *Ṭabīkh*, p. 7, n. 3

242 Ibn Bayṭār, *Mufradāt*, s.v. *milḥ*

243 Azdī, *Ḥikāyāt*, p. 39. "Milḥ Durrānī" in the text should be read "Milḥ Andarānī"

244 *Ṭabīkh*, pp. 7–8f. (Eng. Tr. p. 13f.)

245 Ibid., p. 10ff.; Warrāq, fol. 13a

Iṣfahān were of an excellence unequalled in the world.[246] Rose-water obtained as a part of the *kharāj* from Fārs amounted to 30,000 flasks (*qārūra*).[247] Apart from these two flavourings, the Abbasids frequently added to their dishes dried fruits such as almonds, walnuts, raisins, dried figs, pistachios, currants, and filberts.[248] In the preparation of sour (*ḥāmiḍ*) dishes, fruit juices such as sumach juice, lemon juice, grape juice, pomegranate juice or a mixture of lemon and grape juice or vinegar were used.[249] Lemon juice and sumach juice were also sprinkled on the cooked food, especially on roasted meat.[250]

In the list of flavourings we also find the names of *murrī* (brine) and *aẓfār al-ṭīb* (literally, "perfumed nails").[251] *Murrī*, according to the *Tāj*, was a type of *idām*[252] like sauce and pickle.[253] *Murrī*, which was used as spice, was a mixture of pennyroyal-flour, salt, cinammon, saffron, and some other aromatic herbs. A dough of all these things was made with rose-water and put in the sun for about forty days, kneaded every dawn and evening.[254] *Murrī* could also be used as *idām*.[255] One of the specialities and items of commerce of Merv was *murrī* brine for pickling.[256] *Aẓfār al-ṭīb* was an odoriferous substance "of the nature of the shards of shells". Its Latin equivalent was *strombus lentiginosus*.[257]

---

[246] *Laṭā'if*, pp. 178–81; *Thimār*, p. 537

[247] Jahshiyārī, *Wuzarā'*, p. 282; *Laṭā'if*, p. 179; cf. also, *Thimār*, pp. 537–8, where 27,000 flasks have been mentioned

[248] Warrāq, fol. 13b; *Ṭabīkh*, p. 10ff.

[249] *Ṭabīkh*, p. 10ff. During the early days of the Caliph Hārūn al-Rashīd, Fārs sent 1,000 manna (about 2,000 pound) of raisin juice, 40,000 manna of pomegranate juice, and 1,000 manna of *anbijāt* (jam). Cf. S. A. El-Ali, *A New version of Ibn Muṭarrif's list of revenues in the early times of Hārūn al-Rashid*, *JESHO*, 1971, p. 307

[250] Ḥamadānī, *Maqāmāt*, p. 64

[251] *Ṭabīkh*, pp. 12–13 (Eng. Tr. p. 16)

[252] On *idām* see above, p. 97

[253] *Tāj*, s.v. *Murrī*

[254] *Ṭabīkh*, p. 12 (Eng. Tr. p. 16, n. 1); cf. also, Shayzarī, *Nihāya*, p. 59. Jāḥiẓ is said to have written a treatise on *murrī* entitled "*Risāla fi'l-murrī*". Cf. Yūsuf b. 'Umar al-Turkamānī, *al-Mu'tamad fi'l-adwiya al-mufrada*, (Cairo, 1951), p. 492 cited by Bosworth, in Tha'ālibī's *Laṭā'if*, Eng. Tr. p. 135, n. 112

[255] Jāḥiẓ, *Bukhalā'*, p. 48

[256] *Laṭā'if*, pp. 202, 226

[257] Arberry, *A Baghdad Cookery Book*, p. 16

Sauces, relishes and savouries

These items, as Baghdādī states, were taken with principal meals "to cleanse the palate of greasiness, to appetize, to assist the digestion, and to stimulate the banqueter".[258]

Mukhallalāt, or sauces, were made with vegetables such as egg-plants, turnips, and mint. Hence they were known after these vegetables as *bādhinjān mukhallal, lift mukhallal.*[259] All these were prepared in a more or less similar way. Fresh vegetables were taken, boiled, cut into small pieces and steeped in vinegar with some seasonings and aromatic herbs. The sauces were kept in glass bottles for a few days until they were ready to be served.[260]

Ṣibāgh, or relishes, were made with vegetables and milk. The excellent relish which both awakens and stimulates the appetite was called *shīrāz bi-buqūl* (dry curds with vegetables). It contained mint, celery, leek, dried curds, ground mustard, walnuts and salt.[261] Other relishes were *bādhinjān bi-laban* (egg-plant with milk), *qarʿ bi-laban* (gourd with milk), *silq bi-laban* (a variety of chard with milk).[262] Jāḥiẓ mentions a relish of olive water (*mā' al-zaytūn*), which was the favourite relish of some niggardly people.[263]

Of all the savouries, *kāmakh* (from Persian *kāma, kāmak*) appears to have been the most popular. *Kāmakh*, in fact, was so important that it was always served, even at banquets.[264] It was prized so highly that it was exchanged as a valuable gift in higher circles. It is reported that Ibn Abī Khālid, on a suggestion by the Caliph Ma'mūn, sent a set of presents, among them poisoned white *kāmakh*, to Ṭāhir b. Ḥusayn (died 207 AH). Ṭāhir is reported to have died within two days of eating this relish.[265] Baghdādī in his *Kitāb al-Ṭabīkh* mentions a special *kāmakh* called *kāmakh rījāl* (relish with confection) which was prepared with a large dry pumpkin

---

[258] Baghdādī, *Ṭabīkh*, p. 65

[259] Ibid., pp. 65–6; Azdī, *Ḥikāyāt*, p. 38

[260] Ibid., pp. 65–6; also Warrāq, fols. 56–60

[261] For the preparation of these dishes of relish, see Baghdādī, *Ṭabīkh*, p. 67

[262] For the methods of preparation of all these relishes, see ibid., p. 67

[263] Jāḥiẓ, *Bukhalā'*, p. 91

[264] Rāghib, *Muḥāḍarāt*, ii, p. 615; *Murūj*, viii, pp. 392–4

[265] Shābushtī, *Diyārāt*, pp. 147–8

shell, fresh and sour milk and some aromatic ingredients. All the ingredients were mixed, and the mixture was left in bright sunshine for some days. In fact, it was the heat of the sun which cooked the *kāmakh*, which is why it was made generally in the month of June, at the beginning of midsummer. It was usually kept for a month and was ready to be served at the beginning of August.[266] Since it was kept in sunshine over a period of a month, the *kāmakh* presented a dark brownish colour, which people of refined taste found repellent.[267] A man compared it with excrement (*khur*', *kharā*').[268]

Oil and fat

The oil commonly used in cooking at this time was *shīraj*, or sesame oil.[269] Clarified butter (*saman*) and butter (*zubda*) were also used.[270] The fat of animals was sometimes used in some plain dishes. The animal-fat was chopped and then melted on a fire, and the resultant was preserved after removing the impurities.[271] Common people used this fat of animals (*shaḥm*) in preparing soup (*maraq*).[272] The Arabs, from ancient times, were fond of the fat procured from the fat tail (*alya*).[273] The Abbasid recipe books often give *alya* as one of the best parts of animals, which was cooked with other kinds of meat.[274]

Olive oil was also used for cooking. The manuals of guidance on *ḥisba* advised the use of olive oil in the absence of sesame oil.[275] But it basically and chiefly remained a poor

---

[266] Baghdādī, *Ṭabīkh*, pp. 68–9; cf. also the verses of Ibn Mu'tazz describing the various types of *kāmakh* in *Murūj*, viii, pp. 392–4; see also C. E. Bosworth in the Eng. trans. of *Laṭā'if*, p. 65

[267] Washshā', *Muwashshā*, p. 192

[268] *Muḥāḍarāt*, ii, p. 615

[269] Baghdādī, *Ṭabīkh*, p. 33ff. Cf. also, Ashtor, *JAH*, 1970, p. 4

[270] Jāḥiẓ, *Bukhalā*', pp. 44, 47; *Imtā*', iii, p. 77

[271] *Ṭabīkh*, pp. 17, 26; cf. also, Shayzarī, *Nihāya*, p. 40

[272] Jāḥiẓ, *Bukhalā*', index

[273] *EI*², s.v. *Ghidhā*' (M. Rodinson)

[274] *Ṭabīkh*, pp. 19ff; cf. also Azdī, *Ḥikāyāt*, p. 40

[275] *Nihāya*, p. 25ff. Syria was famous for its abundant growth of olive and the exportation of olive oil to various provinces in great quantities (cf. Muq. p. 180; Dimashqī, p. 193; also Ashtor, *JAH*, 1970, p. 4; *AESC*, 1968, 1023). Olive oil was therefore widely used in the diet of the Syrians, and according to Maqdisī the native Christians prepared a special dish of "oil-meat" during their fast (Muq. pp. 183–4; Ashtor, op. cit.).

man's *idām*, which he took with bread.[276] Almond oil (*dahn al-lawz*) and pistachio oil (*dahn al-fustaq*) were applied in cooking costly sweet dishes such as *lawzīnaj*[277] and *zalābiya*.[278]

Fruit

Fruit was taken at the table either before or after the meal.[279] Dates, of numerous varieties and very cheap, were often consumed by the common people, who bought great quantities of them.[280] Among the fruit taken at the table of the rich, apples, grapes, pomegranates, melons, oranges, citrons, peaches and bananas were prominent.

Iraq and Syria produced many excellent kinds of fruit. The horticulture of Syria was highly specialized, and was renowned for its sweet apples, pomegranates, plums, figs, sycamores and apricots.[281] The Abbasid caliphs received a great quantity of these from Syria as part of the *kharāj*.[282] Upper Mesopotamia had plenty of pomegranates, almonds, sumach, and other fruits, which were also exported to other regions.[283] In spite of that, Iraq imported fruit in great quantities from Syria, of better quality and perhaps more competitive in price.[284] Syrian fruits were also exported to Egypt.[285]

Apples were widely consumed; those from Syria were considered to be of the best quality during this period.[286]

---

276 Jāḥiẓ, *Bukhalā'*, pp. 20, 86, 186; *Murūj*, vi, p. 228; *Fakhrī*, p. 243

277 On *Lawzinaj* and *zalābiya* see earlier in this chapter, pp. 99 and 100

278 Azdī, Hikāyāt, p. 41; *Tabīkh*, p. 71

279 Ṣābī, *Wuzarā'*, p. 261; Warrāq, fol. 37b; *Murūj*, viii, p. 270; Ibn Ḥawqal, p. 206; *Muntaẓam*, v, pt. 2, p. 126

280 Cf. for example, Jāḥiẓ, *Bukhalā'*, Index, s. vv. *tamr*, *rutab*. The *sukkar* variety of dates was often served at the dining table of the well-to-do people (cf. *Bukhalā'*, pp. 108, 122; *Murūj*, vi, p. 363).

281 Muq. pp. 172, 174, 176, 180, 181; Ibn Ḥawqal, p. 172; cf. also E. Ashtor, "The diet of salaried classes", *JAH*, 1970, p. 6

282 *Thimār*, pp. 531–2; *Laṭā'if*, p. 156

283 Ibn Ḥawqal, pp. 220, 227; Muq. pp. 136, 145; E. Ashtor, op. cit., p. 6

284 Muq. pp. 180–1; E. Ashtor, op. cit., p. 6

285 Suyūṭī, *Ḥusn al-Muḥāḍara*, ii, p. 229, cited by Mez, p. 334

286 *Murūj*, viii, 270; *Laṭā'if*, 156, 237; *Nishwār*, ii, in *RAAD*, xiii, 50–2

"Syrian apples" therefore became proverbial.[287] Syria sent 30,000 apples to Baghdad as part of the *kharāj*.[288]

Grapes held a prominent place among fruit. These were of different varieties and were usually named after the localities of origin, such as Ukbara, Dayr al-Ākūl, Ma'lathāya, Sarūj, Ḥulwān.[289] Grapes were also known by names such as "cow-eyes", "sugar", "tiny flasks".[290] According to Ibn Ḥawqal, in the middle of the 4th century Iṣfahān was noted for its abundant production of very cheap grapes.[291] A new variety called "rāziqita" was introduced by the Arabs from Ṭā'if.[292]

Citrons (*utruj*) and oranges (*nāranj*) were used during this period only in the higher circles, as they were rare fruits in Baghdad in the third century.[293] The orange and lemon trees, according to Masʿūdī, appeared in Mesopotamia only in the fourth century. They were brought some time after 300 AH from India to Oman, and thence imported to Basra and Syria.[294] Basra, in the fourth century, became famous for its good oranges and citrons.[295] Jāḥiẓ mentions that citrons in the third century were imported from Sūs to Baghdad.[296] Citrons of Tabaristan are particularly noted by Thaʿālibī for their good flavour.[297]

The pomegranates of Sinjar were highly prized in Iraq.[298] During the early Abbasid period Qumis and Tabaristan were noted for their abundant growth of pomegranates. In the

---

287 *Thimār*, p. 531; cf. also, Ḥ. Zayyāt, "The apples of Damascus", *Mashriq*, 35 (1937), pp. 29–32

288 *Thimār*, pp. 531–2

289 Muq. pp. 122, 123, 125; Ibn Ḥawqal, p. 230

290 Mez, p. 432, Sāmarrā'ī, *Agriculture in Iraq*, p. 138

291 Ibn Ḥawqal, p. 261

292 Khawārizmī, *Rasā'il*, p. 49 cited by Mez, p. 432. See, for some verses praising "Rāziqī" grapes, Azdī, *Ḥikāyāt*, p. 43; see also, Ashtor, *A Social and Economic History* . . ., p. 44

293 *Diyārāt*, p. 152; *Nishwār*, i, p. 146; Sāmarrā'ī, op. cit., p. 140

294 *Murūj*, ii, p. 438f.; cf. also, Mez, p. 432. E. Ashtor observes that since citrons were grown in Egypt in the 9th century, Masʿūdī had only certain kinds in mind which were introduced in the 10th century AD (cf. *JAH*, 1970, p. 7).

295 Muq. p. 145; *Laṭā'if*, p. 238; cf. also Nuwayrī, i, p. 37

296 Jāḥiẓ (?) *Tijāra*, p. 42; see also Azdī, *Ḥikāyāt*, p. 44

297 *Laṭā'if*, pp. 186, 238

298 Ibn Ḥawqal, pp. 220–1. According to Thaʿālibī (*Laṭā'if*, p. 237) Ray was also famous for pomegranates.

days of Hārūn al-Rashīd, the former yielded 40,000 and the latter 100,000 pomegranates as parts of their *kharāj*.[299] Peaches were cultivated chiefly in Basra,[300] while Rahba, Syria and Sinjar were famous for their olives.[301] An excellent kind of quince was produced too in Rahba.[302] The figs of Ḥulwān were much appreciated.[303] From the revenue lists of the Caliph Hārūn al-Rashīd it is known that Fārs sent 150,000 quinces and Tabaristan 1,000 ratls of peaches to Baghdad in partial fulfilment of their *kharāj*.[304]

Melons were the favourite fruit in Baghdad, so much so that the fruit market was known as "the melon house".[305] The melons of Khwārazm were proverbial for their sweet taste and fragrance. The sweetest and best tasting variety of melon was called *bāranj*.[306] The Caliph Ma'mūn had these brought from Khwārazm by post.[307] Melons were imported to Baghdad either cut and dried or packed in leaden ice-chests.[308] On safe arrival a piece of melon kept in ice was sold at 700 dirhams.[309]

The people of sophisticated taste in Baghdad were very fastidious in their choice of fruit at ceremonial meals. They took only delicacies such as Indian olives, pistachios, sugar-cane washed with rose-water, quince from Balkh, and apples from Syria. Pomegranates, figs, water melons, being cheap,

---

299 Jahshiyārī, *Wuzarā'*, p. 284

300 Jāḥiẓ, *Bukhalā'*, pp. 114–15

301 Muq. p. 141; Ibn Ḥawqal, pp. 220–1

302 Muq. p. 145. The quinces of Nishapur were also highly prized (cf. *Laṭā'if*, p. 238).

303 Ibid., p. 123; *Laṭā'if*, p. 237; Jāḥīẓ (?) *Tijārā*, p. 42; cf. also Nuwayrī, i, p. 371

304 Jahshiyārī, *Wuzarā'*, pp. 282, 284

305 Jāḥiẓ, *Dalā'il*, p. 23; *Eclipse*, iii, p. 51; *Nishwār*, ii, in *RAAD*, 13 (1933–35), p. 179; cf. also, Mez, p. 433. For an interesting article on the "melon house" of Baghdad and Damascus, see, Ḥ. Zayyāt, *Mashriq*, 27 (1929), pp. 761–4. On the cultivation of melons see also Sāmarrā'ī, op cit., p. 140

306 *Laṭā'if*, p. 226. See also the note on *bāranj* given by C. E. Bosworth, p. 142, n. 157

307 Ibid., pp. 226, 238. Another variety of melon called "Ramashī" was highly prized by the Baghdadis (cf. Azdī, *Ḥikāyāt*, p. 43; cf. also *Aghānī*[1], viii, p. 10).

308 Mez, p. 433. Ibn Ḥawqal remarks that, to his knowledge, Marv was the only country wherefrom dried melons were exported in huge quantities to various lands (cf. p. 316).

309 *Laṭā'if*, p. 226

were left to the common folk. Fruit having stones (olives, dates, apricots, peaches) were also disliked by these *ẓurafā'*. Dried, unripe and cleft fruits were also despised and rejected.[310]

Drinks

As is mentioned in the section on Table Manners, no alcoholic drink was taken at the table. In Baghdad generally Tigris water was taken after the meal.[311] There were, however, some special drinks taken after the meal, but no alcoholic drink was included. These drinks were known simply as *nabīdh*, with the addition of the principal ingredient's name: *al-nabīdh al-ʿanabī* (of grapes), *al-nabīdh al-zabībī*, *tamarī*, *ʿasalī*, *dūshābī*, (*nabīdh* of raisins, dates, honey, *dūshāb*).[312] The special drink recommended after meals for health was called *fuqqāʿ*.[313] It was made from white sugar, honey or treacle, mixed with rose-water and musk, and was cooled with ice.[314]

In convivial parties, generally held in the houses of the rich, various types of drink were taken. Those who did not take wine, for pious or other reasons, took sherbet and fruit juice.[315] *Nabīdh* was widely taken during this period by people from all walks of life. There was a fierce controversy among the scholars and *fuqahā'* as to whether or not *nabīdh* belonged to the category of wine.[316] The common people and those who belonged to lower social groups were addicted to a

---

310 *Muwashshā*, p. 194; cf. also Mez, pp. 395–6

311 Khaṭīb, *Ta'rīkh*, iii, p. 183; Ḥamadānī, *Maqāmāt*, p. 66; Bayhaqī, *Maḥāsin*, p. 321–2. There are however reports to the effect that people joined a drinking party after having a meal; but that was not done in the dining room itself, rather it was organised in some other apartments of the house (see, for example, *Irshād*, v, p. 260). For a general discussion on drinks and matters related to them see also the German translation of the *Iḥyā'* of Ghazālī, by H. Kindermann, Bk. ii

312 *Muwashshā*, p. 196; *Murūj*, viii, p. 243; Majūsī, *Kamāl al-Ṣanaʿa*, i, pp. 203–6; ii, pp. 14–17; cf. also Badrī, *ʿĀmma*, p. 133

313 *ʿUyūn*, iii, p. 280; Warrāq, fol. 9a; Ghazūlī, *Maṭāliʿ*, ii, 88. Ibn Qutayba notes that *fuqqāʿ* was to be taken before a meal (cf. *ʿUyūn*, iii, p. 298). For the sellers of *fuqqāʿ* in the markets of Samarra, see Yaʿqūbī, *Buldān*, p. 261

314 Ibid., *Maṭāliʿ*, ii, p. 88

315 *Irshād*, v, pp. 260–1; cf. also, Mez, p. 398

316 *ʿIqd*, vi, pp. 352–78; *Quṭub al-Surūr*, p. 444ff.; Charles Pellat, *The life and works of Jāḥiẓ*, pp. 52–5

particular type of drink known as *dūshāb al-maḥsūrī.*[317] The culinary manuals such as Warrāq's *Ṭabīkh* give various recipes for preparing drinks from fruit, milk, sugar, honey, and even from some vegetables such as gourds and carrots.[318]

People of sophisticated taste took only those drinks which were not blackish in colour, not stale or turbid, and not popular among the common folk.[319] Therefore, they favoured drinks made of apricot juice, raisins and honey, cooked (*maṭbūkh*) together probably as kinds of wine with the necessary ingredients (*muʿaddal*).[320]

Fruit juice was sold in the market sealed in bottles with a label mentioning the name of the fruit and the name of the producer.[321] Baghdad imported most of its fruit drinks from Iṣfahān.[322]

Nuql

Nuql (or "nogalmata", served as an hors d'oeuvre) was as important as other items of food at the table. It consisted of dried fruit such as nuts, almonds, or dried figs, taken with drink and also after the meal as *taʿallul* (savoury).[323] The materials used for *nuql*, at this period, are known from an anecdote of the Caliph Wāthiq. On one occasion he asked his courtiers what was the best of the *nuql*. The replies were varied. Some said vegetables (*nabāt*), some suggested pomegranates, some sugar soaked in rose-water, while others recommended salt and biscuits. A young boy who happened to be there suggested *khushknānaj*, a kind of cake, as the best *nuql*. The Caliph appreciated the boy's answer and rewarded him.[324]

Men of refined taste were very careful in choosing things

---

317 *Muwashshā*, p. 196

318 Warrāq, fol. 9a; Ibn al-Ukhuwwa, *Maʿālim al-Qurba*, p. 115ff.; Ḥamadānī, *Maqāmāt*, pp. 60–1

319 *Muwashshā*, p. 196; cf. also M. Ghazi, *Un groupe social: "les raffinés"* (*Ẓurafāʾ*). *SI*, xi (1959), p. 61

320 Ibid., p. 196; M. Ghazi, op. cit., *SI*, 1959, p. 61

321 *Irshād*, v, p. 260

322 Jāḥiẓ (?) *Tabaṣṣur*, p. 39

323 Jāḥiẓ, *Bukhalāʾ*, Index, s.v. *nuql*; Ḥamadānī, *Maqāmāt*, pp. 132, 216; *Muwashshā*, pp. 193–4; 196–7; Azdī, *Ḥikāyāt*, pp. 48–9; *Laṭāʾif*, p. 192

324 *Murūj*, vii, pp. 170–1; *Quṭub al-Surūr*, pp. 290–1

as *nuql*. They mixed their *nuql* with a bit of mint for fragrance, and did not take too much at a time. They avoided eating chicory, *ukshūsh* (a kind of herb), radish, cress, leeks, onion, *qaddāḥ* (a kind of herb) and melilot as *nuql*, because some of these have the property of inducing colds and coughs, others emit a bad odour, and some colour the teeth and gums.[325] They favoured salted hazel-nuts, peeled pistachios, scented salt, edible earth of Khurāsān, and other costly delicacies.[326] Beans, acorns, chestnuts, roasted sesame seeds, and unripe dates were not considered up to their standard, and were therefore left to the masses and the less sophisticated.[327]

Preservation and conservation

The Abbasids inherited the art of food preservation from the ancient east and the classical civilizations. The drying process was widely used and the least expensive.[328] Even the Arabs of the remote past were fond of dried meat called *qadīd*.[329] In the *adab* literature where the food habits of the Arabs are described, interesting anecdotes regarding the *qadīd* are also presented. The common people of the time used this method extensively. Like meat, fish was also dried in the sun and used throughout the year.[330]

In one process of food preservation, antiseptic agents, especially salt and vinegar, were used. The meat thus preserved was known as *namaksūd*,[331] a Persian compound word indicative of the Persian origin of the method. To make *namaksūd*, the meat was cut into slices, seasoned with salt, and left in the sun on a plank to dry.[332] When required, the slices were moistened with water and cooked. Salting seems to have been the most common practice, as the manuals of

[325] *Muwashshā*, p. 193

[326] Ibid., pp. 196–7; Azdī, *Ḥikāyāt*, p. 48; *Laṭā'if*, p. 192

[327] Ibid., *Muwashshā*, p. 196; *Ḥikāyāt*, pp. 48–9; cf. also, Mez, p. 397

[328] *EI*², s.v. *Ghidhā'* (M. Rodinson)

[329] Jāḥiẓ, *Bukhalā'* p. 28; *Muḥāḍarāt*, ii, p. 627; cf. also, *EI*², s.v. *Ghidhā'*

[330] *EI*², s.v. *Ghidhā'*; cf. also, Ibn Ḥawqal, p. 248

[331] Jāḥiẓ, *Ḥayawān*, i, p. 299; Azdī, *Ta'rīkh al-Mawṣil*, p. 210. In Shayzarī's *Nihāyat al-Rutba* (p. 33) the word is read as *Maksūd*.

[332] Ḥuṣri, *Jam' al-Jawāhir fi'l-mulaḥ wa'l-nawādir*, p. 239; cf. also, Ḥ. Zayyāt, in *Mashriq*, 1969, p. 536

ḥisba often enjoin the *muḥtasib* to make sure, for example, that no unsold fish was left unsalted.[333]

The culinary manuals (e.g., *Wuṣlā*) contain some recipes for preservation of food which are so elaborate and costly that common people could never even think of using them. According to these recipes vegetables, fruit, small fishes, and birds (*ʿuṣfūr*) were preserved by means of various spices and condiments. This was called *naqāniq* or *luqāniq* (cf. Aramaic, *Naqnīqa*).[334] In addition to impregnation with salt and vinegar, a great deal of honey or its substitutes such as sugar and treacle, lemon juice, oil, mustard, walnuts or hazelnuts roasted and crushed, various kinds of herbs and spices were used in these preparations.[335] Mutton, beef, and goat were made into sauces with the use of spices and a little semolina, and were eaten for several days.[336] The best sauce was that which contained only mutton and not too much semolina.[337]

Fruit such as figs, pistachios, and nuts were mainly preserved by drying them in the sun.[338] Dried fruit in large quantity was sent, at this period, to Baghdad from Palestine and Damascus as a part of the *kharāj*.[339] Fruits which could not be dried were preserved in several ways. Sometimes in order to preserve them, air-tight containers, often buried in the ground, were used.[340] There were store-houses for fruit, such as the water-melon house of Basra, where all types of fruit were available.[341]

The crystallizing of fruit in honey or sugar, a process handed down from ancient Rome, may have been used by the Abbasids at this period, as various medical works of the Greeks were in vogue in Arabic translation during this period. The Muslim travellers of the third and fourth centuries, describing the products of various lands, often

---

333 *EI*², s.v. *Ghidhā*'; cf. also, Shayzarī, op. cit., p. 33

334 Ibn al-Ukhuwwa, *Maʿālim al-Qurba*, pp. 94f., 107; cf. also Ḥ. Zayyāt, *Khizānat al-Sharqiyya*, iv, pp. 21, 23

335 *EI*², s.v. *Ghidhā*', (M. Rodinson)

336 Ibid.

337 *Maʿālim al-Qurba*, pp. 94f., 170

338 *Thimār*, p. 539; *EI*², s.v. *Ghidhā*' (M. Rodinson)

339 Cf. for example, *Thimār*, p. 539

340 Ibn al-ʿAwwām, *Filāḥa*, i, pp. 662f., 664f. Cf. also, *EI*², s.v. *Ghidhā*' (M. Rodinson)

341 Muq. p. 425; cf. also Mez, p. 481

mention the fruit preserves made with honey or sugar. Herat, for example, produced preserves of raisins, pistachios, and various syrups.[342] Harrān made a special preserve called *qubbayt.*[343] Balkh and its neighbourhood yielded a preserve of pomegranate kernels.[344]

Ice was the chief refrigerating agent, and was commonly used to keep things fresh. For example, we know that melons at this time were transported from Khwārazm to Baghdad packed in ice inside lead boxes.[345] *Thalj* (ice, or perhaps snow) was brought from the mountains. It was brought either from Syria or from the mountains of Hamadhān and Māsabdhān.[346] The method of transport of ice from the mountains over long distances to the cities and its preservation from the heat of the sun, all along the way and in storage, are problems which the ancient writers have dealt with only cursorily. Nevertheless, from some scattered information we know that snow was collected, hardened by pressing, and perhaps kept in the *khaysh* canvas and fully covered with sawdust (*nushāra*), a method still widely in vogue in the underdeveloped countries.[347] In Jibāl and at some other places there were pits dug for storing ice.[348] In Baghdad there were several dealers in ice. They were called *thallāj.*[349] Their method of preservation was so efficient that they could store it in large quantities for several days without any danger of its melting. A story about a merchant in Baghdad is recorded in Tanūkhī's *Nishwār*, and Ibn al-Jawzī's *Muntaẓam* says that he could preserve five ratls of ice in the burning heat of summer without any fall whatsoever in its weight.[350]

Ibn al-Jawzī, writing about the events of the year 330 AH, records that once during the month of February Baghdad had heavy rain accompanied by a hailstorm. The ice dealers

[342] Muq. p. 425; Le Strange, *Eastern Caliphate*, p. 429

[343] Le Strange, op. cit., p. 124

[344] Ibid., p. 430

[345] *Laṭā'if*, p. 226; Ibn al-Faqīh, p. 255; cf. also, *EI*², s.v. *Ghidhā'* (M. Rodinson)

[346] Shābushtī, *Diyārāt*, p. 88

[347] *Muntaẓam*, vi, p. 335

[348] Le Strange, *Eastern Caliphate*, p. 211

[349] *Nishwār*, i, p. 63; Ibn al-Jawzī, *Ḥumaqā*, p. 75; cf. also R. Kahhala, *Muʿjam al-mu'allifīn*, index, s.v.

[350] *Nishwār*, i, pp. 63–4; *Muntaẓam*, vi, pp. 118–19

of the city collected the large hailstones and pressed them together (*kabashūhu*).[351] This report throws light on two points: snow or hail was collected and pressed into slabs of ice, and ice was sold even in winter.

A considerable amount of money was spent on ice in the caliphal palace and in prosperous households. Expenditure on ice formed an integral part of the annual palatial budget of the caliph.[352] The wazir Ibn al-Furāt was so lavish in this respect that immediately after his assumption of office of *wizārat*, the price registered an increase.[353] It is reported that in the year 304 AH he entertained all the visitors who came to congratulate him on his appointment as wazir, and that at this entertainment 4,000 ratls of ice were consumed.[354] Not only among the rich, ice was commonly used in the household for cooling various drinks.[355]

But ice was by no means the only thing wherewith the Abbasids preserved food. For instance, they kept vegetables fresh by using earthenware. We are told that Jamīla bint Nāṣir al-Dawla, in her famous pilgrimage journey in the year 366 AH, entertained the public with, among other things, fresh green vegetables contained in earthenware crocks.[356] The vegetable *hilyawn* (asparagus) was imported from Damascus for the Caliph Muʿtaṣim packed in lead containers (*al-marākin al-raṣāṣ*). It took six days to reach the capital.[357] Merchants kept their vegetables green in their shops by sprinkling water and spraying salt and ground *ṣaʿtar* (thyme) on them.[358]

Cooked green vegetables were preserved in vinegar or other acid liquids.[359] Some vegetables such as egg-plants and gourds were also preserved in the form of sauces and relishes (*ṣibāgh*).[360]

---

351 *Muntaẓam*, vi, p. 335
352 See, for example, Ṣābī, *Rusūm*, p. 24; *Dhakhā'ir*, p. 219
353 *Fakhrī*, p. 312; cf. also, Bowen, *Life and Times of Ali* . . ., p. 154
354 Ṣābī, *Wuzarā'*, p. 73; ʿArīb, p. 61; cf. also Mez, p. 402
355 Ibn al-Jawzī, *Ḥumaqā*, p. 75
356 *Laṭā'if*, p. 82 (Eng. Tr. by C. E. Bosworth, p. 82)
357 Ṣābī, *Rusūm*, p. 18
358 Shayzarī, *Nihāyat al-Rutba*, p. 116
359 *EI*², s.v. *Ghidhā'* (M. Rodinson)
360 *Ṭabīkh*, pp. 65–7

Cereals were stored and preserved mainly in silos (*maṭmūra*) and granaries (*aghādir*).[361] Oil was stored in special huge cisterns.[362] It is reported that in the year 351 AH, when Greeks captured Aleppo, they poured water into such cisterns, causing the oil to overflow.[363]

The principal method of preserving milk was its transformation into cheese.[364] Sometimes it was coagulated and made into curd.[365]

Diet and dietetics

The caliph and the educated class in general, during the period under review, paid a great deal of attention to dietetic precepts, with the result that this science became of no small practical importance.[366] The study of nutrition and dietetics has always been one of the subjects of the medical works[367] and even of some of the *adab* literature,[368] in which the description of what were known as the virtues and the harmfulness of the herbs, cereals and garden plants can be seen. Though ordinary people were not gourmets, popular herbal remedies would seem to have been in great repute and many dishes were eaten for their alleged health value as much as for their taste and nutritive properties.

From the *Kitāb al-Ṭabīkh* of Warrāq, it appears that the Abbasid caliphs, the members of their families, their wazirs and singers had individual recipe-books containing instructions for the preparation of the dishes suited to their health.[369] Thus we find that the Caliph Wāthiq asked his Christian physician, Ḥunayn b. Isḥāq, to write a book in which to make clear the differences between foods, drugs and laxatives, and to describe the organs of the human body. Ḥunayn wrote the

---

361 *EI*², s.v. *Ghidhā'*

362 *Muntaẓam*, vii, p. 9; Mez, p. 434

363 Misk. v, p. 255; Mez, pp. 434–5; also, *Muntaẓam*, vi, p. 9

364 *EI*², s.v. *Ghidhā'*

365 *Ṭabīkh*, p. 23

366 *Murūj*, vii, pp. 105, 182; cf. also, *EI*², s.v. *Ghidhā'*

367 See, for example, Ibn Bayṭār, *Mufradāt*; Ibn Jazala, *Minhāj al-Bayān*, svv.

368 See, for example, Ibn Qutayba's *Uyūn al-Akhbār* (iii, 281–99) and Ibn 'Abd Rabbih's *'Iqd al-Farīd*, vi, pp. 314–34

369 Warrāq, fol, 26ff.

book and called it "The Book of Physical Cases".[370] Similarly, Muʿtaṣim always followed, in matters of eating, the recipe-book written by his physician Yaḥyā b. Māsawayh. If he ate fish, Ibn Māsawayh made for him a sauce of vinegar, caraway, cumin, rue, celery and mustard.[371] The intimate companion of the Caliph Muʿtaḍid, Aḥmad b. Ṭayyib al-Sarakhsī, was also the author of a culinary manual for the use of the Caliph, which he compiled according to months and days.[372]

The Abbasid caliphs and some of their wazirs could not do without dieticians at their table. The Caliph Hārūn al-Rashīd was so dependent on his private physician, Jibra'īl b. Bakhtīshūʿ, that the physician was authorized to have a dish, which in his opinion was injurious to the Caliph's health, removed from the caliphal table even if the Caliph objected.[373] Once, finding his physician absent from the dining table, the Caliph Hārūn reportedly became so alarmed that he did not touch the food until his physician joined him.[374] This physician, according to Ṭabarī, would be the first person to greet the Caliph in the morning for investigation into his health.[375] It is reported that the physicians of the Abbasid courts often appeared at the dining table with digestives (*jawārish*) and various types of *maʿjūn*, a confection made of various herbs, and with cold and hot drinks: those generating heat and natural strength in winter and those having cold properties in summer.[376] Sick persons were not given the usual food; they were given a special invalid meal called *muzawwara*, a kind of soup of various ingredients.[377]

Fuel

Wood formed the common fuel of the Abbasids. The culinary manuals of the Abbasid period commend dry wood which

[370] *Murūj*, vii, p. 182

[371] *Murūj*, vii, p. 105; cf. also H. I. Hasan, *Islam*, pp. 381–2

[372] *Fihrist*, p. 367

[373] *Murūj*, vi, pp. 305–8; vii, p. 274; Ṭabarī, iii, pp. 1455–56; *Irshād*, v, p. 469

[374] *ʿUyūn al-Anbā'*, ii, p. 34; cf. also Ḥ. Zayyāt, in *Mashriq*, 1947, pp. 10–11

[375] Ṭabarī, iii, p. 735

[376] Qifṭī, *Akhbār al-ʿUlamā'*, p. 249; *ʿUyūn al-Anbā'*, i, p. 128

[377] Warrāq, fols. 28, 46; Khālidiyyān, *Tuḥaf*, p. 127

does not give forth an acid smoke.[378] Olive-wood, ilex (*sindiyān*), palm-tree (*daqal*) and the like were, therefore, regarded as very suitable for cooking as they gave forth little smoke. All kinds of sappy wood, and especially that of the fig-tree, were avoided, for they produced much smoke and spoiled the cooking.[379] Ḥamadānī mentions a wood called *ghaḍā* as most suitable for ovens,[380] for it was regarded as one of the hardest of woods, whose hard charcoal offered a long continuance of heat.[381]

Coal was used as fuel where it was found abundantly. The neighbourhood of Farghana has been particularly noted by the geographers and travellers of the ninth and tenth centuries AD as an area where people burned coal as fuel.[382]

Those who could not afford to buy wood had recourse to dry leaves, palm leaves (*saʿf*), dry sugar-cane and the like.[383] The people of Iraq, according to Masʿūdī, commonly used thorns and spikes (*shawk*) for their ovens and furnaces.[384] Apart from the wood-shops there were several shops in Baghdad where *shawk* was sold.[385]

Animal dung also appears to have been a common fuel in the less affluent houses.[386] From a passage in Ibn Qutayba's *ʿUyūn*, it appears that human waste was also dried and put to use as fuel.[387] A group of people in Basra are reported to have taken a contract for cleaning night soil from the privies, which they dried and sold in the market.[388]

Sawdust (*nushāra*) has also been mentioned as a kind of fuel.[389] At the time of the marriage of the Caliph Ma'mūn with Būrān, the daughter of his wazir, when the supply of

---

[378] Baghdādī, *Ṭabīkh*, p. 7 (Eng. Tr. by Arberry, p. 13)

[379] Ibid., p. 7. Cf. also *Ṭabīkh*, Br. Mus. MS. No. Or. 5099, fol. 6b

[380] Ḥamadānī, *Maqāmāt*, p. 196; cf. also Ibn Abī ʿUṣaybiʿa, *ʿUyūn al-Anbā'*, i, pp. 139–40

[381] Lane, *Lexicon*, s.v. *Ghaḍā*

[382] Ibn Ḥawqal, p. 362; Muq., p. 325; cf. also Le Strange, *Eastern Caliphate*, p. 488

[383] *Irshād*, vii, p. 207; Jāḥiẓ, *Bukhalā'*, p. 23

[384] *Murūj*, vii, p. 113; viii, p. 159; cf. also *Muntaẓam*, x, p. 171

[385] Khaṭīb, *Ta'rīkh*, i, p. 112; Ibn al-Jawzī, *Mudhash*, p. 295

[386] Jāḥiẓ, *Bukhalā'*, p. 28

[387] *ʿUyūn*, i, p. 221; Yāqūt, *Buldān*, i, p. 647

[388] Ibid, i, p. 221; *Buldān*, i, p. 647

[389] Mez, Arabic Translation, ii, p. 30, quoting from al-Qushayrī, p. 168

wood ran short, the *khaysh*-canvas soaked in oil was reportedly used as fuel.[390]

Utensils

Of all the utensils commonly used in the kitchen,[391] *qidr* (plural *qudūr*), the cooking-pot or cauldron, was the most important.[392] It was made of various materials and in various sizes for the cooking of different dishes. It was generally made of clay (*fakhkhār*), stone (*barām, ḥijāra*), copper (*nuḥās*), or lead (*ānuk*).[393] The cooking-pots made of stone were considered to be the best and those of baked clay the second best.[394] Those made of tinned copper (*al-nuḥās al-mubayyaḍ*) were sparingly used.[395] Food cooked in a copper pot which had lost its tinning was regarded as something deadly.[396]

The big *qudūr*, we are told, were made with handles (*ādhān*).[397] These (*al-qudūr al-kibār*) were used in cooking food grains (*ḥubūb*), *sikbāj*,[398] *ṣilāqāt*,[399] and the like.[400] These *qudūr* were often very big, and a large quantity of food could easily be cooked at one time. It is reported that in the kitchen of Yaʿqūb b. Layth al-Ṣaffār, the flesh of four goats could be cooked at a time in each of such *qudūr*.[401] The medium-sized cooking-pots were generally used in cooking *zīrbāj*,[402]

---

390 *Nishwār*, i, p. 147; Ibn Zubayr, *Dhakhā'ir*, p. 101; *Laṭā'if*, p. 121 (Eng. Tr. by Bosworth, p. 99)

391 The cooking utensils were sometimes simply called *ṣufr*: copper. cf. *Irshād*, i, p. 392; see also Mez, p. 386

392 *'Uyūn*, iii, pp. 265–69; *Murūj*, viii, p. 54; *Diyārāt*, pp. 80–81; Jahshiyārī, *Wuzarā'*, p. 309

393 Warrāq, fol. 11; Baghdādī, *Ṭabīkh*, p. 7; *Murūj*, viii, p. 54

394 Baghdādī, *Ṭabīkh*, p. 7

395 Ibid., p. 7

396 Ibid., p. 7

397 *'Uyūn*, iii, p. 267

398 For *Sikbāj* see, above, p. 83

399 *Ṣilq* is meat roasted and thoroughly cooked; cf. *Lisān* and Lane, s.v. *ṣilq*

400 Warrāq, fol. 12b. On special occasions such as wedding parties, *qudūr* were hired perhaps from the shop at a nominal rate. Cf. Jāḥiẓ, *Bukhalā'*, p. 56; also Mez, p. 386

401 *Murūj*, viii, p. 54

402 *Zīrbāj* is a sour dish made from fat meat, peeled chickpeas, wine vinegar, sugar, sweet almonds, cinnamon, brayed coriander, pepper, sifted mastic, saffron and rose-water. cf. *Ṭabīkh*, pp. 13–14 (Eng. Tr. p. 16); also Dozy, *Supp.* s.v.

isfidbāj[403] and other varieties of light dishes. The small size *qudūr* were employed in preparing *qalāya* (fried dishes), *ṭabāhajāt*,[404] and the like.[405]

The base of the *qidr*, it would seem, was coated with some greasy material to increase its resistance to the heat of the fire.[406] The cooking-pots described as Syrian (*al-qudūr al-Shāmiyya*) were perhaps of comparatively better quality.[407] The large cooking-pots made in Tus, Marv and Sughd were highly prized.[408]

The *miqlā*, or frying-pan, made of steel or stone, was commonly used for frying fish, eggs and such other things.[409] The one made of steel was considered to be the best for frying fish and that of stone for preparing *narjisiyāt*[410] and *ʿijaj*.[411]

Though the *furn* was the common appliance used for baking bread,[412] another appliance used for the purpose was known as *ṭabaq* (an Arabicized form of the Persian *Tāba*).[413] The *ṭabaq* was a flat piece of metal, iron or copper, which could also be used as a frying pan.[414] The baker's board whereon dough was rolled into various forms of bread was called *lawḥ*, or plank.[415] The *shawbaq*, the rolling-pin, was usually made of the wood of the jujube-tree (*ʿannāb*).[416]

Another device for the baking of bread was the *tannūr*, or

403 For *Isfīdbāj* see above, p. 83

404 *Ṭabāhaja* was a dish cooked with chopped slices of meat, fat of melted tail (*alya*), usual seasonings, wine vinegar, grape juice and lemon juice. It was finally garnished with yolks of eggs and sprayed with rose-water. Cf. *Ṭabīkh*, pp. 14–15 (Eng. Tr. p. 17); cf. also Dozy and Lane s.v. *ṭabāhaj*

405 Warrāq, fol. 12b

406 Jāḥiẓ, *Bukhalā'*, p. 28

407 Ibid, pp. 28, 38

408 Le Strange, *Eastern Caliphate*, pp. 429, 471

409 Warrāq, fol. 12; *Ṭabīkh*, p. 56ff.

410 *Nirjisiyya*—from *nirjis*—narcissus, was a plain dish (*sādhij*) cooked with fat meat, fresh melted tail, peeled chick-peas and carrots. For details see *Ṭabīkh*, p. 41 (Eng. Tr. p. 31)

411 Warrāq fol. 12; *ʿujja* (pl. *ʿijaj*) is an egg fritter or omelette, also a certain food made of eggs or flour kneaded with clarified butter and then fried or roasted. cf. Lane, *Lexicon*, s.v. *ʿujja*

412 *Ṭabīkh*, p. 78f.

413 *Irshād*, vii, p. 207

414 *Murūj*, viii, p. 399; *Nishwār*, i, p. 74; Lane, s.v. *Ṭabaq*

415 Warrāq, fol. 12a

416 Ibid., fol. 12a; cf. also *Aghānī*², v, p. 342

oven made underground.[417] *Tannūr*, as described by Lane, is a kind of oven, open at the top, in the bottom of which a fire is lighted, and the bread, in the form of flat cakes, is generally stuck against the sides. The *tannur* may be portable, made of baked clay, wide at the bottom and narrow at the top where it is open, and the bread is sometimes stuck upon the outside to bake; or it may be fixed, also made of baked clay or constructed of bricks; or it may be a hole made in the ground, lined with bricks or tiles or the like, against which the bread is stuck to bake; and sometimes meat, cut into small pieces, is roasted in it, or upon it, on skewers.[418]

For roasting, *saffūd* (plural *safāfīd*) or *sīkh ḥadīd*, an iron appliance with curved prongs for holding meat, was used.[419]

Ṭinjīr, another vessel made of copper or brass and resembling a *ṭabaq*,[420] without a cover, was used in cooking sweet dishes.[421] The *ṭinjīr*, according to Lane, is now used as a saucepan.[422] The *khabīṣ*, *fālūdhaj*,[423] and the like were cooked in the *ṭinjīr*.[424] Ladles of iron were used to lift out the cooked sweets.[425] To clear off the scum (*raghwa*) from the vessel a strainer called *miṣfāḥ* was employed.[426]

The utensils (*awānī*) used at the table were numerous and of varied material. Those imported from China and known as *al-Ṣīnī* were highly esteemed.[427] The Arabs held the Chinese vessels in such high esteem that they applied the term "Chinese" to every delicately or curiously made vessel.[428] As late as the eleventh century AD the situation remained unchanged. Thaʿālibī (died 1038 AD) reports that the word "Chinese" was used for the finest quality of vessels in his time.[429] The Chinese vessels included fine, translucent

[417] Ibid., fol. 13b; Ḥamadānī, *Maqāmāt*, p. 197
[418] Lane, *Lexicon*, s.v. *tannūr*
[419] Warrāq, fol. 12a; *Ṭabīkh*, p. 60; *Lisān* and Lane, s.v. *safad*
[420] For *ṭabaq* see below, p. 123
[421] Warrāq, fol, 13b; *Nishwār*, i, pp. 171–72
[422] Lane, *Lexicon*, s.v. *ṭinjīr*
[423] For *Khabīṣ* and *Fālūdhaj* see above, pp. 100, 99
[424] Warrāq, fol. 13b; *Nishwār*, i, p. 172
[425] Ibid., fol. 13b
[426] Ibid., fol. 13b
[427] *Nishwār*, viii, p. 149; cf. also Mez, p. 386
[428] *Laṭā'if*, p. 220 (Eng. Tr. by C. E. Bosworth, p. 141); *Thimār*, p. 543
[429] Ibid, p. 220; *Thimār*, p. 543. The Caliph Wāthiq abolished customs on Chinese goods; cf. Yaʿqūbī, *History*, p. 590

pottery which was used for cooking, boiling and frying. It could, at the same time, be employed simply as a dish to eat from. The best of these "Chinese" vessels are the delicate, evenly-pigmented, clearly-resounding, apricot-coloured ware, or the cream-coloured ware with similar characteristics.[430]

The plate which the Abbasids used for taking meals was known as *ṭabaq*. The *ṭabaq* may be, in the words of the mediaeval lexicographers, defined as a household utensil in the form of a plate, a dish, or a round tray upon which or from which one eats. It could also be used as a fruit-bowl.[431] The word *ṭabaq* in the sense of a plate is perhaps derived from the original word, which meant lid or cover of a cooking-vessel, and was also used as a plate to eat from.[432] Wooden trays (*aṭbāq khaizurān*) were used as fruit bowls.[433]

There were some bowls whose capacity determined their names. A bowl or dish large enough for more than ten persons was called *jafana* (plural *jifān*).[434] Some of these were so large that a small child could be easily drowned in one.[435] Their huge size can well be judged from the fact that men could eat from them only in a standing position.[436] These gigantic utensils were made of various metals or wood.[437]

Next to the *jafana* in capacity came the *qasʿa*, from which ten persons could easily be fed.[438] A bowl called *ṣaḥfa* was large enough for a group of five persons; the *miʾkala* was sufficient for two or three persons; last came the *ṣuḥayfa*, which contained food just enough for one man.[439] People ate directly from these voluminous vessels or served food from them onto smaller plates.[440]

---

430 *Laṭāʾif*, p. 221 (Eng. Tr. p. 141)

431 *Lisān* and Lane, s.v. *ṭabaq*; see also Jāḥiẓ, *Bukhalāʾ*, pp. 38, 108, 111, 121, 134, 180; *Murūj*, vi, p. 353; vii, p. 33; *Quṭub al-Surūr*, pp. 70, 305

432 Lane, *Lexicon*, s.v. *Ṭabaq*

433 *Murūj*, vi, p. 353

434 *Mukhaṣṣaṣ*, i, Chap. 5, p. 57; cf. also Lane, s.v. *jafana*

435 *ʿUyūn*, iii, p. 269

436 Ibid., iii, p. 269

437 Jāḥiẓ, *Rasāʾil*, p. 386

438 The picture of a *Qasʿa* can be seen in *Excavations at Samarra* (1936–39), ii, pl. 28

439 *Mukhaṣṣaṣ*, i, Chap. v, p. 57; Lane, s.v. *Jafana*

440 Jāḥiẓ, Bukhalāʾ, pp. 64, 67, 85, 182; *ʿUyūn*, iii, p. 268 Baghdādī, Bukhalāʾ, pp. 90, 107, 184

Ghaḍāra was another vessel which belonged to the class of large utensils. It was often made of cohesive (*lāzib*) green clay, and was usually of a size similar to that of a *qaṣʿa*.[441] Jāḥiẓ has mentioned a *ghaḍāra* which, he says, was made of Kaimākish (Turkish) khalanj-wood[442] and was as good as the highly prized glazed Chinese bowls (*ghaḍār al-mulammaʿ al-ṣīnī*).[443] The khalanj-wood was, at this period, widely used for carving bowls and beakers.[444] Kaimākiya, according to Yāqūt, was a district of China and was inhabited by the Turks.[445] Thaʿālibī mentions khalanj hardwood among the specialities of the Turkish lands.[446] Corroborating this view Maqdisī and Qazwīnī tell us that large bowls were made from this fine-grained wood, which was imported from Tabaristān.[447]

Another vessel in common use for serving food at this period was known as *ṭayfūriya* (pl. *ṭayāfīr, ṭawāfīr*).[448] From some passages and anecdotes found in the chronicles and the *adab* literature, it appears that the *ṭayfūriya* was a vessel similar to a *ṣaḥfa* or a *ṭabaq*,[449] and that it was generally used to serve *harīsa*.[450]

The pot in use for sauces and salt at the table was called *sukurruja* or *sukurraja*,[451] originally a Persian word arabicized to mean a saucer.[452] According to Lane, *sukurruja* was a small varnished bowl-shaped vessel for sauces served at the table with meat dishes, to incite appetite and to aid

[441] *Lisān* and Lane, s.v. *Ghaḍāra.*; see also Jāḥiẓ, *Rasāʾil*, i, p. 392; *Nishwār*, i, pp. 55, 63

[442] Khalanj is described as a tree that produced a variegated and sweet-smelling wood, of which the beads of chaplets were sometimes made, and the best kind grew only on the Tabaristan mountains (cf. Muq. p. 357; also, Le Strange, *Eastern Caliphate*, p. 376).

[443] Jāḥiẓ, *Bukhalāʾ*, p. 47; see also Mez, p. 386

[444] *ʿIqd*, iii, p. 296; *Lisān*, s.v.; cf. also Bosworth, in the Eng. Tr. of the *Laṭāʾif*, p. 142, n. 154; also *Eastern Caliphate* pp. 369, 376, 459

[445] Yaqūt, *Buldān*, vii, p. 307

[446] *Laṭāʾif*, p. 224 (Eng. Trans. p. 142). Khalanj has been read in this passage as Khadanj.

[447] *Eastern Caliphate*, pp. 227, 376, quoting both Maqdisī and Qazwīnī.

[448] *Murūj*, viii, pp. 243–45; *Diyārāt*, p. 124; *Nishwār*, i, p. 249

[449] *Murūj*, viii, pp. 243–45; *Diyārāt*, p. 124, note given by the editor on the *ṭayfūriya*. See also Baghdādī, *Bukhalāʾ* pp. 143-4

[450] Ibid., viii, pp. 243–45; *Diyārāt*, p. 124

[451] Ibid., viii, pp. 244–45, 269–70, 392; *Diyārāt*, p. 186; Nishwār, i, p. 53; *Quṭub al-Surūr*, pp. 70, 145–55; Ṭab. iii, p. 548; Bayhaqī *Maḥāsin*, p. 19

[452] Lane , Lexicon, s.v. *Sukurruja*

digestion.[453] The *sukurruja* was found in two sizes, the larger holding six ounces and the smaller three ounces or four mithqāls.[454] The well-off families used saucers made of onyx (*jazaʿ*).[455]

To prepare sauces and relishes and to hold ground spices, a vessel made of glass, porcelain or baked clay was used, which was known as *baraniyya*, a thick vessel with a wide mouth, bulky and green-coloured, similar to a *qārūra*: a flask or bottle.[456] A crystalline *baraniyya* was also a familiar sight in well-to-do houses.[457] Warrāq commends a glass *baraniyya* as the most suitable vessel for ground spices, or in its absence an *abzār-dāna* (spice-box) made of willow-wood (*ṣafṣāf*).[458]

A receptacle made of sheepskin for dry substances such as salt or saltwort (*ushnān*) was known as *jarāb* or *jirāb*.[459] The name is also applied to a provision bag of a traveller or a common receptacle for carrying goods and utensils.[460]

For sweets, a special vessel called *jām* (pl. *jāmāt*),[461] made of silver or glass,[462] was used. In shape it was more or less like a dish or tray or a *faʾthūr* (a basin, or a tray used as a table).[463] Masʿūdī mentions a *jām* made from onyx (*jazaʿ*), the borders decorated with gold.[464] A *jām* could also be used as a sort of saucer or as a coin box, which generally held the money the caliph or the wazir distributed among people on happy occasions.[465]

The bowl used at banquets as a dish or a plate to serve meals and also as a wine tankard was called *qadaḥ*,[466] and

---

453 Ibid. See also *Diyārat*, note given by K. ʿAwwād, p. 186, and H. Zayyāt, in *Mashriq*, 1969, p. 483

454 Ibid., Lane

455 *Murūj*, viii, pp. 269–70

456 Warrāq, fol. 12a; *Ṭabīkh*, pp. 65–66; cf. also Lane, s.v.

457 *Quṭub al-Surūr*, p. 57

458 Warrāq, fol. 12a

459 *ʿUyūn*, iii, p. 39; Khālidiyyān, *Tuḥaf*, pp. 120, 192; *ʿIqd*, vi, p. 284; *Muḥāḍarāt*, ii, p. 262; cf. also *Lisān*, s.v.

460 Lane, *Lexicon*, s.v. *Jarāb*

461 *Murūj*, viii, pp. 226, 243, 269–70; *Diyārāt*, pp. 157, 296; Nishwār, i, p. 61, viii, p. 146; *Quṭub al-Surūr*, p. 70

462 *Murūj*, vi, p. 295; cf. also Lane, s.v. *Jām*

463 *Lisān* and Lane, s.vv. *Jām*

464 *Murūj*, viii, p. 269

465 Ibid., vi, pp. 295, 350

466 Ibid., vi, pp. 306, 427; *Aghānī*[1], iv, p. 189, ix, p. 58; *Quṭub al-Surūr*, pp. 12, 22, 33, 36, 70, 92, 191

was large enough to quench the thirst of two persons.[467] These drinking cups were usually made to suit some special measure of capacity: two ratls, five ratls.[468] The Caliph Amīn used to drink from a cup having the capacity of five ratls;[469] hence the name *khumāsiya.*[470] The vessel with the capacity of one ratl was known as *raṭliya.*[471] The well-to-do people used cups made of crystal (*billawr*).[472] The *qadaḥ* has also been defined as a vessel resembling the *ʿulba*, a pot used for milking, sometimes made of camel skin and sometimes of wood.[473]

A drinking cup called *ka's*[474] has also been mentioned among the utensils of the period. Apparently it was used for drinking, but apart from this the term *ka's* also has a general connotation, and as such it means a goblet containing wine, full or otherwise.[475] To differentiate a *ka's* from a *qadaḥ*, the former sometimes referred to a brimful goblet, whereas the latter was used for any empty tankard only.[476]

Another vessel used generally for drinking was *kūza* (pl. *kīzān*).[477] It was a type of mug with a handle.[478] In prosperous houses *kīzān billawr* (mugs made of crystal) were used for drinking-water.[479]

Drinking-water was usually kept in an earthenware pitcher or a jar called *jarra.*[480] The *jarra* imported from Madhār, a village in Maysān between Wāsiṭ and Basra, was highly prized at this period.[481] Yāqūt (died 626) also mentions the

[467] Lane, s.v. *qadaḥ*

[468] *Murūj*, vi, p. 427; *Quṭub al-Surūr*, p. 12

[469] *Murūj*, vi, p. 427

[470] Yāqūt, *Irshād*, v. p. 260

[471] Jahshiyārī, *Wuzarā'*, p. 261; Ṣābī, *Wuzarā'*, p. 240; *Tajārib*, v, p. 259

[472] *Murūj*, vi, p. 427; *Aghānī*[1], iv, p. 189; *Muntaẓam*, v., pt. 2, p. 126

[473] Lane, *Lexicon*, s.v.; some pictures of the *qadaḥ* found in the excavation at Samarra can be seen in F. Sarre, *Die Keramik von Samarra*, pls. xii, xix, xxxiii. The picture of a cup or dish with stands can also be seen (ibid, pl. x) and also in *Excavations at Samarra* (1936–39), ii, pl. 58

[474] *Diyārāt*, pp. 41, 68; *Quṭub al-Surūr*, pp. 18, 211; *Nishwār*, i, p. 256

[475] Lane, s.v. *Ka's*

[476] Ibid.

[477] Jāḥiẓ, *Bukhalā'*, pp. 101, 328; *Murūj*, vii, p. 69; *Diyārāt*, p. 143

[478] Lane, s.v. *Kūza*

[479] *Nishwār*, viii, pp. 149–50

[480] *Murūj*, vii, p. 69; Jāḥiẓ, *Bukhalā'*, pp. 70, 77, 90, 188

[481] Jāḥiẓ, *Bukhalā'*, p. 38, see, in particular, the note given by Ṭāha Hājirī, pp. 277–78; Yāqūt, *Buldān*, s.v. *Madhār*

village of Madhār as famous for its pitchers.[482] The *jarra al-Madhāriya* was also used as a water cooler.[483] A passsage in the *Bukhalā'* of Jāḥiẓ shows that the *jarra* was provided with a loop-shaped handle called *'urwa*.[484] It is noteworthy that though the *jarra* was originally designed for storing drinking-water, its use for keeping liquids such as oil and clarified butter was not uncommon.[485] The large water-jar which an ordinary man could hardly carry was known as *khābiya*.[486] The gigantic jar which was generally kept in the mosque for public drinking and also used in big families was called *ḥabb* (pl. *ḥibab*).[487]

A special vessel which was used as a flask was called *muzzammila* (lit. "the enveloped one"). It appears that the *muzzammila* was commonly used for storing water and keeping it cold.[488] The vessel *muzzammila* has been described as a green jar-shaped pot (*jarra, khābiya*) with a silver or lead tap, its outer surface being lined with layers of straw which were wrapped in the *khaysh* canvas. At night water was cooled in a special cooling-jar, *barrāda*, then poured into the *muzzammila* to keep it cold and unaffected by hot weather.[489] Ṣābī has mentioned many water-pots (*muzzammilāt*) kept in the royal palace for storing, it would seem, iced water.[490] In

---

[482] Yāqūt, *Buldān*, s.v. *Madhār*

[483] Jāḥiẓ, *Bukhalā'*, p. 38

[484] Ibid., p. 188

[485] Ibid., pp. 44, 134

[486] Ibid., p. 183. A picture of a blue glazed pottery storage-jar (*khābiya*) can be seen in *Excavations at Samarra* (1936–39), ii, pl. 55

[487] Ṣābī, *Wuzarā'*, pp. 26, 391; Jāḥiẓ, *Bukhalā'*, pp. 70, 101, 177. See for a picture of a *ḥabb*, *Excavations at Samarra*, ii, pl. 23

[488] Jāḥiẓ, *Bukhalā'*, p. 101; *Imtā'*, iii, p. 69; *Muntaẓam*, vi, p. 9; *Nishwār*, i, pp. 23, 60; Muq, p. 394

[489] Aḥmad Taymūr, *Tafsīr al-alfāẓ al-'Abbāsiya RAAD*, ii (1921), pp. 324–25 quoting from *Shifa' al-Ghalīl* and *Sharḥ Maqāmāt al-Harīrī*. See also H. Zayyāt, *Mashriq*, 1969, pp. 478–80; also the note given by Ṭāha Hājirī in Jāḥiẓ's *Bukhalā'*, p. 331. A pear-shaped *muzzammila* with trefoil mouth and modelled handle, covered with transparent turquoise glaze with an inner container, the outer shell being pierced with decoration showing inscriptions and foliate background (belonging to the 2nd half of 12th century AD, from Rayy, height $9\frac{3}{8}$ in.) can be seen in the collection of Sir Alan & Lady Barlow (cf. A. Lane, *Early Islamic Wares*, London, 1950, pl. 42).

[490] Ṣābī, *Wuzarā'*, p. 216

modern Arabia, however, the word *muzzammila* (pronounced in spoken language *mazmala*) is used for a tap, attached to a water pot or otherwise.[491]

The vessel *barrāda*, as the name shows, was used for cooling water by placing mugs (*kīzān*) on it.[492] According to Aḥmad Taymūr a *barrāda* was an earthenware vessel which was exposed to wind for cooling water.[493] The use of mugs, along with other pots for cooling, is mentioned by Ghazūlī, who writes: "Kāfūr [the Fatimid General] was averse to the use of ice, so mugs were placed on the *barrāda* and water thus cooled was used by him for drinking. This saved him from harm associated with the use of ice while giving him water just as cold."[494] In Ṣābī's *Kitāb al-Wuzarā'* another water-cooler known as *thaljiyya* is mentioned, and it deserves special notice.[495] We do not know definitely whether it was a sort of contraption used for making ice or was just an ordinary pot for keeping water cool. A passage in Ibn Abī ʿUṣaybiʿa's *ʿUyūn al-Anbā'*, where a prescription from an earlier source for freezing (solidifying) water even in June or July is reproduced,[496] suggests that the Abbasids were not unfamiliar with the art of ice-making. Thus it is reasonable to assume that the word *thaljiyya* indicates a pot used for making ice rather than an ordinary cooling jar, or a vessel used to keep ice.

The *ṣīnī*, a large round metal plate with raised sides, was also commonly used as a tray.[497] G. Van Vloten writes that this plate was made of copper.[498] In the royal palace, among other golden utensils, the golden *ṣīniyya* is also mentioned.[499] The word *ṣīniyya* is still used for a tray, whatever its material: glass, copper, or any other metal.[500] In his *Kitāb al-Bukhalā'*,

491 Wadīʿ a Ṭāha Najm, (SOAS. Thesis, 285), p. 311

492 Nishwār, i, p. 264; Jāḥiẓ, *Bukhalā'*, p. 73; Lane, s.v. *barrāda*

493 Aḥmad Taymūr, *RAAD*, iii (1930), pp. 269–70

494 Ghazūlī, *Maṭāliʿ*, ii, p. 71

495 Ṣābī, *Wuzarā'*, p. 239

496 *ʿUyūn al-Anbā'*, i, p. 83; cf. also Aḥmad Taymūr, *RAAD*, iii (1930), p. 269

497 *Aghānī*[1], iv, p. 189; vii[2], p. 299; *Diyārāt*, pp. 151, 169, 411; *Tajārib*, v, p. 259

498 Jāḥiẓ, *Bukhalā'*, ed. Van Vloten, Preface, p. xv

499 Nishwār, i, pp. 145–6, 150

500 Wadīʿa Najm, (Thesis, SOAS, No. 285), p. 311

Jāḥiẓ uses the word *al-ṣīniyya* in accompaniment with the word *al-ṣalāḥiyya*,[501] which in the *Muḥīṭ al-Muḥīṭ* of Bustānī was described as a vessel used by common folk. He says, "They use it and it is a big pot large at the bottom and narrow at the top."[502] From this description we may safely conclude that it had a resemblance to what nowadays is known as *al-ṣarāhiyya* or *al-ṣurāhiyya*, a pitcher made of glass which is used as a water-container. It is also large at the bottom and narrow at the top, usually with no handle. We should point out here that the plates and pots imported from China were also known as *al-ṣīnī*: for example, Azdī mentions coloured plates as *al-ṣīnī*.[503]

The water-pot used for washing the hands was called *ibrīq*,[504] an arabicized word from Persian *āb*+*rīz*.[505] The vessel *ibrīq* was a ewer with a handle and a long and slender spout.[506] The first thing that a guest is given in a house is the facility of washing hands and mouth: a ewer and a basin generally carried by two servants, one holding the basin and the other pouring water while guests washed their hands.[507] At dinner parties guests were also provided with an *ibrīq* and a *ṭast* to wash their hands before their meals, an important part of the table manners of Muslim society. The *ṭast* was a round flat-brimmed basin which was generally made of tinned copper, brass or silver.[508] It was provided with a perforated cover and with a raised receptacle for the soap or *ushnān* (saltwort) in the middle; the water being poured upon the hands passed through this cover down into the underpot. Thus a man washing his hands in the basin was spared the sight of the water used by someone before him.[509]

---

[501] Jāḥiẓ, *Bukhalā'*, pp. 93, 129

[502] *Muḥīṭ al-Muḥīṭ*, s.v. see also Dozy, *Suppl.* s.v.

[503] Azdī, *Ḥikāyāt*, pp. 38–41; *Laṭā'if*, p. 220; *Thimār*, p. 543; cf. also Wadī'a Najm, op. cit, pp. 310–11

[504] *Nishwār*, i, p. 193; viii, p. 149; Ḥamadānī, *Maqāmāt*, pp. 118–19

[505] Lane, *Lexicon*, s.v.

[506] Ibid. A pictorial representation of a bronze ewer belonging to the 9th or perhaps early 10th century AD can be seen in *IC*, 14 (1940), p. 432. Representations of two other ewers belonging to 10th and 12th centuries can also be seen in *EI*, Suppl. s.v. *Ceramics* (J. H. Schmidt), pl. 11, n. 1, 3

[507] *Nishwār*, i, p. 193; viii, p. 149

[508] Ibid., viii, p. 149

[509] Lane, *Modern Egyptians*, p. 142

The receptacle used for carrying food was known as *salla*.[510] It was a basket sometimes covered with red skin.[511] The shopping bag was known as *zanbīl* or *zabbīl*. Sijistan was noted for its date baskets (*zanābīl*), which were mainly made for export.[512]

The kitchen utensils were washed clean and thoroughly, and there were several substances known to the Abbasids for removing the burns from vessels.[513] The utensils were rubbed with brick dust, then with dry powdered potash and saffron, if possible, and finally rinsed with fresh leaves of citron or lemon.[514] In the houses of the well-to-do, the utensils were also rinsed with scented water.[515]

Spices were pounded in the mortar called *hāwan* or *minḥāz*.[516] A copper mortar was considered most suitable for spices, and a stone mortar was used for pounding meat.[517] Seasonings were also ground in a mill.[518]

The markets of Baghdad were famous for all kinds of curious country-made articles, and wares from foreign lands. These utensils, as has been mentioned above, were generally made of clay, glass, silver and gold. The third and fourth centuries form a bright period in the history of Mesopotamian pottery.[519] Small and large jars for water and wine, pots, dishes, oil lamps, spouts of wells, and similar articles were made of glazed and unglazed pottery, either plain or artistically decorated.[520]

Food common to rich and poor

Of the dishes popular among the poor and the wealthy alike we can mention the following.

---

510 *Murūj*, viii, pp. 392, 394; *Tuḥaf*, p. 105; Jahshiyārī, *Wuzarā'*, pp. 119–20

511 Lane, s.v. *salla*

512 Le Strange, *Eastern Caliphate*, p. 351, quoting from Maqdisī, pp. 297, 303–4, 324

513 Warrāq, fol. 15

514 Baghdādī, *Ṭabīkh*, p. 8

515 Ibid., Br. Mus. MS. No. Or. 5099, fol. 7

516 Jāḥiẓ, *Bukhalā'*, pp. 73, 104, 318; Baghdādī, *Ṭabīkh*, p. 8

517 Ibid., p. 8

518 Ibid., p. 8

519 *EI*[1], *Suppl.* s.v. *Ceramic*, p. 44; cf. also Dūrī, *Mesopotamia*, p. 110

520 Ibid., *Suppl.* Jāḥiẓ, *Bukhalā'*, p. 218; cf. also Ghanīma, *Majalla Ghurfa al-Tijāra*, 1941, pp. 569–70

Harīsa

This was, and still is, one of the popular meals with the masses of Baghdad.[521] It was prepared in two similar ways. Six ratls of fat meat were taken and cut into long strips and then thrown into a saucepan of water. When it had been boiled for a considerable time it was taken out, stripped from the bones, shredded and put back into the saucepan. Then four ratls of washed, cleaned and ground wheat were added. The pot was kept on a steady fire for a quarter of a night, in the course of which it was constantly stirred. It was then left to simmer on a higher blaze. A quartered chicken was added along with cinnamon bark and the mixture was left till midnight, when it was stirred well until it set into a smooth paste. Hot water was added if needed, and it was left until dawn, when it was stirred again and removed from the heat. Before serving, melted fresh tail was poured on it, and cumin and cinnamon, ground separately, were sprinkled. It was served with *murrī* (brine) and fresh lemon juice. It was better when made in an oven than over an open fire.[522]

Harīsa was dear to the young and old alike. Guests were entertained with it. It is reported that a man (in 351 AH) went for breakfast to the house of a moderately well-to-do friend. The meal consisted solely of an excellent dish of *harīsa* followed by some sweet dishes.[523] At dawn, in the city of Baghdad, the shops of *harīsa* were found crowded.[524] It was because of its popularity that they invented several proverbs praising it, such as "*Inna khair al-baqā'i' thalāth: dukkān al-rawwās wa'l shawwā' wa'l-hirās*" (the best places are three: the shop of animal heads, the shop of roasted meat and the shop of *harīsa*).[525] They even ventured to concoct a *ḥadīth* connecting it with the Prophet, in which the Prophet is supposed to have said, "Gabriel fed me *harīsa* to enable me to withstand the difficulties of the midnight prayer

---

521 Jāḥiẓ, *Bukhalā'*, index; *Nishwār*, i, pp. 55, 173; viii, 40; Shābushtī, *Diyārāt*, p. 123

522 *Ṭabīkh*, p. 52; Shayzarī, *Nihāya*, p. 36; Ibn Jazla, *Minhāj al-Bayān*, Br. Mus. Ms. 5934, fol. 217; *Murūj*, viii, pp. 402–3

523 Ibn al-Jawzī, *Muntaẓam*, vii, p. 12

524 Tawḥīdī, *Imtā'*, iii, p. 57; Khaṭīb, *Ta'rīkh*, xi, p. 178; Maqdisī, *Aḥsan al-Taqāsīm*, p. 129

525 Baghdādī, *Taṭfīl*, p. 53

(*tahajjud*)."[526] The Abbasids gave it the agreeable names of *shahīda* and *hadīya*, as a mark of appreciation.[527] In Baghdad, the first wedding dish, according to the local custom, was invariably the *harīsa*.[528] The Baghdādīs even picked quarrels with those who did not like it. We are told that in a debate Ibn Muqla, the wazir, vanquished his opponent Al-Yazīdī, who preferred *judhāba* to *harīsa*.[529] We are also told that Abū Muḥammad al-Kātib al-Dīnawarī died of excessive consumption of *harīsa*.[530]

'Aṣīd or *Judhāba*

'Aṣīd was prepared in various ways, the most popular being the *'aṣīd al-tamr*.[531] This was prepared with four ratls of dried dates placed in ten ratls of water and boiled until cooked. The dates were then kneaded well by hand, strained through a sieve and returned to the pot with half a ratl of crumbled pulp, a ratl of sesame-oil, and a quarter of a ratl of peeled walnuts. These were stirred until almost cooked and then placed between two thin cakes. This was sometimes garnished with almonds.[532] It was also known by its nickname "*Umm al-Razīna*".[533]

There were two varieties of *'aṣīd* (known as *Manṣūriya* and *Barmakiya*) commonly used in Baghdad. It appears that the Caliph Manṣūr and the Barmakid wazirs were very fond of it.[534] *'Aṣīd* may not have been a costly food, as a dish sufficient for an individual could be bought for one dirham only.[535]

Kabāb

This was also one of the popular and cheap dishes. The people's love for it is expressed by one who exclaimed that his eyes were appeased to see the *kabāb* over the fire.[536] It was

526 Khaṭīb, *Ta'rīkh*, ii, pp. 279–80
527 Qāḍī Jurjānī, *Muntakhab*, p. 95
528 Mez, p. 428, n. 5, quoting from Ibn al-Hajjāj, x, p. 70
529 Tawḥīdī, *Imtā'*, iii, p. 57
530 Khaṭīb, *Ta'rīkh*, x, p. 170
531 Tanūkhī, *Nishwār*, i, p. 62
532 Baghdādī, *Ṭabīkh*, pp. 71–72
533 Qāḍī Jurjānī, *Muntakhab*, p. 96
534 Azdī, *Ḥikāyāt*, p. 41
535 Khaṭīb, *Ta'rīkh*, xiv, p. 395
536 Shayzarī, *Nihāya al-Rutba*, p. 30

prepared with thin sliced meat, with salt to taste, and put in a frying pan without grease. The slices were turned repeatedly till they were browned and cooked. Al-Ghazūlī, after describing this procedure, adds that it was exactly the process (without the addition of spices) by which the kabāb was prepared for Khālid b. Yaḥyā and his sons.[537] One of the varieties of kabāb known as *al-kabāb al-rashīdī* seems to have been in large demand among the people of Baghdad, but we are not sure whether its preparation differed in any way from that of the Barmakids.[538]

Animal Heads and Trotters

These were prepared in the following way. They were scalded with hot water and then washed with cold water. After thorough cleaning they were cut into pieces and boiled. They were served with ground salt and sumach.[539]

From Jāḥiẓ's *Bukhalā'* it appears that people were particularly inclined to buy heads and trotters on Saturday, for in Islamic society animals are slaughtered mostly on Fridays. On Saturday, the heads and trotters were thus in abundant supply and their prices were consequently reduced.[540]

Food of the poor

The food of the poor was simple and inexpensive. Considerations of price restricted their diet both in quality and quantity. The dinner of the poor consisted generally of one course, such as a cheap variety of meat, with bread, treacle, saffron, pickle, olive, or vinegar.[541] Fish, rice-bread, and some fruit were cheap and therefore also accessible to them.[542] Even locusts were eaten, especially in times of hardship. In 331 AH, when locusts swarmed, the poor ate them as "one of

---

537 *Maṭāli'*, ii, p. 55

538 Azdī, *Ḥikāyāt*, pp. 39–40

539 Ibn al-Ukhuwwa, *Ma'ālim al-Qurba*, p. 105

540 Jāḥiẓ, *Bukhalā'* p. 99; cf. also, Ibn Qutayba, *'Uyūn al-Akhbār*, iii, p. 200

541 Ibn al-Jawzī, *Ḥumaqā*, p. 129; *Nishwār*, i, p. 62; *Muntaẓam*, vii, p. 162; cf. also, E. Ashtor, in *JAH*, 1970, pp. 9–10

542 Khawārizmī, *Mafātīḥ al-'Ulūm*, p. 101; Azdī, *Ḥikāyāt*, p. 39; Yāqūt, *Buldān*, s.v. *Baṣra*; *Manāqib Baghdād* (attributed to Ibn al-Jawzī), p. 37

the bounties of God".[543] Tanūkhī tells us about a man in Baghdad who bought a few ratls of locust from a locust seller and ate them all alone.[544]

Sweet dishes (*ḥalwa*) as a dessert were unknown to the poor, but they had dates and oilcakes instead.[545] Once the Caliph Muqtadir was journeying by boat. At lunch time, he was invited by the crew to share their lunch. Having finished the meal, the Caliph asked for *ḥalwa*. The boatmen apologized, saying that they were not accustomed to sweet dishes and therefore offered only dates and oilcakes, their usual fare.[546]

Apart from rice-bread, fish and the like, the poor people also took *sawīq* as a popular type of food.[547] It was a kind of dried barley-meal mixed with water, butter or fat from the tails of sheep. Being in the nature of a gruel or thick tisane, it was not eaten, but rather supped or sipped.[548] *Sawīq* made of chick-peas (*ḥimmaṣ*) was the popular food of the common people of Baghdad during the early Abbasid period. In 360 AH a seller of *sawīq* is reported to have been grinding 360 *kurrs* (one kurr = 500 ratls) of chick-peas yearly and selling all of it during the two or three months when fruit was not available.[549]

The peasants, who were among the poorest in society, took very simple meals. It is reported that on a hunting expedition, the Caliph Mahdī lost his way and was separated from his companions; he came to the hut of a Nabaṭī peasant to ask for some food. The peasant offered the Caliph some barley bread and a dish of small fish. Mahdī enquired whether he had any olives or cress. The peasant answered: "Yes, and some dates too."[550] This meal was probably the best that a peasant could offer to his guest.

The beduins led a hard life and ate almost anything that was obtainable. A townsman asked a tribesman: "What do

---

543 Ṣūlī, *Adab al-Kuttāb*, ed. B. Atharī, Cairo, 1341, p. 237

544 *Nishwār*, ii, pp. 86, 198

545 Ibid., ii, in *RAAD*, 17 (1942), pp. 151–52

546 Ibid., ii, pp. 152–53

547 *Murūj*, vi, pp. 312–13; Jāḥiẓ, *Bukhalā'*, p. 164; *EI*², s.v.

548 Lane, s.v. *Sawīq*; cf. also *EI*², s.v. *Ghidhā'* (M. Rodinson)

549 *Manāqib Baghdād* (attributed to Ibn al-Jawzī), p. 37; cf. also *EI*², s.v. *Ghidhā'* (M. Rodinson)

550 *Murūj*, vi, pp. 227–28; *Fakhrī*, p. 243; Jahshiyārī, *Wuzarā'*, p. 146

you eat and what do you abstain from?" The beduin replied, "We eat all that runs except the reptiles."[551]

The staple food of the tribesmen was bread, dates, milk and its products. Sometimes they took locusts and vegetables. *Waft*, a mixture of dates and milk, and *ḥais*, a preparation of dates with butter and curdled milk, were among their more unusual dishes.[552] Among the poor were the ascetics and the sufis. Their ability to tolerate hunger and their contentment with sparse food were proverbial. To be able to fast for long periods was a necessary qualification for them. The most extreme sufis refrained even from eating bread, and contented themselves with *fatīt*, bread soup.[553] It is said of Bishr al-Ḥāfī (died 227 AH), a renowned ascetic, that he did not taste grilled meat for forty years.[554] Ibn al-Jawzī tells us that among the sufis there was a group which did not eat meat and believed that even a piece of meat worth a dirham made the heart hard and insensitive.[555] It is reported that one extreme sufi, Sahl b. ʿAbdallāh, used to buy treacle for one dirham, ghee for two, and flour for one, mix them and make 360 pellets. This was his food for the whole year, one pellet being sufficient for a day.[556]

We may note that with a reduction in the hardships the diet of the poor man underwent a considerable change. For example, when Ibn al-Qazwīnī, the ascetic, received a gift of two hundred dinars from the Caliph Qahir (381 AH), he changed his usual dishes of egg-plant, vinegar, beans and treacle into *zabādī* (a kind of tender plant with wide leaves), fowls, fine bread and roast chicken.[557]

Food prices

Prices of commodities normally depended on their supply and on the stability of socio-political life in the country. Some

---

551 Jāḥiẓ, *Bukhalā'*, p. 203; *'Iqd*, iii, p. 485; cf. also Dūrī, *Mesopotamia*, p. 303

552 Jāḥiẓ, *Bukhalā'*, pp. 163, 205, 211; cf. also *EI*², s.v. *Ghidhā'*; see also Dūrī, *Mesopotamia*, p. 304

553 Ibn al-Jawzī, *Talbīs*, pp. 223–24

554 Ibid., *Ṣifat al-Ṣafwa*, ii, p. 58

555 Ibid., *Talbīs*, pp. 223–24

556 Ibid., p. 220

557 Ibid., *Muntaẓam*, vii, p. 162

proverbial sayings current in the Abbasid society of the period, such as "everything is cheap when it is plentiful, expensive when it is scarce and needed," and "all goods that multiply have low prices,"[558] clearly reflect the principles of supply and demand. The problems of supply and demand were explained by Jāḥiẓ in the description of the fish-market of Baghdad.[559] The last quarter of the eighth and the first quarter of the ninth centuries AD were a period of happiness and prosperity for the people. Prices were generally low and wages fair. But the civil war between Amīn and Ma'mūn, the recurring flood in Baghdad from the last quarter of the ninth century, and the emergence of turbulent elements in the *'āmma*, together with the evil effects of army interference in the political administration of the country right from the assassination of the Caliph Mutawakkil in AD 861, the Zanj war, (AD 869–883) which paralysed trade and commerce in Southern Iraq, and the menacing Qarmatian revolt (c. AD 890–931), all badly affected the normal life of the people, resulting in inflation, soaring prices and a decrease in the purchasing power and the real income of the common people.[560] In the absence of demographic statistics of Iraq at this period, it is difficult to establish how far the population problem in Iraq was reflected in the decline of agricultural activities and the consequent increase in prices. Certainly, the rising prices with no corresponding increase in wages, and the system of hoarding food supplies practised by the merchants or the wealthy, added to the miseries of the common people.[561]

A great variation in the price of any commodity was found between the regions which produced it and those which lay at some distance from its place of production.[562] This difference was due to the higher profit, the transport cost, and the import duty.

In studying the price lists of the early Abbasid period, we

---

558 Jāḥiẓ (?) *Tijāra*, p. 11; Tha'ālibī, *Khāṣṣ*, p. 70

559 Jāḥiẓ, *Ḥayawān*, iv, pp. 431–3

560 For the disorder and pillage affecting the prices, see Ṭabarī, iii, pp. 1009–10, 1066, 1885; *Muntaẓam*, v, pt. 2, p. 21; vii, pp. 151, 220; viii, pp. 21–2, 44, 47, 50, 54–5, 60, 72–5, 79, 87, 142, 161, etc.

561 See for example, *Kāmil*, viii, pp. 85–6; *Tajārib*, i, pp. 54–5

562 Jāḥiẓ, *Bukhalā'*, p. 21; cf. also, *EI*², s.v. *Ghidhā'* (M. Rodinson)

have to consider various limitations of our source materials. Our sources, both Muslim and *Dhimmī*, quote prices mainly from the years of unusual hardship, such as famine and civil war. Some of the figures are too fragmentary, too disparate and too uncertain to have much value. Hence it is very difficult to arrive at definite conclusions for the price levels in the years of comparative affluence and stability. Moreover, our sources give wholesale prices only. Figures are given for *kurr* and *qafīz*, and not for ratls. The price index is chiefly concerned, too, with the cost of food in urban areas, particularly in certain important cities such as Baghdad, Basra, and Mosul. It is therefore not possible to have a clear idea of the cost of food in rural areas. Nevertheless, the occasional quotations of prices of commodities, however fragmentary, help to give a background to the study of the standard of living and the amenities of life enjoyed by the various groups of the population.

E. Ashtor, who has dealt with the question of cost of living, wages and prices of essential and non-essential commodities of the Abbasid period, has tried to explain the rising trends in prices from the late ninth century AD onward in terms of the devaluation of the currency and the introduction of gold monetary units, along with the failure of the government to introduce any coherent price-control system mainly because of theological opposition. He has also hinted at the rising population and the declining agricultural productivity of Iraq.[563] We may now discuss the prices of essential and non-essential commodities quoted in our sources for the late eighth and the ninth centuries AD.

Prices at normal times

The period of the Caliph Manṣūr has been described as the happiest era with the greatest amenities for the people. The price list found in the writings of several authors brings out a sharp contrast between the prices of the early and the late Abbasid periods.[564] Ashtor concludes from a passage in the *History* of Denys of Tell-Mahré that in the 80's of the 8th

---

[563] E. Ashtor, *Histoire des prix et des salaires dans l'Orient médiéval*, Paris, 1969, p. 42ff.

[564] Ibid., pp. 42–3 Denys de Tell-Mahré, p. 135, Tr. p. 113; Barhebraeus, p. 115; see also Ashtor, *A Social and Economic History* . . ., p. 93

century AD, cereal (perhaps wheat) was sold in Upper Mesopotamia at 0·125 dinars per 100 kg. From Barhebraeus he also quotes a fall of price in 772 when 100 kg. were sold at 0·027 dinar, which compelled the government to give rebates in the land tax.[565]

It is to be noted that cereals, during the early Abbasid period, were weighed by a standard *kurr* known as *kurr muʿaddal*, which was three times the ordinary *kurr*. Though the capacity of the *kurr* varied from place to place, Professor Hinz, calculating from the available sources, found that 1 *kurr* of wheat varied between 2,700 and 2,925 kg.[566] One *kurr* has been calculated to be 7,200 ratls.[567] Similarly, 1 *jarīb* was equal to 10 *qafīz*, 1 *qafīz* was 120 ratls; therefore 1 *jarīb* of cereals was 1,200 ratls.[568]

The staple foods of the people of Mesopotamia were wheat and barley, which were widely cultivated throughout the country, and the *kharāj* of the *sawād* was paid mainly in wheat and barley.[569] Mosul was the granary of Iraq, especially of Baghdad in times of need.[570] Azdī in his *Taʾrīkh al-Mawṣil* mentions some of the normal prices in Mosul towards the end of the 8th and the beginning of the 9th centuries AD, a period characterized by its low cost of food. He says that in AD 791, one *jarīb* (= 1,200 ratls) of wheat was sold at 40 dirhams and one *jarīb* of barley was bought for 20 dirhams only.[571] Thus 40 ratls of wheat cost only one dirham and 60 ratls of barley were worth one dirham only. In the days of Maʾmūn, according to Qudāma, about 34·3 ratls of wheat cost 1 dirham and 11·4 ratls of barley cost 1 dirham.[572] According to Azdī in AD 815, one *jarīb* (1,200 ratls) of flour was sold at the price of 50 dirhams: 24 ratls per dirham.[573] Masʿūdī, recording the events of the year AD 813, notes that the quarters of Baghdad not under siege by the forces of Ṭāhir offered commodities at

[565] E. Ashtor, *Prix*, p. 42

[566] Hinz, *Islamische Masse*, pp. 42–3; cf. also Ashtor, *Prix*, p. 44

[567] Hinz, p. 43; cf. also, A. S. Ehrenkreutz, "The kurr system in medieval Iraq", *JESHO*, 1962, p. 311

[568] Hinz, p. 48; Ehrenkreutz, *JESHO*, 1962, p. 311

[569] Ibn Khurdādhbih, pp. 8–24; Qudāma, pp. 237–9

[570] Muq. p. 136

[571] Azdī, *Taʾrīkh al-Mawṣil*, p. 276

[572] Qudāma, p. 80

[573] Azdī, op. cit., p. 340

their normal prices, as 20 ratls of bread could be purchased for one dirham only.[574] In the year AD 822, it is said, prices in Mosul became so exceedingly low that millers refused to grind wheat in their mills.[575] But from the middle of the 9th century prices began to rise everywhere. In AD 919, there was a serious revolt in Baghdad against the soaring prices. The government was obliged to release its stock and regulate the price. The regulated price, which may be taken as representative of the late 9th century, was fifty dinars per *kurr* of wheat: about 44 ratls per dinar and about 10 ratls per dirham.[576] In AD 928, the standard price for one *kurr* of wheat or one *kurr* of barley was 60 dinars. De Goeje, making calculations on this basis, says that the standard price of a *kurr* of wheat was 545 dirhams or 36·7 dinars and that of barley 355 dirhams or 23·7 dinars.[577] Thus about 13·3 ratls of wheat and about 20 ratls of barley were sold at 1 dirham each.

Extraordinary prices in time of political unrest and economic scarcity

Prices in time of civil war, political turmoil, famine, pestilence, and economic scarcity are abnormal and cannot be taken as a guide to the normal price index. Such prices show a three-fold to ten-fold increase in the cost of food and to a great extent reflect the miseries of the common people. Perhaps the first exceptional rise in price was in the year AD 813, when eastern Baghdad was under siege by the troops of Ṭāḥir. In this part of Baghdad the price of bread was twenty times the price in trouble-free zones.[578] The beginning of the year AD 822 was a period of abundant harvest, and prices fell to their lowest. But when, two months later, a severe famine struck Mosul, Basra, Kufa, Baghdad and other areas, prices soared so high that one *kurr* of wheat cost 3,300–3,900 dirhams, roughly 10,000 dirhams for three *kurr*.[579] Towards the end of

---

[574] *Murūj*, vi, p. 465

[575] Azdī, p. 362

[576] *Tajārib*, i, p. 75; *Muntaẓam*, vi, p. 156; cf. also, Ashtor, *Prix*, p. 43; also Dūrī, *Mesopotamia*, p. 268. At this period 1 dinar was 14½ dirhams (cf. *Tajārib*, i, 71).

[577] De Goeje, *B.G.A.* vi, p. 9; cf. also Dūrī, *Mesopotamia*, p. 268

[578] *Murūj*, vi, p. 465. One ratl of bread in eastern Baghdad was 1 dirham whereas western Baghdad sold 20 ratls for 1 dirham.

[579] Azdī, *Ta'rīkh al-Mawṣil*, p. 362; Ṭabarī, iii, p. 1066

the year, when conditions became more normal, one *jarīb* (1,200 ratls) of wheat at Mosul was sold at 120 dirhams, 10 ratls per dirham,[580] almost triple the normal price.[581] In Baghdad, at this time, one *qafīz* (about 120 ratls) was sold at about 40 to 50 dirhams.[582] In AD 873, again as a result of the Zanj rebellion, prices leaped rapidly. In Baghdad, now, the price of one *kurr* of wheat was 150 dinars,[583] about three or four times the normal.

The price quotations of the 10th and 11th centuries AD have been extensively discussed by E. Ashtor[584] and C. Cahen.[585]

Price of rice

There is very little material on rice prices. E. Ashtor has found only two pieces of evidence on the price of rice from the Abbasid period.[586] Both these come from the beginning of the 10th century. Tanūkhī notes that in AD 912, 1 *kurr* of rice was sold before harvest, near Kufa, at 7 dinars.[587] A year later, in AD 912–13, one *kurr* of rice in Baghdad, at a profit of 7 dinars, was sold at 30 dinars.[588] These two pieces of evidence are insufficient to give any idea of the price of rice in the early Abbasid period. From other sources, however, we know that rice-bread was widely used by the common people and the poor in their daily diet.[589] From Ibn Qutayba we even hear that in Basra a poor man could live on two dirhams a month, eating mainly rice-bread and small fishes.[590] This passage from Ibn Qutayba, which is reproduced by Yāqūt,[591] shows that rice was quite cheap, at least the inferior quality of

---

580 Azdī, p. 363

581 Ibid., p. 276

582 Ṭabarī, iii, p. 1066; *Kāmil*, vi, p. 272; cf. also E. Ashtor, *Prix.*, p. 43. Ṭabarī mentions Hārūnī *qafīz*, for which see Hinz, p. 48

583 Ṭabarī, iii, 1885; *Muntaẓam*, v, pt. 2, p. 21; Ashtor, *Prix*, p. 43

584 Ashtor, *Prix.*, p. 43ff.

585 Cf. Cahen, "Quelques problèmes économiques et fiscaux de l'Iraq buyide d'après une traite de mathématique", *AIEO* x (1952), pp. 326–363

586 Ashtor, *Prix.* p. 45

587 *Nishwār*, viii, pp. 66–67; cf. also Ashtor, p. 54

588 Ibid., viii, p. 92; Ashtor, pp. 45–46

589 See above, p. 133; cf. also, M. Canard, *Le riz, Arabica*, 1959

590 *'Uyūn*, i, p. 221

591 Yāqūt, *Buldān*, s.v. *Basra*

it which the poor could buy at exceptionally low prices. From Būzajānī (d. AD 997) we also know that rice was numbered with the inferior quality of cereals such as barley, varieties of millet, and oats, and was priced at 15 to 20 dinars a *kurr*.[592] If Būzajānī is correct in his assessment, then we can assume that rice was normally sold at half the price of wheat, and was therefore perhaps not beyond the purchasing power of the poor.

Spices and other products

From the *Kitāb al-Manāzil* of Al-Būzajānī, a writer of the late 10th century AD, we can gather useful material on the valuations of various commodities and their approximate prices during the lifetime of the author. On the basis of the materials furnished by him, Ehrenkreutz has tabulated an index of normal prices of agricultural produce in the 10th century AD *sawād*.[593]

According to Būzajānī, various types of grain and some other agricultural and horticultural produce were categorized by fiscal authorities into four basic classes by value: sesame, wheat, barley and *jahjandum* (barley mixed with wheat). The highest class in value was sesame (*simsim*), which included the following spices: cumin, mustard, coriander, caraway, poppy, the seeds of lucerne (*bizr al-ratba*). The value of these spices was always approximately twice that of the class of wheat, being about 60 to 80 dinars per *kurr*. The species classed with wheat were chick-peas, haricot beans, lentils, linseed, garden cress, fenugreek, safflower, raisins, sumach, shelled almonds, shelled hazel-nuts and hemp seeds. This category constituted a middle class, the value of its species being always approximately twice that of barley, and half the value of the sesame class: about 30 to 40 dinars per *kurr*. The species classed with barley were paddy or rice with husk (*aruzz bi-qashrihī*); varieties of millet such as *jawārs*, *dhura*, *dukhn*; a variety of oat called *hurtumān*; kabīs dates; a type of coriander called *kusbara*; and lentil seeds (*majj*) in the Syrian region and beans in the regions of Jabal. This was the lowest

---

592 As cited by Ehrenkreutz in *JESHO*, vii (1964), pp. 49–50

593 A. S. Ehrenkreutz, "The *taṣrīf* and *tasʿīr* calculations in medieval Mesopotamian fiscal operations", *JESHO*, vii (1964), p. 49f.

of the three categories, estimated at half the value of the wheat and one fourth of the value of the sesame class. Thus one *kurr* of items listed in this category was sold at 15 to 20 dinars. The *Jahjandum* category was made up of the last two classes, thus corresponding to half a *kurr* of wheat and half a *kurr* of barley. This constituted a class by itself, to which no other species were related. Its value amounted approximately to one half plus one fourth (three quarters) of the value of the wheat class and to one fourth plus one eighth (three eighths) of that of the sesame. Thus one *kurr* of this material cost between 15 and 20 dinars. This calculation of the price index is tentative, and does not positively establish the exact prices of the species under consideration, but it may nonetheless serve, as Ehrenkreutz claims, as a useful checking guide in our studies of mediaeval economic source materials.[594]

Meat

If we believe the price index given by some Arab authors for the reign of Manṣūr[595] to be substantially correct, meat would seem to have been very cheap, and available to rich and poor alike. At this period one dirham could buy one sheep, 60 ratls of mutton or 90 ratls of beef, while 4 dānaq (about two thirds of a dirham) could buy a camel.[596] This evidence of the Arab authors corroborates, to a great extent, the data furnished by Denys and Barhebraeus for the last quarter of the 8th century. According to Barhebraeus, beef (quantity unspecified) in AD 772 cost 1 dirham, and according to Denys of Tell-Mahré one calf or one goat, in upper Mesopotamia around this period, was sold at 1 dirham, while a cow could be sold at 4 to 5 dirhams.[597] Such low prices were, however, of short duration, and were maintained presumably to enable the workers engaged in the foundation of Baghdad to lead a

594 *Kitāb al-Manāzil* of Al-Būzajānī as quoted by Ehrenkreutz in *JESHO*, vii (1964) pp. 49–50. See also the tabulated price index worked out by Ehrenkreutz, ibid.

595 See, for example, Khaṭīb, *Ta'rīkh*, i, p. 71; Yāqūt, *Buldān*, i, p. 683; *Manāqib Baghdād* (attr. to Ibn al-Jawzī), 24–25

596 Khaṭīb, *Ta'rīkh*, i, p. 71; Yāqūt, *Buldān*. i, p. 683; *Manāqib Baghdād* (attr. to Ibn al-Jawzī), pp. 24–25

597 Barhebraeus, p. 115; Denys, Tr. p. 113, 130; cf. also E. Ashtor, *Prix*, pp. 50–51

comfortable life.[598] In the middle of the 9th century AD, Jāḥiẓ could write that a she-goat cost 7 dirhams, and a calf in Baghdad cost more than 10 dirhams, but in Basra rather less.[599] From his various stories recorded in the *Kitāb al-Bukhalā'*, it would seem that one dirham was an insignificant amount of money for purchasing meat at that period. In one of the stories, a niggardly man in Basra is said to have been in the habit of buying meat every week for one dirham and mixing it with vegetables to form a dish of *sikbāj*.[600] Another miser is said to have bought meat daily for half a dirham, and in times of scarcity for 1 dirham, and fed his family in a niggardly way.[601] These anecdotes indicate that 1 dirham, which bought 60 ratls of mutton in the days of Manṣūr, could not buy even a few ratls of it less than half a century later. In another story, Jāḥiẓ mentions that a man became rich and managed to eat meat,[602] which indicates that the poor could not afford it, except for the cheapest quality, such as beef.

From *Aghānī* we hear that in the early tenth century in Basra sheep were fattened especially for the Sacrifice (*uḍḥiyya*) and were sold at 10 dinars each.[603] Other sheep, for the consumption of daily meat, may have been cheap. A foolish man, perhaps about the middle of the 9th century, bought a goat for 11 dirhams, which evoked criticism from his friends as the price was rather high.[604] From the biography of a 10th-century scholar we know that 20 cows were sold at an extraordinary price of 2 to 3 dirhams.[605] This is an isolated piece of evidence, and cannot be taken as representing the normal price. Ibn Ḥawqal, visiting Ardabil in the second half of the 10th century, found prices very low when he noted that about 3 ratls of meat (probably mutton) were sold at a price of 1 dirham only,[606] indicating that prices in Baghdad and other places were much higher.

---

598 Ashtor, *Prix*, p. 51

599 Jāḥiẓ, *Bayān*, ii, pp. 189–90; *Bukhalā'*, p. 35

600 *Bukhalā'*, p. 110; for *sikbāj* see above, p. 83

601 Jāḥiẓ, *Bukhalā'*, p. 186

602 Ibid., ii, p. 41, as quoted by E. Ashtor, *Prix.*, p. 51, n. 6

603 *Aghānī*[1], iii, p. 62

604 Bayhaqī, *Maḥāsin*, p. 636

605 *Ta'rīkh Baghdād* of Khaṭīb, ii, p. 318; cf. also Ashtor, *Prix*, p. 51

606 Ibn Hawqal, p. 238

Of the prices of chicken we have only a few isolated quotations, which help to give us some idea about their general prices. Kaskar, a place well-known for abundant fowl, fish, rice and other commodities, maintained, throughout the Abbasid period, a very low price. Yāqūt, writing in the 13th century AD, notes that he found 24 big chickens sold at one dirham.[607] Similarly Wāsit, at this period, bought 12 chickens for 1 dirham and 24 young fowls for one dirham only.[608] An anecdote relating to the 9th century shows that francolins at Basra were sold at 1 dinar each.[609] Chickens, therefore, had been cheaper than this. We have another piece of evidence about prices of chicken from the late 9th century AD. This price is rather high, for chicken in Baghdad are said to have been sold at 1 dinar each,[610] a price perhaps to be taken as representing abnormal times.

Fish

Fish were perhaps moderately priced and were consumed by people from all walks of life. There are only a few quotations of fish prices in our sources. Jāḥiẓ, speaking on the fish market of Baghdad, mentions that on certain days, when the Christians frequented the market, fish prices registered an increase, but on other days the price remained normal and low.[611] From the *Maḥāsin* of Bayhaqī we learn an anecdote, probably from the early 9th century AD, which shows that two large fish of unspecified species were sold at Baghdad for one dinar.[612] From Jahshiyārī we hear of an exceptionally high price of an extraordinarily large fish bought by a Baghdadi Christian for 30 dirhams, a fact which led to his arrest and an investigation into his wealth.[613] Small fish were probably very cheap, as they were normally eaten by the poor. A young unmarried man at Basra could live, in the early 9th century

[607] Yāqūt, *Buldān*, s.v. *Kaskar*
[608] Ibid., s.v. *Wāsiṭ*
[609] Ibn al-Jawzī, *Ḥumaqā*, p. 70
[610] Baghdādī, *Taṭfīl*, p. 79
[611] Jāḥiẓ, *Ḥayawān*, iv, pp. 431–32
[612] Bayhaqī, *Maḥāsin*, p. 587
[613] *Wuzarā'*, p. 114. The incident is connected with the reign of the Caliph Manṣūr.

AD, on 2 dirhams a month, feeding himself on rice-bread and small salted fish.[614]

Fruit

Information on fruit prices, especially those of dates, is ample. Dates were an important item of food of the common people and were widely produced in Iraq. The fresh dates of Iraq enjoyed great celebrity.[615] Yet Basra was the most famous region for palm-tree cultivation, producing, according to the estimate of the native author Jāḥiẓ, three hundred varieties that had no equal anywhere else.[616] Dates of Basra were exported not only to Iraq but to India, and to nearer and further China.[617] The people of Baghdad at times of scarcity and famine travelled to Basra to live on its dates.[618] One tray full of dates in this region, in the middle of the 9th century AD, could be had for only two dānaqs (one dānaq being then one sixth of a dirham).[619] At the time of the construction of Baghdad, it is said, 60 ratls of dates were sold at a price of 1 dirham: 720 ratls per dinar.[620] Quotations of date prices coming from the early 10th century show an exceptional fall in prices. In AD 925, we see that 8 ratls of dates were being sold at Baghdad for only one *ḥabba*,[621] or 24 ratls for one dirham.[622] At one time dates became so cheap that 100 ratls were bought for two dirhams only.[623] Kirman, a place noted for date cultivation, which in the time of Hārūn al-Rashīd paid its partial *kharāj* in the form of 12,000 ratls of dates,[624] maintained a very low price over a long period of time. Ibn Ḥawqal, visiting this area about the middle of the 10th

614 Ibn Qutayba, *'Uyūn*, i, p. 221; Yāqūt, *Buldān*, vii, p. 647

615 Muq. p. 118; *Laṭā'if*, p. 237; Nuwayrī, i, pp. 369–71; cf. also Ashtor, *Prix*, p. 52

616 Ibn al-Faqīh, p. 253; see also Dūrī, *Mesopotamia*, p. 64

617 Nājī, *Basra* (thesis), p. 280, quoting from Chau-ju-kua: *Chinese and Arab*, p. 137; Qazwīnī, *Nuzha*, p. 46; Dūrī, p. 134

618 Miskāwayh, ii, p. 95; *Muntaẓam*, vi, p. 344

619 Jāḥiẓ, *Bukhalā'*, p. 121

620 Khaṭīb, *Ta'rīkh*, i, p. 71; Yāqūt, i, p. 683; Ashtor, *Prix*, p. 52

621 36 *ḥabba* = 1 dinar, and 1 dinar at this period was about 12 dirhams (cf. Ṣābī, p. 89; Dūrī, *Mesopotamia*, p. 242).

622 *Tajārib*, i, p. 146; *Muntaẓam*, vi, p. 196

623 *Nishwār*, viii, p. 50; cf. also Ashtor, p. 52

624 S. A. El-Ali, "A new version of Ibn Muṭarrif's list of revenues in the early times of Hārūn al-Rashīd", *JESHO*, 1971 p. 307

century, found dates exceptionally cheap, and he noted that 100 *mann* (about 200 ratls) could be had for only one dirham.[625] From such evidence E. Ashtor notes that dates, during the early Abbasid period, were sold at 0·006 to 0·007 dinar per ratl.[626]

The prices of other fruit depended on supply and season. Peaches, for example, out of season were sold, in the middle of the 9th century, at the rate of 6 a dirham, while during the season 200 could be bought for one dirham only.[627] An anecdote from the late 8th century AD shows that a sack of *kam'a* (truffles), which a beduin carried to the suburb of Mecca, fetched two dirhams.[628] Ibn Ḥawqal, visiting Iṣfahān in the 10th century AD found grapes very cheap, as one hundred *mann* (one *mann* in Iṣfahān was 400 dirhams' weight) were sold for five dirhams and 70 *mann* of grape juice could also be had for 5 dirhams.[629]

Vegetables and other items

The prices of vegetables, as Ashtor mentions, are very rare in our sources, and it is therefore difficult to determine their trend. The references show that vegetables were not too costly in relation to other basic necessities. Jāḥiẓ has written about a man in Basra, early in the 9th century AD, who was in the habit of buying onions for one dānaq, egg-plant for one dānaq, gourd for one dānaq, carrots for one dānaq and meat for one dirham, cooking the lot into *sikbāj*,[630] which he ate for several days.[631] This anecdote, though initially recorded as a portrait of a miser's character, throws sufficient sidelight on the prices of some of the vegetables at this period. At the end of the 9th century, 30 *madd*[632] of beans could be bought for one dirham

625 Ibn Ḥawqal, p. 223

626 E. Ashtor, *Prix*, p. 52

627 Jāḥiẓ, *Bukhalā'*, pp. 114–15

628 *'Uyūn*, iii, pp. 282–83

629 Ibn Ḥawqal, p. 262. A *mann* in Baghdad was 2 ratls (cf. for example, Lane, *Lexicon*, s.v.). According to the author of the *Manāqib Baghdad* (p. 37) fruit in the early Abbasid period was very cheap, as the poor could also afford it almost throughout the year.

630 For *sikbāj*, see above, p. 83

631 Jāḥiẓ, *Bukhalā'*, p. 110

632 1 *mudd* according to Hinz, p. 45, was 810 g.

at Kufa.[633] At about the same period, it is said that 100 egg-plants could be found for only one dirham.[634] The average price of lettuce (*khass*), in AD 956, is described as twenty stalks per dirham.[635] This was apparently a high price.

Honey, at the time of the construction of Baghdad, was sold at 12 ratls a dirham:[636] roughly 0·0083 dinar per ratl.[637] According to Ibn Ḥawqal, Tiflis in the 10th century gave 20 ratls of honey for one dirham,[638] an exceptionally low price, which cannot be taken for other areas. About the price of sugar we know only one quotation, which was mentioned as evidence of rising prices. According to this, in the year 975 a *mann* (about two pounds) of sugar cost 4 dirhams.[639]

The price of clarified butter (*samn*) in the early period of Manṣūr has been recorded at double the price of olive oil. At that time 16 ratls of olive oil and 8 ratls of *samn* were each sold at 1 dirham.[640] In the 13th century AD Yāqūt wrote that in Wāsit one pot of butter cost 2 dirhams[641]—still very cheap. Ashtor concludes that 0·0052 and 0·001 dinar had to be paid for one ratl of olive oil and one ratl of butter respectively.[642]

Ibn al-Jawzī quotes a price of ice in Baghdad for an unspecified year, when 1 to 1½ ratl of ice sold at 1 dirham.[643] This price would seem a reasonable one, as ice was brought to Baghdad from far-off lands.[644]

Cooked food was also inexpensive. Maqdisī notes that in the 10th century in Baghdad a man could eat *harīsa*[645] in a restaurant with full service for one dānaq only.[646] In the early

---

633 Ibn Abī Ya'lā, p. 316, as quoted by Ashtor, p. 51
634 Baghdādī, *Taṭfīl*, p. 79
635 *Nishwār*, i, p. 65
636 Khaṭīb, *Ta'rīkh*, i, p. 70; Yāqūt, *Buldān*, s.v. *Baghdād*
637 E. Ashtor, *Prix*, p. 51
638 Ibn Ḥawqal, p. 242
639 *Muntaẓam*, vii, p. 76. 1 *mann* according to Hizn, pp. 16–17 was 816.5 g.
640 Khaṭīb, op. cit., i, p. 70
641 *Buldān*, s.v. *Wāsiṭ*
642 Ashtor, *Prix*, p. 51
643 *Ḥumaqā*, p. 75
644 Muq. pp. 160, 181. An exceptionally high price of ice in 10th century AD Baghdad has been given by Tanūkhī (cf. *Nishwār*, i, pp. 63–64; also *Muntaẓam*, vi, 118–19).
645 For *Harīsa*, see above, pp. 131
646 Muq. p. 129

9th century a dish of *sikbāj*[647] containing a number of vegetables cost 2 dirhams to prepare.[648] Luxurious food, however, cost a lot, and was therefore out of the common people's reach. The cost of a highly luxurious meal, consisting of roast-meat, fine bread, sauces, and one ratl of the finest quality of sweet, in a Baghdad food shop was just 10 dirhams.[649] In a story referring to the first half of the 9th century we see that a delicious sweet dish of *lawzīnaj* cost 80 dirhams: $3\frac{1}{2}$ dinars.[650] According to another text, in AD 941 a similar dish of *lawzīnaj* cost 5 dinars, or about 65 dirhams.[651] The price of bread was linked with the price of wheat, and fluctuated sharply.

Some anecdotes found in various works indicate that during this period 10 dinars, or about 150 dirhams, a month were thought to be sufficient for a modest living.[652] A substantial proportion of this was spent on food. In the time of the Caliph Hārūn al-Rashīd 300 dirhams a month was a sum quite sufficient for a middle-class workman and his family.[653] One anecdote shows that 5 dirhams a day were considered sufficient for a person to lead a decent life with his family. In AD 895, a notorious thief was employed by the Caliph Muʿtaḍid to spy on the Caliph's former associates in Baghdad for 10 dinars a month. The Caliph is reported to have said on his appointment, "I have set for you ten dinars a month to provide for your food, drink, dress and perfume."[654] A certain jurist (died AD 942), anxious to insure his son's future, declared, "I have decided to give him a dinar daily for life, as 1 dinar is sufficient for a middle class man and his family."[655]

People with a low income and the sufis spent very little on

---

647 For *sikbāj* see above, p. 83

648 Jāḥiẓ, *Bukhalā'*, p. 110

649 Ḥamadānī, *Maqāmat*, p. 67

650 Ibn Abī Yaʿlā, *Ṭabaqāt*, p. 65; cf. also Ashtor, p. 63. 1 dinar in the early 9th century was 20–22 dirhams (cf. Jahshiyāri, *Wuzarā'*, p. 364; cf. also Ashtor, p. 40).

651 *Nishwār*, i, p. 61. 1 dinar at this time was 13 dirhams (cf. *Eclipse*, ii, p. 54).

652 *Murūj*, viii, p. 156; *Mashāriʿ al-Ushshāq*, p. 159

653 *Mashāriʿ al-Ushshāq*, p. 159

654 *Murūj*, viii, p. 156

655 *Muntaẓam*, vi, p. 333; cf. also, Dūrī, *Mesopotamia*, p. 283

their food and living. From a biography of a scholar of the 9th century we learn that 4 dirhams were regarded as sufficient for a man to live on for one month.[656] He could spend less than 10 *ḥabba*, 0·166 dinar, for the nourishment of his body. A sufi woman, the sister of the famous Bishr al-Ḥāfī (died AD 841), is said to have spent only 1 dānaq a week on her food.[657] A certain pious Muhammad b. Yūsuf (d. AD 899) is also reported to have lived on a daily expense of one dānaq only. He gave the rest of his earnings to charity.[658] From a passage in the *Ṭabaqāt al-Ḥanābila* it is known that in the second half of the 9th century, during the month of Ramaḍān, one had to spend one dirham and 2½ dānaqs for a meal after the *ifṭār* (breakfast).[659] A craftsman who afterwards became a famous philologist states that, in the same period, he could live on half a dinar per month: approximately 10–15 dirhams.[660] At about the same period, a scholar who was said to be money-conscious spent two thirds of a dinar a month for his subsistence.[661]

These statistics quoted from various anecdotes refer only to the cost of nourishment; other necessities, such as clothing and housing, required a lot of money and were not included in the figures quoted. Concluding from such facts and figures, E. Ashtor states that the minimum amount required for a man to feed himself amounted to 0·2 dinar at the beginning of the 9th century AD, and 0·5 dinar in the second half.[662] From the middle of the 9th century onwards the cost of living went up, and food, as it appears from the various references quoted in the preceding pages, became expensive. The well-to-do people spent a lot of money on their food and were little affected by the rising prices and the high cost of living. People with little income and limited resources suffered much, which was to some extent reflected in sporadic uprisings and also in the activities of the *shuṭṭār* and the *ʿayyārūn*.[663]

---

656 Khaṭīb, *Taʾrīkh*, i. p. 366; cf. also Ashtor, p. 61f.

657 Ibid, xiv, p. 437

658 *Muntaẓam*, vi, p. 24

659 Ibn Abī Yaʿlā, p. 51; *Muntaẓam*, vi, 5; cf. also Ashtor, *Prix*, p. 62

660 *Nishwār*, i, p. 134; see also Ashtor, *Prix*, p. 62

661 Khaṭīb, *Taʾrīkh*, vi, p. 76; Ashtor, p. 62

662 Ashtor, *Prix*, p. 62

663 *Manāqib Baghdād* (attributed to Ibn al-Jawzī), p. 37. On the activities of the *ʿayyarūn* and *shuṭṭār* see *EI*², s. vv. *Futuwwa, Baghdād,* and the

Markets, shops, restaurants and supply

Markets occupied an important place in urban life. When the cities of Baghdad (in the 8th century AD) and Samarra (in the 9th century) were planned, markets received great attention.[664] When Mutawakkil (AD 846–61) built Al-Jaʿfariyya, north of Samarra, "he founded in every quarter a market".[665]

Each craft or trade had its separate market or lane (*darb*).[666] The western part of Baghdad appears to have been commercially more developed than the eastern side. The "great market" of western Baghdad was al-Karkh, two *farsakh* long and one *farsakh* wide,[667] divided into several blocks, each class of merchants and merchandise being placed in a special street,[668] such as the fruit market, *dār al-biṭṭīkh*, and the food market, "*sūq al-ṭaʿām*". On the eastern side there was a variety of markets, including a flower market, a food market, a goldsmith's market, a sheep market, a bookseller's market, and a market for Chinese merchandise.[669] Moreover, in the great Ruṣāfa market all kinds of goods were sold.[670] The allotment of shops was carefully planned. The butchers' block was kept to the furthest corner of the street, for hygienic reasons.[671]

Food products such as wheat, which were consumed in large quantities, were transported on a large scale from the surrounding countryside to the city markets. The heavy products regularly consumed were, however, transported from the region in which they were originally grown, for considerable distances by caravan, or by ship on river or

---

sources quoted there; see also Badrī, *ʿĀmma*, pp. 286–309. For some other references on the cost of food and living of the 10th century, see Ashtor, *Prix*, p. 43ff.

664 *EI*², s.v. *Baghdād* (A. A. Dūrī). See details in Yaʿqūbī's *Buldān*

665 Yaʿqūbī, *Buldān*, p. 267

666 *EI*², s.v. *Baghdād*

667 Yaʿqūbī, *Buldān*, p. 246; Ibn Ḥawqal, p. 242

668 Ibid., pp. 241, 246; cf. also Dūrī, *Mesopotamia*, p. 141

669 Ibid., pp. 241, 246, 248, 254; *Manāqib Baghdād* (attributed to Ibn al-Jawzī), pp. 26–27, 28; Ibn Ḥawqal, p. 242; cf. also *EI*², s.v. *Baghdād* (A. A. Dūrī)

670 Ibid., *Buldān*, p. 253

671 *Manāqib Baghdād* (attr. to Ibn al-Jawzī), p. 13; Khaṭīb, Ta'rīkh, i, p. 80

sea.[672] The products of all the regions of the Muslim world were thus available throughout every part of it for those who could afford to pay their prices.[673]

The peasant producers came to sell their produce either in the country, in temporary regional markets, or in the towns, in markets which were more or less permanent. In the large towns there were wholesale markets which served the whole of a large urban district, and also the small local markets. Consumers bought their provisions from retailers of the large or small city markets.[674]

Every town, in fact, served as a market for the surrounding countryside, as a storehouse for its products, and as a shopping centre for its needs. The country folk either visited ordinary markets or attended fairs regularly held on certain days.[675] For example, a suburb of Mosul held fairs at definite periods, when merchants, peasants and semi-nomad Kurds met to buy or sell goods.[676] Mosul had also a Wednesday market (*sūq al-arbaʿa*) in the large open square within its castle, which farmers frequented.[677]

Apart from these markets, there were small dealers and pedlars who sold their commodities either sitting along the roadside or moving from door to door. A greengrocer is reported to have set up his shop in front of a house for a nominal rent.[678] A man could buy a stick for two dirhams from a pedlar trading at the roadside.[679] The water carriers (*saqqā'*) moved from street to street to sell their iced water.[680] Because of their profession these vendors and pedlars were commonly known as *ṭawwāfūn*.[681] The pedlars sometimes even took their merchandise to the mosque and sold it to the *muṣalliyūn* (persons coming for prayers), sitting in the corner

---

672 *EI*^{2}, s.v. *Ghidhā'*, (M. Rodinson); Yaʿqūbī, *Buldān*, pp. 250, 263; *Tajārib*, ii, p. 91

673 *EI*^{2}, s.v. *Ghidhā'* (M. Rodinson)

674 Ibid.

675 Dūrī, *Mesopotamia*, p. 147

676 Ibn Ḥawqal, p. 217

677 Muq. p. 117

678 Jāḥiẓ, *Bukhalā'*, p, 29; Khaṭīb, *Bukhalā'*, p. 94; ʿ*Iqd*, vi, 178

679 *Nishwār*, i, p. 60

680 Ḥamadānī, *Maqāmāt*, p. 67; Ibn al-Jawzī, *Akhbār al-Ẓirāf*, 31

681 *Muntaẓam*, ix, p. 44

of a courtyard.[682] The regular shopkeepers, however, did not like these pedlars selling their commodities sitting in the vicinity of their shops. There are reports which suggest that the pedlars were not tolerated by the shop-holders, who considered their presence a potential danger to their business, and so often drove them out of the market.[683]

There were a number of food shops and restaurants in the food markets of the towns. Food could be taken away or eaten in the restaurant.[684] In the *Maqāmāt* of Ḥamadānī there is a lively description of a restaurant where people could eat all kinds of food including sweets.[685] Maqdisī notes that in the shops selling *harīsa* people took their meal on the upper floor.[686] The proprietor of the restaurant provided the customers with perfect service, each visitor having waiters (*khuddām*) to attend to his needs and ever ready with a ewer and a basin. Soap and *ushnān* were provided by the owner of the restaurant for washing the hands.[687]

The expenses of the royal kitchen

The Abbasid caliphs, their wazirs, their high ranking officials and people of wealth used to take a meal marked by its expense, by elaborate preparations and by a lavish use of spices. Several caliphs were noted for their extravagant expenditure on food, and even for gluttony. The Caliph Manṣūr is reported to have died of a stomach ailment which, as his physician pointed out, was a direct result of his gluttony.[688]

From a passage in the *Kitāb al-Wuzarā'* of Ṣābī, it would seem that there were two types of kitchen in the caliphal palace: the *khāṣṣa*, the private kitchen; and the *'āmma*, the

---

682 Baghdādī, *Ta'rīkh*, xiii, p. 191
683 Ibid., xiii, p. 191; cf. also Badri, *'Āmma*, p. 80
684 *EI*², s.v. *Ghidhā'* (M. Rodinson)
685 Hamadānī, *Maqāmāt*, p. 66
686 Muq. p. 129
687 Ibid., p. 129
688 H. I. Hasan, *Islam*, p. 380 (quoting from Tabarī, ix, pp. 290–91). The Caliphs Mu'taṣim and Wāthiq were also well known for their gluttony. Cf. *Murūj*, vii, p. 170; viii, p. 302; *'Iqd*, vi, p. 300; *Quṭub al-Surūr*, p. 290

public kitchen.[689] The private kitchen, it appears, catered for the needs of the caliph himself and of his friends and companions. The other members of the court and the visitors took their meal from the *maṭbakh al-ʿāmma*, the public kitchen.

The annual budget for the royal kitchen and the daily expenses for the caliph's food indicate the unusual interest shown in the procuring of sumptuous dishes. The yearly expenditure of the Caliph Mutawakkil's kitchen was two hundred thousand dinars.[690] This expenditure, it would seem, did not include the money spent on such items as drinks, ice, and kitchen utensils. From Ṣābī we know that the monthly expense of the Caliph Muʿtaḍid's kitchen, both *khāṣṣa* and *ʿāmma*, amounted to ten thousand dinars.[691] The cooks (number unidentified) of this royal kitchen received thirty dinars a day.[692] It is said that the Caliph Ma'mūn's daily expenses amounted to 6,000 dinars, a large amount of which was spent on his kitchen.[693] How many people were fed from this kitchen is not precisely known, but from the fact that the Caliphs did not usually take food alone, it can be assumed that a large amount was spent on the food of the caliph's *nadīms* (intimate companions), physicians and guests.[694]

The caliphs, wazirs and other men of wealth preferred to have a wide range of dishes on their table. Special occasions such as wedding parties and banquets called forth the fullest manifestation of extravagance.[695] A banquet which Ibrāhīm b. al-Mahdī, a member of the Abbasid house, gave in honour of the Caliph Hārūn contained one dish prepared from the

---

689 Ṣābī, *Wuzarā'*, p. 20; idem, *Rusūm*, p. 22; see also, Yaʿqūbī, *Buldān*, p. 240

690 Ibn Zubayr, *Dhakhā'ir*, p. 219

691 Ṣābī, *Wuzarā'*, p. 20

692 Ibid., p. 23

693 *Fakhrī*, p. 312; cf. also Hasan, *Islam*, p. 381

694 That physicians were often numbered amongst the table companions of the caliph is clear from the evidence of various authors (cf., for example, Ibn Abī ʿUṣaybiʿa, ii, p. 34). *Aghānī* notes that the Caliph Hārūn al-Rashīd, however, was careful in his choice of table companions and allowed none other than an Amīr or *ʿĀlim* to sit with him (cf. *Aghānī*[1], v, p. 24).

695 See, for example, the account of the wedding party of the Caliph Ma'mūn, Chapter 7 of this book

tongues of fishes, which cost over 1,000 dirhams.[696] One of the companions of the Caliph Ma'mūn, Ja'far b. Muḥammad, notes that one day he found Ma'mūn seated at a lunch comprising dishes which he thought to exceed three hundred in number.[697] The Caliph Muhtadī, on the other hand, is reported to have cut down the daily expenses of the royal kitchen from ten thousand dinars to one hundred dinars only.[698] Similarly, the Caliph Qāhir is said to have reduced the number of main dishes to twelve, allowing thirty varieties of sweet and allotting only one dinar for the fruit destined for his dining-table.[699]

Well-to-do people in general were also extravagant in their food. Abu'l-'Atāhiya tells us that, being invited by Mukhāriq, the singer, he went to his house and was served there with numerous dishes. The menu included the following kinds of food: fine bread, vinegar, vegetables, roast mutton, roast fish, sweet dishes, desserts, fruits and a variety of drinks.[700] On the dining table of Isḥāq b. Ibrāhīm, the singer, a certain Aḥmad b. 'Abd al-Raḥmān al-Ḥarrānī found thirty birds cooked for three guests only, the number of dishes, sweet and sour, cold and hot, being, in his recollection, uncountable.[701]

Personnel

Our sources are silent about the staff engaged in the kitchen

---

696 *Murūj*, vi, pp. 349–50

697 Ibn Ṭayfūr, *Baghdād*, p. 36. From Tanūkhī we hear that the Caliph Muqtadir, finding a particular dish absent from his dining table, admonished the cook and asked him not to leave a single dish unprepared (cf. *Nishwār*, ii, p. 152).

698 *Murūj*, viii, p. 20

699 'Arīb, p. 183

700 *Aghānī*[1], iii, p. 180; cf. also Abū Naṣr, *al-Hawā wa'l-shabāb fī 'ahd al-Rashīd*, p. 201

701 *Tāj* (attributed to Jāḥiẓ), p. 13. The kitchen expenses of some of the Abbasid wazirs are also to be noted. Ibn al-Furāt's extravagance is well known. His great kitchen, it is said, was open to all (cf. *Eclipse*, i, 120). Hāmid b. al-'Abbās used to set 40 dinner tables daily for those who entered his residence, whether officials, ordinary people, or even servants. Meals included meat and fine wheat bread (cf. *Nishwār*, i, 14). Ibn Muqla (in 317) spent 500 dinars a week on fruit alone (*Eclipse*, i, 203). In 324 the Barīdī's table expenses amounted to 1,000 dinars a day (*Eclipse*, i, 348, n. 2; cf. also Dūrī, *Mesopotamia*, p. 298).

of the royal or wealthy people. From Masʿūdī, however, we know that in the caliphal kitchen there was one supervisor, or head of the kitchen (*qayyim* or *wakīl ʿalaʾl-maṭbakh*), whose duty it was to prepare the menu, arrange the material and employ others to run the kitchen.[702] He had several cooks and servants (*khuddām*) under him. It was the *ṭabbākh* (cook, or perhaps head cook) who was solely responsible for the quality of food cooked in the kitchen. We hear of a cook being severely punished by his master for a slight negligence in cooking.[703]

In the mediaeval period, when Egyptian cuisine acquired a high reputation,[704] Indian cooks also enjoyed a considerable fame. Jāḥiẓ, praising their trustworthiness and ingenuity in the art of cooking, says "one does not find among the slaves cooks better than the Sindis, who have the most natural gift for preparing tasty dishes."[705] As a matter of fact, renowned cooks from distant regions were employed in the royal kitchen. Ṭāhir is reported to have brought to Baghdad a Khurāsānī cook.[706] Cooks generally came from slave stock, the slave girls being the most expert.[707] Black slaves may have been preferred for the kitchen, for a man is mentioned to have purchased especially a black cook from the slave market.[708] In a middle-class home the wife did most of the cooking for the family,[709] including pounding of spices and washing of utensils.[710]

From a passage in Ṭabarī it would seem that the cooks wore a distinctive dress.[711]

The chief of the servants or waiters in the dining room was called *murāqib khādim* (*ʿalā al-māʾida*).[712] It was perhaps he who was responsible for a clean and orderly service at the

---

[702] *Murūj*, vi, p. 227; *Dhakhāʾir*, p. 103; *Nishwār*, viii, p. 40

[703] *Diyārāt*, p. 124

[704] H. Zayyāt, in *Mashriq*, 1947, pp. 14–15; cf. also *EI*², s.v. *Ghidhāʾ*

[705] Jāḥiẓ, *Fakhr al-Sūdān* (ed. Van Vleten, in *Tria Opuscula*, Leyden, 1903), p. 85

[706] *EI*², s.v. *Ghidhāʾ* (quoting from Ṭayfūr, *apud*, Spular, Iran, 510)

[707] *Nishwār*, i, 22; Ḥamadānī, *Maqāmāt*, 221; H. Zayyat, op. cit., 14–15

[708] Khālidiyyān, *Tuḥaf*, p. 172; *Nishwār*, i, p. 22

[709] Ḥamadānī, *Maqāmāt*, p. 111

[710] Ibid., p. 11

[711] Ṭabarī, iii, p. 1224

[712] *Murūj*, vi, p. 350

table and for the care of the guests. Our sources have laid down various qualifications for two posts in the royal kitchen. The person holding the one was called *ṣāḥib ṭaʿām* or *māʾida*, and the other was called *ṣāḥib sharāb*, or master of the drinks.[713] "They should be trustworthy, intelligent, free, aware of the pleasure and displeasure of the ruler in matters of eating, and should not serve a dish twice. They should be able to look after each and every requirement of the royal table carefully, place the food very neatly in the best and cleanest available utensils. They should be fully aware of the varieties of dishes, their sequence and season. They should also be aware of the best things drawn from different countries and be well versed in the manners of social gathering. Finally they should carefully keep up the supply of such things as their ruler would like most."[714] The master of the cellar or in charge of the drinks in the palace was also known as *sharābī*.[715]

Timing of meals

The usual meals in ordinary life were two: a midday meal or luncheon (*ghadāʾ*), and an evening meal or supper (*ʿashāʾ*), which was the more important.[716] Breakfast does not seem to have been a formal repast.

The midday meal or luncheon was at noon. There would be a good margin between luncheon and the *ẓuhr* or *jumʿa* prayer. A man is reported to have been in the habit of taking his Friday luncheon in a garden, after which he had a siesta and a bath. In spite of this he was never late in reaching the mosque for the *Jumʿa* prayer, usually held between one and two o'clock.[717]

---

713 *Nishwār*, ii, in *RAAD*, 12 (1932), p. 695; 17 (1942), 151–52; cf. also Munajjid, *Khulafāʾ*, p. 83

714 Ibn Abī Rabīʿ, *Sulūk al-mālik fī tadbīr al-mamālik*, p. 136, cited by Munajjid, *Khulafāʾ*, pp. 83–84

715 Mez, p. 398

716 *Mukhaṣṣaṣ*, i, chap. iv, p. 122. The morning meal taken for medical reasons was called *sulfa* (ibid., i, chap. iv, 121). Early drinking of wine in the morning is reported as a regular habit of the pleasure-loving people, hence the term *ṣabūḥ* (cf. *Quṭub al-Surūr*, 25, 38, 61, 66, 71, 200, 205, 213, 429. *Diyārāt*, Index, s.v. *Ṣabuḥ*).

717 Jāḥiẓ, *Bukhalāʾ*, pp. 19–20

Supper was taken after the *Maghrib* prayer. Having finished their supper, people went perhaps to the mosque for *'Ishā'* or late night prayer, after which they went to bed, except those who were accustomed to singing and drinking and therefore went to convivial parties instead.[718]

The Caliph Ma'mūn reportedly took only three meals in two days: one at late noon; the second the following morning, and the third in the evening.[719] There are reports suggesting that some people took only one meal in twenty-four hours.[720] According to Washshā', people of refined taste took not more than one meal in a day.[721]

Ādāb al-Mā'ida: Table manners

Very few books have been written by Muslim scholars on this particular aspect of study. Most of the books written exclusively on this subject, such as *Kitāb Adāb al-Mawā'id* by Qāḍī al-Ḥasan b. 'Abd al-Raḥmān b. Khallād al-Rāmhurmuzī,[722] and *Kitāb Adāb al-Ṭa'ām wa'l-Sharāb* by Abū Naṣr al-Iṣfahānī,[723] seem to have been lost to the world and are known to us only through the writings of succeeding scholars. Two other books on the subject, *Fawā'id al-Mawā'id* and *Risāla Adāb al-Mu'ākala*, written respectively by Jamāl al-Dīn Yaḥyā b. 'Abd al-'Aẓīm b. al-Jazzār (d. AD 1280) and Shaikh Badr al-Dīn Muḥammad al-Ghazzī (AD 1499–1577), are still extant. The former is in manuscript form[724] while the latter has been edited and published in *Majalla al-Majma' al-'Ilmī al-'Arabī*.[725] In addition to the above, books on *ḥadīth* and *fiqh* also contain special chapters dealing with the rules for table manners. Books on culinary art such as Al-Warrāq's *Kitāb al-Ṭabīkh* also contain a few chapters on this topic.

[718] See for various stories on drinking parties *Aghānī*² (e.g., xii, p. 70); cf. also H. Zayyāt in *Mashriq*, 43 (1949), pp. 503–11

[719] Warrāq, fol. 16

[720] *Nishwār*, i, p. 271

[721] *Muwashshā*, pp. 192–93

[722] *Fihrist*, p. 221

[723] H. Zayyāt, *Ādāb al-Mā'ida fi'l-Islām*, *Mashriq*, 37 (1939), p. 162

[724] The MS. is preserved in the British Museum, No. Or. 6388

[725] The editor of the *Risāla* is Dr. 'Umar Mūsā Pāsha, published in Vol. 42 (1967).

Kushājim's *Adab al-Nadīm*, Al-Ghazzālī's *Iḥyā' al-'Ulūm*,[726] and similar works also throw some light on it.

From the information scattered in different sources at our disposal it appears that the term *mā'ida* in Islamic literature includes two types of dining-table, one known as *sufra* and the other as *khiwān*. During the period we are discussing, the *sufra* was usually made of cloth, or copper, or palm-leaves in round shape, and was put on the ground where people sat around it.[727] In course of time, however, an improvement was introduced when people started using a *sufra* made of leather, which facilitated its cleaning.[728] The word *khiwān* was applied to a *mā'ida* which was raised from the ground.[729] It was generally made of wood and stone.[730] Affluent people preferred it to be of marble or onyx.[731] Large round trays of brass, set on a low table and often inlaid with ebony, mother-of-pearl or tortoise-shell, were also a common sight in the houses of the rich.[732] The Abbasid caliphs, however, had some of their dining tables made of gold or silver.[733]

Generally the Abbasids washed their hands together at the table, before the meal, which was done with a single bowl. In compliance with the Prophetic traditions the *ṭast* was presented from the right to each successive guest; the servant simply let the water run from the ewer upon the fingers of the right hand only, since the left hand was not used for touching the dishes except for holding the bread. The practice of the "hand-bath" prior to eating was considered indispensable, and no time was allowed between hand-washing and eating. It is said that at a banquet given in honour of the Caliph Ma'mūn, one of the guests present touched his head after he had had his hand washed. At this Ma'mūn asked him to have his hand rewashed. The man then touched his beard, whereupon Ma'mūn admonished him for not observing the rules of table

[726] See the German Translation by H. Kindermann, with many useful notes.

[727] Ibn Zubayr, *Dhakhā'ir*, p. 63; H, Zayyāt, *Mashriq*, 37 (1939); idem, in *Khizānat al-Sharqiyya*, iii, p. 133

[728] Ṣābī, *Wuzarā'*, p. 261; cf. also H. Zayyāt, *Mashriq*, 1939, p. 164

[729] *Mukhaṣṣaṣ*, i, pt. v, p. 11

[730] *Dhakhā'ir*, p. 256

[731] Ibid., pp. 27, 179, 195, 261; *Murūj*, viii, p. 269

[732] Hitti, *History of the Arabs*, p. 335

[733] *Dhakhā'ir*, pp. 19, 170, 185, 231

manners, and asked him to wash his hand the third time.[734]

With a view to making the guests feel at home, and so that "no one need feel ashamed" (of undue haste in starting the meal), it was a general convention that in a banquet the host first washed his hands and the guests followed him.[735] On other occasions, however, people themselves washed their hands, presumably in a basin kept outside the dining-room or near a drain (*bālūʿa*) in the courtyard.[736] It was the chief guest or the oldest man in the assembly who began eating, and others followed him.[737]

As regards the serving of food at the dining table, two practices were commonly in vogue among the people of this society. The old Muslim practice was to serve all the food, and it was left to the discretion of each individual to take what he pleased.[738] This old practice would seem to have been common among the masses. In the higher circles, at this period, instead of all the food being served at once, a menu was presented to the guests and everyone was served with what he desired.[739]

While eating, the people particularly observed the following etiquette and manners.

Everybody started eating with the introductory phrase, *basmala.*[740]

It was considered a mark of culture and good breeding to indulge in conversation, in particular narrating stories of the table-manners of pious predecessors.[741] There was some disagreement as to whether the host should make any conversation with the guests or not. According to Arab custom, as Abshīhī points out, they believed in freedom and informality to put the guests at ease. Guests and hosts indulged in long conversations.[742] The evidence available

734 Warrāq, fol. 164a; Ghazzī, *Ādāb al-mu'ākala*, *MMII* 42 (1967), p. 506; *Adab al-Nadīm*, p. 28

735 Ibid., fols. 164–65; *Adab al-Nadīm*, p. 28; *Iḥyā'*, ii, p. 16; *'Iqd*, vi, p. 298; cf. also Mez, p. 394

736 Azdī, *Ḥikāyāt*, p. 43

737 Warrāq, fol. 164a

738 *Mustaṭraf*, p. 149; cf. also Mez, p. 394

739 *Adab al-Nadīm*, p. 17

740 See, for example, *'Iqd*, vi, p. 298

741 *Adab al-Nadīm*, pp. 7–8; cf. also Badrī, *'Āmma*, p. 135

742 *Mustaṭraf*, i, p. 21; cf. also, Mez, p. 395

relating to this period shows that the Abbasids talked freely at the dining table. Meals lasted for hours at a time.[743] It was the host who carried on the conversation, to enable the guests to enjoy their meal undisturbed. Jāḥiẓ, however, criticizes a miser who used to involve his guests in conversation while he alone ate all the food.[744] The *ẓurafā'* (men of refined taste), who habitually abstained from joking and indulging in loose talk, conversed or laughed but little at the table.[745]

Staring at others was considered ignominious. People looked at their own dishes and did not raise their eyes to see how others were eating. People in the habit of eating swiftly waited until the last man of the company finished his meal.[746]

While eating from the same bowl one particularly took care of one's neighbour, encouraging him by invitation: "please have some more". The diner did not extend his hand in front of his neighbour, he did not do anything which might offend the feelings of the neighbour, such as shaking hands over the bowl at the time of taking a morsel, or dipping into the pot the remains of a morsel.[747] Jāḥiẓ recommends as a table companion one who does not pick marrow from the bone; who does not grab at the egg lying upon vegetables; who does not appropriate to himself liver and breast of the fowl, brains or kidneys, or the choicest piece of mutton or chicken.[748]

Just as at the beginning, so also at the end of the meal, the people of this society said the *ḥamdala*. As it was an indication of finishing the meal, offering of this prayer in the midst of eating was considered unpleasant. Warrāq in his *Kitāb al-Ṭabīkh* records the story of a man unaware of this custom who uttered this phrase in the midst of eating. At this people became disgusted and were about to beat him. Jaḥẓa (died 324 AH), who was present on the occasion, instantly composed

---

[743] Ṣābī, *Wuzarā'*, p. 262; *Quṭub al-Surūr*, pp. 154–55; *Aghānī*², xiii, p. 179

[744] *Bukhalā'*, p. 87

[745] Washshā', *Muwashshā*, p. 193

[746] Kushājim, *Adab al-Nadīm*, pp. 8–9; Ghazzī, *Ādāb al-Mu'ākala*, pp. 741–42; cf. also Badrī, *'Āmma*, p. 136

[747] *Ādāb al-Mu'ākala*, pp. 741–42, 748, 750; Warrāq, fol. 164; Jazzār, *Fawā'id al-mawā'id*, Br. Mus. MS. Or. 6388, fols. 13–14; *Muwashshā*, pp. 191–93; Khaṭīb, *Taṭfīl*, p. 79

[748] Tha'ālibi, *ZDMG*, viii, p. 518, cited by Mez, p. 395

a few verses to teach the man the appropriate manners of social gatherings and the etiquette of eating.[749]

Unlike the *zuhhād* (ascetics), who grabbed meat with their teeth and licked their fingers at the end of the meal, the men of elegant taste cut their meat with knives and avoided licking their fingers.[750]

They took particular care to make their morsels as small as possible, and avoided making sounds while eating. Therefore, they did not take two morsels of different kinds into the mouth, nor did they sip their soup. They did not soil their hands with fat, nor did they take an excessive amount of salt. This was regarded as vulgar. They did not dabble about in vinegar, make the bread lying before them greasy, reach out from their places, or take huge pieces which made their lips greasy.[751]

An important convention was to wash hands and mouth after the meal. This was rather different from the washing which preceded eating, and particular attention was paid to complete cleanliness. To remove grease, people generally used *ushnān* (saltwort). To make it more effective and scented the well-to-do people added to it various ingredients such as ground rice, Khurāsānī clay, frankincense, cyperus (*su'd*), sandalwood, musk, camphor, or rose-water.[752] This made a sort of washing-powder, which was kept in a pot known as *ushnāndān*.[753] Any one intending to wash his hands took out a spoonful for the purpose.

The ablution after the meal began from the left of the host and proceeded onward so that the host's turn came last.[754] The Khurāsānian author Al-Qummī (died 381 AH) testifies to another custom, presumably of Khurāsān. Here they began from nearest to the door, no matter whether the first was a

---

749 Warrāq, fol. 167b; cf. also Ghazzī, op. cit., pp. 737–38

750 *Muwashshā*, pp. 191–92; Miskāwayh, *Tahdhīb*, p. 50

751 *Muwashshā*, p. 191f.; Warrāq, fols 165, 166; Khaṭīb, *Taṭfīl*, p. 79; cf. also Mez, pp. 395–96

752 Azdī, *Ḥikāyāt*, p. 41; *Wuṣlā*, Br. Mus. MS. Or. 6388. fol. 90. In the fourth century the shop of a Jewish merchant known as Ibn 'Adara was famous for the best quality of *ushnān*, basin and ewer (cf. Azdī, *Ḥikāyāt*, p. 42).

753 Ghazūli, *Maṭāli'*, ii, p. 66; Ṭabarī, iii, p. 416; cf. also Badrī, *'Āmma*, p. 139; H. Zayyāt. *Mashriq*, 37 (1939), p. 167

754 *Kitāb al-'ilal*, Berlin, fol. 112b, cited by Mez, p. 394

slave or a free man.[755] This hand-washing, in the early Abbasid period, was not performed in the dining room, as it presented an unsightly scene. Since it was an elaborate ablution, it was done in a side room.[756] In the houses of the common and less cultured people, the guests were taken for this purpose to a drain (*bālūʿa*) flowing at the end of the courtyard of a house.[757] The practice of washing the hands at a place other than the dining-room goes back as far as the time of the Caliph Mahdī. It is reported that Ibn Da'b, an intimate companion of the Caliph Mahdī, declined to dine with the Caliph, saying "I don't eat where I cannot wash my hands." Because of his protest he was, however, given permission to wash his hands in the presence of the Caliph.[758] On the other hand, Afshīn, the military commander of the Caliph Muʿtaṣim, is reported to have fallen into disfavour with the Caliph because he failed to comply with the rules of table manners and washed his hands in the presence of the Caliph.[759] If, however, all were equal in a *majlis*, it was not inadmissible to wash hands at the table.[760]

Unlike the people of the early Islamic period, who dried their hands by rubbing them on the upper part of their feet, the common people of the Abbasid society generally used towels, while those fond of the luxurious life preferred fine Dabīqī silken kerchiefs.[761]

At the end of the meal, after the washing of hands, the guests took their seats on the couches placed all round the room, while the servant or the master of the house passed around small graceful ewers containing rose-water or other fragrant water, which was sprayed over one's face or over one's clothes. This refinement was followed by the fumigation of perfumes, incense, or sandalwood burnt in a censer.[762]

The supply of tooth-picks (*khilāl*) at a banquet was

---

[755] Ibid., quoted by Mez, p. 394, n. 2

[756] Ṣābī, *Wuzarā'*, pp. 261–62; *Nishwār*, viii, p. 135

[757] Azdī, *Ḥikāyāt*, p. 45

[758] *Irshād*, vi, p. 105

[759] Warrāq, fol. 164; cf. also *Maṭāliʿ*, ii, p. 67

[760] Mez, p. 394

[761] Ṣābī, *Wuzarā'*, p. 262; H. Zayyāt, *Mashriq*, 37 (1939), p. 167; Azdī, *Ḥikāyāt*, p. 42

[762] Ibid., *Wuzarā'*, p. 262; *Murūj*, viii, p. 158; Warrāq, fol. 165 a.; *Iḥyā'*, ii, p. 5

considered one of the important social manners of eating.[763] Its indelicate use, however, was despised. A guest was to pick his teeth only when alone. Ibn Muʿtazz criticizes an undesirable table-companion in these words: "He continually picks his teeth with a tooth-pick."[764]

The people of this society commonly used their fingers for eating, as is evident from the elaborate rites concerning the washing of hands after a meal; however, the use of the spoon and the knife was not unknown to the more sophisticated among them.[765] We do not have as yet any reference to the use of the fork. For the purpose of keeping their clothes tidy they laid a kerchief on their chest, as the modern napkin is used. We are told that the wazir Ibn al-Furāt and his companions used Dabīqī kerchiefs soaked in scented water.[766]

It appears that the use of the spoon was popular among the upper classes. Some of them were so fastidious as to use thirty spoons at one meal.[767] We are told that when the wazir Al-Muhallabī dined, there stood two servants on his right and left, with a bundle of spoons. He took one morsel of food with a spoon and passed it to the servant on his left. The servant on the right handed to him another spoon, with which he took his second morsel. This process continued till he finished his dinner.[768] Spoons were generally made of glass, copper, silver, or gold.[769]

It was not the custom to give a single plate to each individual. The guests instead took food from a common plate kept in the middle of the table.[770] The practice of sharing food from a common plate made them very conscious of the *ādāb* of the *mā'ida*. Numerous adjectives were coined for those who did not observe the strict rules of the table and indulged in practices unpleasant to their table-companions.[771]

---

763 Azdī, *Ḥikāyāt*, p. 41; Warrāq, fol. 164a

764 Ibn Muʿtazz, *Dīwān*, ii, p. 6, quoted by Mez, p. 395

765 Ibn Ḥājj, *Mudkhal*, pp. 185–86, 191; *Quṭub al-Surūr*, pp.154–55

766 Ṣābī, *Wuzarā'*, p. 262

767 *Irshād*, v. pp. 153–53

768 Ibid, v, pp. 152–53

769 H. Zayyāt, *Ādāb al-Mawā'id, Mashriq*, 37 (1939), p. 168

770 Jāḥiẓ, *Bukhalā'*, pp. 14, 19, 67ff.; *Aghānī*^{2}, xiii, p. 179; *Quṭub al-Surūr*, pp. 154–55; cf. also Mez, p. 396

771 See, for example, Jāḥiẓ, *Bukhalā'*, pp. 66–68; Jazzār, *Fawā'id al-mawā'id*, fols. 3ff.; Ghazzī, op. cit., p. 741ff.

Offering guests a variety of food became a sign of luxury and hospitality. Therefore, it was expected that the surface of the table would not be exposed to the eyes of eaters; rather it should be covered with bread.[772] Jāḥiẓ blames several persons for their shortage of bread on the table. A man was labelled a miser simply because the bread-loaves which he offered were of the same number as the eaters, in spite of the fact that food was carefully prepared and neatly laid out.[773]

Water was taken to drink with the meal.[774] "Even in the most dissolute period, wine was never taken with meals."[775] The Abbasid caliphs at dinner did not take wine, nor did they allow it to appear on their dining tables. It is reported that the Caliph Manṣūr refused Bakhtīshūʿ, the Christian physician of the Abbasid court, when he asked permission to take alcoholic drink at the caliphal table.[776] Non-alcoholic drinks in the form of sherbet, consisting of water sweetened with sugar and flavoured with extracts of violets, bananas, roses or mulberries, were served at table or at drinking-parties.

---

[772] Jāḥiẓ, *Bukhalāʾ*, p. 47

[773] Ibid., p. 47

[774] Ibid., pp. 85–86; Ḥamadānī, *Maqāmāt*, 66; Khaṭīb, *Taʾrīkh*, iii, p. 183

[775] Mez, p. 396; cf. also Hasan, *Islam*, p. 380

[776] Bayhaqī, *Maḥāsin*, pp. 321–22; cf. also Ḥasan, *Islam*, pp. 380–81

Chapter 4

Housing

Residential houses

Siting of Houses in Abbasid Society

The social structure of Abbasid society is reflected in the housing pattern of the urban centres of Abbasid Iraq. In Baghdad there were aristocratic quarters such as Ẓāhir, Shammāsiya, Ma'mūniya and Dār ʿAwn. There were also poor quarters such as Qaṭīʿa al-Kilāb and Nahr al-Dajāj.[1] Whereas the caliphs, bureaucrats and rich men lived in palaces and palatial buildings, the poorer people lived in small huts and hovels. The houses of the rich generally included a private bath, a garden and other features, and were usually divided into three quarters surrounded by a wall: the women's quarter, the servants' quarter, and the reception rooms.[2]

There was another group of people who lived in rented houses.[3] Since the rent was high relative to the income of the people, it was not always feasible for the poor tenants to hire a house and consequently they had to be content with an apartment or had to share a house with other tenants.[4] There were some others who could afford neither to build huts nor

---

[1] Azdī, *Ḥikāyāt*, pp. 23, 106; *EI*², s.v. *Baghdād* (A. A. K. Dūrī); cf. also S. A. El-Ali, "The Foundation of Baghdad" in *The Islamic City*, ed. Hourani & Stern, Oxford, 1970, pp. 87–102. For Samarra, see J. M. Rogers, "Sāmarrā: a Study in Medieval Town-Planning" in *The Islamic City*, pp. 119–56

[2] *Aghānī*¹, ii, 73, iii, 31, ix, 144, v, 38, xvii, 129; Ṣābī, *Rusūm*, p. 32; cf. also, *EI*², s.v. *Baghdād*

[3] Jāḥiẓ, *Bukhalā'*, pp. 73ff.; *ʿUyūn*, iii, p. 259; Bayhaqī, *Maḥāsin*, p. 642

[4] Shaybānī, *Ḥiyal*, pp. 68–72; Khaṭīb, *Ta'rīkh*, vi, p. 256; Ghazūlī, *Maṭāliʿ*, i, p. 193; Bayhaqī, op. cit., p. 248

to hire houses or apartments, and were consequently forced to spend their nights in ruined houses, or in mosques.[5]

The building of a house was the primary concern of those who had the means to do so. This is beautifully expressed in the proverbs which were used, stressing such a need. They used to say "*Wa'l-takun al-dūr awwal mā yushtara wa ākhar mā yubā'*" (houses should be the first thing to be bought and the last thing to be sold).[6]

A special feature of life in the important cities of the early Abbasid period was the vast number of mosques. Since these as well as the palaces of the caliphs have been vividly described by different scholars and are easily available, we do not consider it necessary to describe them here. However, it is to be noted that in the capital cities, especially in Baghdad, each quarter generally had a homogeneous group, ethnically (Persians, Arabs, Turks, Khwārizmians), or by vocation; merchants and craftsmen lived on one side of the city, and soldiers on the other, generally outside the wall.[7] On account of the wonderful gardens of Baghdad, its splendid high palaces with sumptuous decorations on the gates, and in the halls and their exquisite rich furniture and other beauties, poets extolled Baghdad and called it a "Paradise on earth",[8] while Samarra was designed by its founder "to please everyone who saw it" (*surra man ra'a*).

The Price of Houses

With regard to the cost of land and of building, and the prices of houses, Arab authors have furnished very little detail, and only isolated anecdotes can be cited as evidence of house prices.

In the late second century a man of Baghdad appears to have asked a price of two thousand dirhams for his house.[9] In the third century the wife of a *faqīh* sold a house for 30 dinars, about 400 dirhams.[10] At the beginning of the fourth century,

[5] *Muntaẓam*, x, 189; Khaṭīb, *Ta'rīkh*, vi, 254; Tha'ālibī, *Tamthīl*, 199; cf. also, Badrī, *'Āmma*, pp. 166–67

[6] *'Uyūn*, I, p. 311; *Tamthīl*, p. 297. Another proverb compares owning a house with paradise "*Jannatu'l-mar' dāruhū*" (cf. *Tamthīl*, p. 297).

[7] *EI*², s.v. *Baghdād*

[8] Ṭabarī, iii, p. 873; cf. also *EI*², s.v. *Baghdād*

[9] Khaṭīb, *Ta'rīkh*, iii, p. 268

[10] Ibn Abī Ya'lā, p. 42; Ashtor, *Prix*, p. 56

a potter in Basra, asked about the price of the house he rented at five dirhams a month, replied that such a house would cost only 500 dirhams.[11] Thus five hundred dirhams was regarded as almost a minimum for the building or purchase of a house of somewhat moderate standard.

The huts (*kūkh*, pl. *akwākh*) in which the poor people lived were generally made of inexpensive materials such as mud, and did not cost much, but their purchase was clearly beyond the means of the poor.[12] From some evidence on house prices, E. Ashtor suggests that a village hut cost between six and eight dinars in the 10th–11th century AD, and possibly rather less in the 9th century, as prices at that time were comparatively lower.[13]

The houses of the well-to-do would cost a lot of money, depending on site, area and condition. In 307, Ibrāhīm, the son of the Caliph Muqtadir, purchased the house of Muḥammad Isḥāq Kindāj for 30,000 dinars.[14] The building which belonged to the wazir Ḥāmid b. ʿAbbās at the Sarāt canal was bought from Nāzuk for 12,000 dinars.[15] The extravagant wazir Ibn al-Furāt is said to have spent (about 300 AH) three hundred thousand dinars for his palace. He further paid half a million dinars for the building of a garden-house where his womenfolk, his nieces, and his small children resided.[16] The Caliph Hārūn al- Rashīd is said to have offered 3,000 dinars to one of his courtiers to purchase a house.[17] He is also said to have offered the Barmakid Faḍl b. Yaḥyā 35,000,000 dirhams to build a mansion in Baghdad.[18]

A report from outside Baghdad would suggest a similar expense on house building. An acquaintance of Iṣṭakhrī (died 346) built an excellent dwelling house at Sīrāf, the port town of the Arabian Gulf, at a cost of 30,000 dinars.[19] According to

---

[11] Tanūkhī, *Nishwār*, i, p. 39

[12] Jāḥiẓ, *Bukhalā'*, p. 22; cf. also Begg, *The Social History of the Labouring Classes in 'Iraq under the Abbasids*, Section "The cost of housing"

[13] Ashtor, *R.S.O*, 1961, pp. 58–59

[14] Ibn al-Jawzī, *Muntaẓam*, vi, p. 153

[15] Ibid., vi, pp. 183–84

[16] Ṣābī, *Wuzarā'*, p. 199; cf. also, Mez, p. 382

[17] *Iḥyā'*, i, p. 23, cited by Ashtor, *Prix*, p. 57, n. 2

[18] Jahshiyārī, *Wuzarā'*, p. 289

[19] Iṣṭakhrī, p. 127; cf. also Mez, p. 512

the fashions of Sīrāf, the building might have been two-storied or multi-storied.[20]

People in Abbasid Iraq seem to have been very particular about their choice of neighbourhood. This consciousness was reflected in the saying "*Al-jār thumma al-dār*" ("The neighbour is the first [consideration] and the house is the next.")[21] Prices of houses, therefore, would go up because of a good neighbour. It is reported that the neighbour of the *Muḥaddith* Abū Hamza al-Sukkarī (died 167) wanted to sell his house. When asked about the price, he said: "Two thousand for the house and another two thousand for the neighbourhood of Al-Sukkarī."[22]

Repairing and furnishing a house also called for huge expenditure. A young man belonging to an official circle, who inherited from his maternal side 40,000 dinars, spent 1000 dinars for repairing, decorating and restoring his ancestral home, whereas he spent 7000 dinars for carpets, dresses, and slave-girls.[23] The famous singer Isḥāq al-Mawṣilī received a grant of 10,000 dinars for furnishing a house which was a gift from the Caliph.[24]

The cost of land for building houses has also received very little attention by authors of the Abbasid period and is therefore insufficiently documented for an authoritative statement. The price of plots of land purchased by the Caliph Muʿtaṣim at Samarra has been recorded by contemporary historians and geographers, but they do not mention precisely the area of the land nor the general prices of land in the third century. According to the reports of Arab authors, Muʿtaṣim paid, among other prices, 5000 dirhams for a plot of land belonging to a Christian monastery, and the same amount for

---

[20] See Iṣṭakhrī, pp. 127f.; also, the excavation reports of Sīrāf, published in *Iran*, 1968–71

[21] Thaʿālibī, *al-Tamthīl wa'l-Muḥāḍara*, p. 297.; cf. also Jāḥiẓ, *Bukhalā'*, p. 75; Bayhaqī, *Maḥāsin*, p. 225

[22] Khaṭīb, *Ta'rīkh*, iii, p. 268

[23] Tanūkhī, *Faraj*, ii, p. 17; cf. also Mez, p. 379. At the beginning of the 10th century AD the wage of a builder who built a wall in one day was reported to be 20 dirhams (cf. *Imtāʿ*, 1, p. 28). In another report it is said that a man in Basra paid 20 dinars for wages of the labourers engaged in erecting a house (cf. Ibn al-Jawzī, *Ẓirāf*, p. 50).

[24] *EI*[1], s.v. *Isḥāḳ al-Mawṣilī*

the adjacent garden.[25] Ashtor, citing a Jewish source, states that a garden belonging to an Armenian person was valued, in the sixties of the 9th century AD, at 27 dinars:[26] an isolated incident providing no conclusive evidence. From a passage in the *Kitāb al-Wuzarā'* of Ṣābī, however, we get more precise and conclusive evidence about the prices of land in early fourth-century Baghdad. Ṣābī notes that in AD 905 a *dhirā'* of land at an inferior site near the Tigris was normally sold at the price of one dinar.[27] Thus, in the absence of other corroborative evidence, 1 dinar per *dhirā'* (about 1 square yard)[28] might be regarded as a normal price in Baghdad in the 9th century AD.

Rent of Houses

The rent of a house, it would seem, depended on its amenities and its location in the city. An anecdote relating to early 9th-century Baghdad[29] and a report of the early 10th century AD connected with Basra[30] perhaps show that 5 dirhams a month per head was a normal rent. In the first half of the 9th century AD we also find that a shop was rented at the rate of 3 dirhams per month.[31] A savant of Baghdad (died 295) is reported to have lived a very hard life on the earnings of a shop (*yastaghill*) amounting to 17 dirhams per month.[32] The shop was perhaps let or leased for a period. A report of an unspecified time, recorded by Bayhaqī, shows that a man rented a house, probably in Baghdad, for two dinars, or about 30 dirhams a month.[33] This report, however, does not indicate whether the man was a bachelor or living with his family, whether occupying one room or more. Nevertheless, from other evidence at our disposal it can be assumed that 2 dinars for a single man was too high a rent, and therefore the man must have been living with his family.

---

[25] Ṭabarī, iii, p. 1180; Yāqūt, *Buldān*, iii, p. 16; cf. also Ashtor, *Prix*, p. 56

[26] Ashtor, *Prix*, p. 56, n. 6, quoting from *T'shūbhōt ha-g'ōnīm mi-tōkh ha-genīzah*, ed. Assaf (Jerusalem, 1929), p. 36f.

[27] Ṣābī, *Wuzarā'*, p. 312; cf. also Ashtor, *Prix*, p. 56

[28] On *Dhirā'*, see *EI*², s.v. *Dhirā'* (Hinz)

[29] Jāḥiẓ, *Bukhalā'*, p. 71

[30] *Nishwār*, i, p. 39

[31] *Ḥilya*, ix, p. 179; cf. also, Ashtor, *Prix*, p. 57

[32] *Muntaẓam*, vi, p. 76; Ashtor, p. 57

[33] Bayhaqī, *Maḥāsin*, p. 642

However, from a proverb[34] current in fifth-century Baghdad and possibly much earlier,[35] it can be gleaned that the rents of houses were beyond the means of many, and ordinary people could not afford even 5 dirhams a month.

From a passage in Jāḥiẓ's *Bukhalā'*, it appears that some people considered it to be against etiquette to invite guests to rented houses and allow them to stay overnight. According to this text, not supported by corroborative evidence, if the guests stayed more than a few days (presumably three days, a tenure recommended by Islam for hospitality), the tenant was obliged to pay rent on their behalf.[36] Maʿbad, the theologian, a contemporary of Jāḥiẓ, was once tenant of the house of one Al-Kindī. Maʿbad kept a cousin and his son in the house as guests. Kindī sent a note saying that he would not mind their staying there for a day or two, but would not tolerate a longer stay. Maʿbad informed him that the guests would stay only for a month. Kindī wrote back demanding an extra ten dirhams for the guests, saying: "The rent of your house is thirty dirhams; and since there are six of you, that comes to five dirhams a head. Now that there are two more of you, that will be another ten dirhams; so from today your rent will be forty dirhams."[37] The rent was paid at the end of each month, seldom in advance.[38] The landlord was supposed to repair any damage and the wear and tear were his responsibility.[39] According to Ibn al-Jawzī, the cleaning of the house was one of the duties of the landlord.[40] The landlord, according to Jāḥiẓ, charged a nominal amount of about 10 dirhams a year for recurrent repairs and for sweeping and cleaning.[41]

The relationship between lodger and landlord was not always cordial. Bad tenants would delay payment of rent and would not take proper care of the building. For these reasons, house-keeping and house purchasing for renting were not

[34] "Heavier than the rent of a house" (*athqal min kirā' al-dār*)
[35] Ṭaliqānī, *Amthāl al-Baghdādiya*, n. 77, p. 7
[36] Jāḥiẓ, *Bukhalā'*, p. 71
[37] Ibid., p. 71; cf. the English translation of this passage in Ch. Pellat, *Life and Works of Jāḥiẓ*, p. 241f.
[38] Ibid., p. 74; Ibn al-Jawzī, *Dhamm al-Hawā*, p. 453
[39] *Bukhalā'*, pp. 73, 75
[40] *Dhamm al-Hawā*, pp. 453–54
[41] Jāḥiẓ, *Bukhalā'*, p. 73

considered very profitable business.[42] At times of calamity and unstable conditions, the landlord, in order to protect his property, was obliged to exempt tenants from their rent. In the year 330, as a result of heavy rain, hailstorm and famine, the landlords of Baghdad offered their tenants extra money to protect their estates from burglars and thieves.[43]

Thus the amount of money spent on housing constituted, as Ashtor points out,[44] a significant proportion of total family expenditure. The lower income groups probably paid relatively more for housing than the higher income groups. The two major exceptions to this rule are of course the *fuqarā'* and the ṣūfīs, on the one hand, who were content to live in inns or mosques, and on the other hand the moneyed group who paid exorbitant rents to maintain their standard in society.

An interesting question that arises at this stage is the extent to which people tended to move from the category of tenant to that of house-owner. It has been noted that houses were not considered a good investment,[45] which would probably hold for any commercial, as opposed to industrial, society. However, there seem to have been a number of important inducements for building houses for personal use: rents were quite high, but the cost of building was not prohibitive. Hence we witness a spate of building in Abbasid Iraq. The well-to-do people of the community were especially interested in constructing lavish dwellings for themselves.

Types of Houses

As has already been observed, people in some areas possessed impressive multi-storied buildings with attractive gardens and elegant furniture; the common people, in general, lived in single-storied houses and huts.[46] There is little information about the area of ground occupied by a house, the dimensions of the floors of a building, or the number of persons per dwelling.

---

[42] Ibid., p. 76; cf. the English translation in Pellat's *Life and works of Jāḥiẓ*, p. 245

[43] *Muntaẓam*, vi, p. 335

[44] Ashtor, *Prix*, p. 61ff.; idem., in *AESC*, 1968, p. 1029; in *JAS*, iv (1970), p. 9f. For a discussion on the earnings of various social groups see Ashtor, *Prix*, p. 64f.; idem, *A Social and Economic History . . .*, p. 154

[45] See above, p. 167

[46] See above, p. 167

Very little archaeological and historical evidence is available on the dwelling houses of the common people in Baghdad; but the reports of Herzfeld and Creswell on Samarran houses, and more recent ones on the houses of Sīrāf by David Whitehouse, throw some light on the houses of the 9th century AD. Samarran art, a departure from the Hellenistic influence of Persia, was a development of a new phenomenon in the history of Muslim art and architecture which extended its influence to places such as Egypt, Nīshāpūr and Baḥrayn.[47]

The dwelling houses at Samarra and other places were built on a definite plan. From Yaʿqūbī, it would seem that before the reign of Wāthiq (227–32) people considered Samarra a camp town and "built their houses temporary and unstable. But when they realized that Surra-man-ra' was to be a regular town they improved their style of building and made it strong and good."[48] These houses were often very large, sometimes containing fifty rooms, and were all built to a similar plan.[49] A covered passage led from the street or the lane into a rectangular court of proportions 2:3, which was surrounded by small living rooms and offices, and with a T-shaped main room and two corner rooms on the narrower side. This grouping of rooms was occasionally repeated in a second court, which most probably represented the *serai* and the *harim*, but when repeated on opposite sides of the same court it indicated summer and winter dwellings. The rest of the court was surrounded by rectangular dwellings and store-rooms. In most houses a number of small side courts with store-rooms were to be found. Some houses had open pillared halls and underground living rooms (*sīrdāb*)[50] with ventilating arrangements. All the houses had baths and drainage; a few had wells.[51]

Almost all big houses in Baghdad and other places had

---

[47] *EI*², s.v. *Architecture* (Creswell)

[48] Yaʿqūbī, *Buldān*, p. 265. At the time of the construction of Samarra, the workers were temporarily sheltered in tents (cf. Ṭabarī, iii, p. 1180; Azdī, *Ta'rīkh al-Mawṣil*, p. 422).

[49] Yaʿqūbī, *Buldān*, p. 263; cf. also Ernest Kühnel, *Islamic Art and Architecture*, p. 54; *Excavations at Samarra*, i, 13f.

[50] On *Sirdāb* see below in this chapter, p. 184

[51] Creswell, *Early Muslim Architecture*, ii, pp. 282–83, quoting from Herzfeld; see also E. Kühnel, *Islamic Art*, pp. 54–55; *EI*¹, s.v. *Samarra*; *Excavations at Samarra*, i, p. 9ff.

gardens.[52] The roofs, generally flat and mostly made of timber,[53] were used to sleep on in summer nights.[54] In some regions, however, such as Āmūl in the north, roofs were made sloping, to shed the frequent rain.[55] The doors nearly always had horizonal lintels, only rarely pointed arches. Windows were filled with great protruding discs of coloured glass, usually of 20 to 50 cm. in diameter.[56]

The houses of Baghdad had projections and bay-windows on the ground floor, opening onto the street, which were a potential source of danger for heedless donkey-riders.[57] In the narrow streets of Shīrāz, where two animals could not pass side by side, people were often colliding with these projections.[58] It was one of the duties of the *muḥtasib* in the mediaeval period to look after the problems of streets and highways. On the basis of the mediaeval *ḥisba* text, Scanlon observes that newer cities and those undergoing reconstruction generally opted for at least two wide cross-streets, between 15 and 30 feet wide. Such highways were related to the arrangement of city walls, to Friday mosques, to military needs, or were moves towards sounder administrative organization, particularly in capital cities. Otherwise the beast of burden or the ridden animal was the gauge of width. The *muḥtasib* could fine merchants for not keeping the streets fronting their shops well-watered and free of dust, or could hold them responsible for repairing and heightening the streets when ordered to do so.[59]

The excavation reports at Sīrāf show a similar pattern of dwelling houses. For example, the houses excavated in 1967

---

[52] *Murūj*, viii, p. 269; *Aghānī*², xiv, p. 20; *Quṭub al-Surūr*, 64

[53] *Nishwār*, viii, p. 31; cf. also Bowen, *ʿAlī b. ʿĪsā*, p. 22 quoting from Herzfeld

[54] Khaṭīb, *Ta'rīkh*, ii, 148; iv, 72; *Muntaẓam*, vi, 139, 156, ix, 157; *Irshād*, vi, 271; *EI*², s.v. *Baghdād*; Mez, p. 381

[55] Iṣṭakhrī, p. 211; cf. also, Mez, p. 381

[56] Creswell, *Early Muslim Architecture*, ii, p. 283

[57] *Yatīma*, ii, 253; *Jamh. al-Islām*, Leiden, fol. 77a, cited by Mez, p. 385, n. 6

[58] Muq. p. 429; cf. also Mez, p. 385

[59] G. T. Scanlon, *Housing and Sanitation: Some Aspects of Medieval Public Service*, in *The Islamic City* (Papers on Islamic History, 1), ed. A. H. Hourani and S. M. Stern, Oxford, 1970, p. 183f., quoting mainly from Ibn al-Ukhuwwa's *Maʿalim al-Qurba*. Cf. also Serjeant, "A Zaidī manual of *ḥisba* of the 3rd century AH" in *RSO*, 28 (1953), pp. 18, 28–29

and 1968 were rectangular, approximately 27 m. long and 18 m. wide. The ground floor had a symmetrical plan with a courtyard 12·7 m. long and 9·5 m. across, surrounded by rooms on all four sides, up to fourteen in number. On the north side of the house there was a narrow yard with a well at the east and a group of structures to the west. The main entrance of the house was in the north wall. Another house at Siraf having a symmetrical plan and a courtyard had eight ground-floor rooms on three sides only. Like other houses it had both front and rear entrances; it had a well near the centre of the west side.[60]

The flat-roofed houses of Baghdad, Samarra, Sīrāf and other places were protected against storm and rain by a series of drains of earthenware pipes which carried rainwater into stone-lined pits at the foot of the outer walls.[61] Wherever possible, the pits were dug in the alleys, rarely in the main street. In later Abbasid periods people seem to have been more careless, and dug pits in the streets, causing considerable inconvenience to the passers-by. Imām Ghazālī is said to have issued a *fatwa* prohibiting the digging of pits and drains in the street, especially where the road was narrow.[62] There were some types of soak-aways with corbelled tops, which absorbed the water.[63]

In the middle of the third century, the Ḥīra style of architecture was adopted for larger buildings: frontages on three sides, with a door in the centre and in each of the two wings. The Caliph Mutawakkil built his palace with three huge gates "through which a rider could pass with lance in hand."[64] According to Mas'ūdī, this style found general favour.[65]

[60] David Whitehouse, *Excavations at Siraf, Iran*, vii (1969), p. 51f.; viii (1970), p. 9ff.

[61] Ibid., viii (1970), p. 14; *Nishwār*, i, p. 38; Ṣābī, *Wuzarā'*, p. 84; Ibn al-Jawzī, *Ḥumaqā*, p. 53; Khaṭīb, *Ta'rīkh*, viii, 241

[62] *Iḥyā'*, ii, p. 334

[63] David Whitehouse, op. cit.

[64] Ya'qūbī, *Buldān*, p. 266; cf. also, Mez, p. 381

[65] *Murūj*, vii, p. 192f. According to Ya'qūbī (*Mushākalāt*, Eng. tr. in *JAOS*, 1964, p. 343) the Caliph Mutawakkil occasioned the building of "prisons and buildings with heavy doors" and the population imitated him, perhaps prompted by desire for security.

Upper Floors

As has been mentioned above, the houses of the wealthy people in Baghdad, Samarra and some other places usually consisted of two stories. The people of Sīrāf made their homes multi-storied, as has been attested by recent excavations.[66] At Fustat there were houses five, six, seven, and even eight storeys high, and Nāṣir Khusraw remarks, perhaps with exaggeration: "He who sees the town from a distance takes it for a mountain, for some houses are fourteen storeys high."[67]

The upper rooms of the house were called *ʿāliya* or *ghurfa*.[68] They were the most desirable part of the establishment, and were given to guests who were to be treated with honour. A scholar (died 182) who was on a short visit to Baghdad stayed in the *ghurfa* of a local savant. The students visited him there and studied *ḥadīth*.[69] It seems likely that the *ghurfa* were used as bedrooms, especially in summer. Those who had one-storey buildings slept on the roof.[70]

Dihlīz

An important feature of the houses of this period was the *dihlīz*.[71] This was a veranda or corridor which stretched from the gate of the house to its interior court. Special attention was paid to the ostentatious decoration of this *dihlīz*, as it was considered "the face of the house", "the alighting place of guests", and the "waiting room" for visitors.[72]

The men's quarters, consisting of one or more rooms, generally adjoined the *dihlīz* which led to the main gate.[73] The corridor could be spacious, and it was possible to build a study or guest room there. Ibrāhīm al-Ḥarbī (d. 285) is

---

[66] See, David Whitehouse, op. cit., *Iran*, 1968–72

[67] Iṣṭakhrī, p. 49; Ibn Ḥawqal, p. 96; Muq., p. 198; Nāṣir Khuṣraw, p. 50; cf. also, Mez, p. 412

[68] *Aghānī*[1], iii, p. 30; Khaṭīb, *Taʾrīkh*, viii, 214–15; vi, 222; Bayhaqī, *Maḥāsin*, p. 249

[69] Khaṭīb, *Taʾrīkh*, vi, p. 222

[70] Ṣābī, *Rusūm*, p. 40; *Muntaẓam*, vi, pp. 139, 156; *EI*[2], s.v. *Baghdād*; Mez, p. 381

[71] *Quṭub al-Surūr*, pp. 1, 164, 292; Ghazūlī, *Maṭāliʿ*, i, p. 35; Khaṭīb, *Taʾrīkh*, v, pp. 21, 281; xii, pp. 89–90; Ibn al-Jawzī, *Ḥumaqā*, p. 52

[72] *Maṭāliʿ*, i, p. 35; Khaṭīb, *Taʾrīkh*, v, p. 281; ix, p. 41; Ḥuṣrī, *Jamʿal-Jawāhir fī mulaḥ waʾl-nawādir*, p. 127

[73] Khaṭīb, *Taʾrīkh*, v, pp. 21, 281; xii, pp. 89–90

reported to have built a small apartment in the *dihlīz* of his house "to write and to study".[74] Teachers holding classes at their residence accommodated the students in the *dihlīz* if necessary.[75] Students often waited for their teachers in the corridor of the teacher's house.[76] A professional copyist of a teacher in 332 had his seat in the corridor.[77]

Doors

In our sources we often come across the phrase "*fajalasa alā bāb dārihī*" ("He sat at the door of his house"),[78] which suggests that people in this period frequently utilized the place adjacent to the doorways. It is evident from some reports that people sat "at the side of the door" on mats or carpets, or on raised platforms (*dukkān*) usually constructed just outside the doorway.[79] The *dukkān* was made, it would seem, mainly for sitting in hot summer evenings. People of sophisticated taste made their outdoor platforms ostentatious, with verses inscribed on the canopy in beautiful colours. Washshā' once found a secretary in Baghdad sitting in a hot summer evening on such a *dukkān*, made of teak-wood profusely decorated with verses written in lapis lazuli.[80]

The *dukkān* was also used as a classroom by the ulema and the teachers. A scholar (died 219) taught his three students there. The platform was small; therefore only two students sat with him, while the third student had his seat on the ground.[81]

People greeted their friends and seated them at the side of the door, probably on the carpets or mats generally used in the house. In a report we see that three savants used to sit in the evenings "at the door of a fellow savant".[82] The famous scholar Ibrāhīm al-Harbī (died 285) was also in the habit of sitting at his door, and his visitors had to sit there too.[83] A

[74] Ibid., vi, p. 32
[75] Ibid., xii, pp. 89–90
[76] Ibid., v, p. 281
[77] Ibid., v, p. 21
[78] Ibid., vi, pp. 29, 31; xii, 55, 354; *Quṭub al-Surūr*, p. 163
[79] Khaṭīb, *Ta'rīkh*, xii, p. 354; vi, p. 29; Ḥuṣrī, op. cit., p. 153
[80] *Muwashshā*, p. 268
[81] Khaṭīb, *Ta'rīkh*, xii, pp. 353–54
[82] Ibid., xii, p. 55
[83] Ibid., vi, p. 31

man is reported to have sat at his door simply to watch and enjoy the movements of the passers-by.[84]

Houses in Baghdad, especially those nearer to the Tigris, had balconies (*rawshan*).[85] People retired there to sit in comfort.

Decoration of houses

Under the Abbasids, stucco, because of its association with brick, was the principal form of decoration.[86] Samarra, the crucible in which Hellenic, Syro-Coptic and Indo-Persian arts were fused, produced an individual Abbasid style of decoration signifying no less than a complete ornamental revolution. The stucco ornament was used profusely in the interior decoration of the palaces and houses of Samarra.[87] High carved panels and a decorative frieze always ornamented the public rooms and sometimes all the rooms in the house. The courtyards also were sometimes ornamented, but not the outer walls. Elaborate panels ran all round the rooms at a height of three feet with ornamental alcoves and niches of various shapes above. The door frames and the embrasures of windows were ornamented, the ceilings adorned with cornices and friezes. The material of the dado decoration was fairly pure gypsum with a slight admixture of earth, and the decoration was made in plaster finely designed and executed, sometimes set off with paintings.[88]

The designs were of various types: some were simple, with large veins somewhat coarse in workmanship, some others were finely chiselled without relief, and some others, accentuating the relief, treated the principal motif in round bosses.

---

[84] *Quṭub al-Surūr*, p. 163

[85] *Muntaẓam*, viii, pp. 117, 149; *Nishwār*, i, p. 39

[86] Ernest Kühnel, *Islamic Art and Architecture*, p. 54; Creswell, *Early Muslim Architecture*, ii, pp. 234f.; 258; cf. also *EI*[1], s.v. *Samarra* (H. Viollet); *EI*[2], s.v. *Architecture* (K. A. C. Creswell); see also D. Whitehouse, *Excavations at Siraf* (third interim report), in *Iran*, viii (1970), p. 14

[87] Abdul Aziz Hameed, *The Stucco ornaments of Samarra*, Ph.D. thesis, SOAS, 1962, p. 2ff.

[88] See for the Arabic sources, Azdī, *Ḥikāyāt*, p. 35ff.; Yaʿqūbī, *Buldān*, s.vv. *Baghdād* and *Sāmarrā*; for archaeological evidence, see Creswell, op. cit, ii, pp. 234–35; Herzfeld, *Samarra*, pp. 14, 73; Rogers, *Samarra*, in *The Islamic City*, p. 119ff.; *Excavations at Samarra* (1936–39), i, p. 9ff.

Some were carved out of the mass *in situ*, others were cast in a mould on a bed of matting and then fixed to the wall.[89]

The forms of the designs also varied. Some were very simple and severe, in fine lines without arabesques, a form regarded as the prototype at Samarra. But others, probably inspired by fauna and flora, were more elaborate and rich: conventionalized flowers occupied the centre of geometrical figures repeated again and again and connected by ribands; headings, intermittent or interwined, taking the shape of a vase, a lyre or a cornucopia.[90]

From a passage of Ṭabarī, it would seem that gold and silver were also sometimes applied in the decoration of the houses of the ostentatious and the wealthy.[91] The Caliph Mahdī, visiting a house of a wealthy man whose house was modestly built, became much impressed with his simplicity, and admonished his own family in the following words: "I did not expect his house to be built of materials other than gold and silver; but [you are so ostentatious that] whenever you get some money you build houses of teak and gold."[92]

Building materials

The building materials employed in the early Abbasid period were varied, ranging from rammed earth to sun-baked and kiln-burnt bricks, wood, rubble and stone. The use of these depended, it would seem, on the availability of the resources and, to a great extent, "on local traditions or foreign traditions brought by foreign builders".[93]

Bricks and wood formed the major part of the building materials. There were two types of bricks: kiln-burnt bricks (*ājurr*) and sun-baked bricks (*libn*). They were made in two sizes, each having specific dimensions and weight. Thus we hear that in the buildings of Baghdad the large-sized bricks were 1 cubit square and weighed 200 ratls, whereas the half

---

89 *EI*[1], s.v. *Sāmarrā*', quoting from Creswell and Herzfeld

90 Ibid., s.v. *Sāmarrā* (H. Viollet); see also, Creswell, *Early Muslim Architecture*, ii, p. 282f.

91 Ṭabarī, iii, p. 537; cf. also *Muwashshā*, p. 268

92 Ibid., iii, p. 537

93 cf. *EI*[2], s.v. *Binā*' (G. Marçais)

brick was of ½ cubit and weighed 100 ratls.[94] According to the Khaṭīb Baghdādī, a mud brick with a red inscription indicating its weight as 117 ratls was found in the demolished wall adjacent to Bāb al-Muḥawwal. It was weighed and found to be correct.[95] The bricks even bore the name of the contractor or the person for whom the bricks were being moulded.[96] Bricks were generally cemented with clay,[97] and where burnt brick was used, a lime mortar was employed.[98] Although burnt bricks were not so porous, when combined with quicklime (*ṣārūj*) their strength improved considerably. They were, therefore, mostly used in foundations, at the base of retaining walls, especially wherever good insulation was necessary, and in tunnel-vaults and domes.[99] Reeds (*qaṣab*) were set in as a bond between courses.[100] This method, as Creswell points out, was an ancient Babylonian practice which continued into Sassanian times.[101] Bricks, as a rule, were covered with plaster, but they might remain visible and add an element of colour, either pink of baked earth or that of some enamel applied to their edge.[102]

Wood, the best being teak (*sāj*), was frequently used in

---

[94] Ya'qūbī *Buldān*, p. 238; *EI*², s.v. *Binā*'; cf. also, Creswell, *Early Muslim Architecture*, ii, pp. 8–10, 363; Iraq Antiquity Department, *Excavations at Samarra (1936–39)*, i, p. 9. The kiln-baked bricks laid in gypsum used in the construction of the palace of Huwayṣilāt (perhaps the *Qasr al-Jiṣṣ* of the late third century; cf. Ibn Serapion, p. 127; also, A. A. Hameed, *The Stucco ornaments of Samarra*, Ph.D. thesis, SOAS, 1962, i, p. 26) at Samarra, were 25 × 25 × 7 centimetres; whereas the large kiln-baked bricks were flat and generally square of 36 × 36 cm. (cf. *Excavations at Samarra*, i, pp. 6–7; cf. also Pl. 5)

[95] Khaṭīb, *Ta'rīkh*, i, p. 72; Ṭabarī, iii, p. 322; cf. also, Yāqūt, *Buldān*, i, p. 483

[96] Cf., for example, Ja'farī bricks in Khaṭīb's *Ta'rīkh*, i, p. 72, and Yāqūt's *Buldān*, i, p. 683

[97] Ya'qūbī, *Buldān*, p. 238; cf. also, *EI*², s.v. *Binā*'

[98] Khaṭīb, p. 79; cf. also, J. Lassner, *The Topography of Baghdad in the early Middle Ages*, p. 238; also, *Excavations at Samarra*, i, p. 9

[99] R. J. Forbes, *Ancient Technology*, i, pp. 72–74, quoted by Lassner, op. cit., p. 238, n. 17. According to Ya'qūbī (p. 239) and Ibn Rusta (p. 108) the great arcades (*ṭāqāt*) of Baghdad were vaulted with *ājurr* (burnt brick) and *jiṣṣ* (gypsum).

[100] Yāqūt, *Buldān*, i, p. 681

[101] Creswell, op. cit., ii, pp. 22–23

[102] *EI*², s.v. *Binā*' (G. Marçais)

roofs, windows, and doors.[103] The people of Sīrāf, Ṭabaristan, and Bukhāra built their dwelling houses mostly of wood.[104] Sīrāf, situated on the Arabian Gulf, imported wood from East Africa,[105] whereas Ṭabaristan and Bukhāra had forests producing an abundant supply of wood.[106] Longitudinal beams were sometimes sunk in walls, whereas small beams formed ceilings and sometimes lintels.[107]

Apart from bricks and wood, stones (*ḥijāra*), clay (*ṭīn*), and gypsum (*jiṣṣ*) seem to have been in popular use in houses in the East, in such places as Iṣfahān, Jibāl, Ray, Nīshāpūr, Marv, and Mawṣil.[108] The use of mosaic (*fusayfisā'*) and marble (*marmar*) was limited to the wealthy houses.[109] In the Yemen the roofs and the walls were built of marble, and the houses were always full of light. Indeed, where pure marble was used for the roofing "the shadow of the flying birds was visible within."[110] Lime was used for whitewashing the interior of a house.[111] Sometimes slabs of limestone set in gypsum mortar constituted the wall of a building, while mud-bricks were hidden by thick coats of stucco.[112]

Tiles were also used as building materials. Damascus was the centre of an extensive mosaic and *qāshānī* tile industry. *Qāshānī*, a name derived from *Qāshān* in Media, was given to square or hexagonal glazed tiles, sometimes figured with conventional flowers and used in exterior and interior decoration of buildings. The predominant colours were indigo blue, turquoise blue, green, and less frequently red and yellow.[113] The glazed *qāshānī* tiles were of such high quality

---

103 Jāḥiẓ, *Bukhalā'*, p. 72; *Nishwār*, viii, p. 31; Ḥamadānī, *Maqāmāt*, pp. 113, 122; *EI²*, s.v. *Binā'*; M. Jawād et al., *Baghdād*, p. 229; cf. also, Mez, p. 385

104 Ibn Ḥawqal, p. 271, 198, 335; cf. also David Whitehouse, *Excavations at Siraf*, in *Iran*, vi (1968), pp. 51–52

105 Iṣṭakhrī, p. 127; Ibn Ḥawqal, p. 127

106 Ibn Ḥawqal, p. 271

107 *EI²*, s.v. *Binā'* (G. Marçais); *Nishwār*, viii, p. 31

108 Ibn Ḥawqal, pp. 144, 262, 264, 268, 269, 324; *EI²*, s.v. *Binā'*. On *Jiṣṣ*, see, *EI²*, s.v. *Djiṣṣ*

109 Ḥamadānī, *Maqāmāt*, p. 122. For details on mosaic, see, *EI²*, s.v. *Fusayfisā'* (G. Marçais)

110 Hamadānī, p. 196; cf. also, Mez, p. 381

111 *Aghāni²*, x, p. 283

112 *EI²*, s.v. *Architecture* (K. A. C. Creswell)

113 Yaqūt, s.v. *Qashān*; Ibn Baṭūta, i, p. 415; ii, pp. 46, 130, 225, 297; iii, 79

that in 248 a consignment of them was dispatched from Baghdad to Qairawān for the decoration of its mosque, where the tiles can still be seen.[114]

Methods of cooling

Several devices were adopted by the Abbasids for making their homes cool in summer. The use of *khaysh*-canvas was a general practice of the Abbasids.[115] It was a device designed for refreshing the air, in the form of a "punka" which was kept wet; the evaporation produced a cool breeze.[116] A poet described the use of the *khaysh*-punka in the following verses.[117]

> "The *khaysh* was made wet inside the dome,
> Which called forth winter and removed the heat of summer;
> And the cord caused drops of water to fall
> From it on the ground as if pearls were being scattered.
> If the *khaysh* were set in hell,
> Its coolness would certainly overcome the burning heat of the fire."

As appears from these verses and also from the explanation of Sharīshī in his *Sharḥ al-Maqāmāt al-Ḥarīrī, khaysh* was a piece of thick linen hung (*ʿulliqa*) from the ceiling of the room in the form of a ship's sail; a cord was attached to put it into action. It was made wet with water, rose-water being also sprinkled from time to time for fragrance.[118] The fourth-century Muslim traveller Maqdisī notes a slightly different method of wetting *khaysh* at Shīrāz. He says: "I have seen the

---

[114] *EI*², s.v. *Architecture*; Dūrī, op. cit, p. 111

[115] Jāḥiẓ, *Bukhalā'*, pp. 90, 187; *Ḥayawān*, i, p. 14; *Rasā'il*, i, p. 398; Ṭabarī, iii, pp. 418, 536; *Diyārāt*, p. 133; *Nishwār*, i, pp. 174, 250, viii, p. 135; Miskāwayh, *Tahdhīb*, p. 51; Khaṭīb, *Ta'rīkh*, iii, p. 183; *Irshād*, vi, p. 99; Bayhaqī, *Maḥāsin*, p. 394; Ibn Rusta, *Aʿlāq*, p. 198; cf. also Mez, 380

[116] C. Pellat, *Livre des avares*, p. 316; cf. also Mez, 380

[117] Ibn al-Nadīm, *Quṭub al-Surūr*, p. 359

[118] *Sharḥ Maqāmāt al-Ḥarīrī*, ii, p. 318; Ghazūlī, *Maṭāliʿ*, ii, p. 65; see also a long note given by Ṭāhā Hājirī on *khaysh* in Jāḥiẓ's *Bukhalā'*, pp. 322–23; cf. also Pellat, *Le livre des avares*, pp. 316–17. From a poem recorded in Thaʿālibī's *Laṭā'if* (p. 182), it would seem that people fitted the *khaysh*-canvas on a framework and sold it in the markets as a ready-made dome of *khaysh* (*qubbat al-khaysh*).

buyūt al-khaysh where water flows constantly from pipes which surround the room."[119]

Sources declare Hajjāj b. Yūsuf to be the first man for whom the *khaysh* was suspended from the ceiling.[120] If Ṭabarī is correct, the use of *khaysh*-canvas for cooling houses was widespread in Baghdad right from the early Abbasid period.[121]

The Caliph Manṣūr is reported to have lined a dome-shaped pavilion with a cloth of coarse thick linen (*khaysh*), which was wetted constantly.[122]

A considerable amount of money was kept in the caliphal annual budget for the purchase and use of *khaysh* in the palace buildings.[123] The apartments in the caliphal palace provided with the *khaysh* punka were called *bayt mukhayyash*, where visitors could stay and take their siesta.[124]

In Jāḥiẓ's *Bukhalā'*, a miser is reported to have adopted an inexpensive method of cooling which, according to his claims, "served the purpose of the *khaysh*-canvas." He simply put sodden rugs on the floor and poured over the floor of the house water which he fetched from his own well. The hot wind entering the house touched the water on the floor and produced a cooling evaporation.[125]

Khaysh was used by the soldiers in their camps and garrisons.[126] At the beginning of the fourth century, a general considered the proceeds from a levy which he was allowed to collect in Baghdad inadequate for the sustenance of his army, as his men were accustomed, among other luxuries, to wet

---

[119] Muq. p. 449; *EI*², s.v. *Khaysh* (C. Pellat).

[120] Bayhaqī, *Maḥāsin*, p. 394; see also Pellat, *Avares*, p. 316

[121] Ṭabarī, iii, p. 418; cf. also, Tha'ālibī, *Laṭā'if*, p. 20

[122] Ibid., iii, p. 418; *Laṭā'if*, p. 20

[123] *Dhakhā'ir*, p. 219. At the marriage of the Caliph Ma'mūn with Būrān, when the supply of wood ran out, *khaysh*-canvas soaked in oil was used as fuel (*Nishwār*, i, p. 147).

[124] Khaṭīb, *Ta'rīkh*, iii, 183. The expression *bayt makhayyash* may mean a "summer room", the wall and ceiling of which were lined with *Khaysh* canvas which was constantly moistened. It may also mean, as suggested above, a large *Khaysh* punka hung from the ceiling to which a cord was attached to set it in motion. Wealthy people may have used rose water to sprinkle and moisten the *Khaysh* punka (cf. *EI*², s.v. *Khaysh*).

[125] Jāḥiẓ, *Bukhalā'*, p. 90

[126] Ibn al-Jawzī, *Muntaẓam*, v, pt. 2, p. 134

khaysh. [127] Ice and wet *khaysh*-felts were even taken in the pleasure boats on the Tigris, curtains of coloured gauze draping them.[128]

In addition to such means of avoiding heat in summer, wealthy people of Abbasid society had another method of bringing down the temperature of their rooms, a method which gave more comfort but entailed a large expense. Big slabs of ice were placed in the dome (*qubba*) of the central room of a house and fanned by porters; this considerably lowered the temperature of the house.[129] Sometimes *khaysh*-canvas was also used with this cooling process. It is reported that a man came to see the physician Jibra'īl b. Bakhtīshū' at the midday of a burning summer. To his surprise he found the physician sitting in the room wearing winter apparel. Within a few moments, the visitor showed signs of cold and began to shiver. Perceiving this, the physician offered him the warm clothes. On enquiry the physician revealed that he merely had some slabs of ice fanned by his slaves at the corner of the dome.[130] By this method one could cool other rooms as well without incurring any extra expense, for the proximity of the central room and the cold wind passing through the doors and windows made the adjoining rooms quite cool and comfortable.[131]

Following the methods of the Persian monarchs, the Abbasids also used double roofs, and had the roof of their summer houses plastered over with clay each day. The wet deposit easily absorbed the heat and kept the temperature down.[132]

The Caliph Manṣūr reportedly adopted this method for the first time in Abbasid history.[133] The idea of using ice-slabs is said to have come to the Abbasids from the Persians,

---

[127] De Goeje, *Carmatians*, p. 218, citing from Misk. Cf. also, Mez, pp. 380–81

[128] Bayhaqī, *Maḥāsin*, p. 447; cf. also *Jamhara* of Shayzarī, Leiden, fol. 199a quoted by Mez, p. 381

[129] Ibn Abī 'Uṣaybi'a, *'Uyūn al-Anbā'*, i, p. 139; cf. also Ṭabarī, pp. 418, 536; *Laṭā'if*, p. 19

[130] *'Uyūn al-Anbā'*, i, p. 139

[131] Ibid., i, p. 139

[132] Ṭabarī, iii, pp. 417–18; *Laṭā'if*, pp. 19–20

[133] Ibid., iii, p. 753; *Laṭā'if*, p. 20

who took their siesta in a room with double walls, the intervening space being filled with ice.[134]

Apart from the *bayt* or *qubbat al-khaysh* (house or dome of *khaysh*) and the using of ice-slabs, a *sirdāb* or *sardāb*, an underground apartment, was another means of combating the heat. The writers of the third and fourth centuries make references to the *sirdāb* as a summer-house for rich people, which is corroborated by the archaeological reports of Samarra and Baghdad.[135] In the later Abbasid period the use of the *sirdāb* was widespread in Baghdad, as is evident from the statement of Maqrīzī, who declares that "in summer the people of Egypt need not, like the people of Baghdad, go into underground dwellings."[136]

The idea of building a *sirdāb* for sheltering oneself from the intense heat of summer is said to have come from Central Asia.[137] Thereafter, neighbouring Muslim places such as Zereng, capital of Afghanistan, and the Persian town of Arrajan adopted this cooling method, and built *sirdābs* with running water for their summer dwellings.[138] The word *sirdāb*, however, suggests the device to be of Persian origin, from *sard*, cold, and *āb*, water: a place cooled with running water.[139] In course of time, the device spread to Baghdad and other Muslim lands. In the beginning the use of the *sirdāb* was limited: it was used extensively as a dungeon where prisoners, outlaws, and others were confined.[140]

---

[134] Ibid., iii, p. 418; *Laṭā'if*, p. 19; cf. also Mez, p. 380 In fact they used to have willow laths placed upright round the walls of the buildings, and large lumps of snow would be placed in the interstices (cf. *Laṭā'if*, p. 19; English translation by C. E. Bosworth, p. 48).

[135] *Aghānī*², v, pp. 193–94; Ibn Ḥawqal, p. 299; *Excavations at Samarra*, Iraq Antiquity Department (1936–39), i, p. 11, Pl. 96. Creswell, *Early Muslim Architecture*, ii, pp. 82, 241–42, 282–83; M. Jawād et al., *Baghdād*, p. 229; *EI*², s.v. *Dār* (G. Marçais). This evidence refutes the statement of Mez when he says that "in the Mesopotamian literature of the fourth/tenth century we find no reference to summer underground dwellings" (cf. p. 380).

[136] *Khiṭaṭ*, i, p. 28, cited by Mez, p. 380

[137] Mez, p. 380, quoting from *JRAS*, 1898, p. 819

[138] Ibn Ḥawqal, p. 299; cf. also, Mez, p. 380

[139] Lane and Steingass, s.v. *sardāb*

[140] *Murūj*, vi, 200; see, for some other references of *sirdāb* being used as a hiding place or a prison, Arīb, p. 10; *Muntaẓam*, vi, p. 206; x, p. 20; cf. also Mez, p. 380, n. 1

In the days of Manṣūr, we hear of a man imprisoned in a *sirdāb*, "who could not distinguish the light of the day from the darkness of the night."[141]

The number of *sirdābs* in Baghdad, even in the fifth century, was not large, and those who could afford it built not more than one basement room for their use. The fifth-century Muslim traveller Nāṣir Khusraw found it peculiar that in Arrajan some houses had as many rooms below as above the earth.[142]

The depth of these underground dwellings varied from house to house. Usually the *sirdāb* was constructed at a depth of ten steps from the ground floor.[143] The Little *Sirdāb* of Muʿtaṣim's palace in Samarra was a cavity cut into the rock, 21 metres long and about 8 metres deep.[144] A staircase (*daraja*) running from the ground floor to the basement offered entrance.[145] The *sirdāb* of the celebrated singer Ibrāhīm al-Mawṣilī had also a water pool (*birkat mā'*), which originated from a place nearby and reached the garden of the house.[146] He used to drink there during the day and sleep there at night.[147] The entrance of the Little *Sirdāb* of Samarra palace formed a square room, on the walls of which was a frieze of double-humped camels walking, executed in painted stucco, with a circular fountain. The Great *Sirdāb* of this palace had also a circular hollow basin of 70 metres diameter, connected with a deep underground canal.[148]

Heating

Since the weather of Baghdad and the whole of Iraq was mostly dry and hot, there was very little need to heat homes except for a brief period in winter. The general method of heating rooms was to use braziers (*kānūn*) with a charcoal

---

[141] *Murūj*, vi, p. 200

[142] Nāṣir Khuṣraw, Text, ed. Schefer, p. 91 (trans. p. 250); cf. also Mez, p. 380

[143] Ḥarīrī, *Durrat al-Ghawās*, p. 29

[144] Creswell, *Early Muslim Architecture*, ii, p. 241

[145] *Aghānī*², v, pp. 193–94; cf. also M. Jawād et al., *Baghdād*, p. 229

[146] Ibid., v, pp. 193–94

[147] Ibid.

[148] Creswell, *Early Muslim Architecture*, ii, p. 241

fire.[149] Braziers were usually of stone and iron, but the caliphs and some wealthy people are mentioned in our sources as possessing braziers of gold and silver.[150] Since braziers were light in weight and portable, they were not fixed at a particular place to make a hearth. From a passage in Masʿūdī's *Murūj*, however, it would seem that the ***kānūn*** or brazier was, in some houses, fitted on two side posts, each in the form of a giraffe, the feet of which served as support and the two bent necks as a handle.[151] The bodies of the giraffes were covered with red brocade (*dībāj*).[152] Some people put their braziers at the side of the dome of the central room in the same fashion as ice-slabs were placed for cooling in summer.[153] This is evident from a story narrated by Ibn Abī ʿUṣaybiʿa in the *ʿUyūn al-Anbā*'. The person whom we have mentioned as visiting the physician Jibra'īl b. Bakhtīshūʿ in summer came to see him in winter and found him clad in a light summer costume. On enquiry he was shown the fire-place in the dome and the methods the servants were using to impel the warm draught to the farthest corner of the room.[154]

Water supply

The people of Baghdad, Samarra and other cities brought their drinking-water mainly from the rivers and canals. The river Tigris was the main source of water for Baghdad and Samarra, which was either brought in skins directly from the river on camels, mules and donkeys, or taken to the houses of the well-to-do by water-carriers. Water-carriers using donkeys or their own backs are mentioned in mediaeval Arabic literature as moving to and fro fulfilling the needs of houses, shops, ateliers, baths, mosques and public fountains.

There were several canals in Baghdad which "passed through the streets, side streets, and suburbs, flowing without

[149] *Murūj*, viii, p. 268; Jāḥiẓ, *Bukhalā*', p. 34; *Nishwār*, i, pp. 60, 257; Ṭabarī, iii, 584; *Quṭub al-Surūr*, p. 60; *Laṭā'if*, p. 182; *Fakhrī*, p. 259; *ʿUyūn al-Anbā*', i, p. 139; see, for some verses on *Kanūn*, *Nishwār*, i, p. 257

[150] *ʿUyūn al-Anbā*', i, 139–40; Ṣābī, *Rusūm*, 16; *Dhakhā'ir*, 183, 217

[151] *Murūj*, viii, 268; see also the note given by C. Barbier de Meynard, on p. 428 (of the *Murūj*, viii)

[152] Ibid., viii, p. 268

[153] *ʿUyūn al-Anbā*', i, p. 139

[154] Ibid., i, p. 139

any interruption in summer and winter."[155] Among them were four major canals leading to the general vicinity of Baghdad. They were Nahr ʿĪsā, Nahr al-Mālik, Nahr Sarsar and Nahr Sarāt,[156] which were used for boat traffic unloading foodstuffs from Egypt, Syria, Mosul and other distant lands.[157] There were various conduits constructed of burnt brick and quicklime in Baghdad which supplied drinking water to the city.[158] According to Khaṭīb they were all above ground except for the conduit of Ḥarbiyya, which connected underground with the canal of Dujayl.[159] The Caliph Manṣūr had conduits built of teak wood which extended from the Khurāsān Gate to his palace.[160]

To obtain water for domestic use, wells were also dug, preferably within the house premises.[161] In Samarra digging wells was not practicable, as the water level was very low, and the water in them was salty and disagreeable to the taste; moreover it was not abundant.[162]

The Abbasid caliphs had cisterns built in various parts of the empire, one of which, built in 172 by the orders of the Caliph Hārūn al-Rashīd at Ramla in Palestine, has been excavated and vividly described by Creswell. This Abbasid monument, locally known as *Biʾr al-ʿAniziya*, consisted of "a subterranean excavation, lined with strong retaining walls

---

[155] Khaṭīb, *Taʾrīkh*, i, p. 79; Yāqūt, *Buldān*, s.v. *Baghdād*, cf. also M. Jawād et al., *Baghdād*, p. 23, also p. 86f.

[156] Muq., p. 124; cf. also, J. Lassner, *The Topography of Baghdad*, p. 279 n. 2

[157] Yaʿqūbī, *Buldān*, pp. 250, 263; Iṣṭakhrī, 85; Ibn Ḥawqal, 165; Muq., p. 120

[158] Yaʿqūbī, p. 250; Mez, p. 413; M. Jawād et al., op. cit., p. 23; cf. also, Rogers, *Sāmarrā: a Study in Medieval Town-Planning* and G. T. Scanlon, *Housing and Sanitation: Some Aspects of Medieval Public Service*, in "The Islamic City" Oxford, 1970

[159] Khaṭīb, *Taʾrīkh*, i, pp. 113–14

[160] Khaṭīb, *Taʾrīkh*, i, p. 78

[161] Jāḥiẓ *Bukhalāʾ*, p. 90; Ibn al-Jawzī, *Ḥumaqā*, p. 64; M. Jawād et al., *Baghdād*, p. 23; cf. also, *Excavations at Siraf*, in *Iran*, ix (1971), p. 14. Within the domestic complex, distinction would be made between water for cleaning and cooking and that for drinking. The former would simply be put into a channel flowing into the *gabal*, bricked round and brought up to floor level; the latter into holes meticulously cut into the rock, smoothed, plastered and in some cases covered by vaulting (cf. Scanlon, op. cit., 192).

[162] Yaʿqūbī, *Buldān*, p. 263

and divided into six aisles by five arcades of four arches each, running from east to west and resting on cruciform piers".[163]

A staircase 1·02 metres wide starts in the north-east corner and runs down the north side to the bottom of the cistern. It rests on two segmental arches. Water was drawn by means of the staircase, and a series of holes averaging 55 cm. square, pierced in the vault of each bay, enabled twenty-four people at the same time to draw water by means of ropes and buckets.[164]

It was an act of great merit to supply water to travellers and to make some permanent arrangements by building aqueducts where necessary. Thus we hear that Hārūn's wife Zubayda had constructed an underground aqueduct in Makka which was later restored by the mother of the Caliph Mutawakkil.[165] Similarly, the wazir ʿAlī b. ʿĪsā purchased a great number of animals and endowed a sum of money for their upkeep. At the same time he had a large well dug which supplied sweet water.[166] He also caused another abundant spring to be opened up and its channels widened.[167]

In the East, water circulated in an old moat of a fortress. It was carried to the middle of the market by a stone dam whence it was distributed further by means of lead pipes. The expenses of such water-supply systems were realized from the income of neighbouring lands. Non-Muslims were generally made supervisors and administrators, and for their services were exempted from *Jizya*.[168]

Toilets

Almost every house had a toilet (*mustarāḥ*; *kanīf* in Kufan

[163] Creswell, *Early Muslim Architecture*, ii, pp. 161–62, 164

[164] Ibid., ii, p. 163

[165] Ṭabarī iii, p. 1440; cf. also Ibrāhīm al-Mashhadānī, *Mawārid al-miyāh fi'l-waṭan al-ʿArabī*, (*ʿAyn Zubayda*) in *Majalla al-Jāmiʿ al-Mustanṣiriyya*, i (1970), pp. 535–45

[166] Ṣābī, *Wuzarāʾ*, p. 286; cf. also, Mez, p. 414

[167] Bowen, *Life and Times of ʿAlī b. ʿĪsā*, p. 128

[168] Iṣṭakhrī, p. 216; Ibn Ḥawqal, p. 366; cf. also, Mez, 414. Perhaps it was one of the duties of the *muḥtasib* in the early Abbasid period (as it was in the Ayubid and Mamluk periods) to see that drinking water was available in those purlieus of the city lacking any public fountain, and that all fountains be working and the water therein potable (cf. Scanlon, op. cit., p. 183).

dialect, *ḥushsh* in Basran, *madhhab* in Syrian, *bayt al-khalā'* in Medinian and *mirḥāḍ* in the Yemeni dialect).[169] Although no specific information on the forms of toilets is available, it is known from the information scattered in different sources that there were two forms of latrines: "well-latrines" and "service latrines". For well-latrines, which would seem more common, pits were dug and slabs of stone were placed to sit on.[170] In this system when the privies were full and disagreeable, the well was filled in and put out of use.[171] According to Tanūkhī, well-to-do people had their privies reserved for their exclusive use and would not let anyone else enter them.[172]

The existence of a group of people known as *kannās, ḥashshāsh, kannāf* (privy cleaners) indicate that service latrines were also in use.[173] In this system, presumably the privy cleaner would come at regular intervals to collect the human excreta and transport it to some place outside the city. The existence of service-latrines is also attested by the fact that in Basra there was a group of people who had undertaken the contract of cleaning privies; they collected the human excreta and dried it in the sun to sell in the markets as fuel.[174]

A hemistich of a poem of Ibn Mu'tazz, saying that "a privy is either cleaned or filled in and closed down,"[175] supports our assumption that toilets, in the Abbasid period, existed in the two forms.

Though the poor people and especially those living in the countryside used bushes and barren lands as their privies, the wealthy people built their lavatories at lavish expense.[176] A merchant of Baghdad had his privy plastered on the top with gypsum and at the bottom with mortar; the roof was made

---

[169] *'Iqd*, vi, p. 394; see also p. 449

[170] Ibid., vi, p. 449; *Nishwār*, i, p. 18; Creswell, *Early Muslim Architecture*, i, 359. For the picture of a latrine stone, see ibid, i, p. 359

[171] *Nishwār*, i, p. 15

[172] Ibid., i, p. 15

[173] Tawḥīdī, *Imtā'*, ii, p. 54; *Aghānī*², i, p. 415; *'Iqd*, vi, pp. 449–50 Ibn 'Abdūn, *Thalāth Rasā'il*, p. 48

[174] *'Uyūn*, i, p. 221; Yāqūt, *Buldān*, s.v. *Baṣra*

[175] *Dīwān*, p. 341

[176] Ḥamadānī, *Maqāmāt*, pp. 122–23; *Aghānī*², v, p. 216; *Nishwār*, i, pp. 39, 54, 204; Azdī *Ḥikāyāt*, 7, 8, 12; *Quṭub al-Surūr*, 403

flat and the floor paved with marble. It had a door of which the slats were made alternately of teak and ivory.[177]

Toilets were built either at a corner of the house or at the extreme end of the garden,[178] so that cleaners could approach the latrine from outside the building without causing any disturbance to the inmates of the building. Ibrāhīm al-Mawṣilī once hid himself near the latrine of Ibrāhīm al-Mahdī and picked up the tune which Al-Mahdī was rehearsing there to sing in the caliphal assembly.[179]

Water was used to clean the private parts in latrines.[180]

Furniture

Mediaeval Muslim houses possessed very little large furniture such as tables, chairs, cupboards, bedsteads and the like. The Muslims were accustomed to squatting on the floor and depending for their comfort entirely on cushions and pillows without frames and supports; the only solid furniture were chests to hold clothes and household linen.[181] Recesses in the wall, often as large as cupboards and closed by wooden doors, held the household utensils. People anxious to display some luxury pieces or other treasures divided up a wall surface into ornamental niches, each containing a single object and sometimes even shaped to fit it.[182] The value of a room was assessed by the carpet on the floor, by the niches over a tiled dado in the wall, by the coffering or stalactite moulding in the ceiling.

During the early Abbasid period, a *dīwān*, a sofa extending

---

177 *Maqāmāt*, pp. 122–23

178 Ibid., pp. 122–23; *Aghānī*², v, p. 216

179 *Aghānī*², v, p. 216

180 *Nishwār*, i, p. 15. Fustat, a city of multi-storied buildings, had, according to the findings of Professor Scanlon, a complex system of privies. The buildings had flues constructed within the walls. All of these flues gave on to deeply cut canals in the *gabal*, which ran beneath walls, floors and courtyards; all covered, at times vaulted, running individually or *en système* to cess-pools which were cleaned from without the complex. These canals were constantly watered from within, and the cess-pools covered daily with sand (cf. *The Islamic City*, p. 188).

181 *Nishwār*, viii, pp. 190–91; Miskāwayh, i, p. 244; Ṣābī, *Wuzarā'*, p. 172; Mez, p. 384; cf. also, E. Kühnel, *Islamic Art*, pp. 1–2

182 Ṭabarī, iii, p. 536; E. Kühnel, *Islamic Arts*, pp. 1–2

along three sides of the room, was also to be seen in the houses of the wealthy.[183] A pictorial representation from the *Maqāmāt al-Ḥarīrī* shows the use of bedsteads not unlike those of our day.[184] It is, however, not clear when such bedsteads were introduced in Abbasid society. Chairs and tables for dining were common in the houses of the well-to-do,[185] the tables being of course very low to suit the need of people accustomed to sitting on floor cushions.

A great deal of attention was paid to the interior decoration of the house with carpets, cushions, mats, hangings, and curtains. The carpet industry was therefore developed to meet the ever-increasing need of the wealthy in various Muslim lands. Carpets, being a symbol of luxury as well as a practical necessity, were woven in almost all the important Muslim cities.[186] Since they were made for different social classes and to satisfy varying standards and requirements, they could be divided into three general groups; for court and caliphal use; for officials of high rank, wealthy merchants, and for export; for the simpler people in towns and villages and also for nomads. The variety, size and quality of the carpets determined the name: *bisāṭ* and *zūlliya* for large carpets; *ṭinfisa*, a knotted carpet; *zarbiya*, a striped, multi-coloured carpet; *namaṭ*, a sur-carpet; and so forth.[187]

Carpets of Armenia and Tabaristan are mentioned with great admiration by contemporary writers.[188] The caliphs' palaces were adorned mainly with Armenian carpets, which aroused general appreciation in the Islamic world and were cited repeatedly from Umayyad times as very precious objects.[189] The high regard was due to their characteristic

---

[183] *Aghānī*[1], iii, p. 145; Lane, s.v. *dīwān*; cf. also, Hitti, *History of the Arabs*, p. 335

[184] Arnold and Grohmann, *The Islamic Book*, A Scene from *Maqāma* 19, MS. dated 734/1334, in the National Library, Vienna.

[185] *Murūj*, p. 269; *Dhakhā'ir*, pp. 27, 179, 195, 261; Mez, p. 386

[186] See, for example, *EI*[1], *Suppl.* s.v. *Ḳālī* (R. Ettinghausen)

[187] W. H. Worrel, "On Certain Arabic terms for 'rug'", *Ars Islamica*, i (1934), pp. 219–22; ii (1935), pp. 65–68; cf. also, *EI*[1] (Suppl.) s.v. *Ḳālī*

[188] See, for example, *Aghānī*[2], v, pp. 428–29; vi, p. 181; Jāḥiẓ (?) *Tabaṣṣur bi'l Tijāra*, pp. 21, 34; *Murūj*, vi, pp. 234, 433; Ṭabarī, iii, pp. 536, 602; Azdī, *Ḥikāyāt*, p. 36; Muq. p. 374, 380; Ibn Ḥawqal, pp. 244, 246; Yaʿqūbī, p. 277

[189] *Aghānī*[2], vi, p. 181; *Murūj*, vi, pp. 234, 433; cf. also, *EI*[1] (Suppl.), s.v. *Ḳālī*

red colour, *qirmiz*, and to their fine wool.[190] The consort of Hārūn is said to have sat on an Armenian carpet, her women on Armenian cushions.[191] A vassal is said to have presented the Caliph Muqtadir with seven Armenian carpets.[192]

The Persian woollen carpets, especially those of Iṣfahān, matched the splendid Armenian carpets and were highly esteemed in this period.[193] The "Art carpets" (*al-busūṭ al-ṣanīʿa*) were sometimes woven with the technique of Susanjird, a technique much prized in this period.[194] *Aghānī* mentions in the hall of Faḍl b. Rabīʿ a large glistering Susanjird carpet of satin embroidered with gold.[195] The city of Āmūl in the province of Mazendaran was an important centre of carpet-weaving which started in the third century and continued for centuries together.[196] One of the famous varieties of carpet known as *qālīqalā* does not seem to have been in use in the third century. Thaʿālibī, however, mentions it as equal to Armenian carpets.[197]

Apart from the carpets of Persia, Tabaristan and Armenia, there were good carpets produced in Ḥīra and Nuʿmāniyya.[198] The Hīra carpets are described as having designs of elephants, horses, camels and birds; these were imitated in Nuʿmāniyya with the result that the local product itself came to be known as Ḥīra carpets.[199] Similarly the districts of Maysān and Dast Maysān were also celebrated for manufacturing good-quality carpets and curtains.[200] According to Jāḥiẓ, Wāsit too produced tapestry-woven carpets.[201]

---

[190] Jāḥiẓ (?) *Tabaṣṣur*, p. 31; Ibn Ḥawqal, p. 244; *Laṭā'if*, pp. 183, 236

[191] ʿArīb, p. 48; cf. also, Mez, p. 464

[192] Elias Nisib, p. 202 cited by Mez, p. 464

[193] Ibn Rusta, p. 153; Iṣṭakhrī, p. 153; cf. also, Mez, 464–5

[194] Azdī, *Ḥikāyāt*, p. 36; *Laṭā'if*, p. 111; Mez, p. 464

[195] *Aghānī*², v, p. 371

[196] *EI*¹ (Suppl), s.v. *Ḳālī*, cf. also Serjeant, *Islamic Textiles*, Index

[197] *Laṭā'if*, pp. 183, 236; *Thimār*, p. 538. The word *Kālī* is derived from Qaliqala, Erzerum, where large carpets were made, but on account of this long name, they were referred to by the short *nisba*: cf. Yāqūt, *Buldān*, iv, p. 20. Serjeant suggests that it was introduced into Abbasid society by the Buwayhids; cf. *Islamic Textiles*, Chap. vi, p. 97

[198] *EI*¹ (*Suppl.*), s.v. *Ḳālī*. Mez, p. 465; Serjeant, *Islamic Textiles*, Index. Cf. also, Dūrī, *Mesopotamia*, p. 106

[199] Ibn Rusta, p. 186; *Hira*, p. 83, quoted by Dūrī, *Mesopotamia*, p. 106

[200] Ibn al-Faqīh, p. 253; cf. also, Dūrī, op. cit., p. 106

[201] *Tabaṣṣur*, p. 346, quoted by Dūrī, op. cit.

Ibn Zubayr in his *Kitāb al-Dhakhā'ir wa'l-Tuḥaf* mentions the list of the articles left by the Caliph Hārūn al-Rashīd in the caliphal palace, an inventory which shows the extravagance and the splendour of the Abbasid court. The number of the carpets, curtains and cushions mentioned is as follows:[202]

1,000	Armenian carpets (*bisāṭ*)
500	carpets (*bisāṭ*) of Tabaristan manufacture
1,500	knotted carpets (*ṭinfisa*) of *khazz* (beaver skin)
1,000	carpets (*bisāṭ*) of Dārābjird manufacture[203]
300	Maysānī large carpets (*bisāṭ*)
100	sur-carpets (*namāṭ*) of *khazz*
4,000	curtains (*sutūr*) of unspecified material
1,000	curtains of *khazz* silk
300	curtains of brocade (*dībāj*)
5,000+ 1,000	cushions (*wisāda*)
5,000	pillows (*mikhadda*)
1,000	cushions (*wisāda*) of brocade
1,000	cushions of *khazz* silk
1,000	cushions of *khazz raqam* (perhaps with some inscriptions)
1,000	pillows (*mirfaqa*)

After carpets, mats were the common *farash* which was spread on the ground. They could be spread on the floor with or without the carpets; they were made of rush (*ḥalfa*), reeds, papyrus and palm-tree leaves.[204] The most reputed mat, which was commonly used in this period by the wealthy class, was that made in Abbādān, a small island at the mouth of the Shaṭṭ al-ʿArab.[205] Some of these Abbādānī mats were thin, neatly woven and very soft, and could be folded like cloth.[206] They were copied in Persia as well as in Egypt.[207]

202 *Dhakhā'ir*, pp. 214–17

203 Dārābjird was an important city noted for valuable kinds of costly robes, mats, carpets etc. (cf. Muq. 442–3).

204 Mez, p. 465; cf. also Ghanīma, in *Majalla Ghurfa al-Tijāra*, iv (1941), p. 580

205 Muq. p. 118; Azdi, *Ḥikāyāt*, p. 36; cf. also, Mez, p. 465

206 Azdī, op. cit., p. 36

207 Muq. pp. 442, 203; Mez, p. 465

Later on (probably in the fourth or fifth centuries) the reed-mats woven in Baghdad acquired wide popularity and became proverbial for their excellence.[208] Maysān, too, produced excellent mats.[209]

It will be perhaps of some interest to quote here a passage found in Abu'l-Qāsim of Baghdad, an author of the early fourth century, who satirizes the Isfahanis and boasts about the splendid furnishing of Baghdadi houses.

> "By Allah . . . nor do I see your houses with their public rooms furnished with carpets (*zulliya*) of the Maghrib, nor with Khurāsānī carpets (*ṭinfisa*), nor carpet-strips of Andalus (*nakhākh*) and Cordova, and Armenian carpets (*miṭraḥ*), and Rūmī (Byzantine) velvets (*qaṭīfa*), and Tustari cushions (*miqʿad*), nor Maghribi carpets (*anṭāʿ*), nor gold embroidered pillows (*makhādd mudhahhaba*) of Dabiq, nor square carpets (*ṭarrāhāt*) of Cyprus, nor Susanjird, nor Abūqalmūn, and cushions (*namāriq*)—a house full of which looks like ground covered with flowers.
>
> "Nor have you Sāmān or Abbadānī mats (*ḥuṣr*) which fold in two as cloth does, lovelier than carpets (*zurbiyya*), and softer than Sus *khazz* silk, of fine workmanship, perfect craftmanship (*qushayrī*) picked out (*mufaṣṣal*) with gold, and cushions (*dusūt*) of *mamzūj* mixed with Iraqi gold, and gold embroidered with pictures of elephant (*mufayyal*) and horse (*mukhayyal*), and carpets (*miṭraḥ*) stuffed with feathers of the Indian bullfinch and Tustar brocade embroidered (*muqaṣṣab*) with gold."[210]

The Abbasids, as a rule, did not sit at times of distress on the carpets; rather they sat, on sad occasions, on floors or under-carpets.[211] This practice, according to Thaʿālibī, goes back to the time of the Caliph Hārūn al-Rashīd. On the death of Ibrāhīm b. Ṣaliḥ b. ʿAlī, he went to Ibrāhīm's house for condolence and refused to sit down on any of the mattreses or cushions which were arranged on the under-carpet, but only supported himself by leaning on his sword. He ordered the mattresses and cushions to be taken away and took his seat directly on the under-carpet, commenting that "It is not

[208] Thaʿālibī, *Thimār*, p. 428

[209] Nuwayrī, p. 370; cf. also, Dūrī, *Mesopotamia*, p. 106

[210] Azdī, *Ḥikāyāt*, pp. 36–7; English translation by Serjeant, *Islamic Textiles*, Appendix, i, *Costume*, p. 76

[211] Thaʿālibī, *Laṭāʾif*, p. 21; Eng. Tr. by C. E. Bosworth, p. 50

seemly that anyone should sit down on mattresses and cushions in the house of a dear friend and relative on such a day of misfortune."[212]

The best type of curtain for hanging on the windows and the walls was produced at Wāsit.[213] Wāsiṭī curtains are mentioned by Khaṭīb among the furniture of Muqtadir's palace.[214] Maysān, Mawṣil and Amil also produced and exported excellent qualities of curtains.[215] Curtains were frequently embroidered and sometimes woven with gold thread.[216]

Ḥammām (Public baths)

One of the most conspicuous features of the social life of the period we are studying is the abundance of *ḥammāms*. The ritual use of the *ḥammām* in the purification of the believer, the fulfilment of the laws of hygiene, and the need for social recreation explain why it has always been considered one of the essential amenities of Muslim society. During the period of our study the *ḥammām* became a source of considerable revenue for the individuals or the authorities who established them,[217] which furthermore explains the very large and sometimes perhaps exaggerated number of baths mentioned in our sources.[218]

---

[212] *Laṭā'if*, p. 21; Eng. Tr. p. 50

[213] Muq. pp. 128–9

[214] Ibn al-Faqīh, p. 253; *Tabaṣṣur bi'l-Tijāra*, pp. 344, 347 (edited ʿAbd al-Wahhāb Hasanī, Cairo, 1354/1935, pp. 41–2). *Laṭā'if*, p. 183

[215] *Muwashshā*, p. 265; cf. also, Dūrī, *Mesopotamia*, p. 106, quoting from Khatīl, p. 52

[216] *Dhakhā'ir*, pp. 214–17; *Muwashshā*, p. 265

[217] It is said that Muslim b. Abī Bakra had a daily income of one thousand dirhams plus one *kurr* of wheat and barley (*ṭaʿām*) from his bath in Baṣra (cf. *Dhakhā'ir*, p. 222).

[218] Both Hilāl al-Ṣābī (d. 448) and Khaṭib al-Baghdādī (d. 463) tried to do a demographic study of Baghdad by enumerating the number of baths that existed in the third–fifth centuries AH. It is claimed that 60,000 baths existed during Muwaffaq's regency (AD 870–891); 27,000 under Muqtadir (AD 908–952); 5,000 under ʿAḍud al-Dawla (d. AD 983); 3,000 under Bahā' al-Dawla (AD 989–1012); 1,500 in the year 993; only 170 in AD 1029 and at the time of Ṣābī only a few more than 150. Cf. *Rusūm*, p. 21; *Nishwār*, i, p. 65; Khaṭīb, *Ta'rīkh*, i, pp. 117–19; *Manāqib Baghdad*, attr. to Ibn al-Jawzī, p. 24; *EI*², s.v. *Baghdād* (Dūrī); cf. also Begg, op. cit., s.v. Section, *Ḥammām*.

There were two types of baths: private baths[219] installed in the precincts of palaces or within large town houses, and public baths run commercially.[220]

The majority of the public baths served both men and women. It appears that on certain days or at certain times they were reserved for men, and at others for women.[221] To indicate the turn of women, most probably a curtain was stretched in front of the entrance hall.[222] When women were bathing the entire staff was replaced by women.[223] In addition, baths strictly reserved for women were not uncommon. References to *Ḥammām nisawī*,[224] *Abwāb ḥammāmāt al-nisā'*,[225] and *al-Ḥammāmāt al-nisawiyya al-milliya al-ʿāmma*[226] in the sources at our disposal are a clear proof of their existence.

The Bath and its Apartments

Bath houses generally consisted of a number of rooms with mosaic pavement and marble-lined inner walls, clustering round a large central chamber.[227] The rooms may, as in

---

The figures given for the reigns of Muwaffaq and Muqtadir would seem highly exaggerated, implying various complications in determining the population estimate of Baghdad. Yaʿqūbī (d. 897) (*Buldān*, 254), however, makes the number 10,000 not long after the foundation of Baghdad, which, compared to the figures of the Buwayhid period, comes to double and treble. The fact that all sources show a fall in the number of baths to be found in Baghdad over the years indicates that as time passed the relative affluence of Baghdad declined perceptibly. It is possible that in counting the baths of Baghdad, authors in the different periods, confused between the public and household baths, recorded the number sometimes taking account of both private and public baths together, and sometimes counting the public baths exclusively; hence this difference between the numbers of baths.

219 Ṣābī, *Rusūm*, p. 21; *Nishwār*, i, pp. 193, 195, 205; cf. also Creswell, *Early Muslim Architecture*, ii, p. 282

220 *Dhakhā'ir*, p. 222; Ḥamadānī, *Maqāmāt*, p. 171

221 *EI*², s.v. *Ḥammām* (J. Sourdel-Thomine)

222 Hitti (*History of the Arabs*, p. 338) notes this fact without quoting his source.

223 *EI*², s.v. *Ḥammām* (J. Sourdel-Thomine)

224 *Muntaẓam*, viii, p. 228; cf. also, Badrī, *ʿĀmma*, p. 180

225 Shayzarī, *Nihāyat al-Rutba*, p. 109

226 Ghazālī, *Iḥyā'*, ii, p. 334

227 Miskāwayh, *Tajārib*, i, p. 314; Jāḥiẓ, *Rasā'il*, i, p. 388–9; *ʿIqd*, iii, p. 492; *Murūj*, viii, pp. 4, 7–8; *EI*², s.v. *Ḥammām*

modern times, have had different names in different countries, but their functions remained the same everywhere. The first room was used for undressing and rest; the second was the first heated room or warm room, and the third was the second heated room, or tepidarium (*ḥarāra*).[228]

The first room was a cool chamber with stone benches covered with mattresses and carpets.[229] Here the owner sat behind his counter to receive the clients. Here, also, the clients put off their outer garments and hung them on pegs.[230] Then they were taken to the second room, the atmosphere of which was warmed by its proximity to the tepidarium.[231] In the second chamber the clients were given loin-cloths composed of towels knotted together (*mi'zar*). As soon as they became sufficiently accustomed to the heat and the humidity, they proceeded to the third room.[232] The tepidarium had a number of stone benches for the staff who attended the bathers, and was provided with numerous *maqṣūras* (cubicles, alcoves) furnished with earthenware pipes bringing supplies of hot and cold water, and also with stone basins which served as small swimming pools.[233] In the centre of this chamber there was a big swimming pool where the bathers completed their purification.[234]

After sweating abundantly, for which they sometimes used to drink hot water,[235] the clients entered the *maqṣūras* for the scouring of the skin. This was done by the clients themselves or by specially trained staff-members who washed them clean with soapy lather, rubbed them vigorously, removed their body-hair, shaved them, and if the customer wished, massaged them.[236] After this vigorous treatment of the body, the bathers

---

228 Shayzarī, *Nihāyat al-Rutba*, p. 86; Ibn al-Ukhuwwa, *Ma'ālim al-Qurba*, p. 154; cf. also *EI*², s.v. *Ḥammām*; David Whitehouse, *Excavations at Siraf, Iran*, x (1972), 78

229 Shayzarī, op. cit., p. 86; cf. also *EI*², s.v. *Ḥammām*

230 Dimashqī, *Tijāra*, p. 35; *Muwashshā*, 221; Badrī, *'Āmma*, p. 180

231 *EI*², s.v. *Ḥammām*

232 Ibid.

233 Ghazālī, *Iḥyā'*, ii, p. 334; *EI*², s.v. *Ḥammām*; cf. also Hitti, *History of the Arabs*, p. 338

234 *EI*², s.v. *Ḥammām*

235 *Muwashshā*, p. 222

236 Ghazāli, *Iḥyā'*, ii, p. 334; *Nishwār*, i, pp. 193–95; *EI*², s.v. *Ḥammām*.; *A Zaidi manual of ḥisba of the 3rd century AH, RSO*, 28(1953), p. 27

proceeded to the big swimming pool to complete their purification. After all these attentions there came a brief period of relaxation in little rest rooms generally disposed around a pool with a fountain, and provided with wooden benches covered with luxurious cushions.[237]

The tepidarium was built with thick walls with steam-proof linings of marble. Sometimes the lower portion of these walls was faced with bitumen, which looked like black polished marble, while their upper portion was plastered with white mortar.[238] Inscriptions and drawings of animals, plants and human faces formed simple decorative motifs.[239] To protect the floor against damage by the continual use of water, it was generally coated with bitumen brought from a well between Basra and Kufa. This oozed a fluid which was scooped up and, after congealing, could be used for plastering.[240] To carry off the water used by the bathers, the tepidarium was provided with several runnels. It had neither windows nor ventilation, so that heat and steam could be ensured. A conspicuous feature of the tepidarium was its thick cupola or dome, studded with small round apertures glazed with thick pieces of glass through which the light penetrated.[241]

The heat and the steam of the tepidarium were supplied from a furnace room next to it,[242] and separated from it by a thin partition pierced with numerous holes through which the steamy air passed, rising from cauldrons of boiling water or from a central jet of water in the middle of a basin. To maintain a balance, cold air was also supplied to the bath by a system of ventilation from the stove. Earthen pipes were embedded in the walls or beneath the floor for the supply of water.[243] The supply of water from outside to the *ḥammām* was obtained either from wells worked by a draught animal,

---

237 *EI*², s.v. *Ḥammām*

238 Ibn Jubayr, *Riḥla*, p. 228; cf. also, Creswell, op. cit, i, 276

239 *Murūj*, iii, p. 29; Ibn Sīna, *Ḥifẓ al-Ṣiḥa*, quoting from Ghazūlī, ii, p. 7; cf. also Mez, p. 387; M. Jawād et al., *Baghdād*, p. 183. To judge by those of the Umayyad baths, see Creswell, *Early Muslim Architecture*, i, pp. 253–84

240 Ibn Jubayr, *Riḥla*, p. 228; cf. also Mez, p. 387; Muq. p. 146

241 *Tajārib*, i, p. 314; *EI*², s.v. *Ḥammām*; D. Whitehouse, op. cit., p. 78

242 Ibn al-Jawzī, *Dhamm al-Hawā*, p. 474; Jāḥiẓ, *Rasā'il*, i, p. 388; *EI*², s.v.

243 *EI*², s.v. *Ḥammām*

or from canals through pipes.[244] The waste water of the *ḥammām* was carried off to nearby ditches dug especially for this purpose, and was never allowed to flow into the canals and rivers which supplied the drinking-water.[245]

Personnel

The number of regular employees of the bath varied generally from five to six. Ṣābī, quoting from a third-century writer Ibn Mihmandār, gives six names of bath attendants: the *qayyim* (*ra'īs al-ḥammām, ṣāḥib al-ḥammām*), the lessee of the bath, whose duty was to welcome the clients at the entrance and to receive payments at the exit; *ṣāḥib al-ṣundūq*, the superintendent of the changing or dressing room; *waqqād*, the stoker who was in charge of the supply of fuel for the furnace; *zabbāl*, the sweeper who was in charge of the cleaning; *muzayyin* (or *ḥallāq*), the hairdresser, who, in addition to his usual duties, removed the body-hair; and *ḥajjām*, the cupper or blood-letter.[246] Khaṭīb's account differs from that of Ṣābī both in the number of workers and in the designation of the employees. According to his account every bath had five workers: *ḥammāmī, qayyim, zabbāl, waqqād, saqqā'*.[247] In smaller towns we find even fewer attendants in the baths. For example, it is known from the *Maqāmāt* of Ḥamadānī that in Ḥulwān there were only three members of the staff of the bath.[248] The staff was generally assisted by a number of servants such as cubicle-stewards and the *dallāk* (masseur).[249]

Among the most important objects used by the bathers for cleanliness of the body were: *nūra*, a depilatory agent which, according to common belief, was an aphrodisiac;[250] *ṭīn Khurāsānī*, a kind of clay brought from Khurāsān and applied for cleaning hair, perfumed by the more fastidious with rosewater, essence of rose geranium, or orange-flower

---

[244] Dimashqī, *Tijāra*, p. 35; cf. also, *EI*², s.v. *Ḥammām*

[245] *Muntaẓam*, ix, p. 129

[246] Ṣābī, *Rusūm*, p. 19; Ibn Mihmandār, *Faḍā'il Baghdād*, p. 17; cf. also, *Nishwār*, i, p. 193; Jāḥiẓ, *Rasā'il*, i, pp. 388–89; *Bukhalā'*, p. 37; *EI*², s.v. *Ḥammām*; Mez, p. 387

[247] Khaṭīb, *Ta'rīkh*, i, p. 117

[248] *Maqamāt*, p. 171

[249] *EI*², s.v. *Ḥammām*

[250] Jāḥiẓ *Bukhalā'*, p. 37; Makkī, *Qūt al-Qulūb*, iv, p. 180; Serjeant, *A Zaidi manual of Ḥisba, RSO*, 28(1953), p. 27

water;[251] *miḥakka*, a curry-comb for scouring the legs;[252] *khirqa*, cloths used by the common people, and *mandīl* (towel) used by the men of elegant taste, for rubbing their bodies;[253] *khiṭmī*, marsh mallow, and leaves of lotus trees for washing the body.[254] The use of soap was not unknown,[255] though sieved *ushnān* (saltwort) was commonly used.[256]

Maintenance and Supervision of the Bath

In view of the importance of the *ḥammām* as a hygienic centre of social life, the government paid assiduous attention to its cleanliness and to the observance of the rules of hygiene by the staff as well as by the clients. One of the duties of the *muḥtasib*, for example, was to look after the *ḥammām*; to issue orders for sweeping and washing the *ḥammām* properly with clean water before closing it; to issue orders preventing the washing of utensils or clothes in the pool of the tepidarium; to keep an eye on the waste water so that it did not flow into the canal or the river to pollute the water. The owner of the bath (*qayyim*) also maintained the rules of hygiene, for he cleaned the tank of water at least once in a month; fumigated the *ḥammām* twice a day; soaked the curry-comb in saline water; and washed the loin-cloths every day.[257] The *muḥtasib* was also responsible for seeing that the bathers entered the *ḥammām* in proper dress. The bath-owner might not allow anybody in the bath without a *mi'zar* (loin-cloth).[258] The common people, it would seem, did not observe this restriction properly.[259] Maqdisī, writing in the last quarter of the 10th century AD, notes that he found the people of Shīrāz, Khūzistān, Fārs and the Maghrib infringing this regulation by entering the *ḥammām* without a *mi'zar*.[260]

---

[251] Ḥamadānī, *Maqāmāt*, p. 171; cf. also, *EI*², s.v. *Ḥammām*

[252] Saqaṭī, *Fī adab al-ḥisba*, p. 67

[253] *Muwashshā*, p. 221

[254] Shayzarī, *Nihāya*, p. 78

[255] Khaṭīb, *Ta'rīkh*, i, p. 118; Jāḥiẓ, *Bukhalā'*, p. 56; *Manāqib Baghdād*, p. 24; *Muntaẓam*, vi, p. 5

[256] *Muwashshā*, p. 221

[257] Ghazālī, *Iḥyā'*, ii, pp. 87, 334; Saqaṭī, *Fī Adab al-Ḥisba*, p. 67; Shayzarī, *Nihāya*, p. 68; cf. also, *EI*², s.v. *Ḥammām*

[258] *A Zaidi manual of ḥisba of the 3rd century AH, RSO*, 1953, p. 27

[259] *Muntaẓam*, vii, p. 222.; Bayhaqī, *Maḥāsin*, p. 584

[260] Muq. pp. 239, 416, 429, 440

The popularity of the *ḥammām* in this society was due to its manifold benefits. It was a place of ritual purification, of salutary effects, and of social recreation; and above all, it was a silent doctor. Its warm atmosphere producing abundant perspiration, and the hygienic care and caution taken by its staff helped to cure ailments such as coughs and colds, all kinds of fever, and especially various forms of rheumatism.[261]

Ḥammāms, which according to the local beliefs and superstitions were the favourite haunt of *jinn* during the night, remained open from dawn to sunset throughout the year.[262]

[261] Ibn Jazla, *Minhāj al-Bayān*, Br. Mus. Ms. No. 5934, fol, 78b; Shayzarī, *Nihāya*, p. 86

[262] Khaṭīb, *Ta'rīkh*, vi, p. 122; Ibn al-Jawzī, *Dhamm al-Hawā*, p. 474; Shayzarī, p. 87; Ghazālī, *Iḥyā'*, i, p. 144; Ibn al-Ukhuwwa, *Ma'ālim al-Qurba*, p. 155

Chapter 5

Hunting

Hunting literature; popularity of hunting

Hunting was a favourite pastime of Abbasid society. It was a recreation, a physical exercise, a source of income and food, and above all, a well-accomplished art. Summarizing the benefits of the hunt, the author of *Al-Fakhrī* notes that the highest objective of hunting is the exercise of troops in charge and in defence, in aggression and in retreat; training them to chivalry (*furūsiyya*) and in shooting with the bow and arrow, fighting with the sword and the mace; it also accustoms the huntsmen to killing and to bloodshed; provides excellent opportunity for physical exercise which promotes digestion and keeps the constitution in health.[1] Hunting trips were, therefore, utilized at this period to give military training to the soldiers. The enthusiasm of the early Abbasids in hunting, chiefly with the help of animals, made it a special subject of study. Treatises written during this period and even afterwards on the art of hunting, some of which have survived and many have been lost,[2] present a graphic and interesting

[1] *Fakhrī*, p. 75. A more or less similar statement can be seen in *al-Bayzara* (attributed to Abū ʿAbd Allāh al-Ḥasan) pp. 18, 21, 24

[2] Presumably the first treatise written on this subject was that of the famous philologist Abū ʿUbayda Maʿmar b. al-Muthanna (114–210). Ibn Nadīm attributes two books to him viz: *Kitāb al-Bāz* (Book on Hawks) and *Kitāb al-Ḥamām* (Book on Pigeons) (cf. *Fihrist*, p. 80). During Hārūn al-Rashīd's reign a certain expert huntsman called Ibrāhīm al-Baṣrī wrote a book on hunting called *al-Bayzara*. According to Mangalī it dealt more with tonics and medicinal properties of birds and beasts of prey than with the hunting art (cf. Mangalī, *Uns al-Malā'*, p. 81). Similarly Aṣmaʿī compiled a book called *Kitāb al-Wuḥūsh* (Book of Wild Animals); Abū Ḥātim al-Sijistānī (d. 255) wrote books on beasts, birds, entomology, and

picture of their skill, especially in the art of training birds and beasts of prey and protecting their lives from ailments. These treatises also throw sufficient light on zoological information and on legal and religious questions arising from this pastime.

Hunting in one form or another was practised by the Arabs even in the pre-Islamic period. To the pagan Arabs it was more a training in the art of fighting and a source of food than a recreation.[3] During the early age of Islam large-scale

---

hunting-weapons (cf. *Fihrist*, pp. 82, 87). Several other books written during the third and fourth centuries, relating to hunting, trapping and falconry, are *Kitāb al-Ṣayd* by Khālidiyyān (d. late fourth century); *Kitāb al-Maṣāyid* by Ṭabīb'Īsā al-Raqqī, one of the physicians of Ṣaif al-Dawla (ruler at Aleppo, AD 944–67); *Kitāb al-Jawāriḥ* by Muḥammad b. ʻAbdallāh b. ʻUmar al-Bazyār (d. late third century); *Kitāb al-Jawāriḥ wa'lla'b bihā* (also called *Kitāb al-Buzāt wa'l-ṣayd*); *Kitāb al-Silāḥ* by Abū Dalaf al-Qāsim b. ʻĪsā (226 or 227); *Kitāb al-Jawāriḥ wa'l-ṣayd* by Ibn al-Muʻtazz (d. 296); *Kitāb al-Ṣayd wa'l-Jāriḥ* by Fatḥ b. Khāqān (d. 247 or 248); *Kitāb al-Ṭard* by Aḥmad b. Abī Ṭāhir (d. 280); *Kitāb al-Ṣayd* by Muḥammad b. Masʻūd al-ʻAyyāshī (probably 4th century); *Kitāb al-Ṣayd wa'l-dhabā'iḥ*, by Abū Yūsuf (d. 182); *Kitāb al-Ṣayd wa'l-dhabā'iḥ*, by Qāḍī Muḥammad b. Ḥasan (d. 189); *Kitāb al-Ṣayd* by Shāfiʻī (d. 204); *Kitāb al-Ṣayd* by Dāwūd b. ʻAlī (d. 270); *Kitāb al-Jawāriḥ wa'l-Ṣayd bihā* by Aḥmad b. Muḥammad al-Sarakhsī (d. during the reign of Muʻtaḍid) etc.; cf. *Fihrist*, pp. 222, 438; 169, 170, 210, 276, 286, 288, 296, 304, 366–67. Jāḥiẓ is also said to have written a treatise on hunting, entitled *Kitāb al-Jawāriḥ* (cf. Ch. Pellat, *The Life and works of Jāḥiẓ*, Eng. Tr., p. 10). Ḥājī Khalīfa and Brockelmann have mentioned some more books written on the art of falconry and chase. These compilations do not seem to have survived. The earliest available book so far known is *al-Maṣāyid wa'l-Maṭārid*, by the encyclopaedic writer Kushājim (d. after 358). This book has fortunately been edited and published by an Aleppan scholar, Asʻad Ṭalas, in 1954. A year before, the Syrian scholar Kurd ʻAli published a treatise called *al-Bayzara*, by an anonymous author, devoted to the falconry of the Fatimid Caliph ʻAzīz Billāh (975–96), Damascus, 1953. The book was written, according to its editor, thirty years after Kushājim's *Masāyid wa'l-Maṭārid*, and gives us a vivid description of the art of hunting. The book has been translated into French (Leiden, 1967) by François Viré. Similarly the hawking-sport memoirs of Usāma b. Munqidh (d. AD 1188) contained in his autobiography, *Kitāb al-Iʻtibār*, the work of the Mamluk author Mangalī, *Kitāb Uns al-Malā' bi waḥsh al-Falā'* (Paris, 1880) and the *Kitāb al-Manṣūrī fi'l-Bayzara* (published in *Mashriq*, 1968), and an unpublished manuscript of Kushājim named *Al-Bayzara*, and several other *ṭardiyāt* poems throw much light on the art of chase and hunting during the middle ages.

[3] Cf. the pre-Islamic poetry, especially the poems of Imru' al-Qays in the *Sabʻ al-muʻallaqāt*; cf. also Mercier, *Chasse*, p. 13ff.

hunting was not practised. It was the Umayyad Caliph Yazīd I who appeared to be the first to operate large-scale hunting. He spent much money on the maintenance of birds and beasts of prey.[4]

The Abbasid caliphs in general seem to have been very fond of hunting, which was one of their favourite amusements. What made them conspicuous in this field was their skilful use of trained birds and beasts in their hunts. The influx of wealth, the intimate connections with the Persians and their non-expansionist policy perhaps explain the ever-increasing enthusiasm of the Abbasid caliphs for such costly and complicated sports.

The Caliph Mahdī used to take a special interest in going out on regular hunting trips in company with his close friends, his horsemen armed with swords, and followed by a regiment of soldiers and pages.[5] His keen interest in hunting is reported to have cost him his life.[6] The Caliph Amīn, like the Umayyad Yazīd I, was excessively given to pleasure and hunting.[7] He spent lavish sums of money to purchase bear-skins, beasts and birds for the hunt, and the best animals for the royal zoo.[8] He was particularly fond of hunting lions,[9] and a brother of his is said to have met his death pursuing wild boars.[10] The Caliph Muʿtaṣim was so interested in hunting that he is said to have built a special horseshoe-shaped wall along the Tigris and used his men to drive the game inside, thus shutting it in between the wall and the river.[11] Like Muʿtaṣim, the Caliph Muʿtaḍid was very fond of this pastime. It was his practice to engage in a hunting expedition at the conclusion and the beginning of each

[4] *Murūj*, v. p. 156; *Fakhrī*, p. 76

[5] *Murūj*, vi, pp. 227–28; *Fakhrī*, pp. 243–44; *Bayzara* (attr. to Abū ʿAbdallāh al-Ḥasān), p. 43

[6] *Fakhrī*, pp. 245–46

[7] *Murūj*, vi, 431–32; *Maṣāyid*, p. 5; *Bayzara*, p. 46; Mangalī, 69

[8] Ṭabarī, iii, p. 951; cf. also *EI*², s.v. *Bayzara* (F. Viré)

[9] *Murūj*, vi, pp. 432–33. Most of the *ṭardiyāt* (cynegetic) poems of Abū Nuwās are said to have been composed relating to Amīn's hunting pastime (cf. *Maṣāyid*, 5; *Bayzara*, 46).

[10] *Aghānī*², x, p. 190

[11] *Fakhrī*, pp. 73–74; Ibn al-Kāzrūnī, *Ta'rīkh*, p. 139; *Nishwār*, viii, p. 28f.; *Maṣāyid*, p. 5; *Bayzara*, p. 46

military campaign.[12] In lion-hunting he was such an expert that, in the words of Kushājim, "he seldom came back leaving behind lions that were not dead."[13] Likewise the Caliph Mustakfī was so keenly interested in hunting with cheetah and falcons that he would personally take care of the beasts and birds.[14]

It appears that, because of the interest in hunting, the early Abbasid caliphs established a special zoo (*ḥayr al-wuḥūsh*) attached to the royal palace.[15] It was here that they brought and preserved every kind of animal known to them.

Hunting-animals exchanged as gifts

The Caliphs, wazirs and wealthy people who were fond of hunting delighted in exchanging gifts of falcons, hawks, cheetah and dogs.[16] The Abbasid caliphs often received such gifts both from their wazirs and governors and from monarchs of friendly countries. According to Ṭabarī, in the year 190 AH Hārūn al-Rashīd received a set of presents from the Byzantine king among which were included twelve falcons and four hunting dogs.[17] The Queen of Ifranj, Bertha, is said to have sent, among other magnificent presents, ten big dogs of unequalled species, seven falcons and seven saker falcons to the Caliph Mustakfī in 293.[18]

Ibn Zubayr in his book *Treasures and Gifts* records a number of instances when the Caliph Muʿtaḍid received, among various things, gifts of falcons and cheetah from ʿAmr

---

[12] *Maṣāyid*, pp. 5–6; *Bayzara*, 46; *Muntaẓam*, v, pt. 2, pp. 123, 129

[13] Ibid, *Masāyid*, p. 6; see also, *Bayzara*, p. 46. For a story of a duel fought by this Caliph with a lion, see *Muntaẓam*, v, pt. 2, p. 129

[14] *Maṣāyid*, p. 7; *Bayzara*, p. 48

[15] Jāḥiẓ, *Ḥayawān*, iv, p. 422; Ṣābī, *Rusūm*, p. 7; *Muntaẓam*, v, pt. 2, p. 144; Creswell (*Early Muslim Architecture*, ii, pp. 241, 292) calls it "game preserve". On game reserves of Samarra, see Rogers, *Samarra* in "The Islamic City", ed. by Hourani and Stern, Oxford, 1970, p. 151f. It is in this zoological garden that the Byzantine embassy was brought, during the reign of the Caliph Muqtadir, and shown herds of wild animals, lions, elephants (cf. *Rusūm*, p. 11f; Khaṭīb, i, p. 103).

[16] *Al-Maḥāsin wa'l-Aḍdād*, p. 197; *Dhakhā'ir*, p. 39f; Khālidiyyān, *Tuḥaf*, p. 14

[17] Ṭabarī, iii, pp. 710–11

[18] *Dhakhā'ir*, p. 49

b. al-Layth al-Ṣaffār. In 281, ʿAmr presented to the Caliph fifteen falcons; in 282, thirty; in 283, twenty; in 286, a large number.[19] In 280, this Caliph is also reported to have received eleven falcons and three cheetahs from the Samanid ruler Ismāʿīl b. Aḥmad.[20] In 298, Ismaʿīl again sent 50 falcons and 100,000 furs of sable (*sammūr*), foxes and marten (*fanak*) to the Abbasid court.[21] The enthusiasm of the Abbasid caliphs for hunting with predatory animals is also reflected in their demand that the *kharāj* be paid partly in the form of hunting animals. For example, the Caliph Hārūn received thirty falcons from Armenia, ten falcons and twenty dogs from Babr and Taylasan per annum.[22]

Social classes engaged in hunting

The literature on the subject shows that the art of hunting was in essence practised by two distinct social groups.[23] On the one hand the caliphs and their court dignitaries indulged in hunting as a lively pastime. They spent large sums of money and conducted elaborate hunting expeditions for pleasure almost throughout the year.[24] On the other hand, the poorest social classes took to hunting as a vocation. These professionals looked upon hunting as a means of earning their livelihood.[25] The methods and technique they used depended upon their meagre resources. Interestingly, we find very little evidence in the literature about the practice of hunting by the common people. It seems that both city and country dwellers of ordinary means did not engage in hunting regularly. This conclusion of course may be erroneous, as the existing social literature does not usually concern itself with describing the customs and the culture of the common people. Hence it is difficult to speak authoritatively on the extent to

[19] Ibid., pp. 40, 41, 43

[20] Ibid., p. 42

[21] Ibid., p. 59

[22] Jahshiyārī, *Wuzarā'*, p. 286; cf. also Saleḥ A. ʿAli, *JEHSO*, 14 (1971), p. 309

[23] *Maṣāyid*, pp. 15–16; *Bayzara*, pp. 19–20

[24] Ṣābī, *Wuzarā'*, p. 24; *Diyārāt*, p. 164; *Nishwār*, viii, 28; *Murūj*, vi, 227–229; *Maṣāyid*, p. 3ff.; *Bayzara*, 41f.; *EI*², s.vv. *Bayzara* & *Fahd* (F. Viré); cf also, Serjeant, *South Arabian Hunt*, pp. 13, 23–5

[25] *Bayzara*, p. 19; Jāḥiẓ, *Ḥayawān*, v. pp. 439–40

which the commoners engaged in hunting as a profession or as a temporary or seasonal vocation. The evidence about the expense involved in the undertaking of hunting expeditions would, however, point to the conclusion that it made hunting prohibitive for the ordinary people. On the other hand it is likely that the small farmers and the beduins may have engaged in hunting as a temporary means of sustenance, especially during periods of famine, drought, and agricultural inactivity.

Beasts and birds employed in hunting

It is worth mentioning here that a reader of works on *al-Maṣāyid wa'l-Maṭārid* written during the mediaeval period frequently comes across the terms *al-ḍawārī* and *al-jawāriḥ* to indicate beasts and birds of prey respectively. Lexicographers do not appear to make any distinction between the two, and modern writers on hunting confusingly use them interchangeably. But a study of Arabic sources makes it clear that *al-ḍawārī* was used particularly to denote the beasts trained to the chase, while *al-jawāriḥ* was used to mean only the birds trained to hunt.[26]

Among beasts employed in hunting were hounds, horses, ferrets, wolves, panthers, weasels, lynx-caracal, jungle cats, tiger cats and the like. But the most prized and desired animal trained to the chase was *fahd*, or cheetah.

Cheetah

The cheetah, the most somnolent animal on earth, is the swiftest of all quadrupeds, attaining a speed of about seventy miles an hour over a distance of five or six hundred yards.[27] Modern mammalogists, in fact, "recognize it as a greyhound with the fur of a big cat from the form of the cranium, teeth like those of the canidae, non-retractile claws, its habit of running in strides, each step being a leap of five to six yards, and its peaceful nature; the cheetah does not experience the blind atavistic ferocity shown by the big felines at the sight of

---

[26] *Maṣāyid*, pp. 7, 18, 21, 61, 49ff.; *Bayzara*, pp. 18, 29, 48ff.; cf. also Anonymous, *Al-Manṣūrī fi'l-Bayzara* in *Mashriq*, 1968

[27] Kushājim, *Al-Bayzara*, SOAS. Ms. no. 2091, fol. 10; cf. also *EI*², s.v. *Fahd* (F. Viré)

blood." This beautiful animal, found mostly in Iraq, Syria, Persia and India, was almost unknown to contemporary Europe and was surprisingly not used by the Muslims in the Maghrib and Spain. It was at the time of the Crusades in the 14th century AD that the cheetah was introduced to the courts of Sicily and Italy, and subsequently from there to the courts of France, Germany and England.[28]

The methods of snaring and trapping a cheetah and giving it proper training for the chase, and the techniques of its hunting have been vividly narrated by Arab writers such as Kushājim and Mangalī.[29] The information contained in these treatises has been analysed and paraphrased by F. Viré in his article *Fahd* in the new Encyclopaedia of Islam, and also by Mercier in his book on chase and sports. Therefore there is hardly any need to repeat them here. When a cheetah was caught by the trailers by the *kadd* and *itʿāb* (tease and fatigue) method,[30] it was carried home with extreme caution and care, where it was subjected to vigorous and sometimes painful training to become efficient at the chase. Through a gradual process of taming it became accustomed to take food in front of people, to jump on the pillion and ride on horses without any fright or hesitation. It was also given some "bagged quarry", preferably in the jungle, and the quarry was slaughtered under its feet to enable the cheetah to lap the blood, to bring out hunting instincts quickly.[31]

When the cheetah-master (*fahhād*) thought that the cheetah

---

[28] *EI*², s.v. *Fahd* (F. Viré)

[29] *Maṣāyid*, pp. 183f.; *Bayzara*, pp. 118f.; *Uns al-malā'*, pp. 61–62

[30] *Maṣāyid*, p. 183; *Al-Manṣūrī fi'l-Bayzara*, p. 185. For the description of snaring the cheetah, see *EI*², s.v. *Fahd*. The Arab authors, who are apt to believe fabulous ideas inherited from Greek writings through Arabic translations, mention that cheetahs and other wild animals were caught with the help of "beautiful voice" (*ṣawt ḥasan*) cf. Jāḥiẓ, *Ḥayawān*, vi, pp. 471–72; *Maṣāyid*, p. 183; *Al-Manṣūrī fi'l-Bayzara*, p. 185; Damīrī, *Ḥayawān*, s.v. *Fahd*. Though these Arab writers have not substantiated their statements by citing any example, it is not quite impossible that the cheetah, like some other wild beasts, would allow itself to be approached when it heard music (cf. *EI*², s.v. *Fahd*). That wild animals are responsive to music and singing is supported by experiments in the field, and is illustrated by the example of countries such as India, where it is still practised successfully by some people.

[31] *EI*², s.v. *Fahd* (F. Viré) based on the materials found in the *Maṣāyid*, p. 183f.; *Uns al-Malā'*, p. 61f. Cf. also, Mercier, *Chasse*, pp. 72–73

had become efficient at the chase, it was taken to the hunting ground, hooded, on its pillion, and was kept untied except for its sleep.[32] Hunting treatises mention three ways of hunting with this predatory animal, called *mukābara* (hunting by force), *dasīs* (stalking) and *mudhānaba* (trailing). The best method, said to be the princely prerogative, is *mukābara*, also called *muwājaha* (confrontation). This involves more hardship and more risk for the cheetah-master than for the cheetah: the huntsmen, having reconnoitred a herd of animals from a distance, select a buck and run it down until it becomes fatigued; now the cheetah is cast on the exhausted quarry and brings it down without difficulty or fatigue.[33]

The second method, stalking, depends mostly on the animal itself. It is often greatly admired for the thrilling spectacle that it presents. The cheetah is kept unhooded on the ground and is set off by a signal to take its quarry by surprise when it has reconnoitred from a distance the gazelle grazing in the field. While stalking towards its quarry, the cheetah takes every precaution to conceal its scent and not to startle the quarry. The huntsmen usually conceal themselves in order not to be seen by the quarry, while the cheetah creeps up to the gazelle very carefully, remaining stock-still at the first signal, moving step by step, and taking full advantage of every undulation of the ground until it comes up quite close to the quarry, when it attacks swiftly, without giving its quarry any chance to be on the alert. This careful stalking movement of the cheetah is known by the technical term *da'lān*.[34]

The third method commonly used by huntsmen, and said to be the popular hunting technique of the *dahāqīn*[35] (gentlemen farmers), is *mudhānaba* or "trailing". The cheetah-keeper usually recognizes the herd by the footprints, and trails it upwind as far as its cover without disturbing it. When

[32] *EI*², s.v. *Fahd*. See a picture of the cheetah being taken to the hunting ground on horseback, Mercier, *Chasse*, facing p. 73 (copy from an Indian illustration).

[33] *Maṣāyid*, p. 183; *Bayzara*, p. 119; *Al-Manṣūrī fi'l-Bayzara*, p. 186; cf. also *EI*², s.v. *Fahd* (F. Viré)

[34] *Maṣāyid*, p. 184; *Bayzara*, pp. 120–21; *Al-Manṣūrī fi'l-Bayzara*, pp. 186–87; cf. also *EI*², s.v. *Fahd*, also Mercier, p. 73

[35] On *dahāqīn* see, *EI*², s.v. *Dihḳān* (A. K. S. Lambton); cf. also, *Fahd*, in *JESHO*, viii (1965), p. 185f.

he is within striking distance, he releases the cheetah, which succeeds in hunting down a number of animals from the herd.[36]

It is very important that after every chase (*ṭilq*) the cheetah keepers do not forget to cut the quarry's throat under the cheetah's feet and let it lap up the blood caught in the bowl, in order to remove it from its quarry. Similarly, the huntsmen must hood the cheetah as soon as it remounts the pillion, lest it jump on animals of its own accord.[37]

Whichever hunting method is applied, the cheetah-master should not call for more than ten chases from his cheetah in one day, though it could be twenty as a maximum with some exceptional cheetahs. If this is not observed strictly, the cheetah becomes useless and sometimes it loses its rapine instinct. This is why it is advised by hunting experts that this animal should be taken to the hunting ground only on alternate days.[38]

As the cheetah was highly prized as a rare animal in Abbasid Iraq, it was regarded as a status symbol. The Abbasid wazir Abū Muslim al-Khurāsānī (AD 718–55) and some Abbasid and Fatimid caliphs showed such uncommon interest in this animal that they frequently took it in their official processions.[39] It was also an article of gift exchanged amongst wealthy and high dignitaries.[40]

ʿAnaq al-Arḍ (Lynx-Caracal)

From the various synonyms used for the lynx-caracal (*ʿanaq al-arḍ*) it appears that it was perhaps one of the most popular beasts of prey used during this period. The caracal, resembling the cheetah in appearance, but smaller than a dog and having a wonderful jumping capacity of twenty feet high and forty feet long, lighter in weight than the cheetah and less exacting in its requirements, seems to have been used for "fur-hunting", and appears equally adept with birds, such as partridges, wild

---

36 *Maṣāyid*, p. 184; *Bayzara*, pp. 120–21; *EI*², s.v. *Fahd*

37 *Maṣāyid*, p. 184; *Bayzara*, pp. 120–21; *Al-Manṣūrī fi'l-Bayzara*, pp. 186–87; cf. also *EI*², s.v. *Fahd* (F. Viré); see also Mercier, *Chasse*, p. 73f.

38 Ibid.

39 *EI*², s.v. *Fahd*; cf. also Mercier, *Chasse*, p. 71 apparently quoting from al-Faqīhī, Paris MS. No. 2834

40 *Dhakhā'ir*, p. 42; *Al-Maḥāsin wa'l-Aḍdād*, p. 197

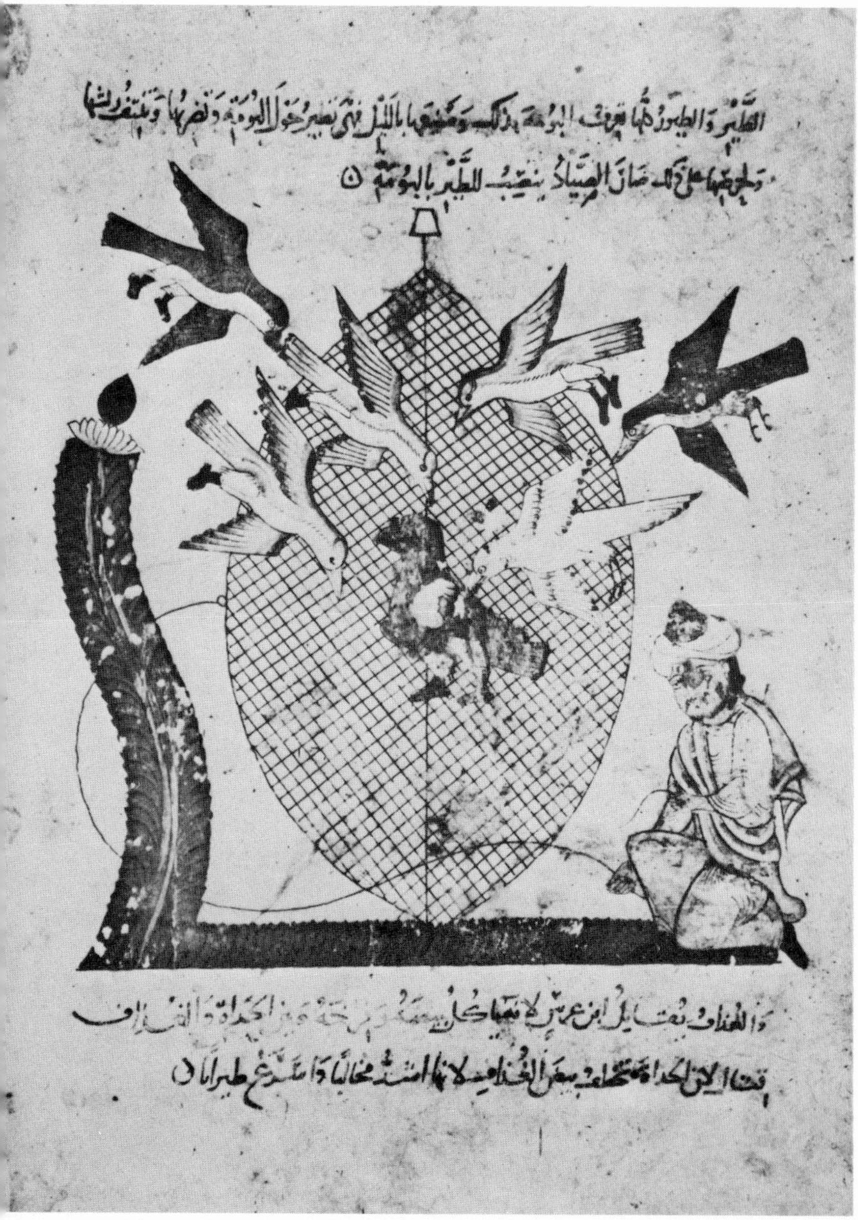

ig. 6. *Snaring Birds in a Net.* A hunter snaring the birds with a net, using an owl as decoy.

Fig. 7. Salūqī Dogs Employed for Hunting

Fig. 8. A Hunting Party. Note the huntsman, accompanied by a cheetah riding o
the pillion.

geese, bustards, and cranes.[41] Al-Mangalī informs us that it was trained to the chase like the cheetah.[42] From Kushājim it would seem that the popular hunting method with this animal was the *dasīs* or stalking.[43]

The Arab authors mention, though not at all convincingly, that lions could not harm the lynx-caracal, as it was apt to slip between the legs of the lion and catch hold of its neck with its forelegs, hurting the chest of the lion with its back until the lion was compelled to jump into water to get rid of it.[44] For such unique tricks and artifices of the *ʿanaq al-arḍ*, the author of *Al-Manṣūrī fi'l-Bayzara* holds it superior to the cheetah.[45]

Dogs

The next important animal widely used in hunting, during the period under review, was the hound.[46] Hounds were usually employed to retrieve the game and to assist the falcons attacking gazelles or hares. It was for their wonderful smelling power, their loyalty to the master, and other characteristics rarely found in beasts of prey, that the hounds were regarded as essential for hunting. On frosty and snowy days none but hounds could discover the lair of hares, gazelles and other animals. Moreover, unlike the cheetah the dog is a light sleeper and a keen watcher, and unlike beasts of prey it habitually pursues the chase for the master and not for itself.[47] According to the beliefs of some Arab writers, the hunting dog can easily distinguish between a dead animal and an

---

[41] *Maṣāyid*, pp. 186, 224f.; Mangalī, *Uns al-Malā'*, pp. 73–74; *Al-Manṣūrī fi'l-bayzara*, pp. 159–88. *ʿAnaq al-Arḍ* was often known as *Tuffa* or *Tiffa*; *al-Ghunjul* or *Funjul*; *ʿUnfut*; *Hanjal, Farāniq al-Asad* etc. Cf. *Maṣāyid*, pp. 224, 227; Damīrī, *Ḥayawān*, s.vv. *ʿanaq al-arḍ, tuffa*; Lane and the *Muḥīṭ al-Muḥīṭ*, s.vv. *Ghunjul* and *Funjul*; see also *EI*^{2}, s.v. *Fahd* (F. Viré)

[42] *Uns al-Malā'*, pp. 73–74

[43] *Maṣā'id*, pp. 186, 225–26

[44] *Uns al-Malā'*, pp. 73–74

[45] *Al-Manṣūrī fi'l-Bayzara*, p. 159

[46] See, for example, the *ṭardiyāt* poems of Abū Nuwās, which are mostly devoted to hunting dogs, their merits and their hunting methods; *Dīwān*, pp. 206–23

[47] *Maṣāyid*, p. 134; *Bayzara*, pp. 142–43; Jāḥiẓ, *Ḥayawān*, ii, pp. 118–119; *Al-Manṣūrī fi'l-Bayzara*, pp. 164–68; Kushājim, *Al-Bayzara*, SOAS. MS. No, 2319, fol. 12 (Extracts published with English translation by Phillott and Azoo, in *JASB*, 1907, pp. 47–49)

animal that feigns death. These dogs are so expert that even foxes, clever in counterfeiting death, cannot escape their eyes. Moreover, if several dogs are slipped and one seizes the quarry while the other fails, the latter does not dispute possession, but seeks another quarry.[48]

The best hounds employed in hunting during the early Abbasid period were those imported from Salūq, a village in the Yemen.[49] Mercier believes that the Salūqī was the only dog with which the Arabs hunted in the mediaeval period.[50] But his observation that these dogs were used to retrieve animals rather than to engage in hunting is erroneous and seems contrary to our sources.[51] Several traditions, poems, and writings of hunting experts point to the conclusion that the Salūqī dogs were successfully employed to hunt hares, foxes, francolins, gazelles and even oryx.[52] The last was the biggest quarry against which hounds were matched, and it involved great risk, as the sharp horns of the oryx could badly injure the dogs. For big quarries, as a rule, two or three dogs were released at a time, and sometimes falcons were slipped to assist them.[53]

The Zaghūrī hounds (drawn from the Byzantine territory called Zaghūr), often cited by Usāma and Mangalī as equally good hunting animals,[54] do not appear to have been employed in hunting during this period.

An anecdote connected with the Caliph Ma'mūn shows that the good points of hounds are similar to those of horses.[55]

---

[48] *Maṣāyid,* 134; *Bayzara,* 43; *Al-Bayzara,* fol. 12; *Al-Manṣūrī fi'l-bayzara,* p. 162

[49] Ibid., *Maṣāyid,* p. 131; *Bayzara,* 140f.; cf. also Mercier, 67

[50] Mercier, *Chasse,* p. 68. It is interesting to note that the beduins in the Arab desert still use Salūqī pure-bred greyhounds for hunting hare and gazelle (cf. Dickson, *The Arab of the Desert,* London 1972, pp. 374–78).

[51] Ibid., p. 67

[52] For Traditions see *Concordance,* s.v. *ṣayd*; cf. also the *ṭardiyāt* poems of Abū Nuwās, *Dīwān,* pp. 206–23; see also *Maṣāyid,* p. 141; Jāḥiẓ, *Ḥayawān,* ii, p. 23

[53] *Maṣāyid,* p. 141; *Al-Manṣūrī fi'l-Bayzara,* p. 193

[54] Usāma, *I'tibār,* p. 212; Mangalī, *Uns al-Malā',* p. 37

[55] See the anecdote in the existing hunting treatises: e.g. *Maṣāyid,* p. 13; *Bayzara,* p. 145; *Al-Manṣūrī fi'l-bayzara,* p. 168; *Kitāb Jamhara fī 'ilm al-bayzara* by an anonymous author of the 10th century; extracts of this book published and translated by D. C. Phillott and F. Azoo in *JASB,* 1907, p. 599

As outlined by the mediaeval writers on the chase, these are that the animal should be light coloured and black-eyed; long between the forelegs and the hind-legs; short in the back; small in the head; long in the neck; pendant-eared, with breadth between the ears; that it should possess large prominent eyes and a long slender muzzle; and be deep-mouthed. It should have a loud and fierce bark; a prominent and broad forehead with a few hair-warts under the chin and on the cheeks. Moreover, it should be long in the thighs and short in the forelegs.[56]

The mediaeval writers on hunting have mentioned, perhaps through their observation and experience, a number of methods for selecting the pup most suitable for training to the chase. They hold that if the bitch produced only one pup, it was regarded as better than its parents; if two, the male was thought to be better than the female; if three, the one resembling the mother was thought to be the best of the three; if among the three there was only one male, it was regarded as the best.[57] In another method of determining the best pup it is said that the dog keeper should take a number of newly born pups into a room and call them to approach him at a distance. The one that moved on all four legs without much stumbling was regarded as the best.[58]

The training method for Salūqī dogs for taking to quarry was not complicated. For this purpose they were matched against a muzzled fox. The dog, encouraged by the fox's inability to bite, easily tore it to pieces, and thus became an efficient chaser after a few repetitions.[59] As a precaution against having it frightened by the sight of game during its immaturity and consequently losing its rapine instinct, a hound was generally not taken to the hunting ground before attaining ten months.[60]

---

[56] *Maṣāyid*, pp. 136–37; *Bayzara*, pp. 144–45; Kushājim, *Al-Bayzara*, SOAS, MS. No. 2091, fol. 11; extracts of this MS. with English translation by D. C. Phillott and R. F. Azoo, *JASB*, 1907, pp. 47–49

[57] Ibid., *Al-Bayzara*, fol. 11; extracts, op. cit., pp. 47–49; see also the extracts of *Kitāb al-Jamhara*, op. cit., 599–600; also *Maṣāyid*, p. 137; *Bayzara*, p. 145

[58] *Maṣāyid*, pp. 137–38; *Bayzara*, p. 145

[59] Mercier, 69; cf. also, Zaky Ḥasan, *Hunting as practised . . .*, 11–12

[60] *Al-Manṣūrī fi'l-bayzara*, p. 171

Horses

Horses were frequently employed by the huntsmen to chase the prey. The horse was employed to meet the lion and other ferocious animals. To train it not to take fright at the sight of a lion, it was supplied with fodder in front of a dummy wooden lion for a few days, and then it was fed near a real lion placed in a cage, to whose smell and roar it became gradually accustomed. Finally, to make it more familiar with lion, the horse was ridden to the forest and was made to approach the caged lion to within a spear's length.[61]

The method of provoking and attacking a lion, with the hunter mounted on a trained horse, with spear and bow in hand, presents a thrilling scene. The lion, infuriated by the teasing of the horseman, usually runs after him. But since the horse runs faster than the lion, the latter becomes fatigued, and the horseman, taking the opportunity, wheels round with a rapid and deft movement and waits for the lion to approach. As soon as the lion comes within arrow-range, the horseman shoots it in the foot. The lion, though roaring in pain, continues to pursue the horseman, who continues to shoot arrows at it from shorter and shorter distances, until, when the lion is overpowered with fatigue and wounds, the horseman brings the combat to an end by further use of arrows, spears and swords or knives if necessary.[62]

Lion-hunting appears to have been a favourite pastime of the early Abbasid caliphs[63] and other members of the *futuwwa* organizations.[64] Some recent archaeological evidence has corroborated the practice of lion-hunting in the Abbasid period.[65]

Weasels *(Ibn ʿirs)*

Not unlike dogs, weasels were used by the hunters as an

[61] *Uns al-Malā'*, pp. 41–42; cf. also Zaky Ḥasan, *Hunting as practised in Arab countries of the Middle Ages*, p. 4; also Mercier, *Chasse*, p. 20, quoting from Mangalī

[62] *Maṣāyid*, pp. 170–71, Usāmā, *Iʿtibār*, pp. 106, 109; Zaky Ḥasan, op. cit., p. 4; Mercier, p. 20 quoting from Mangalī

[63] *Maṣāyid*, pp. 5–6; *Bayzara*, p. 46; *Muntaẓam*, v, pt; 2, pp. 123, 129

[64] *Muntaẓam*, ix, p. 47; cf. also, Badrī, *ʿĀmma*, pp. 245–46

[65] See, for example, Abdur Rāziq, *Annales Islamologiques*, ix, 1970, pp. 109–21. I am indebted to Professor Claude Cahen for drawing my attention to this article.

indispensable aid in hunting.[66] This animal has often been confused with the ferret, which, according to the scientific data of modern mammalogy, is essentially of European origin.[67] Weasels, found in almost all countries of Islam, with slight difference of coat and size, possess uniform character. It was for the extremely bloodthirsty instincts of this miniature wild beast, its feline suppleness, its agility in creeping noiselessly into the narrowest fissure, the lightning speed of its leap, the inexorable vice-like grip of its jaws, its great aptitude for being trained, the little attention that it required, and the extreme ease of carrying it about on account of its small size, that the weasel played an important part in Abbasid hunts.[68]

Weasels were generally used to retrieve game-birds from impenetrable thickets, or to terrify and flush them out from dense coverts to be taken by the falcons, and to dig out fox, badger and porcupine. To dislodge foxes hiding in their earths, the weasel, fastened at the neck or waist to a long leash, was released. Its appearance terrified the foxes and forced them to flight, or else, having been seized by the throat by the little steel-jawed weasel, they were forcibly dragged out by the leash fastened to their assailant, which would never release its hold.[69]

The avid interest in hunting during the early Abbasid period is evident from reports that some people even trained wolves, lions and panthers to the chase and used them as *ḍawārī* (beasts of prey).[70] But these are isolated instances which cannot be generalized as common practice. Jāḥiẓ mentions a wolf and a lion, presumably during the caliphate of Mutawakkil, having been trained to the chase and having hunted wolves, foxes, asses, cows, and wild animals quite freely.[71] Similarly, Usāma b. Munqidh (*c.* 584 AH) tells us of a trained lion-cub which often used to attack horses and caused harm to people.[72] He also speaks of a lynx (*washaq*)

[66] *Maṣāyid*, pp. 19, 48, 227–28; *Al-Manṣūrī fi'l-Bayzara*, p. 188; cf. also Jāḥiẓ, *Ḥayawān*, vii, Index, s.v. *Ibn ʿIrs*

[67] *EI*², s.v. *Ibn ʿIrs*. (F. Viré)

[68] Ibid.; cf. also, *Maṣāyid*, pp. 227–28

[69] *EI*², s.v. *Ibn ʿIrs*, (F. Viré); cf. also, *Maṣāyid*, pp. 227–28

[70] *Maṣāyid*, p. 42; Jāḥiẓ, *Ḥayawān*, vii, pp. 252–53; *Iʿtibār*, 106–7

[71] *Ḥayawān*, vii, pp. 252–53

[72] Usāma, *Iʿtibār*, pp. 106–7

which was employed for hunting hares.[73] Kushājim also speaks of a black expert hunter who was reported to have trained wolves and lions to hunt deer, asses and similar animals.[74]

Birds of Prey *(Jawāriḥ)*

Like the hunting beasts, the hunting birds were very skilled hunters among the Abbasids, who generally used four types of bird: *bāzī* (the goshawk), *shāhīn* (the peregrine falcon), *ṣaqar* (the saker falcon) and *ʿuqāb* (the eagle). The abundance of technical words designating sporting birds in accordance with their age, sex and habitat must be noted.

Broadly speaking, the *bāzī* were of three species, each having some special and peculiar characteristics readily recognized by the expert falconers. They were: *bāz* (female goshawk), *zurraq* (male goshawk), *bāshiq* (sparrow-hawk). Similarly the *shāhīn* had three species, known as *shāhīn* (peregrine falcon), *anīqī* (inferior to *shāhīn* and used for sparrow-hunting), and the *qaṭāmī* or *quṭāma* (a large species, similar to *shāhīn* in hunting instinct). The *ṣaqar* had again three species: *ṣaqar, kubaj* and *yū'yū'*.[75]

The preferred colour for the *bāz* and *shāhīn* was *al-asbahraj*, a colour in which whiteness is predominant; the next was deep black.[76] According to the author of the *Tabaṣṣur bi'l-Tijāra*, the best *bāz* was the light coloured one drawn from Turkistan and Jilan; next the deep black imported from parts of Zanj, the Yemen, and India. The red ones, or those having two colours intermingled, were considered to be of inferior quality. Among the *shāhīn* the black and the light-coloured peregrines brought from Jurjan were considered the best. In *bawāshiq* (sparrow hawks) black was much sought after. Next preferred was the light-coloured of India, and the red with red back and spotted breast.[77] In the *ṣaqar* and the eagle, generally red and black colours were preferred.[78] However,

---

[73] Ibid., p. 193

[74] *Maṣāyid*, p. 42

[75] *Maṣāyid*, pp. 48–103; *Bayzara*, p. 50f. Cf. also *EI*², s.v. *Bayzara* (F. Viré); also, Mercier, *Chasse*, chapter "Falconry"

[76] *Bayzara*, pp. 65, 104; *Maṣāyid*, pp. 55, 79; Mangalī, *Uns al-Malā'*, pp. 92–93

[77] *Tabaṣṣur bi'l-Tijāra*, pp. 35–36

[78] *Maṣāyid*, pp. 85, 96; *Bayzara*, pp. 95, 108

other colours were not disliked; it was only a matter of preference and sometimes of personal taste.

The usual weight of a preferred *bāzī*, as stated by the grand falconer of the Fatimid ʿAzīz Bi'llāh, was 3 to 3½ Baghdadi ratls;[79] of a *shāhīn*, 2½ to 3 ratls;[80] of a *ṣaqar*, 2½ ratls;[81] of an *ʿuqāb*, 10 to 14 ratls.[82]

Of all the hawks, the goshawk or *bāz* has been traditionally regarded as the best of its species, for its rapid stooping to its quarry, its unexcelled patience in holding the quarry and, above all, its delicate temperament. It was widely believed that the *bāz* was born to the flying art.[83] That is why the enthusiasts of hawking did not hesitate to import it from far-off lands such as Greece, Turkistan, Persia, and India.[84]

These hawks were generally snared or limed, or caught when young by means of nooses and flying decoys.[85] They were given extensive training to make them useful to the huntsmen.

The young hawks (*ghiṭrīf*) when caught are seeled, kept awake, and weakened by fasting for several days. The bird is generally kept for about a week in a dark room and offered its necessary diet, preferably flesh of some birds such as sparrows, doves and pigeons, or a piece of lamb; the food is always accompanied by a certain sound to which the falcon gradually becomes accustomed. It is thus induced to step onto the fist of its own accord. During this period, the eyes are generally not unseeled, though sometimes progressive unseeling might be employed. Some trainers unseel the bird at night only, but

[79] *Bayzara*, p. 65

[80] Ibid., p. 104

[81] Ibid., p. 95

[82] Ibid., p. 110. It is the largest of all the hunting birds. It binds to all birds, and hunts four legged animals such as the hare, the fox, and the lynx (cf. ibid., pp. 110–12; *Maṣāyid*, p. 93ff.). According to Damīrī it is the swiftest of all birds of prey and can fly from Iraq to Yaman between morning and evening (cf. Damīrī, *Ḥayawān*, s.v.).

[83] *Maṣāyid*, p. 52f.; Shawkat, *Ṣayd gāhe shawkatī*, pp. 12–14; *EI*², s.v. *Bayzara* (F. Viré); cf. also the poems of Abū Nuwās (*Dīwān*, pp. 223–25) and Ibn Muʿtazz (*Dīwān*, p. 186), describing the various qualities of falcons and their hunting skill

[84] See, for example, Jāḥiẓ (?), *Tabaṣṣur bi'l-Tijāra*, pp. 35–36

[85] *EI*², s.v. *Bayzara* (F. Viré). See for some methods of snaring hawks by means of nets and decoy used by beduins in modern times, Dickson, *The Arabs of the Desert*, pp. 368–70.

seel it again as soon as it is day. When it is tame enough to step on the fist, its eyes are unseeled, and a hood is provided instead; then, in order to make it bold and ready for more taming, it is taken to noisy places where there are music and dancing, where drums are beating, and to smithies, where it hears the ring of hammers on the iron.[86]

After the necessary taming, the primary training for stooping at game begins. Now it is carried for several successive days on the gloved fist to open places, preferably the hunting grounds; it is kept on the ground and fed there by accustoming it to respond to the trainer's call to step onto his fist. The trainer usually waits on horse-back or stands on the ground. Having finished this training, the bird is taken out in the field, hooded and mailed in the sock (*qabā'*), with bell and creance[87] tied to the leather band round its leg, along with game birds (*kāsira*) selected from the species which it is being trained to hunt. To start with, it is usually released on porphyro (a sort of water fowl) or pigeons. The trainer, on horse-back with the hawk on his fist unhooded, waits for the servant hidden nearby to release the game bird in flight as soon as the drum is beaten.[88] Sometimes a long cord is fastened to the feet of the game with its end held by a servant, who shakes it several times to cause the bird to flutter and thereby attract the falcon's attention. The falcon, cast off by the trainer, stoops at the captive bird and seizes it, whereupon the falconer cuts the bird's throat under its feet and gives it the flesh soaked in blood to provoke its carnivorous instinct and awaken its keenness (*faraḥa*) to take the quarry. Generally

---

[86] *Maṣāyid*, pp. 50–1; *Bayzara*, pp. 49–113; *Uns al-Malā'* pp. 83–107; *EI*², s.v. *Bayzara*; cf. also Mercier, *Chasse*, Chapter "Falconry", p. 80ff.

[87] The creance is tied and held by the falconer to keep the hawk in control; because, if it is neglected and the hawk takes fright and flies up into the air to a height greater than the length of the creance and then comes down, it will almost certainly injure itself. In that case the falconer probably will never be able to overcome its nervousness (cf. Shawkat, *Ṣayd gāhe shawkatī*, p. 81). Bells are fastened, generally in the tail, presumably for two reasons: first, it helps the falconer to discover the whereabouts of a hawk when it flies in pursuit of its quarry to bush or thick cover and goes out of sight of the owner; secondly, sometimes bells cause the quarry which is being pursued to look around as the hawk gets nearer, thus reducing its speed and making it an easy prey for the falcon (cf. ibid., pp. 122–3).

[88] Drums are usually beaten to frighten the birds and make them fly, so that the hawk can easily take them.

it seems that the falconer does not allow the hawk to catch more than one bird a day for the first week, two a day for the second, and three for the third, after which it is allowed, at the falconer's discretion, to take as many as it can fly at. The hawk is, however, allowed to "take its pleasure" (*ishbāʿ*) on one of its captures. After repeating these exercises patiently, each time at a greater distance, the hawk is estimated "assured" (*mustawin li'l-irsāl*) and is flown "for good" (*ṣāda ṭalqan*) at waterfowl, sparrows, and other birds.[89]

The training of the hawk, especially the saker falcon, to attack gazelles is interesting. For this purpose a gazelle hide is procured and carefully stuffed with grass and straw until it looks like a real gazelle. A piece of meat is tied on the head of the dummy between the ears, and the saker is fed there for several days, with a gradual diminution of the quantity until one day nothing is put there. Now a real gazelle is taken to the field with a cord tied to the feet and held by a hidden man, who moves it frequently to cause the gazelle to move. The hawker with the hawk on his fist remains facing the wind until he comes within the smell and the sight of the gazelle, when he casts off the hawk, who readily attacks the prey. As soon as the man hidden with the cord in hand sights the falcon stooping at the quarry, he comes out, screams and makes the sounds general in hunting. This sort of screaming and noise is used to encourage the hawk to be bold on the quarry. Now the animal is seized and thrown to the ground, and its throat is cut under the feet of the hawk, which is allowed to eat its fill of the gazelle. This exercise is repeated several times on successive days, until the bird becomes habituated to flying at the quarry unhesitatingly.[90] A similar method is applied by the falconers to train their falcons on hares, wolves, foxes and other animals. Sometimes hounds are employed to help the falcons in seizing the animals. However, on no account must the hooding be forgotten before taking the hawk up after it has fully fed on the quarry.[91]

[89] *Bayzara*, pp. 49–113; Kushājim, *Maṣāyid*, pp. 50–61; Mangalī, *Uns al-Malā'*, pp. 83–107; *Ṣayd gāhe shawkatī*, pp. 56–93; cf. also *EI*², s.v. *Bayzara*, (F. Viré)

[90] *Bayzara*, pp. 99–101; cf. also Tīmūr Mirza, *Bāz Nāma-e-Nāṣirī*, Eng. Tr. by D. C. Phillott, London, 1968, p. 99ff.

[91] Ibid., *Bayzara*, pp. 101–3; *Maṣāyid*, pp. 84–5; *Ṣayd gāhe shawkatī*, pp. 42–3

It is evident from our sources that the falconer during the Abbasid period used to take special care of the health of the birds (*jawāriḥ*), their food and their perches. This accounts for the fact that our treatises on falconry have devoted long chapters to the diagnosis of diseases of sporting birds, and their cure with various types of tonics, medicines, pills, pessaries and ointments.

To assure their good health the hawks were never given stale flesh or fish, though sometimes in the absence of flesh, fish was taken as the only alternative.[92]

When set down to rest, the falcon was placed on the perch or block, and was weathered (*tashrīq*) in the sun, near the bathing pool. Great care was taken of the feathers, and caution was used in releasing the bird to quarry. During the period of moult (*qarnaṣa*) the hawks were kept away from noise and their mutes (*dharq*) were carefully examined.[93]

The Abbasid caliphs and the well-off members of this society seem to have been very interested in hunting water fowl (*ṭayr al-mā'*), grouse, and francolins with hawks and falcons.[94] The Caliph Wāthiq, as reported by Abu'l-Faraj al-Iṣfahānī, was in the habit of paying frequent visits to the Qāṭūl, a river flowing into the Tigris, for hunting francolins and water fowl with his regular hunting associates.[95] Generally the huntsmen and the falconers used to encircle the pond, lake or riverside. The drum was beaten to make the waterfowl fly. As soon as the birds rose, falcons were set on them, which stooped to their quarry speedily and did not relinquish the chase as long as there was any chance of success; when the falcon seized the quarry it waited for the hounds or the servants to approach. The hawks were then fed something from the quarry and were hooded.[96] It appears that the falconer generally kept a small drum (*ṭabal*) attached to his saddle, and beat it when he intended to call the falcons, which readily responded to the drum's sound and jumped on the fist.[97]

---

92 *I'tibār*, p. 199
93 *Bayzara*, pp. 59–64; *Maṣāyid*, pp. 108–130; *EI*², s.v. *Bayzara*, (F. Viré)
94 *Aghānī*², vii, pp. 158–9, x, pp. 227–8
95 Ibid., vii, pp. 158–9
96 *Maṣāyid*, pp. 57–8; Usāma, *I'tibār*, pp. 202–5
97 L. Mercier, *Chasse*, p. 98; cf. also *EI*², s.v. *Bayzara*, (F. Viré)

Hunting-weapons

The weapons traditionally used by the Arabs in warfare were also employed in hunting ferocious animals. The Abbasids, in accordance with their elegant taste, appear to have effected certain advanced modifications in the shape and size of these weapons, which resulted in their elaboration and their more successful operation. These weapons generally consisted of double-edged swords, various types of bows and arrows known as *sahm, nushshāba, nabl, julāhiq, bunduq*; spears fitted with flint heads (*ḥirāb*), lances (*rumḥ*); shields, knives, daggers, and spades.

The word *sahm*, it would seem, was generally used to denote all types of arrows, whereas the word *nabl* was used for Arab arrows made of bamboo.[98] The most effective and deeply penetrating arrow was the *nushshāba*, probably of Persian origin. This arrow was generally made of wood.[99] Usāma b. Munqidh (AD 1095–1188) tells us that it was so effective that if it pierced the body of a man he would meet an instantaneous death.[100] This seems to be the reason why *nushshāba* was frequently used in lion-hunting.[101]

The arrows were usually dressed with birds' feathers (*rīsh*).[102] The strings (*watar*) of the bows were generally made of twisted silk cords or of leather; the former was suitable for winter and the rainy season. During rainy and damp weather

---

[98] Lane, *Lexicon*, s.v. *sahm*; E. Renatsek, "On some old arms and instruments of war", *JRAS* (Bombay Branch), xiv (1880) pp. 219–63; cf. also, Latham and Paterson, *Saracen Archery*, where *sahm* and *nabl* are well described (Glossary s.vv.). According to them, *nabl* is a dart designed to be shot from a hand-bow with the aid of an arrow-guide, whereas the word *sahm* denotes general arrows, to be followed by adjectives to mean particular types of arrows, such as *sahm tamām* (a full-length arrow), *sahm ṭawīl* (long arrow), *sahm sibāq* (flight arrow) etc. For details see *Saracen Archery*, Glossary, p. 190

[99] *Maṣāyid*, p. 163. A 12th century AD manual of warfare (*Tabṣira*, fol, 94b) defines the *nushshāba* as a collective term applied to arrows complete with wood, fletching, and head. Cf. *Saracen Archery*, Appendix 3, p. 164, where the reference is supplied.

[100] Usāma, *I'tibār*, p. 194

[101] *Maṣāyid*, pp. 170–1

[102] In fact trimming feathers on an arrow controls the motion and speed of its flight. Generally three or four moderately sized and straight feathers of eagle, vulture or falcon were fixed on to the shaft back to belly in position (cf. *Arab Archery*, pp. 110–13).

the bow-string, especially the leather one, had to be drawn with force, while in warm and dry weather there was no need for great exertion of strength.[103] That is why the length of the *nushshāba* was kept within the span of the archer's outstretched arms (*ṭūl al-bāʿ*).[104]

The process of shooting and handling the bows and arrows as outlined by mediaeval writers is interesting. The archer should hold the arrow with his middle, little and ring fingers and lock the *nushshāba* with his index finger, and release the arrow smoothly at his mark. This method of spanning the bow-string with three fingers is known to Arabs as *daniyyāt*; while releasing with two fingers (the thumb and the index finger) is known as *bazm.*[105] It appears that the archers, as a precautionary measure, sometimes set two strings to their bows, one small and the other large, to use either of them according to advantage and necessity.[106]

In shooting, the archer should hit the animal in the muscle beneath the shoulder-blades (*farīṣa*) because the arrow reaches the heart and renders the quarry powerless. Nevertheless, if the archer was very skilled, he might aim at the front part of the animal, preferably the neck.[107] The professional hunters were so skilled in shooting that they could hit birds in flight, and could hit the quarry at any point they chose. Kushājim narrates that he saw an archer who set a ring between the thumb and index fingers of his slave and released several arrows from his cross-bow through the ring without causing any injury to the fingers of the slave.[108] Similarly, it is reported that two enthusiastic archers of Basra, once confronting a lion in their way, each fired an arrow from his *julāhiq* aimed at one eye of the lion, blinding it and escaping thereby.[109]

The Turks, during this period, were great masters of archery. Comparing their skill with the Khārijites and the

---

[103] *Maṣāyid*, p. 163; *Al-Manṣūrī fi'l-Bayzara*, p. 188 which quotes from Kushājim's *Maṣāyid* almost verbatim

[104] *Maṣāyid*, p. 164; *Al-Manṣūrī*, p. 189

[105] Ibid.

[106] Ibid.

[107] *Maṣāyid*, pp. 165–6; *Al-Manṣūrī fi'l-bayzara*, p. 189

[108] *Maṣāyid*, p. 248

[109] Ibid., p. 248; *Al-Manṣūrī fi'l-bayzara*, p. 190. On *Julāhiq* see below in this chapter, p. 223

beduins, Jāḥiẓ says that "the Khārijites and the beduins have no skill worth mentioning in shooting from horseback, but the Turk can shoot at beasts, birds, hoops, men, sitting quarry, dummies, and birds on the wing, and do so at full gallop to fore or to rear, to left or to right, upwards or downwards, loosing ten arrows before the Khārijites can fire one."[110]

The training of archers for hunting running animals was interesting. In this, a moving target known as "imitation beast on a chariot" (*ʿajala*) was preferred. For this purpose generally a four-wheeled chariot was taken; tied firmly to its front was the skin of a jackal or hare stuffed with straw, and at the rear was a small skin stuffed similarly. The front skin represented the beast to be shot, while the hind skin represented the archer's dog, which was usually let loose to chase the beast. The chariot was now pulled to a high place, preferably a hill, and pushed down the steep incline. As the chariot started rolling down the hill, the archer shot at the front skin. If he hit it correctly then he was estimated a good archer; if not, he was regarded as unfit for the hunt, and it was feared that he might kill his own dog.[111] Sometimes, as an alternative method, a long cord was tied to the chariot, and a rider on horseback pulled it at speed, while an archer mounted behind him was invited to shoot at the chariot. This was repeated several times, until the archer became skilled.

The next important weapon was *al-julāhiq*, which has often been confused with *al-bunduq* (cross-bow). *Julāhiq* is a word most probably of Persian origin. Kushājim, being unable to trace its origin in the Arabic language, asked an expert philologist, who was equally unable to find its origin in Arabic.[112] It has been said that this instrument was first used in Arabia during the caliphate of Uthmān, who, receiving complaints, prohibited its use in the country.[113] In describing this weapon, lexicographers such as Ibn Manẓūr, Lane and

[110] Jāḥiẓ, *Rasāʾil*, i, p. 45 (English translation by C. T. H. Walker, in *JRAS*, 1915, p. 666)

[111] *Maṣāyid*, pp. 166–7; *Al-Manṣūrī fiʾl-bayzara*, p. 190; cf. also, *Arab Archery*, pp. 146–7

[112] *Maṣāyid*, p. 247. The term *julāhiq* does not occur either in *Arab Archery* or in *Saracen Archery*, books written by the scholars of the Mamluk period and translated into English by N. A. Faris, and Latham and Paterson.

[113] *Maṣāyid*, pp. 247–8

others do not mention more than the fact that *julāhiq* was like *bunduq* and that bullets were fired by it. A careful study of this weapon, however, makes clear that it was a bow-like weapon for throwing round earthen pellets, extremely effective for hunting birds. Our study also suggests that it was not generally used by the Arabs. Perhaps foreigners, presumably the Persians, were best acquainted with the use of this weapon.

Hunting with the *bunduq* has frequently been recorded by our sources. The *qaws bunduq* would seem an ancient weapon frequently used in hunting and warfare in the early mediaeval period.[114] It was a type of crossbow that shot pellets (*bunduq*) of clay or metal.[115] The phrase (*khamsīna bunduqa raṣāṣ*), recorded in Masʿūdī's *Murūj*, indicates lead pellets which were fired by a crossbow.[116] In warfare, the pellets were sometimes heated to glowing point in a fire and used as incendiaries. Other kinds of projectile made out of naphtha were also used.[117]

Shābushtī, in his *Kitāb al-Diyārāt*, has mentioned another type of hunting weapon, called *sabṭāna*, which is explained by Qalqashandī as a long straight instrument like a spear. This was made of wood, hollowed into a tube; small earthen bullets were fired from it, presumably with the help of a trigger.[118] This was reported to be a very effective weapon for hunting birds.

Tricks and devices used in hunting

Other types of instruments and devices used in hunting birds were flying decoys, nets, and bird-lime. For beasts, mostly *zabī* or *ukar* (hidden ditches), fire, whistle (*ṣafīr*), traps (*fikhākh*), hidden nets (*shirāk mastūra*), nooses (*ahwāq*) and the like were adopted. These devices were not used on all

[114] *Maṣāyid*, pp. 26, 165, 247; cf. also Bashford Dean, *Handbook of Arms and Armour*, p. 161

[115] Reinord, pp. 217–18 and Hein, *Isl.* xiv, p. 304, quoted by Latham and Paterson in *Saracen Archery*, p. 19; cf. also L. A. Mayer, *Saracenic Heraldry*, pp. 13, 83; also *EI*², s.v. *Bārūd*

[116] *Murūj*, viii, p. 17

[117] *Saracen Archery*, p. 139

[118] *Diyārāt*, p. 9; Qalqashandī, *Ṣubḥ al-Aʿshā*, ii, p. 138

sorts of animals uniformly; various methods were adopted to trap different sorts of animal.[119]

Catching birds in nets was done in several ways. Generally, in the fields and in between the branches of trees and the sides of rocks a net was set, with a lure or decoy of small birds such as sparrows or doves fastened in it. The birds, not observing the net from a distance, stooped at the lure and were trapped in the net.

The method of snaring hawks is not mentioned by our contemporary sources. Usāma, however, writing in the twelfth century AD, mentions some eye-witness accounts of hawk-snaring by professional hunters. He says that the snarer used to build a little stone house about his own height, cover it with branches and conceal it under tufts of straw and dry grass. He made an opening in it, took a dove, tied its feet to a spar of wood and sent it out through the hole, shaking the piece of wood. The bird opened its wings; the falcon saw it and darted at it to take it. As soon as the hunter saw the falcon was there, he pulled in the spar, put out his hand, seized the falcon's feet, which were grasping the dove, captured it, and seeled its eyes.[120]

Ṣayd al-dibq (bird-lime) is also reported to have been an effective and safe means of catching sparrows, serins, starlings, and other small birds. The wood of *dihq* (a very glutinous tree) was put on the branches of a tree; birds touching it were trapped, and glue stuck to their wings. Sometimes lime was prepared from a mixture of materials, drawn out into longish strings, and put upon trees; birds were caught by it. It was more free from hazard than the *shubbāk* (net), because the latter often caused bruising to the wings of birds.[121]

Ibn Qutayba and Ibn ʿAbd Rabbih, quoting the author of *Al-Filāha,* describe a strange method of hunting common birds with the help of *hiltīt* (asafetida), *banj* (henbane) and *kharbaq aswad* (black hellebore). It is said that the birds became unconscious on eating grains mixed with such medicinal herbs and recovered only when the hunters

---

119 *Maṣāyid*, pp. 47–8; *Iʿtibār*, p. 210; cf. also Mercier, *Chasse*, pp. 77–8

120 *Iʿtibār*, p. 200

121 *Al-Manṣūrī fi'l-Bayzara*, p. 190; *Uns al-malā'*, pp. 81–2; Lane, *Lexicon*, s.v. *dibq*; Mercier, *Chasse*, pp. 78–9

provided them with a food prepared with special drugs.[122] Arab authors quite often narrated stories from Greek sources without putting them to experiment or observation, and became victims of fabulous beliefs and popular imaginations. The use of anaesthetic herbs may therefore be a legacy of naive ideas perhaps widely believed in ancient times.

For catching sparrows an easier method was adopted. A basket in the shape of a lobster-pot (*miḥbara*) was taken, and a sparrow fastened at the bottom, luring other sparrows to enter, which found no way out. In this way one could snare hundreds of sparrows in one day.[123] Jāḥiẓ tells of similar instruments for catching pigeons, known as *baikathīr quffāʿ*, *milqaf* and *dū-shākh.*[124]

For trapping waterfowl, contemporary Arab writers mention the following curious method. A dry gourd was thrown into a pool where waterfowl were in abundance. The birds, at first frightened at the sight of the gourd, gradually became familiar with it and regarded it as a plaything. Now, the huntsman, putting on his head a gourd with two holes in front for the eyes, quietly entered the pool and approached the birds playing there. Approaching a bird the huntsman would seize it by its feet, drag it under water, bruise its wings and let it swim in the water helplessly. He would then move to other birds and do the same, until in the end he would throw off the gourd and collect the game.[125] This method is reported as so effective that one could catch hundreds of birds in one hour. It is narrated that seeing one hundred water-fowl captured in one day Jāḥiẓ asked the hunter how he had caught so many. The hunter, to the great astonishment of Jāḥiẓ, replied that he had caught them by this method in a single hour.[126]

For trapping animals, hidden ditches were much used by professional hunters. They had various names, mostly from their various sizes and from the types of animals they caught.[127] The ditches, it would seem, were of two types: one

---

[122] *ʿUyūn*, ii, pp. 94–5; *ʿIqd*, vi, pp. 246–7

[123] *ʿUyūn*, ii, pp. 94–5; *ʿIqd*, vi, p. 246

[124] Jāḥiẓ, *Ḥayawān*, iii, pp. 218–19

[125] Ibid., v, pp. 439–40; *ʿUyūn*, ii, pp. 94–5; *ʿIqd*, vi, pp. 246–7

[126] *Ḥayawān*, v, pp. 439–40

[127] The ditches used for trapping wolves were called *laḥma*; for gazelles,

which trapped the animal, and the other where huntsmen used to conceal themselves and wait for the animals to approach. In the first type, it seems, the ditch was covered with iron rods, probably in the shape of nets with big holes. These were covered with earth.[128] Details of this hunting method are not given by our sources. But it is likely that the animals were driven from thickets and dens, and were trapped in the ditches. This sort of ditch is reported as so effective that the animal once entangled could not escape by any means. These ditches were generally dug for such animals as wild asses, cattle, deer, and boars.[129] Likewise, *zābiya*, a pitfall on an elevated piece of ground, was used for lion and wolf.[130]

The second type of ditch (*mawāḍiʿ al-qāniṣ*) was known as *qarmūs* (trapper's hollow underground ambush), *nāmūs* (hunter's ditch like a *ghurfa* or room), *qatra* (hunter's *bayt*, or place for concealment) and *zarība* (hiding-place like a lion's den).[131] Kushājim tells us that these were all excavations (*biʾār*) used as an ambuscade, which the huntsmen fumigated with animals' fur to conceal their smell from wild animals. A sportsman who thus fumigated his lurking place was called by Arabs "*mudammir*": one who captures the game unperceived.[132]

Hares, antelopes, mountain goats and the like were frequently hunted with nets. The huntsmen stretched nets (*fikhākh, shirāk*) across valleys, then chased the animal until it fell into them. Hunting by nets was safer because it seldom caused injury to the animal.[133] Fire, whistle and animal calls

---

ḥibāla; for lions, *zābiya*; for mountain goats *dāghūt*; for foxes, *dāḥūm* etc. (cf. *Al-Manṣūrī fīʾl-bayzara*, p. 201)

128 *Maṣāyid*, p. 47; cf. also Mercier, *Chasse*, p. 77

129 *Maṣāyid*, p. 47; *Al-Manṣūrī fīʾl-bayzara*, p. 201; *Iʿtibār*, 214

130 *Maṣāyid*, p. 47; *zābiya* means a hill which water does not flow over; but in hunting terminology it applies to the hunter's ditch dug in elevated ground for trapping beasts such as lions. Since the ditch is in a place which water cannot reach, it is named by the Arabic phrase used for a thing exceeding the ordinary bound or limits; "*balagha al-sail al-zubā*"—the torrent covered the top of the hill which it did not usually reach (cf. *ʿUyūn*, ii, 84; *ʿIqd*, vi, p. 247).

131 *Maṣāyid*, pp. 241–2

132 Ibid., p. 242

133 Ibid., p. 47

have also been recorded as devices for attracting and trapping the animal.[134] They would seem hardly practical. Perhaps the Arabs derived such ideas from the imagination of the Greeks through Arabic translations. According to these fantastic beliefs, fire was generally kindled facing the animal, who stared at it until it became puzzled and startled. Sometimes, in addition to fire, a bell was rung to bewilder the animal quickly.[135] Jāḥiẓ speaks of the *ṭisās* (a kind of vessel or basin of tinned copper or brass) which was sometimes beaten for hunting both birds and beasts: a statement for which there is no practical evidence. It was believed that on hearing the sound of this vessel the lions approached it and listened to it with delight.[136] The call and the whistle were also believed to produce similar effects.

Some other tricks, such as stalking a horse or a camel (*darīya*), using a lariat (*wahaq*) and slipping a noose by taking a turn on the quarry (*muḥāwada*) were also employed by the huntsmen.[137] Lariats were often used for catching zebra and even lions.[138] Following the fabulous beliefs of the Greeks, Arab authors mention the use of anaesthetic herbs. In this method a large fish was taken and cut into pieces, which were put one by one in the ditch, where a fire was kindled to carry the smoke and the odour of the fish to the animal's lair. Now some pieces of meat mixed with black hellebore and opium were scattered around the fire. The animal, smelling the aroma (*qutār*), approached and ate the meat and became unconscious. The men in ambush would now come out and take the quarry.[139]

In books on hunting and snares we occasionally come across the word *ḥibāla* or *ḥabā'il* used in the trapping of birds and beasts. It was some sort of snaring tool made of rope often attached to a piece of wood called *jurra*, having a snare at the head and a cord in the middle, with which gazelles were

---

134 Ibid., p. 47

135 Ibid., pp. 47, 207; Jāḥiẓ, *Ḥayawān*, iv, p. 484; *Al-Manṣūrī fi'l-bayzara*, p. 194

136 *Ḥayawān*, iv, p. 193

137 *Maṣāyid*, pp. 48, 207; *Al-Manṣūrī fi'l-bayzara*, pp. 194, 199; cf. also, Mercier, *Chasse*, p. 77

138 Zaky Ḥasan, *Hunting as practised in Arab countries of the Middle Ages*, p. 3; Mercier, *Chasse*, p. 199

139 *'Uyūn*, ii, p. 84; Ibn 'Abd Rabbih, *'Iqd*, vi, p. 247

caught. When a gazelle was trapped in it, it strove with it for a while, struggling in vain to escape. This seems to be the origin of the proverb "*nāwaḍa al-jurra thumma sālamahā*" ("He struggled with the *jurra* and then made peace with it"), about a man who opposes the counsel of a wise man and then is obliged to agree with him.[140]

A *ḥibāla* with cords of sinew was sometimes tied to a stick hidden in the earth. When the foreleg of the gazelle entered the snare, it became knotted in the cords, and when the animal leaped to escape and stretched out its foreleg, it struck the stick with its other foreleg and its hind legs and broke them.[141] The question put to the Imām Shāfiʿī regarding the legality of killing animals by blows of iron in the *ḥibāla* suggests that iron was sometimes used in this snare.[142] *Ḥibāla* does not seem a very heavy or complicated snare, for boys could use it for catching birds. Abu'l-Faraj al-Iṣfahānī tells us of a boy who used to snare birds with *ḥibāla* in the suburb of Medina, using his *izār* for stalking by putting one end over his head.[143]

In addition to the above, several other tricks and devices were adopted in hunting big animals such as lions and ostriches. Sometimes in lion-hunting the hunter lying in ambush provoked the lion to come out of its den by unusual sounds or by hurling stones. The hunter then stretched out his left arm bound in rolls of wool to be bitten by the lion. The lion thus enraged and tempted came to bite, exposing itself to the hunter, who used his sword on it.[144] Some other methods have been recorded, such as encircling the lion by a group of people with spears in hand while it slept in the afternoon, or attacking by two men, one acting as decoy and the other as assailant, or blinding it by throwing blankets.[145]

---

140 *Maṣāyid*, p. 211; cf. also, Lane, *Lexicon*, s.v. *jurra*

141 Lane, *Lexicon*, s.vv. *ḥibāla* and *jurra*

142 *Maṣāyid*, p. 208

143 *Aghānī*[1], i, p. 22

144 Zaky Ḥasan, *Hunting as practised*, p. 6; Mercier, *Chasse*, 23

145 Zaky, *Hunting*, pp. 5–6; Mercier, pp. 21–3; *Maṣāyid*, pp. 170–1; *Al-Manṣūrī fi'l-bayzara*, p. 199. During the late Abbasid period, lion-hunting would seem a regular pastime of the Baghdadis. From Ibn al-Athīr we learn that enthusiastic lion-hunters often brought out ceremonial processions and marched through different quarters of Baghdad displaying the trophies of the chase. Such processions occasioned rivalries and feuds

Utilization of the game

Dishes prepared with the meat of the hunted animals were highly prized by the Abbasid people. Special dishes were prepared from different types of flesh. Moreover, the utility of feathers, skin, horn and fur of the animals and the beneficial properties of various types of game were not unknown to the age. Zoological books and hunting treatises of the mediaeval period quite often discuss these things with precision and detail. Various *ṭardiyāt* and *urjuza* bear testimony that flesh of game was held superior to all other meat. We quote one such poem.[146]

> "Ghadawtu li'l-ṣayd bi fityān najab
> wa sabab li'l-rizq min khayr sabab"

"I went to the hunt early in the morning in the company of accomplished young men; and it is the best means for seeking subsistence."

It was believed that the natural heat of venison was increased by the terror inspired by the beasts trained for chase, and so it increased the heat of a man.[147] A wise man is reported to have said, "The best meat is that of a hunted beast that has been well terrified."[148]

It appears that enthusiasts found nothing more pleasant than to broil and take the meat hunted in the company of friends and relatives, even in the hunting ground, where they were surrounded by poets and singers who sang or recited poems suitable to the occasion.[149] It is reported by Isḥāq al-Mawṣilī that once he called on the Caliph Muʿtaṣim while he was drinking, and various captured birds and beasts were lying before him to please him. According to the will of the Caliph, Mawṣilī took part in the feast and sang.[150] Thaʿālibī also, in his *Yatīmat al-Dahr*, gives us a vivid description of such parties, and tells how fire was kindled and how the game was broiled and served to the caliph after the hunt.[151] The

among the populace, resulting in bloodshed and violence. (See Serjeant, *South Arabian Hunt*, pp. 23–5)

146 *Maṣāyid*, p. 67; *Bayzara*, p. 170

147 *Fakhrī*, p. 75

148 Ibid., p. 75

149 *Aghānī*[1], v, p. 88; *Quṭub al-Surūr*, p. 44

150 *Aghānī*[1], v, p. 88

151 *Yatima*, ii, p. 200, quoted by H. I. Ḥasan, *Islam*, p. 372

most prized birds were *durrāj* (francolin) and water fowl. Cranes, which were widely hunted, were used in cooking *sikbāj*,[152] after the meat had been thoroughly washed and the blood and saliva drained away.[153] Pheasants and partridges were also greatly enjoyed.[154]

Among other animals whose flesh was liked most were gazelles, buck, hare, wild bull and the like. From venison, a favourite dish called *kushtābiya*[155] (meat-soup) was prepared, which is reported by Kushājim to be of fine taste.[156] Hares' flesh was believed to possess the beneficial property of curing epilepsy, and was liked very much, especially in preparing *zīrnāj*[157] and roast. It is said that its meat was the easiest to digest.[158] The flesh of the wild bull was preferred to that of the cow. The former, it was said, had more dietary properties than the latter. It was cooked with salt and water while the latter was served with vinegar.[159] Medicinal use of the parts of the animals such as gall, fat, flesh and blood was common for curing the diseases of mankind and those of birds and beasts.

The fur of animals such as hares and foxes, and the skins of the cow, buffalo, lion and wolf were utilized for various purposes. The fur was used mainly for garments, whereas the skins made shoes, leather shields, and drums.[160] It is reported that from lion-hide strings of musical instruments were also made.[161] Horns were put to use in making bows, and the bones of large animals for weapons of war. Ostrich-feathers were used for ornament and the tendons and bones for arrows and spear heads.[162]

---

[152] On *sikbāj* and its ingredients, see chapter *Food* above, p. 83

[153] *Maṣāyid*, p. 227; *Al-Manṣūrī fi'l-bayzara*, p. 205

[154] Shābushtī, *Diyārāt*, p. 148

[155] *Kushtābiya* is a Persian compound word from *gūsht*, meat, and *āb*, water, meaning meat-soup.

[156] *Maṣāyid*, p. 208

[157] For the ingredients of *Zīrnāj* and its cooking method, see *Ṭabīkh*, pp. 13–14

[158] Jāḥiẓ, *Ḥayawān*, vi, pp. 359–60; *Maṣāyid*, p. 147

[159] *Maṣāyid*, pp. 143, 161

[160] Jāḥiẓ, *Ḥayawān*, v, p. 477; vii, p. 86

[161] *Maṣāyid*, pp. 171–2

[162] Zaky Ḥasan, *Hunting as practised in Arab countries*, p. 10; Mercier, *Chasse*, p. 56

Times for hunting

For hunting, the most favourable was the day overcast with clouds where there was no rain.[163] The enthusiasts of the hunt usually went out for the chase at dawn, because in the darkness of night animals generally take rest and remain fast asleep.[164] Various hunting poems testify that the hunting-party marched to the fields early in the morning and engaged in hunting for several days.[165] Friday was regarded as the best day for large-scale hunting. There were, however, some people who preferred Saturday to Friday.[166]

Hunting treatises often refer to astronomical calculation and the movements of particular stars, planets, and the moon to be observed by kings and those who sought good omens.[167] It appears that Indian astronomical works and Persian and Greek books made available in Arabic translations had some influence on the cultural life of the Abbasids. The Persians, of course, took every care to seek bad or good omens before hunting. This Persian custom seems to have influenced the Abbasids to some extent, for they too looked for auspicious hours according to astronomical observations. But this does not appear to have been a regular practice of the Abbasid caliphs; and the common people, who had very little access to and sometimes no knowledge of astronomical calculations, did not credit them at all.

Fishing

Several instruments and methods were adopted for fishing. Fish were generally caught by nets (*shirāk, shabaka*) or hooks (*shuṣūsh*).[168] The Caliph Amīn was reportedly very fond of angling. With his favourite slave-girl he used to sit and compete in fishing.[169] Fishing by "locks and dams" (*al-abwāb wa'l-sukūr*) was frequently used. In this method the fishermen

---

163 *Maṣāyid*, p. 235

164 Ibid.

165 See, for example, Ibn Mu'tazz, *Dīwān*, pp. 184, 145, 245–6, 282–3; Abū Nuwās, *Dīwān*, p. 206ff.; cf. also Mercier, 51f.

166 *Maṣāyid*, pp. 235–7

167 Ibid., pp. 235–40

168 *Maṣāyid*, pp. 3, 229f; Barhebraeus, pp. 232, 246

169 *Murūj*, vi, p. 431; Barhebraeus, p. 232

used to close off one side of a pond, pool, or small canal, bail out the water and catch fish in the mud. It is claimed that the "locks and dams" method was the best for fishing.[170] Fishing by net at night was considered very effective because fish at that time were believed to be overpowered with sleep. Fishing on a moonlit night was considered pleasant.[171]

In clear water fish could be caught by hand and by javelins and spears. Masʿūdī tells us of a skilled person who could catch fish by hand.[172]

Jāḥiẓ notes another method of fishing. He says that fishermen sometimes made an enclosure (*ḥaẓīra*) on one side of the river and created noise and clamour by continuous shaking and beating of a stick in the water. On hearing the sound various types of fish approached with curiosity and entered the enclosure.[173]

As a rule, it was considered that the clearer the water the better were the fish. That is why people preferred fish of the Tigris to those of the Euphrates, and those of the Euphrates to those of the Nile.[174] Similarly the fish from deep water were considered better than others, since they did not live on filth, algae, and other dirty things which generally float on the surface of small rivers and ponds. The fish of stagnant, thick and sluggish water were regarded as inferior in quality.[175]

Economic aspects of hunting

Total Estimate

The importance of hunting in Abbasid society can be gauged by some estimate of the expenditure of the court on the chase. Hunting provided a full-time occupation not merely for professional hunters but also for a vast army of organizers, trainers, and servants. The *fahhādīn* (cheetah-keepers), *kallābīn* (dog-keepers), and *bayzār* (falconers) were regular employees of the court. Besides a host of other hangers-on, archers, trappers, and runners also sought and gained

[170] Warrāq, fol. 21a; *Al-Manṣūrī fi'l-bayzara*, p. 213
[171] Warrāq, fol. 21a–b
[172] *Murūj*, vii, pp. 96–9
[173] Jāḥiẓ, *Ḥayawān*, iv, p. 193
[174] Warrāq, fol. 21a; *Al-Manṣūrī fi'l-bayzara*, p. 213
[175] Ibid., fol. 21a; *Al-Manṣūrī*, p. 213

employment. Total expenditure on the hunt by the caliphs was in consequence colossal.[176]

Although hunting was not an official institution in this period, as it was in the Mamlūk and Mughal periods, when a separate department under the direction of the master of the chase was established,[177] a considerable amount of money was set apart for the purchase of predatory animals, their fodder, the staff needed for the upkeep of animals, and the purchase of hunting weapons. Ṣābī and Ibn Zubayr have recorded in comparative detail the expenses of the early Abbasid court. According to Ibn Zubayr, the yearly budget exclusively for the payment of the hunting staff of the Caliph Mutawakkil was 500,000 dirhams.[178] This budget obviously did not include the purchase of animals, equipment, and other necessary provisions. If half a million dirhams were spent for the payment of the staff alone, then certainly a far greater amount would have been allocated for the purchase of animals (both predatory hunters and game-birds), their fodder, and other hunting paraphernalia. Ṣābī, in his *Kitāb al-Wuzarā'*, has given a more detailed estimate of the hunting expenditure of the court of the Caliph Muʿtaḍid (279–289 AH). He says that the monthly estimate of the amount paid to the hunting staff comprising hawkers, cheetah-keepers, dog-keepers, falconers, other hunting experts, lancers, people who knew the habits and disposition of the beasts, trappers, elephant-keepers and other assistants, porters and hangers-on; as well as money spent on fodder and provisions of the predatory animals was 2,500 dinars per month, the month being of 35 days. Apart from this, an instalment of 50 dinars was given for the maintenance of equipment.[179] Regarding the budget of the Caliph Muqtadir's court (295–320 AH), Ṣābī, in another book, *Rusūm Dār al-Khilāfa*, records the total amount required for a host of things. But he does not give an analysis of the expenditure into various commodities and uses. It is therefore very difficult to ascertain the exact portion of the budget

---

[176] Ṣābī, *Wuzarā'*, p. 24; idem., *Rusūm*, pp. 24–5; *Dhakhā'ir*, p. 219; *Fakhrī*, p. 75; *EI*², s.vv. *Bayzra* and *Fahd* (F. Viré); cf. also, E. Ashtor, *Prix*, p. 63

[177] *EI*², s.v. *Bayzara* (F. Viré)

[178] *Dhakhā'ir*, p. 219

[179] Ṣābī, *Wuzarā'*, p. 24

spent on a particular item. Ṣābī notes that the budget for the fodder of the beasts of burden, other animals and birds, and some other items, was 44,070 dinars per month. Similarly 42,007 dinars per annum were spent on purchasing birds, ostriches, and wild cows and their fodder, along with some other items.[180] Thus it is clear that thousands of dinars were spent by the caliphs on hunting.

As a comparison, the annual budget of the nearly contemporary Fatimid Caliph Al-ʿAzīz Bi'llāh (AD 975–96) may be mentioned here. The favourite hunting-companion of this Caliph informs us that a sum of 50,000 dinars was granted to the grand falconer (*al-bayzār*) to pay the salaries of the staff employed in the hunting department, to buy provisions for hunting-animals, and to buy Salūqī dogs and hawks. This amount did not include the extra grant paid to the master of the hunting department for the purchase of other animals.[181]

Effects of Hunting on General Economic Life

Hunting with the aid of animals, a diversion for the rich, was an important source of income for a number of people. The caliphal palace required various sorts of people for the upkeep of birds and beasts and for experts to train them.[182] From the yearly salary of such a staff for the reign of Mutawakkil, it would seem that a good number of people found employment in such work.[183] The economic impact of the royal hunt was also considerable. The organization of the pastime led to the development of markets for animals and birds and for their fodder; similarly, a thriving trade in hunting-equipment also sprang up.[184] From the *Tabaṣṣur bi'l-Tijāra* (attributed to Jāḥiẓ), it appears that dealing in sporting birds was a very profitable business and various types of birds were imported into the Baghdad market to fulfil the need of the wealthy people.[185]

---

180 *Rusūm*, pp. 22, 24–5

181 *Bayzara*, p. 7

182 This is evident from the lists of hunting employees. See, for example, Ṣābī, *Wuzarā'*, p. 24; *Dhakhā'ir*, p. 219

183 *Dhakhā'ir*, p. 219

184 *EI*², s.v. *Bayzara* (F. Viré); cf. also A. Ṭalas, *Al-Ḥayāt al-Ijtimāʿiyya fi'l-qarnayn al-thālith wa'l-rābiʿ*, in *MMII*, (1952), pp. 271–301

185 *Tijāra*, pp. 34–5

To train a hawk was an art; therefore there existed a group of people who earned their livelihood from this occupation.[186] Apart from this, some of the poor people who took to hunting as a profession depended on the income earned by selling game.[187] A report from the early 3rd century shows that francolins at Basra were sold at one dinar each.[188] Though the text does not explain whether these birds were snared or not, it can be assumed that they were game birds, as our sources do not mention the domestication of francolins. The Basran grammarian Khalīl b. Aḥmad al-Farāhīdī (100–70) is especially mentioned as living entirely on the income earned from the hunting profession and never accepting any gratuity from the court.[189] Another anecdote shows that when an ascetic was asked why he had chosen hunting as a profession, he replied that he did not find any other profession so profitable or so enjoyable.

Prices of Birds and Beasts for the Hunt

Some further indirect evidence about the expenses involved in the hunt may be gleaned from scattered information on the prices of birds and beasts. These estimates are of course very limited as a guide to the actual cost involved. It is impossible to give a set of figures that can be dated with precision. Hence it is impossible either to study movements in the prices of these animals or to compare them with the prices of other animals and commodities over a period. However, some conclusions can be drawn about the relative prices of hunting-birds. In general they were highly priced in Abbasid society, and only the rich could afford to buy them.

Our sources do not mention the prices of hunting-animals of the early Abbasid period. Hunting treatises refer to them as very costly and therefore regard hunting with animals as a sport for the wealthy.[190] There are some reports about prices of falcons in the late Abbasid period which may be

---

[186] *I'tibār*, pp. 198, 201

[187] Ibid., p. 200; *Bayzara*, p. 19; see, for an indirect reference, Jāḥiẓ, *Hayawān*, v, pp. 439–40

[188] Ibn al-Jawzī, *Ḥumuqā*, p. 70

[189] *Bayzara*, p. 6.19. On Farāhīdī see *EI*² s.v. (Ch. Pellat); also F. Viré, *Le traite de l'art de volerie*, Leiden, 1967, p. 7, n. 1

[190] *Maṣāyid*, pp. 15–16; *Bayzara*, p. 20

taken as a specimen of the general price level. A report from the sixth century shows that untrained falcons at that period were sold at 10 to 15 dinars each.[191] An anecdote relating to the early Abbasid period (third century) mentions that a foolish man bought a dead falcon for two dirhams. When asked why, he replied that he could not think of buying a live falcon even for 100 dirhams.[192]

The author of the *Tabaṣṣur bi'l-Tijāra* devotes a chapter to hawks and falcons and the better specimens brought from various lands to the Baghdad market, but he does not mention their prices.[193] In his *Kitāb al-Ḥayawān*, Jāḥiẓ compares the prices of hawks and falcons with the prices of pigeons, and says that pigeons fetched a very handsome price; some pairs were sold at 500 dinars, but no hawks fetched such prices.[194] He also notes that pigeons brought from Wāsiṭ cost 30 dinars each.[195] It is obvious that fully-trained birds must have cost more. A tradition recorded by Kushājim in the course of his discussion on the legal aspects of hunting says that "the blood money of a hunting dog (*diya kalb al-ṣayd*) is forty dirhams."[196] If this *ḥadīth* is authentic, 40 dirhams might have been an ordinary price of a trained dog in the early Abbasid period. Jāḥiẓ confirms this to be the value of a hunting-dog by quoting the tradition twice in his *Kitāb al-Ḥayawān*.[197] Unfortunately no quotation is available for the prices of other hunting-beasts such as cheetahs and weasels.

As regards the prices of the captive birds supplied as quarry to the hunting-birds in the course of their training, no more than a few instances can be cited. A francolin at this period is said to have been sold at one dirham.[198] From a legal answer

---

[191] *I'tibār*, p. 200. For the prices of falcons in the Mamluk period, see Mangalī, *Uns al-Malā'*, p. 98–9 and Ashtor, *Prix*, p. 371

[192] Ibn al-Jawzī, *Ḥumuqā*, p. 28

[193] *Tijāra*, (attributed to Jāḥiẓ), pp. 34–5

[194] *Ḥayawān*, iii, p. 212; he quotes 500 dinars as a price for a single bird, therefore a pair might be a thousand dinars. At another place (vi, p. 312) Jāḥiẓ notes apparently very low prices for eagles (*'uqāb*): a male eagle for 1 dirham; a female for half a dirham.

[195] Ibid., iii, pp. 295–6

[196] *Maṣāyid*, p. 25. The same *ḥadīth* can also be seen in Rāghib, *Muḥāḍarāt*, iv, p. 665

[197] *Ḥayawān*, i, pp. 217, 293; cf. also, Ashtor, *Prix*, p. 63

[198] Ibn al-Jawzī, *Ḥumaqā*, p. 70

delivered by the son-in-law and heir apparent of the Caliph Ma'mūn, ʿAlī al-Riḍā', it emerges that an ordinary pigeon was valued at one dirham, a chicken at half a dirham, and an egg at a quarter of a dirham.[199] The trained pigeons used for racing and communication were far dearer, and according to Jāḥiẓ a choice pair could be sold at 30 dinars; a young one fetched three dinars and an egg two dinars.[200]

Compensation

There is no direct reference to the participation of farmers, peasants and beduins in the hunting expeditions organized at the bidding of the caliphs. Therefore it is rather difficult to assess what were the reactions of such people when a hunting-party marched through their fields and habitations. Whatever might be their reaction and the degree of their participation in such expeditions, it is definitely known that the caliphs and other wealthy huntsmen paid full compensation for the damage to the crops and plantations caused during the chase. From Kushājim's advice to the hunters it can be assumed that the peasants and small land-owners expected fair and perhaps lavish compensation.[201] One particular instance of compensation at the orders of the Caliph Mutawakkil is recorded by Kushājim. It is narrated that on the return of one hunting expedition, this Caliph asked one of his secretaries, Ibn ʿItāb, to estimate and pay for the damage to the crops, which amounted to three hundred thousand and eighty dirhams.[202]

The organization and requirements of the hunt

The hunt was traditionally organized as a large party which set out from the metropolis for a specified period. Hunting parties that set out at the initiation or conclusion of a war consisted of the entire army, and were elaborate affairs. The

199 *Maṣāyid*, p. 39

200 *Ḥayawān*, iii, pp. 295–6; cf. also p. 212

201 Kushājim, *Al-Bayzara*, SOAS, Ms. No. 2091, fol. 5. Mercier, in *Chasse*, p. 51f., without mentioning the precise period writes that people from the countryside participated in hunting trips mainly to get food.

202 *Al-Bayzara*, fol. 5

routine hunting parties were modest compared to these grand cavalcades. However, they were quite an imposing sight.

Whenever the caliph or the wazir wished to go out hunting, he instructed the Master of the Chase to make preparations. The master of the royal hunt now sent message to the archers, trappers, runners and servants, and the keepers of cheetahs, falcons, hawks, hounds and horses, who instantly made ready with their trained beasts and birds to march with the hunting party. This party generally consisted of the members of the caliphal family and the intimate companions of the caliph; route guides (*mu'adhdhins*), who were expert at locating places and determining times, and were familiar with rendezvous and movement of stars and planets; the *faqīhs*, who were familiar with the laws of hunting; eloquent Qur'ān readers; secretaries and well-known physicians.[203] All sorts of provisions, drinks and first-aid boxes were taken with the hunting party. Even salt, fire-steel, saltwort, toothpick and iron skewers for grills were not omitted.[204]

Reaching the hunting ground, the whole contingent pitched their tents and made necessary preparations for hunting. Hunting with *ḥalqa*, or close-drive, was a favourite method of the Abbasids.[205] In certain conditions the hunting party would form a ring surrounding and closing in on the spot in which the game abounded. Drums were beaten to drive the animals to the middle. The animals thus driven into the enclosure were attacked by huntsmen with sticks, maces, arrows and other weapons. No sooner did a bird fly or a hare or gazelle raise the dust than the hunter went in pursuit of it. If a grouse flew, the falcon engaged it; if a hare was flushed, the hawk was slipped to engage it or drive it towards the cheetahs which were instantly sent towards it.[206] In this way game was rarely given a chance to escape. The caliphs, who were usually, in the meantime, enjoying the natural scenery of the countryside, were invited by the huntsmen to come and

---

203 Kushājim, *Al-Bayzara*, SOAS, Ms. Fol. 2; idem., *Maṣāyid*, p. 3f.; *Bayzara*, p. 41f.; 101–3; Ṣābī, *Wuzarā'*, pp. 144–5; *Nishwār*, viii, 281; *Diyārāt*, p. 164; *Fakhrī*, pp. 73–4

204 Ibid., *Al-Bayzara*, fol. 2; cf. also Mangalī, *Uns al-Malā'*, p. 10

205 *Fakhrī*, pp. 73–4; Ibn al-Kāzarūnī, *Mukhtaṣar al-Ta'rīkh* (ed. Muṣṭafa Jawād, Baghdad, 1970), p. 139; Mercier, pp. 50–1

206 *I'tibār*, pp. 193, 202; cf. also Mercier, *Chasse*, pp. 50–1

shoot as much game as they could in the enclosure.[207] Such hunting trips of the caliphs lasted for several days.[208]

The hunting of the lower social groups was of course differently organized. Many of the professional hunters, no doubt, were allowed to join and serve in the royal hunting procession; others hunted on their own in much smaller groups and with very modest preparations.

Ṣayd al-Mudāfaʿa: Hunting for the Protection of Lives, Property and Agriculture

The literature of the period does not provide us with instances of hunting being undertaken exclusively in order to protect lives and property. However, permission for such hunting is given in a *ḥadīth*, according to which the Prophet commended a man for killing a mad camel and enjoined the Companions to destroy harmful and dangerous animals.[209] There is little doubt that, especially in the villages of Abbasid Iraq, men frequently resorted to the hunting of animals which threatened crops and lives. Ibn al-ʿAwwām and Ibn Sīda have mentioned some of the harmful animals which were constant sources of trouble for agriculture and plantations. Such animals were wild rabbits, rats, foxes, jackals, wild boars, weasels, hedgehogs, jerboas, and hyenas. Other creatures such as insects, locusts, and snakes have also been mentioned.[210] We find a great deal of evidence on the hunting of these animals in our sources, but they do not mention specifically that these hunts were organized to exterminate harmful creatures. Hunting wild boar was a pastime of many celebrated hunters. A son of Hārūn al-Rashīd met his death while chasing a wild boar.[211] Usāma recollects a number of occasions when he and his party engaged in hunting boar, a task said to be tedious and extremely dangerous.[212] Since

---

[207] *Fakhrī*, p. 74; Abū Naṣr, *Al-Hawā*, p. 207; Mercier, p. 54

[208] Ibn al-Muʿtazz, *Dīwān*, pp. 184, 145, 245–6, 282–3; Abū Nuwās, *Dīwān*, p. 206ff.; cf. also Mercier, *Chasse*, p. 51f.

[209] See *Concordance*, s.v. *ṣayd*; cf. also, *Maṣāyid*, p. 37

[210] Ibn Waḥshīyya, *Al-Filāḥa al-Nabaṭīyya*, Vienna Library MS. fol. 23b; Ibn al-ʿAwwām, *Filāḥa*, fols. 155b–7a; *Mukhaṣṣaṣ*, viii, pp. 91, 98, 117–118, 120, 141–3, 177, 182, cited by El-Sāmarrāʾī, *Agriculture in Iraq, 3rd/9th century*, p. 114

[211] *Aghānī*[2], x, p. 190

[212] Usāma, *Iʿtibār*, p. 214

boars, jackals, and hyenas were not eaten, it is reasonable to assume that the animals were hunted mainly to protect agriculture and probably live-stock too. We find reference to the fact that buffaloes were trained in the hilly border areas of Syria to destroy lions, leopards and other harmful creatures.[213]

Hunting Practice and *Fiqh*

The religious literature of the period discusses various aspects of hunting in great detail. This provides some evidence about the popularity of hunting as a pastime in Abbasid society. The unique position of the scholars and the *'ulamā'* in Abbasid society, which resulted mainly from their control of the judicial and legislative systems of the state, necessitated that their approval be sought on all occasions. The overwhelming importance of the *'ulamā'* is illustrated by the fact that the caliphs had to seek guidance and approval from the *'ulamā'* even when they planned their excursions and pastimes. The *fuqahā'* always accompanied the hunting parties.[214]

The general principle on the basis of which the *fiqh* permitted the *ṣayd* were quite clear. The Qur'ān says: "They ask you what is lawful for them. Tell them all good things are lawful for you, and what you have taught the beasts and birds of prey, training them to hunt, you teach them what Allah has taught you. So eat of that which they catch for you, and mention Allah's name over it, and keep your duty to Allah: Allah is swift in reckoning."[215] There are a number of *aḥādīth* which can be cited to prove that hunting is permissible under Islam.[216] However, the fundamental sources of Islamic law detail the proviso under which hunting is considered permissible. The primary objective for which hunting is allowed under Islam is to provide for the sustenance of the hunters.[217] In fact the social life of the Muslims in the days of the Prophet and the Rightly Guided Caliphs provided very

---

[213] Jāḥiẓ, *Ḥayawān*, vii, p. 131ff; Nuwayrī, *Nihāya*, x, p. 124. There are some references which show that beasts attacked live-stock and killed them (cf. for example Jāḥiẓ, *Ḥayawān*, v, p. 355; Wakī', *Akhbār al-Quḍāt*, ii, p. 269).

[214] See p. 239

[215] *Qur'ān*, V:4

[216] See, for example, Wensinck, *Concordance*, s.v. *ṣayd*

[217] See the *Aḥādīth* relating to hunting and the books on *Fiqh*

little scope for the practice of hunting as a pastime. Hunting was undertaken by the beduins, who considered agriculture demeaning and would not attune themselves to urban life, but they hunted for food. Hence, no direct approval for the practice of hunting as a pastime could be gleaned from the primary Islamic sources. A number of theologians of the early Abbasid period and their successors discussed various legal problems relating to hunting and also provided solutions to a number of hypothetical questions that might arise in the course of a hunt.[218] This is why the legal problems of hunting constitute the introductory part of almost all the works dealing with falconry and venery.[219]

However, the avid interest that the *fuqahā'* took in this field shows the popularity of hunting. The religious literature thus testifies to the fact that in early Abbasid society hunting was a common practice for the rich and had an effect on the social life of the poor.

---

218 The Imām Shāfi'ī (d. 204), Abū Yūsuf (d. 182), Muḥd. b. Ḥasan (d. 189) compiled special treatises entitled *Kitāb al-Ṣayd wa'l-dhabā'iḥ* (cf. *Fihrist*, pp. 286, 288, 296). See, for a clear account of the different positions adopted by each of the four schools of law, Averroes, *Le livre de la chasse*, extr. of the *Bidāya*, text and trans., annotated by F. Viré in *Revue Tunisienne de Droit*, nos. 3–4, Tunis, 1954, pp. 228–59; cf. also the chapter on hunting contained in the books of law (e.g., *Hidāya*, s.v. *Bāb al-ṣayd wa'l-dhabā'iḥ*, Eng. Tr. by Hamilton). Cf. also Mercier, *Chasse*, pp. 38–41

219 See, for example, *Maṣāyid*, pp. 14–40; cf. also *EI*², s.v. *Bayzara* (F. Viré)

ig. 9. A Game of Polo

Fig. 10. The Games of Backgammon and Chess. A disputation between backgammon (*nard*) and chess (*shatranj*).

Chapter 6

Indoor and Outdoor Games

The Abbasids practised a number of sports, some of which were inherited from their forefathers while others were adopted from foreign cultures. Among their outdoor sports, horse-racing, archery, running, polo, and wrestling had a notable place. Chess, backgammon and similar indoor games were also popular. The literature surviving from this period throws insufficient light on such questions as whether or not the Abbasid period saw the emergence of new sports, or even the introduction of improvements into games and pastimes already known.

Outdoor games were played not only for recreation, but also for physical exercise and military training, whilst indoor games were regarded as a means of sharpening the mental faculties.

Outdoor games

Horse-racing

Horse-racing had been a major sport of the Arabs, even in pre-Islamic days. During the Islamic period the breeding, maintenance and training of horses became one of the means of facilitating the prosecution of the *jihād*. The Prophet regarded horse-breeding as a meritorious calling, and assigned to it a share in the booty obtained on the field of battle. This religious sanction fostered a competitive attitude amongst the breeders and encouraged the augmentation of the stock, which suffered considerable depletion in the course of the wars of that time. Cavalry was in fact to become an important factor in the military success of the Muslims. It is not surprising, therefore, that under the Abbasids a rich literature came into being which contained information on hippology, horse-breeding, the genealogies of horses and their various categories, on race-courses, horse-racing, farriery and equitation. No other animal evoked from the writers of the time so large a number of literary works, both in prose and in poetry.[1]

Horse-racing (*sibāq al-khayl* or *ijrā' al-khayl*), a part of equitation (*furūsiyya*), was regarded as essential for military training and also as an object of entertainment for the caliphs, for princes, and the people in other walks of life. Long *maydāns* (hippodromes) were set apart for this purpose in Baghdad, Samarra, Raqqa, Shamāshiya and other places.[2] Islam forbade gambling (*maysir*) but allowed the placing of

[1] Ibn Nadīm mentions the following works on the horse and on matters relating to it: *Kitāb al-Khayl*, of Abu 'Ubayda (died 210); *Kitāb al-Khayl*, *Kitāb khalq al-faras*, and *Kitāb al-sarj wa'l-lijām* of Aṣma'ī (died 213), the famous grammarian (the *Kitāb al-Khayl* has been edited and published by Haffner, Vienna 1875); *Kitāb al-Khayl* of Aḥmad b. Ḥātim (died 231); *Kitāb khalq al-faras* of Ibrāhīm al Zujāj (died 310); *Kitāb khayl al-kabīr* and *Kitāb khayl al-ṣaghīr* and *Kitāb al-sarj wa'l-lijām* of Ibn Durayd (died 321); *Kitāb al-khayl* and *Kitāb nasab al-khayl* of Muḥammad B. Ziyād al-A'rābī (died 231), one of whose books has been edited and published (Leiden 1928) by G. Levi della Vida under the title *Kitāb Asmā' al-khayl wa fursānihā*; *Kitāb khalq al-faras* of Ibn Abī Thābit; *Kitāb khalq al-khayl* of Hishām b. Ibrāhīm al-Kirmānī; *Kitāb khalq al-faras* of Qāsim al-Anbārī; *Kitāb khayl al-sawābiq* of Khawlānī; *Kitāb khalq al-faras* of al-Washshā' (died 325); *Kitāb al-khayl* of Hishām al-Kalbī (died 207), which has been published (Leiden 1928) by G. Levi della Vida under the title *Kitāb Nasab al-khayl fi'l-Jāhiliyya wa'l-Islām*, and re-edited and published by Aḥmad Zakī Pāshā from Dāru'l-kutub al-Miṣriyya in 1946; *Kitāb al-khayl wa'l-rihān* of Al-Madā'inī (died 215); *Kitāb al-ḥalā'ib wa'l-rihān* of Aḥmad al-Khazzāz (died 258); *Kitāb al-khayl bi khaṭṭ Ibn al-Kūfī* of Muḥammad b. Ḥābīb; *Kitāb al-fursan* of Abū Khalīfa (died 305); *Kitāb ṣifat al-khayl wa'l ardiya wa asmā'ihā bi Makka wa mā wālāhā* of Abū al Ash'ath; *Kitāb akhbār al-faras wa-ansābuhā* of Abu'l-Ḥasan al-Nassāba; *Kitāb al-khayl* of Qāḍī al-Ashnā'ī; *Kitāb al-khayl* of Al-'Attābī; *Kitāb al-khayl* of Al-'Utbī (died 228); *Kitāb al-khayl al-kabīr* of Aḥmad b. Abī Ṭahīr (died 280); *Kitāb jamhara al-ansāb al-faras* of Ibn Khurdādhbih (died about 300). Cf. *Fihrist*, pp. 80, 82, 83, 91, 92, 103, 104, 105, 112, 119, 126, 141, 153, 155, 165, 166, 175, 176, 210, 213. Mas'ūdī (*Murūj*, iv, pp. 24–5) mentions a book called *al-Jalā'ib wa'l-Ḥalā'ib*, written by the famous *muḥaddith* and historian 'Īsā b. Lahī'a: a work which, according to him, included a detailed description of almost every race (*ḥalba*) of the Jāhiliyya and the Muslim eras. For further literature of *furūsiyya*, see *EI*², s.vv. *Faras* (F. Viré) and *Furūsiyya* (G. Douillet); D. Ayalon, *Scripta*, ix, pp. 31 ff., and H. Ritter, in *Der Islam*, xviii, pp. 116 ff.

[2] Jahshiyārī, *Wuzarā'*, p. 207; *'Iqd*, i, p. 194; cf. also Jurjī Zaydān,

wagers on archery (*naṣal*), foot-racing (*qadam*) and horse-racing (*ḥāfir*).[3] At horse-racing prizes were offered by the caliphs, by the high dignitaries of the court, such as the wazir, and also by affluent members of society.[4] A special horse called *muḥallil* or *dakhīl* was allowed to take part in a race on condition that its owner made no wager, but received the whole amount staked by all the other entrants if his horse won.[5]

A race could take place only between horses of the same class, age, blood, degree, and training. One could, however, hold a race between a trained and an untrained horse provided that no wager was placed. Moreover, the length of the course was to be precisely defined for the race. According to Aṣmaʿī, the length of the course was fixed according to the age of the horses as follows: at two years, 40 bowshots (about 7500 metres); at three years, 60 bowshots (about 11,300 metres); at four years, 100 bowshots (about 18,800 metres).[6]

Between two competitors, a race was authorized only if it did not take place for a bet, or if the stake was furnished entirely by one of the two competitors, so that he recovered the bet if he won and lost it if he was beaten. The winner of the race was the horse which led the other at the finish at least by an ear, if the two necks were equal in length; if not, he had to be at least a shoulder ahead. In case of a tie the bet would be divided.[7]

Tamaddun, v, p. 158; Rosenthal, *Gambling in Islam*, pp. 46–52. For the description of the *maydān*, see below, pp. 262–4

[3] *Concordance* svv. *ḥafar, naṣal*; cf. also Ibn Hudhayl, *Ḥilyat al-fursān fī shiʿār al-shujʿān*, p. 142; anonymous, *al-Risāla fi'l-rimāya*, SOAS, Ms. No. 46339, fol. 159

[4] *EI*[2], s.v. *Furūsiyya* (G. Douillet); cf. also, Mercier, *La chasse et les sports chez les Arabes*, pp. 200–1

[5] Ibn Hudhayl, *Ḥilya*, pp. 143–4; *ʿIqd*, i, p. 207; *Risāla fi'l-rimāya*, SOAS, Ms. No. 46339, fols. 161–3; *EI*[2], s.v. *Furūsiyya* (G. Douillet); cf. also, Mercier, *Chasse*, 199

[6] Mercier, *Chasse*, pp. 198–9, quoting from Aṣmaʿī and other *furūsiyya* Mss. The Prophet organized races at Madīna from Hafya to Thaniyyat al-Wadā' (60 *ghalwa*) for mature horses and from Thaniyyat al-Wadā', to Banū Zurayq (10 *ghalwa*) for young horses. Cf. *al-Aqwāl al-Kāfiya*, Br. Mus. Ms. Or. 3830, fol. 58; *Ḥilya*, p. 141; also *EI*[2], s.v. *Furūsiyya* (G. Douillet)

[7] Mercier, *Chasse*, p. 199, deriving from Arabic *furūsiyya* manuscripts. See also Ibn Qayyim al-Jawziyya, *Furūsiyya*, pp. 100–1

It is also evident that one man could enter more than one horse in a race. Khālid al-Barmakī is said to have won the first three prizes in a race organized by the Caliph Manṣūr.[8] At the start of a race, as a rule, the horses were arranged side by side in a line, the straightness of that line being determined by stretching in front of them a long thread known as *miqwas*.[9]

It appears that, during the period here under review, two methods of horse-racing were in vogue: long distance races and hippodrome races. In the former a bamboo pole was fixed at a point far distant from the starting-post and the horseman who first plucked it from the ground was considered to have won the race.[10]

In a *maydān* (hippodrome) race the field (*ḥalba*) consisted of ten horses. Seven tokens (*qaṣab*) were placed on lances set within an enclosure (*ḥujra*) large enough to hold only eight horses. The tokens were generally such articles as pieces of clothing or an embroidered garment, or purses containing silver.[11] The first eight horses in the race were allowed to enter the enclosure. Seven received prizes according to their final placing in the race and only the eighth was denied a prize, its admission to the enclosure being regarded as a sufficient reward. According to the order of finishing each of the ten horses was given a special name.[12] Masʿūdī and other

[8] Jahshiyārī, *Wuzarā'*, pp. 207–8

[9] *ʿIqd*, i, p. 207; *Ḥilya*, p. 174; Mercier, *Chasse*, p. 200

[10] *ʿIqd*, i, pp. 194–5; *Irshād*, iv, pp. 116–17; *EI*², s.v. *Furūsiyya*; cf. also A. Ṭalas, *al-Ḥayāt al-ijtimāʿiyya*. in *MMII*, ii, (1952), pp. 277–8

[11] Mercier, *Chasse*, p. 200. The Prophet is reported to have offered the winners of a particular race, organized by him between Thaniyyat al-Wadā' and Masjid Zurayq, prizes as follows: 1st, three Yamani *ḥulla* (pieces of clothing); 2nd, two *ḥulla*; 3rd, one *ḥulla*; 4th, one dinar; fifth, one dirham; sixth, one token, and the others the blessings of God (cf. Kalbī, *Ansāb al-Khayl*, ed. Zakī Pāsha, Cairo, 1946, p. 8, n. 2). Rosenthal quoting from *Faḍl al-Khayl* of the 7th-century author Dimyāṭī gives another tradition which indicates that bunches of dates also formed prizes given by the Prophet to the winners (cf. *Gambling in Islam*, pp. 48–9).

[12] *Ḥilya*, pp. 144–7; *EI*², s.v. *Furūsiyya*; Mercier, *Chasse*, p. 200; cf. also ʿAbd al-Qādir, *Nukhba*, pp. 245–8. A report to be found in Yāqūt's *Irshād*, regarding a horse-race organized at the bidding of the Umayyad Caliph Hishām, is very unusual and difficult to believe. In this particular race, four thousand horses are reported to have participated over a distance of 250 *ghalwa*. A hundred tokens were placed and the row of horses stretched over a distance of six bow shots (cf. *Irshād*, iv, pp. 116–17).

writers have listed these names (with slight variations):[13]

1st: *Sābiq*, the winner.
2nd: *Mutabarriz*, the fighter; the champion.
3rd: *Mujallī*, the horse who, because of its success in a race, removes his master's sorrow.
4th: *Muṣallī* (from *ṣala*: the extreme end of the tail), so named because it sets the front of its head near the tail of the preceding horse.
5th: *Musallī* (from *Suluww*: consolation), because it brings pleasure to its master and dispels some of his anxieties. Tha'ālibī calls the fifth horse *'Ātif*, the comforter.
6th: *Tālī*, the follower. It was also known as *ḥaẓī*, the lucky one.
7th: *Murtāḥ*[14] the contented.
8th: *Mu'ammil*, the hopeful.
9th: *Laṭīm* (excluded from the enclosure), so called because it had sought to reach the goal, but had failed to do so.
10th: *Sukkayt*, the silenced, so called because its master was overcome by humiliation and was unable to talk about the race.

The Muslims used to fasten a rope around the last horse and place a monkey on its back with a whip in its hand to lash the horse, thus putting its master to shame and humiliation, while the owners of the winning horses were welcomed with ovation and received robes of honour.[15]

Horse-racing during the early Abbasid period was popular amongst people from all walks of life. Even the caliphs, the princes and the wazirs vied with each other in the breeding of race-horses. The scattered material available on this topic does not throw sufficient light on the organization of these

[13] *Murūj*, viii, 359–72; he has also recorded a poem which describes the merits of the horses participating in a race, a description which underlines the keen interest of the public in these matters (op. cit). A similar list with slight variations can also be seen in Ibn Hudhayl, *Ḥilya*, pp. 144–6.

[14] *Murtāḥ* has been regarded by some authors as the fifth horse. In that case the word derives from *rawāḥ* the palm of the hand, which signifies five (cf. *Ḥilya*, p. 145).

[15] *Murūj*, viii, pp. 371–2; *'Iqd*, i, p. 208; cf. also Mercier, *Chasse*, pp. 200–1

races, the financing of them and their frequency. Jahshiyārī, however, notes that in the court circle such races were arranged at the bidding of the caliphs. Thus Jaʿfar al-Barmakī organized a horse-race at Raqqa in response to an order from the Caliph Hārūn al-Rashīd, a race in which the horse of the Caliph was beaten by that of the wazir.[16] In another account, given by Masʿūdī, it is known that Hārūn al-Rashīd was overjoyed when he found that his horse came in first and that of his son second.[17]

It is interesting to note that people used to give their horses names;[18] for example, a favourite horse of Hārūn al-Rashīd was called *Mushammir*.[19]

Before competing in a race, a horse had to undergo a period of training, termed *taḍmīr* or *iḍmār*, which lasted for some forty to sixty days. Special care was taken by the trainer to get the horse in good condition. It was supplied with fodder early in the morning and evening: with grass and barley for a week, and then the quantity of grass was gradually decreased, until its fodder consisted only of barley. The horse was ridden daily for a *shawt* (round, or course) or two. The excess weight of the horse was sweated off under a few blankets, a process known as *ijlāl*. Before being entered for a race, horses were generally given a trial run over the distance specified for the stake. If the horse was not over-exhausted and panting, it was considered well-trained and fit for the competition.[20]

With regard to the qualities which the Muslims prized in a horse, Aṣmaʿī states that a thoroughbred should have a high belly (*baṭn*) and a short back (*ẓahr*), long shanks to the front legs (*ṭūl al-waẓīfatain fi'l-rijlain*) and short shanks to the hind legs (*qaṣr al-waẓīfatayn fi'l-yadain*).[21] Other good signs (*shiyāt*)

[16] Jahshiyārī, *Wuzarā'*, pp. 207–8

[17] *Murūj*, vi, pp. 348–9. A similar story can be seen in Ibn ʿAbd Rabbih, (*ʿIqd*, i, pp. 194–5) where it is mentioned that in a race held in the year 185 the Caliph Hārūn al-Rashīd, having won the race, asked the grammarian Aṣmaʿī to extol his horse by describing the various parts of the horse's body in a poem: a poem which contained a rich vocabulary of technical terms relating to the horses.

[18] *ʿIqd*, i, pp. 195, 200; *Aqwāl al-Kāfiya*, Br, Mus. Ms. Or. 3830, fols, 99 seq. Kalbī, *K. Ansāb al-khayl fi'l-Jāhiliyya wa'l-Islām*, pp. 5 ff.

[19] *ʿIqd*, i, p. 200; cf. also ʿAbd al-Qādir, *Nikhbat ʿIqd al-Ajyād*, p. 253

[20] *Ḥilya*, pp. 149–50; *Kitāb al-Bayṭara*, Br. Mus. Ms. Or. 1523, fols. 37–46; cf. also *EI*², s.v. *Furūsiyya* (G. Douillet)

[21] Aṣmaʿī, *Kitāb al-Khayl*, pp. 15–17

of a horse were the blaze (*ghurar*), the stockings (*taḥjīl*) or white markings above the hooves, and the *dawā'ir*, tufts of hair growing in different directions.[22] The shape of the upper parts (*al-aʿālī*), the underside (*al-sāfil*), the fore-quarters (*al-maqādim*), and the hind-quarters (*al-ma'ākhir*), its posture, its manner of walking and trotting, its speed and stamina: all these points were taken into consideration by horse lovers.[23]

Full knowledge of the principles of equitation was necessary for riders wishing to compete in a race.[24] The advice given by mediaeval Arab writers to aspiring riders was simple. The main points observed by the riders were the firmness of the seat (*thubāt*) and the evenness of the reins (*taswiyat al-ʿinān*).[25] There was no specific period for training in horse-riding. The firmness was acquired by riding bareback (*ʿala'l-ʿārī*), the rider being held in position by the grip of his thighs. As soon as the rider had some measure of experience, he was advised to use the saddle-and-fork seat. The rider had to practise riding over short and long distances regularly until he mastered the art and became an efficient rider.[26] The Turks were regarded by Jāḥiẓ as the masters of horse-riding and of fighting with bows and arrows and other weapons.[27]

Under the Abbasids, racing would seem to have been a passionate interest. The people in general, being unable to meet the expenses of horse-racing, held competitions involving camels, donkeys, mules, or dogs.[28] The two-humped racing camels were known as *bukhtī*.[29]

---

[22] *EI*², s.v. *Faras* (F. Viré)

[23] Ibid.

[24] *Ḥilya*, p. 131

[25] Ibid., pp. 131 ff.; cf. also *EI*², s.v. *Furūsiyya*

[26] Ibid.

[27] *Rasā'il*, i, p. 45

[28] Ibn Qayyim al-Jawziyya, *al-Furūsiyya*, pp. 4, 8 ff.; cf. also Asʿad Ṭalas, in *MMII*, 1952, pp. 277–8; Mez, 457. The rules and regulations governing the races between these animals were probably the same as in the case of horses. On the analogy of the legality of horse-racing, the Imām Abū Ḥanīfa and Shāfiʿī regarded it as lawful to organize races of camels, mules, and donkeys, and to place wagers on them. The Imām Mālik and Aḥmad b. Ḥanbal, however, discouraged such races and regarded horse-racing as the only lawful *ḥāfir* (hoof) game mentioned in the famous Prophetic tradition. But the majority of the *fuqahā'* (*Jamhūr*) regarded camel-racing as lawful (cf. Ibn Qayyim al-Jawziyya, *Furūsiyya*, p. 8).

[29] Mez, *Renaissance*, p. 457

Pigeon-racing

Pigeon-racing (*zajl* or *zijāl*) in competitions also enjoyed a wide popularity.[30] Pigeons, like horses, called forth a considerable literature, most of which seems to have been lost.[31] Being less expensive than horses, pigeons offered to many people a readily available means to satisfy their love of gambling. The populace became so infatuated that pigeon-racing became a social problem. The government sometimes had to take repressive measures against it, ordering the demolition of dove-cotes (*abrāj, harādī*) on the grounds that the privacy of the women dwelling nearby might be endangered and that the clamour of pigeon-trainers, and their hurling of stones at pigeons sitting on roof-tops, were a cause of public disturbance.[32] We are also told that in Baghdad there was a market called *sūq al-ṭuyūr*, where the chief articles of sale were pigeons.[33] In this market a young pigeon, according to Ghazūlī, was sold at 20 dinars, and a pigeon's egg at five dinars.[34] The pigeon-fanciers, however, did not hestitate to pay large amounts of money to obtain choice pigeons whose records of pedigree (*dafātīr al-ansāb*) were carefully kept. If the report of Jāḥiẓ is true, the price of such pedigree birds reached 500 dinars each in the Baghdad market.[35] Jāḥiẓ notes that a pair of pigeons is as productive as

---

30 Jāḥiẓ, *Ḥayawān*, ii, pp. 256–7; cf. also, Rosenthal, *Gambling in Islam*, pp. 52–5.

31 Ibn Nadīm, in his *Fihrist*, mentions a number of books written during the time of the early Abbasids, e.g., the *Kitāb al-Ḥamām* of the philologist, Abū ʿUbayda (d. 210); the *Kitāb Ansāb al-Ḥamām* and *Kitāb mā wurida fī tafḍīl al-ṭayr al-hādī* of a certain Ibn Ṭarkhān al-Mughannī; and the *Risāla fī tamwīkh al-Ḥamām*, of al-Kindī (cf. *Fihrist*, pp. 80, 222, 242). Qalqashandī notes that a certain Al-Qawwās al-Baghdādī wrote a book on pigeons for the Abbasid Caliph Nāṣir, an ardent pigeon enthusiast (cf. *Ṣubḥ*, ii, 87 ff; xiv, pp. 369 ff.). The Mamluk scholar Qāḍī Muḥi'l-Dīn Ibn ʿAbd al-Ẓāhir (620–92) is said to have compiled a book called *Kitāb Tamāʾim al-Ḥamāʾim* (cf. *EI*², s.v. *Ḥamām*, by F. Viré).

32 *Muntaẓam*, viii, pp. 294, 308; Ibn al-Athīr, *Kāmil*, x, 85; Damīrī *Ḥayawān*, s.v. *ḥamām*. According to Ḥamadānī (*Maqāmat*, p. 168), thieves and burglars used pigeons as their aids in theft. They released the pigeon onto the roof-top of a house and followed the bird, pretending to be a pigeon-fancier.

33 Jāḥiẓ, *Ḥayawān*, i, p. 118; *Manāqib Baghdād* (attributed to Ibn al-Jawzī), p. 26

34 *Maṭāliʿ*, ii, p. 260

35 Jāḥiẓ, *Ḥayawān*, iii, p. 212

a landed estate, and in the markets of Baghdad and Basra a young male pigeon of good pedigree will fetch 20 dinars or more, a female 10 dinars or more, and an egg 5 dinars.[36] Similarly, pigeons brought from the city of Wāsiṭ were highly prized. A Wāsiṭī pigeon was sold, at this period, at 30 dinars, a fledgling at 3 dinars and an egg at 2 dinars.[37] Jāḥiẓ observes that, although pigeon-racing was popular among people from almost all walks of life, it was the *khiṣyān* (eunuchs) who showed the greatest interest in it.[38]

The method used for training the homing pigeons (*zājil*, plural *zawājil*) was that the moment the young pigeon, having grown its feathers, left the nest and tried to fly, it was compelled to return to the nesting place through narrow holes at the foot of the loft (*burj*). The bird was thus persuaded to climb to the top of the loft by the steps of a ladder. This process was repeated several times, till the muscles of the bird became sturdy and its homing instinct "experienced" (*mujarrab*). To intensify the homing instinct, the bird was mated very early in life. To ensure that the bird's affection for its mate would cause it to come back, when separated, the owner carried the bird in a basket and released it. This manoeuvre was continued for some time, the distance being increased every day.[39]

A second method of training was to raise a long post on the roof of a tall house. Around this post food was scattered and the bird was taken there twice a day. After having been fed, the bird was taken away and released to fly over the nearby houses, the point of release being extended gradually further and further from the food. The bird's owner took special care to see that no pair of birds was released at the same time; if the male was to be released, the feathers of its female were plucked out, and vice-versa. Once the bird was accustomed (*muwaṭṭan*) to this training, it would return easily to the post from distant places.[40]

From the observations of Jāḥiẓ it appears that wide

---

[36] Ibid., iii, p. 212

[37] Ibid., iii, pp. 295–6

[38] Ibid., i, p. 118; cf. also Bayhaqī, *Maḥāsin*, p. 611

[39] *EI*², s.v. *Ḥamām* (F. Viré); Ṣabbāgh, *Musābaqāt al-barq wa'l-ḥamām*, pp. 53 ff.

[40] Jāḥiẓ, *Ḥayawān*, iii, pp. 274–5

publicity was given to each pigeon-racing competition before it was held. We are told that on one occasion a large number of people gathered on a high place merely to enjoy the sight of the pigeons returning home at the end of a particular contest.[41] Despite demands from some quarters that pigeon-racing be declared illicit, some of the *fuqahā'* legalized this sport on the grounds that it was useful as a means of rapid communication, especially during times of war.[42] People of this time, taking advantage of the approval, satisfied their interest in it by placing bets on competitions. The Abbasid Caliphs Mahdī, Hārūn al-Rashīd, Wāthiq and Nāṣir were all known to be addicted to this pastime.[43] It is reported that, realizing the enthusiasm of Hārūn al-Rashīd for pigeon-racing, one narrator of *ḥadīth* concocted a *ḥadīth* by adding the word *ḥamām* to the well-known tradition of the Prophet wherein archery and horse-racing received encouragement. The Caliph, however, ordered the pigeon which had occasioned this deceit to be killed, saying that it had led a man to concoct a *ḥadīth* for him.[44]

Polo

Unlike pigeon-racing, the game of polo (*laʿb bi-ṣawlajān*) was limited to the higher and more sophisticated elements in Abbasid society.[45] The Abbasid caliphs, especially Hārūn al-Rashīd and Muʿtaṣim, were very fond of this pastime.[46] They used to play it often with their *nadīms*. Ṭabarī records that the Caliph Muʿtaṣim was seen playing *ṣawlajān* with his *nadīm* Isḥāq b. Ibrāhīm, both of them wearing a light sports costume called *ṣudra*.[47] Like the caliphs, their wazirs also took keen

[41] Ibid., iii, p. 256. It has been reported that some birds were able to fly from the Bosphorus to Basra, from Cairo to Damascus, or from Tunis to Cairo in a single flight (cf. *EI*², s.v. *Ḥamām*, by F. Viré).

[42] Damīrī, *Ḥayawān*, s.v. *Ḥamām*; Ibn Qayyim al-Jawziyya, *Furūsiyya*, p. 8.; Ṣabbāgh, *Musābaqāt al-barq*, p. 29

[43] *EI*², s.v. *Ḥamām* (F. Viré). See also, *Murūj*, vi, p. 314

[44] ʿAbd al-Qādir, *Nukhbat ʿIqd al-Ajyād*, p. 239

[45] Ṭabarī, iii, pp. 496, 1326–7, 1808; *Murūj*, vii, p. 298; Mez, p. 406

[46] Ibid., iii, pp. 1326–7; *Murūj*, viii, p. 296; *Kāmil*, vi, p. 216; Ibn Qayyim al-Jawziyya, *Aḥkām ahl al-dhimma*, i, p. 220

[47] Ṭabarī, iii, pp. 1326–7. On one occasion, Muʿtaṣim's Turkish General, Afshīn, refused to play against him because Afshīn did not want to oppose the Caliph even in a game (Ibn al-ʿAbbās, *Āthār al-Uwal*, p. 130, cited by Hitti in the *History of the Arabs*, p. 339).

interest in this sport. ʿUbayd Allāh, the wazir of the Caliph Muʿtaḍid, is said to have played it regularly.[48] It is possible that the soldiers also paid much attention to this sport and practised it as a part of their military training. The Turkish soldiers, according to Jāḥiẓ, played it skilfully.[49] The details found in our sources are, however, inadequate to provide a full picture of this game, which was widely played in court circles.

Ṣawlajān (the word is an Arabic version of the Persian *Čawgān*) originated in Persia and came into Muslim usage possibly during the Umayyad period.[50] It was under the early Abbasids that it became a favourite pastime of the caliphs and other affluent members of society. The game was generally played on horse-back.[51] It appears that, to lessen the danger in the game, a limited number of people were allowed to take part at one time. According to the *Qābūsnāma*, four people formed a team.[52] Players were divided into two teams, each carrying a long-handled stick with one end bent back (*ṣawlajān*).[53] The game was started by one of the players throwing the ball as high into the air as possible. Another struck it, and thus the ball passed from player to player. Each team tried to get the ball between two posts defended by the opponents, the posts being located at the end of a pitch so large that it gave ample freedom of movement for the mounted participants.[54]

---

[48] Quatremere, *Mamlukes*, i, 125, quoting from the History of Bibars, Mansouri man. Arab. 668, fol. 38

[49] Jāḥiẓ, *Rasāʾil*, i, p. 21

[50] *EI*², s.v. *Čawgān* (H. Massé). Mercier (p. 226) considers it an "Aryan" invention. On the authority of Ṭabarī he also notes that polo was played in Persia as early as the 4th century before Christ in the court of Darius III (cf. *Chasse*, pp. 223–6).

[51] *EI*², s.v. *Čawgān* (H. Massé)

[52] *Qābūsnāma*, quoted by R. Levy in "A Mirror for Princes". According to Quatremere (*Mamluke*, pp. 122 f.) and Mercier (*Chasse*, pp. 224–5), six men constituted a team: two at the entry of the arena, two in the middle, and two on the far side.

[53] *EI*², s.v. *Čawgān* (H. Massé). Quoting Quatremere, Mercier states that the word *ṣawlajān* corresponds to the modern club, while *chawgān* indicates a kind of small racket with a very long handle (cf. *Chasse*, p. 223).

[54] *EI*², s.v. *Čawgān* (H. Massé); Jurjī Zaydān, *Tamaddun*, v, p. 159. Jāḥiẓ is said to have compiled a book on polo players entitled *Kitāb al-Ṣawālija* which may throw some further light on the organization and rules of this

The players, as a rule, had to be very careful not to injure the other players or smash the ball, even though half a dozen of these balls were worth only one dirham.[55] Balls were generally made of leather.[56] The Caliph Mutwakkil is said to have been in the habit of playing polo with leather balls and wooden sticks.[57] His Christian *nadīm*, Salma b. Saʿīd, once disclosed to the Caliph that his ostentatious wazir ʿAbd Allāh b. Yaḥyā spent thirty thousand dinars on balls and polo-sticks made from silver, information which incurred the displeasure of the Caliph and led him to take drastic action.[58] To prevent any interference with the spectators sitting on the wall of the *maydān* (hippodrome), the polo players "made the course 60 yards broad."[59]

Ṭabṭāb

The game of *ṭabṭāb* was quite common at the court of the Abbasids.[60] It appears to have been one of the most popular of the *furūsiyya* games.[61] The game of *ṭabṭāb*, it would seem, was very similar to polo. It was played on horseback with a broad piece of wood or racket (*ṭabṭāb*) and a ball.[62] The game of *ṭabṭāb* is reported to have been one of the favourite pastimes of the Caliph Hārūn al-Rashīd, who is also believed to be the first among the Abbasid caliphs to have played it in a *maydān*.[63] The Turkish troops of the Abbasids are reported

game. Acccording to Mursī al-Khūlī (quoted by Rosenthal, *op cit.*, p. 56) the manuscript is preserved in a Moroccan library.

[55] Ibn Qutayba, *ʿUyūn*, i, p. 134; cf. also Mez, p. 406

[56] Ibn Qayyim al-Jawziyya, *Aḥkām ahl al-dhimma*, i, p. 220

[57] Ibid., i, p. 220

[58] Ibid., p. 220

[59] *ʿUyūn*, i, p. 134; Mez, p. 406. In the time of the Mamluk sultanate, polo games began, as a rule, after the *Ẓuhr* prayer and continued till the *ʿAṣr* prayer: from about 2 p.m. until 5 p.m. (cf. D. Ayalon, *Scripta*, ix(1961), pp. 53–4, quoting from Qalqashandī, *Ṣubḥ*, iv, p. 47)

[60] *Murūj*, viii, p. 296

[61] Jāḥiẓ, *Rasāʾil*, i, p. 21; ii, p. 376

[62] *Lisān* and Lane, s.vv. *Ṭabṭāb.*; cf. also Aḥmad Taymūr, *Alʿāb al-ʿArab*, pp. 54–5. Hitti's (*History of the Arabs*, pp. 339–40) suggestion that *ṭabṭāb* might have been "tennis in its rudimentary form" does not seem correct, as the game of *ṭabṭāb* was generally played on horseback (cf. Jāḥiẓ, *Rasāʾil*, ii, p. 376). The rules and regulations of the game were probably the same as in polo.

[63] *Murūj*, viii, p. 296

by Jāḥiẓ to have been the champions of the game of *ṭabṭāb*.[64]

Birjās

The game called *birjās*[65] was widely practised at this time.[66] It was more a military exercise than a public game. According to Masʿūdī, the Caliph Hārūn al-Rashīd was the first Caliph to play *birjās* in the hippodrome.[67] It was a game in which the players, mounted on horses, rode one after the other, releasing arrows at a target.[68] It is reported that during the reign of the Caliph Muʿtaḍid regular military training was carried out by means of this game. The mounted troops had to participate as a test by which their proficiency was judged and their rate of pay fixed.[69] Each horseman was asked to shoot at the *birjās* target; if he shot correctly, remaining firm and still, and kept the reins of his horse under control, his name was enrolled in the group "J", an abbreviation of *jayyid*, meaning "excellent"; whereas those who missed the target narrowly were placed in group "T", an abbreviation of *mutawassiṭ*, meaning "mediocre"; and those who arrived late, could not ride well or

---

[64] Jāḥiẓ, *Rasā'il*, i, p. 21

[65] The word appears as *birjās* in Masʿūdī (*Murūj*, viii, p. 296) and as *birjaṣ* in Ṣābī (*Wuzarā'*, p. 17)

[66] *Murūj*, viii, p. 296; Ṣābī, *Wuzarā'*, p. 17

[67] Ibid., viii, p. 296

[68] Dozy, *Suppl.* s.v. *Birjās*; Ṣābī, *Wuzarā'*, p. 17. Redhouse defines *birjās* as "a mark to shoot at". According to Steingass it is "a butt to shoot at, especially elevated high in the air" (cf. D. Ayalon, *Scripta*, 1961, p. 56, n. 141; also, Latham and Paterson, *Saracen Archery*, p. 83). Mercier, from his observation of miniature paintings in the Bibliothèque Nationale, Paris, defines the game of *birjās* as "a particular target, an empty cylinder or barrel set up horizontally on four legs. The horsemen passed at a gallop, normally with an axe and at a certain distance from the cylinder, threw it while arriving in front of its opening, and the axe had to pass straight through" (cf. *Chasse*, p. 205). According to the observations of Latham and Paterson, *birjās* is a "ring or hoop mounted on a spear for use in lance exercises. Under certain circumstances it may also have served as a target for archers in training" (*Saracen Archery*, p. 180). On the authority of a sixteenth-century Paris MS entitled *Kitāb al-makhzūn jāmiʿ al-funūn* (Bibliothèque Nationale, Arabe, 2826, fols. 104 a–b) Latham and Paterson note that in the game of *birjās* the cavalryman, having set up a hoop by means of a wooden truck on top of a short lance, charges and, engaging the target on his left, aims to snatch up the hoop with the end of his full-length "candle-form" lance (*Saracen Archery*, p. 83).

[69] Ṣābī, *Wuzarā'*, pp. 17–18

failed to hit the target, came under group "D", an abbreviation of *dūn* (plural of *adwan*), meaning "inferior".[70] The Turkish soldiers, being traditionally good archers, excelled at the game of *birjās*.[71]

Archery

Archery (*ramī al-nushshāb*) was one of most popular games of this period. Since the bow was a main weapon in war, the sport of archery was always regarded with special favour and esteem. The Abbasids were much devoted to the maintenance of archery, which now assumed sufficient importance to attract the attention of numerous authors who compiled treatises on this subject.

Archery was one of the main elements in the military training and the *furūsiyya* exercises practised under the Abbasids. The sources written during or soon after the third century often refer to archery, but give few details about it. Some valuable information relating to this century can be gleaned, however, from subsequent works of *furūsiyya*, composed in the time of the later Abbasids, the Ayyubids and the Mamluks.

In flight shooting (*ramī al-sibāq*), preference was given to arrows which were round, thin, spindle-shaped, light, hard and strong. They were thinned down near the neck and trimmed with pinion feathers.[72] People practised archery in a number of ways, and on special occasions competitions were held amongst renowned archers. A novice generally practised by shooting against targets of all kinds: near, still and moving. It appears that in trick-shooting the archer used various methods of releasing the arrow and aimed at different

[70] Ṣābī, *Wuzarā'*, pp. 17–18

[71] Jāḥiẓ, *Rasā'il*, i, p. 21

[72] *Arab Archery*, p. 117; *Saracen Archery*, p. 104; *Qiṣṣat qaws wa sahm*, Br. Mus. MS. Or. 3134, fol. 32. These arrows, including the arrowhead and the feathers, equalled in weight six to eight dirhams (cf. *Arab Archery*, p. 118). The Mamluk author Ṭaybughā' notes that the lighter the arrow, the greater its range; the lightest flight arrows in his experience weighed six dirhams (285·6 gr.); cf. *Saracen Archery*, p. 104. The weight of a competition bow was heavier than that of a normal bow by three ratls (cf. *Arab Archery*, p. 118). On weights and measures of Islamic bows and arrows, see *Saracen Archery*, pp. 159–60. For further details on Arab arrows and bows see A. Boudot-Lamotte, *Contribution à l'étude de l'archerie musulmane*, Damascus, 1968.

types of targets.[73] For still targets archers made use of "imitation horsemen" and "opposing targets". In the former case, material the height of a mounted horseman was set in position; a disc about a span in diameter was attached to it, representing a horseman's head; and a shield about three spans in diameter was placed one span below the disc. The target was located at a distance equivalent to the cast of the bow, and arrows were aimed at the shield and the "head". In the second method, four targets were set up, one to the right, another to the left, the third in front and the fourth to the rear. The archer, having planted his feet firmly on the ground, had to stand in the centre, holding four arrows between his fingers, and shoot them at the four targets, moving only his torso and not his feet.[74]

Archery competitions were carried out in two ways, by target shooting and by long-distance shooting; the former was unanimously approved of by the *fuqahā'*, whereas the latter was discouraged by some amongst them.[75] Since betting was allowed on archery, the people showed great enthusiasm for this sport. As in horse-racing, the employment of a *muḥallil*[76] was considered necessary for such wagers.[77]

Some of the rules observed in target shooting were that the number of shots (*rashq*) be determined before starting a competition; the bows and arrows of each competitor should be of the same kind and quality; shooting distance be fixed—according to the Shāfiʿītes of Iraq, the minimum distance was 250 yards and the maximum 350 yards; the prize money should be particularized and not be kept vague. Lots might be cast to determine the man to start shooting; if the prize was being given by a dignitary, he might choose a competitor and ask him to start.[78]

---

[73] *Arab Archery*, pp. 131–45; Rosenthal, *Gambling in Islam*, p. 59. On the procedures, conduct, and principles to be observed by a novice in archery, see Ibn Qayyim al-Jawziyya, *Furūsiyya*, pp. 106 ff.; *Saracen Archery*, pp. 152 ff.

[74] *Arab Archery*, pp. 145–6

[75] Ibn Qayyim al Jawziyya, *Furūsiyya*, pp. 79–80; *Ghunya*, Br. Mus. MS. Or. 1358, fols. 94, 196–9

[76] For *muḥallil* see above, p. 245

[77] *Ghunya*, fols, 196–7; *Risāla fi'l-rimāya*, SOAS, MS. 46339, fol, 159

[78] Ibn Qayyim al-Jawziyya, *Furūsiyya*, pp. 80 ff.; *Risāla fi'l-rimāya*, fols. 163 ff. For details see *Furūsiyya*, pp. 80 f.

Like *ramī al-nushshāb, ranī bi'l-bunduq* (shooting with the cross-bow) was also popular. The projectiles (*banādiq*) were made of earth, stone, steel, or lead.[79] The use of the cross-bow, a weapon popular among the Persians, is said to have made its appearance amongst the Muslims as early as the time of the Caliph ʿUthmān.[80] By the time of the first Abbasids there were men famous for their skill with this particular instrument, who used to visit various parts of the empire, urging other experts to compete with them.[81] It is reported that the Caliph Hārūn al-Rashīd had in his service a group of these archers, known as *al-namal*, who attended him in sport and on hunting expeditions.[82]

Three schools of archery emerged during the Abbasid period, each school being named after a renowned archer of that time: after Abū Hāshim al-Māwardī, Ṭāhir al-Balkhī, and Isḥāq al-Raqqī.[83]

Competitions in archery, both on horseback and on foot, were held usually in autumn, either in the morning or in the

[79] *Ghunya*, fol. 179. For a discussion on the *qaws al-bunduq* see Chapter 5 *Hunting* above, p. 224

[80] Kushājim, *Maṣāyid*, pp. 247–8; cf. also A. Ṭalas, in *MMII*, 1952, p. 278

[81] *Aghānī*[1], xx, p. 93; see also Asʿad Ṭalas, *al-Ḥayāt al-Ijtimāʿiyya*, in *MMII*, 1952, p. 279

[82] Ibid., xx, p. 93; cf. also, J. Zaydān, *Tamaddun*, v, p. 159

[83] *Qiṣṣat al-qaws wa'l-sahm*, Br. Mus. MS. Or. 3135, fols. 11–12; *Kitāb al-ramī*, Br. Mus. MS. Or. 3135, fols. 1–2; *Arab Archery*, p. 16. Some writers (e.g., the author of the *Qiṣṣat al-qaws wa'l-sahm*, fol. 11b, and of the *Kitāb al-ramī*, fol. 1) read Māwardī as Bāwardī and Raqqī as Raffā'. Latham and Paterson think Māwardī to be erroneous and take it as al-Bāwardī, from Bāward, a town and district on the northern slopes of the mountains of Khurāsān in an area now within Turkmenistan (U.S.S.R.); cf. *Saracen Archery*, p. 39. The dates at which these three masters of archery lived are very uncertain, and, in the absence of documentary evidence, impossible to ascertain. The tentative findings of Latham and Paterson may be accepted until some further research proves something conclusive. They observe that "to judge from their names, they were certainly all Muslims and therefore could not have antedated the first quarter of the seventh century AD, and, as they are mentioned by Mardī, the second half of the twelfth century can be taken as a rough *terminus ante quem*. To suppose that they lived no earlier than the middle of the eighth century would, in the absence of evidence to the contrary, be a reasonable guess since it was from early Abbasid times that large-scale recruitment of troops and officials from Khorasan and Transoxiana began." (Cf. *Saracen Archery*, p. 39)

evening. Humid or windy weather was avoided for such contests, since these conditions hindered the best use of the bow and decreased its range.[84]

Wrestling (*Muṣāraʿa*)

Another popular sport was wrestling. The caliphs and the high dignitaries of the court encouraged this pastime, employed famous wrestlers, watched the matches and even joined personally in feats of wrestling.[85] The Caliph Amīn is reported to have been especially fond of this exercise.[86] He fought a duel with a lion and injured his fingers badly in the combat.[87] In order to show his physical strength and prowess the Caliph Muʿtaḍid fought a duel with a lion and killed it. He attacked the lion so suddenly with his sword that it took only two strokes to finish the combat.[88]

Wrestling matches of the fourth century, held at the bidding of the Buwayhid Muʿizz al-Dawla at Baghdad, presented a remarkable scene. On the day of the wrestling competition a tree was set up in the race-course (*maydān*) with prizes of valuable items hanging from it. Purses of dirhams were placed to the foot of the tree. Musicians with drums and flutes made the occasion colourful. The contest continued for hours and the winners received rewards and robes of honour from Muʿizz al-Dawla.[89]

Weight Lifting and Other Sports

Weight lifting was also popular at this time, even with the caliphs and their courtiers. Muʿtaṣim, possessing a well-built body, often took this form of exercise. It is said that he was able to lift a weight of a thousand *raṭl* (about one thousand pounds) which he raised above his head, walking several steps with it.[90] On one occasion he lifted an iron door which weighed 750 *raṭls* (about 750 pounds).[91]

---

[84] *Qiṣṣat al-qaws wa'l-sahm*, fol. 33; Br. Mus. MS. Or. 1358, fol. 98; *Arab Archery*, p. 120

[85] *Muntaẓam*, vi, p. 341; cf. also A. Ṭalas, *MMII*, 1952, p. 279

[86] *Murūj*, vi, p. 432

[87] Ibid., vi, p. 432

[88] *Muntaẓam*, v, pt. 2, p. 129; *Nishwār*, ii, *RAAD*, xvii, p. 453

[89] Ibid., vi, p. 341; cf. also Mez, *Renaissance*, p. 406

[90] *Fakhrī*, p. 316

[91] *ʿIqd*, ii, p. 304; cf. also Munajjid, *Bain al-Khulafā'*, p. 100; Rosenthal, *Gambling in Islam*, pp. 55–7.

Other sports such as running, fencing, boat-racing, swimming and the lance game (*laʿb al-rumḥ*) were also in vogue amongst the populace.[92] As these recreations cost little, people from all walks of life took an interest in them. The military training of the Abbasid troops depended in no small degree on *furūsiyya* exercises of this kind.[93] The Abbasids enthusiastically practised and vied with each other in swimming, with the result that some of them acquired skill in performing the most difficult feats. Expert swimmers could even "swim standing, carrying in their hand a utensil with fire in which food was cooking".[94] The Tigris at Baghdad, with its 30,000 boats employed in passenger and goods transport, offered excellent facilities for boat-racing.[95] Like other sports, this too presented a colourful scene for spectators. On festive occasions, boat-racing may have been one of the main sources of recreation for the people of Baghdad.

Contests of Animals

Amongst the sports of the Abbasid period, contests of animals and bird-fighting have a special place. Such games were welcomed with enthusiasm by the caliphs as well as by the common people. Beasts such as dogs and rams, and birds such as cocks, partridges and quail were used in competitions.[96] The large traffic in these animals at the special markets called *Shāriʿ al-kabsh wa'l-asad* (the street of rams and lions) and *sūq al-ṭuyūr* (bird market) in Baghdad indicates the favour shown to these sports.[97] From information to be

[92] *Muntaẓam*, vi, p. 341; Ibn Qayyim al-Jawziyya, *Furūsiyya*, pp. 7, 106; *Baghdād* (ed. M. Jawād et al.), p. 38, quoting from Abu'l-Wafā' (d. 513); see also, A. Talas, *MMII*, 1952, p. 279. There was much betting on these games, with the result that some of the *fuqahā'* declared these pastimes to be unlawful (cf. Ibn Qayyim al-Jawziyya, *Furūsiyya*, pp. 7–8).

[93] Jāḥiẓ, *Rasā'il*, i, p. 21. According to Ibn Qayyim al-Jawziyya (*Furūsiyya*, p. 106) *furūsiyya* has four branches: horse-riding, archery, lance-throwing and fencing; whosoever masters these exercises, masters the *furūsiyya*.

[94] *Muntaẓam*, vi, p. 341; cf. also, Mez, p. 407

[95] Mez, p. 407; *Manāqib Baghdād* (attributed to Ibn al-Jawzī), p. 27

[96] *Murūj*, viii, p. 230; *Aghānī*[1], vi, p. 75; Ibn al-Ukhuwwa, *Maʿālim al-Qurba*, p. 242; cf. also Mez, p. 404

[97] *Murūj*, viii, p. 184; *Manāqib Baghdād*, p. 26. The common people often laid bets on these competitions (cf. Mez, p. 404); Rosenthal, *op. cit.*, pp. 57–8

found in Masʿūdī it appears that the Abbasid caliphs kept a large number of such animals in their royal zoo.[98]

Contemporary sources throw very little light on the details of animal contests organized perhaps periodically by the enthusiasts. The avid interest of the early Abbasid caliphs, however, led a group of people to find employment in the court chiefly as the keepers of the animals. The *kabbāshīn* (ram keepers), *dayyākīn* (cock masters) and *aṣḥāb kilāb al-hirāsh* (keepers of fighting dogs) were regular employees of the Abbasid court.[99] With reference to the court of the Caliph Mutawakkil, Ibn Zubayr mentions the enormous sum of money spent on the maintenance of such a staff. The annual pay of these employees and three other court servants amounted to five hundred thousand dirhams.[100] This amount did not include the money spent on the purchase of the animals, their food and the like.

Since these contests were not considered lawful by the *Sharīʿa*, there is no mention of the rules and conditions governing the contests in the books of *fiqh* and *furūsiyya*. How far the common people were addicted to these sports is, therefore, difficult to ascertain. There is evidence, however, that in the court circles, contests of animals were frequently organized at the bidding of the caliphs on special occasions such as *Nawrūz*. It is said that a duel of lions and buffaloes was organized at the orders of the Caliph Muʿtaṣim.[101] On special occasions the animals were brought out, perhaps to a *maydān*, and matched one against the other, a contest which thrilled and delighted the spectators. These sports sometimes caused dissension amongst the owners of the animals and birds.[102] Thus we hear of enmity between the Caliph Mustakfī and Faḍl b. Muqtadir, provoked by a dispute which arose in the course of a contest involving pigeons, rams, cocks and quail.[103] It was perhaps to prevent such discord that the

---

[98] *Murūj*, viii, p. 19. About the middle of our period Muʿtazz is said to have shown to his guests, as a great marvel, a fight between the lions and the elephants in the zoological garden (cf. Mez, p. 404).

[99] Ibn Zubayr, *Dhakhāʾir*, p. 220; *Murūj*, viii, p. 19

[100] Ibn Zubayr, *Dhakhāʾir*, p. 220

[101] Jāḥiẓ, *Ḥayawān*, vii, p. 131; Nuwayrī, *Nihāyat al-Arab*, x, p. 124

[102] *Murūj*, viii, p. 379; cf. also Ibn al-Ukhuwwa, *Maʿālim al-Qurba*, p. 242

[103] *Murūj*, viii, p. 379

Caliph Muhtadī Bi'llāh (ruled AD 869–70), after assuming the office of *khilāfa*, banned all fighting between animals, ordering the beasts in the royal zoo to be killed immediately.[104] His decree, however, did not continue long in force, since the court circle rejected such a severe attitude, the earlier state of affairs being restored after the assassination of Muhtadī.

It is reported that the servants of the caliphal palace were greatly addicted to these sports. Their enthusiasm went so far that sometimes it made them indifferent to their duties. Ibn Ṭayfūr records that, although he called them several times, the Caliph Ma'mūn was unable to gain the attention of his servants, then intent on watching cock-fighting and other games in the courtyard.[105] Jāḥiẓ states that the *khiṣyān* (eunuchs) revealed as great an interest in these sports as they did in pigeon-racing.[106]

Maydān (Hippodrome)

It is interesting to note that hippodromes (*mayādīn*) were constructed by the Abbasid caliphs for the practice of various sports and for organized competitions. They also served as *furūsiyya* training grounds for the military elements. From the information of Ṣābī, it appears that there was more than one kind of hippodrome.[107] The caliphs built hippodromes around or inside their palaces, the structures being different no doubt from the *maydāns* erected outside the towns, often on the bank of a river.[108] Thus Ṣābī speaks of the "*maydān al-ṣaghīr*" at Baghdad, an arena which the Caliph Muʿtaḍid Bi'llāh used to visit and where he participated in games with much enjoyment.[109] This *maydān*, which was built near the *birkat al-sibāʿ*, seems to have been a large one, as sumptuous apartments were erected in it for the caliph and his *nadīms* (intimate companions) and a large garden was laid out there. Most probably the *maydān* was surrounded by a stone wall,

104 Ibid., viii, p. 19

105 Ibn Ṭayfūr, *Baghdād*, p. 55; Bayhaqī, *Maḥāsin*, p. 554

106 Jāḥiẓ, *Ḥayawān*, i, p. 118; *Maḥāsin*, p. 611

107 Ṣābī, *Wuzarā'*, p. 17; Ṭabarī, iii, 1808; *Murūj*, vii, 299

108 *Nishwār*, i, p. 70; *Kāmil*, vi, p. 155; cf. also *Sāmarrā'*, Baghdad, 1940, pp. 62–5.

109 Ṣābī, *Wuzarā'*, p. 17. Ṭabarī (iii, p. 1808) mentions a *maydān* called "maydān Bughā al-Ṣaghīr" at Samarra, where Turkish soldiers played polo.

with a large gate protected by an iron chain. Ṣābī speaks of a "garden gate" inside the *maydān* which was shut before any exercise was carried out. This might be a small gate, or else it indicated the main gate which we have assumed to exist there. A number of amenities were provided in the hippodrome, for we hear about a place for ablutions (*ḥujrat al-waḍū'*), a dining room (*khawarnaq*) and a rest room (*majlis*). The room for ablutions was at some height, since we are told that the Caliph Muʿtaḍid ascended some steps to it.[110] From another passage found in Ṭabarī it is known that well-heated and perfumed bathrooms were built in the *maydān* to enable the caliph and others to clean their bodies after exercise.[111] The Caliph Muʿtaṣim is said to have enjoyed a bath in one of these rooms after playing polo, and spent several hours there, talking with his partner.[112]

The first *maydān* in Baghdad for horse-racing was built by the Caliph Mahdī thirty years after the foundation of Baghdad.[113] After the extermination of the Barmakids, Ma'mūn is said to have built a *maydān* for polo within the grounds of the Hārūnī palace.[114] Similarly Amīn, after he became caliph, ordered the building of a *maydān* at the palace of Abū Jaʿfar al-Manṣūr.[115] The Jawsaq Palace of the Caliph Muʿtaṣim had "an almost bottle-shaped race-track, the neck lying on the axis of the palace".[116] The east side of the Jawsaq, with its vast rectangular enclosure and a number of transverse walls behind it, has been identified by Herzfeld and Viollet as the palace polo-ground, the stables being for the polo-ponies, and the lodge for the spectators.[117] The bottle-shaped race-course to the east of this is, according to Rogers, something different.[118] The Caliph Mutawakkil is said to have erected the *Tall-al-ʿAlīj* or *Tall-al-ʿAlīq* and the *burj al-Qā'im*, an

[110] Ṣābī, *Wuzarā'*, p. 17

[111] Ṭabarī, iii, pp. 1326–7; cf. also *Murūj*, vii, p. 299

[112] Ibid., pp. 1326–7

[113] S.A.El-Alī, *The Islamic City*, ed. Hourani and Stern, pp. 93, 101

[114] Yaʿqūbī, 253, quoted by Rogers in *Islamic City*, p. 151

[115] *Kamil*, vi, p. 155

[116] Rogers, *Islamic City*, pp. 151–2; see also Herzfeld, *Geschichte*, air-photographs 3 and 4

[117] Herzfeld, *Mitteilungen*, pp. 196–204; Viollet, *Description*, pp. 695–8; cited by Rogers, *op. cit.*, p. 152, *n.* 109

[118] Rogers, op. cit., p. 152, n. 109

enormous mound, as a grandstand from which to have an adequate view of the race-course. The *Tall-al-ʿAlīq*, it is said, had a nine-roomed kiosk from the top of which the Caliph could watch his horses.[119]

Indoor games

Shaṭranj

Shaṭranj or *shiṭranj* (chess) seems to have been the favourite indoor game of the Abbasids. According to the sources, a certain Abū Ḥāfiẓ al-Shaṭranjī was famous as a renowned *shaṭranj* player who lived in the time of the Caliph Hārūn al-Rashīd.[120] Other renowned chess players of the third and fourth centuries were ʿAdlī, Rāzī, Māwardī and Ṣūlī.[121] ʿAdlī in fact had stood alone in the first class of chess players for some considerable time, until he was defeated by Rāzī in a match which was played in the presence of the Caliph Mutawakkil.[122] Among the caliphs, Hārūn al-Rashīd is said to be the first who played *shaṭranj*. He granted a maintenance allowance to some chess players.[123] His son Ma'mūn, like his father, showed a keen interest in the game. He used to say "*shaṭranj* sharpens the intellect," and is said to have written a poem on it.[124] Of other caliphs of this time, Mutawakkil and Muʿtaḍid were enthusiastic players of chess.[125]

Competitions often took place amongst chess players. The first well-known competition was arranged in AD 819 in

[119] Yāqūt, *Buldān*, iv, p. 22; Qazwīnī, *Nūzha*, 42; cited by Rogers, op. cit., pp. 151–2

[120] Maḥfūẓ, *Shaṭranj*, pp. 7–8

[121] *Murūj*, i, p. 161; viii, pp. 311–12; Munajjid, *Khulafā'*, pp. 108–9; A. Ṭalas, *MMII*, 1952, pp. 276–7; cf. also Murray, *History of Chess*, pp. 198 ff.

[122] *Fihrist*, p. 221; Murray, *History of Chess*, pp. 170, 198

[123] *Murūj*, viii, p. 296. Hārūn's enthusiasm for chess is evident in his own words when he says: "it is impossible to live without some kind of recreation, and for a monarch, I can suggest no better diversion than chess" (cf. Br. Mus. MS. Add. 23, 517, fol. 163).

[124] Munajjid, *Khulafā'*, p. 108; cf. also Murray, *History of Chess*, p. 197, quoting from Ibn Badrūn and Suyūṭī

[125] *Murūj*, viii, p. 271; Ṭabarī, iii, p. 1671; Ḥuṣrī, *Jamʿ al-Jawāhir*, p. 30. For a chess competition organized at the orders of the Caliph Muktafī (289–95), where Ṣūlī beat the then court champion al-Mawardī: *Murūj*, viii, pp. 311–12

Khurāsān between Jābir al-Kūfī and Ziryāb al-Qaṭṭān in the presence of the Caliph Ma'mūn.[126]

The popularity of chess can be judged from the fact that, with a view to increasing the prices of their slave-girls, the merchants took pains to train them in chess. ʿArīb, the slave-girl of the Caliphs Amīn and Ma'mūn, was regarded as an accomplished slave-girl because of her excellence at chess, amongst other attainments.[127]

The wide interest shown in this game made it a subject of special study and writers of the time wrote books about it. According to Ibn Nadīm, the first man to write on the subject was ʿAdlī, who produced two books, called *Kitāb al-Shaṭranj* and *Kitāb al-nard wa-asbābuhā wa'l-laʿb bihā*, on chess and backgammon.[128] Other noted writers of the 9th and 10th centuries AD were Abū Zayd al-Balkhī, Rāzī, Ṣūlī, Muḥammad b. ʿUbayd Allāh al-Lajlāj, Ibn al-Uqlīdasī, Qarīṣ al-Mughannī, and Abū Yūsuf al-Maṣṣīsī.[129]

Chess, originally an Indian game, is said to have been invented by an Indian prince Ṣiṣṣa for a king named Baltīt.[130] Later, it passed from the Indians to the Persians and then to the Arabs.[131] In the country of its origin the game was known as *chatūr anga*, meaning "four members of the army", elephants, horses, chariots and foot-soldiers (the king and queen not being counted among the troops).[132] Arab

[126] Maḥfūẓ, *Shaṭranj*, pp. 7–8; *Muḥāḍarāt*, ii, p. 727

[127] Suyūṭī, *Mustaẓraf*, p. 37; Munajjid, *Khulafā'*, pp. 108–9

[128] *Fihrist*, p. 221; Eng. Tr. by Bayard Dodge, i, p. 341

[129] Their works were: Abū Zayd al-Balkhī: *Kitāb al-Shaṭranj*; Rāzī: *Kitāb Laṭīf fi'l-shaṭranj*; Ṣūlī: *Kitāb al-Shaṭranj* (*nuskhat al-ūlā*: first manuscript) and *Kitāb al-Shaṭranj* (*nuskhat al-thāniya*: second manuscript); Lajlāj: *Kitāb Manṣūbāt al-Shaṭranj*; Ibn al-Uqlīdasī: *Kitāb Majmūʿ fī manṣūbāt al-Shaṭranj*; Qarīṣ: *Kitāb fi'l-shaṭranj*; Maṣṣīṣī: *Kitāb Taḍʿīf būyūt al-Shaṭranj* (cf. *Fihrist*, pp. 199, 221–2, 392; Eng. Tr. by B. Dodge, i, pp. 304, 341–2; ii, p. 665). Ibn Nadīm mentions Ibn Ṭarkhān too among the writers on chess, but forgets to give the title of the work (cf. *Fihrist*, p. 222; Eng. Tr. p. 342). None of these treatises would seem now to be extant (cf. Murray, op. cit., 169 ff.). For existing chess manuscripts of late Muslim mediaeval period and a brief discussion on them, see Murray, op. cit., pp. 171 ff.

[130] *Murūj*, i, p. 159; *EI*[1], s.v. *shaṭrandj* (B. Carra de Vaux); Somogyi, *Table Games*, p. 238; cf. also Murray, op. cit., p. 207 f.

[131] Murray, op. cit., pp. 186 ff.; Firdawsī *Shāhnāma* (ed. J. Mohl, Paris), vi, pp. 385–401

[132] *Table Games*, p. 240, n. 3; Steingass, *Persian-English Dictionary*,

grammarians and philologists in the past, however, tried in vain to find a derivation for the word *shaṭranj* either from the Arabic or from the Persian language. According to Damīrī, the word is derived either from *al-mushāṭara* (halving) or from *al-tashṭīr* (uniting, bringing together).[133] According to Ḥākim, the author of the *Kitāb Nuzhat al-Shaṭranj*, it is derived from the Persian *shash-rang* (six colours), the six kinds of chess-men, or from *hasht-rang* (eight colours), the eight squares of the chess-board.[134]

From the presents of the Rāja of Qanūj given to the Shāh of Persia, Khusraw I, Anūshirwān (AD 531–79) it appears that chess-boards, at first, were generally made of wood.[135] Masʿūdī, referring to the third century, makes mention of a red leather chess-board.[136] An addition to the popular forms of the game introduced at this time was known as *al-Jawāriḥiyya*, or zodiacal chess, played with the human organs,[137] where all the six senses of man[138] were arranged against each other. The game was begun with the throwing of a die, the throw indicating which of the chess-men was to be moved.[139] It was the dice that settled the movement of the pieces and not the skill of the player.[140]

Much attention has been paid in Muslim literature on chess to the qualifications which made a man eligible for the game and also to the etiquette which should be observed in the playing of it. A chess-player ought to be a man of elegance, good memory and probity. He should be well-groomed, well-

London, 1892, p. 734; Majīd Yaktā'ī *Peshīna-e-Tārīkh-e-Shaṭranj*, in *Majalla Bar Rasīha-e-Tārīkhī*, Iran, vol. 26, 5th year, no. 2, pp. 105 ff.

133 Damīrī, as quoted by Somogyi, *Table Games*, p. 240

134 Cf. John Rylands Library, Manchester, MS. 766 as quoted by Somogyi, in the *Bulletin of the John Ryland Library*, vol. 41, No. 2, March, 1959, pp. 431–2

135 Firdawsī, *Shāhnāma*, vi, pp. 385–401; cf. also Murray, op. cit., pp. 150 f. For a detailed discussion on Muslim chess boards see Murray, op. cit., pp. 220 f. Jāḥiẓ mentions *takht al-nard* (backgammon board) in *Bukhalā'*, p. 30.

136 *Murūj*, viii, p. 316

137 Ibid., viii, p. 314; Mez. p. 403; *EI*¹, s.v. *Shaṭrandj* (B. Carra de Vaux)

138 The six senses are those by which we speak, hear, see, grasp and move and the universal sense belonging to the heart (cf. Murray, *History of Chess*, p. 342).

139 Somogyi, *Table Games*, p. 237

140 *EI*¹, s.v. *Shaṭrandj* (B. Carra de Vaux)

behaved, and quick in his answer whenever he is asked a question.[141] This mode of conduct was observed by the players of the time, especially when they competed with the caliphs or the high dignitaries of the court. The Caliph Ma'mūn, however, did not like such formalities in playing, and is reported to have said to the players, who were playing stiffly and formally in front of him, "Chess and politeness do not go well together. Talk naturally as you would among yourselves."[142] It is perhaps because of this fact that, among the qualifications of a prospective companion, the author of the *Kitāb al-Tāj* lists ability in archery, hunting, playing ball and chess, in all of which the companion may equal his royal master with no fear of affronting him.[143]

Nard (Backgammon)

Another indoor game popular at this period was backgammon, or *nard*. It was played on a checkered board divided into twelve points, symbolizing the number of months in a year, thirty pawns representing the number of the days in a month and two dice acting as the divine will and human submission to it.[144] Backgammon was, however, held to be inferior to chess, a game in which the decisive features are the insight

---

[141] Ibn Abī Ḥajala, *Kitāb Anmudhaj al-qitāl fī laʿb al-shaṭranj*, John Rylands Library, MS. 767, fols. 31a–41a; also MS. No. 766, fol. 42a

[142] Rāghib, *Muḥāḍarāt*, ii, p. 727; Mez, p. 404; Murray, op. cit. p. 197

[143] *Tāj* (attributed to Jāḥiẓ) p. 72. Mālik b. Anas, Abū Ḥanīfa and Aḥmad b. Ḥanbal, basing their verdict on specific *ḥadīth*, regarded chess-playing as unlawful; whereas Shāfiʿī and some of the other *fuqahā'* declared it to be legal, resting their judgement on the usefulness of the game, which sharpened the mind and afforded a training in warfare, and on the point that some of the *ulema* active in earlier times had played chess. A more correct opinion, as Damīrī indicates, held the game to be *makrūh* (disfavoured). Even the *ulema* who thought chess to be licit imposed a number of conditions: it should not be played for wagers; it should not be allowed to draw a man from his prayers and his other religious duties; it should not become an occasion for improper language; and it should not be played in the street or in a public place (cf. John Rylands Library, MS. No. 766. fol. 14b; also Somogyi, *Table Games*, pp. 241–3). For a detailed discussion on the legal aspects of chess, see Murray, op. cit., pp. 188 f. who derives information from the traditions recorded in the existing chess literature.

[144] *Murūj*, i, p. 158; *Table Games*, pp. 239–40; Mez, p. 404; Rosenthal, *Gambling in Islam*, pp. 40–3

and choice of the players and their capacity for discrimination between good and bad.[145]

Mediaeval Muslim sources are almost unanimous in stating that backgammon originated in Persia.[146] The historian Masʿūdī, on the other hand, asserts that it came from India, offering, however, no historical evidence for his contention.[147] The Arabo-Persian name of the game, *Narda-shīr*, might be connected with its legendary inventor, Ardashīr b. Bābak (AD 212–241), King of Persia.[148]

Notwithstanding the unanimous opinion of the *ʿulamāʾ* that backgammon was illicit, the people of this time, high and low alike, played it frequently. Since *nard* was a game of chance, it was openly played for money.[149] Muḥammad b. Aḥmad b. Ḥamdūn is said to have gambled away seventy thousand dirhams in one sitting with the Caliph Muʿtaḍid Bi'llāh.[150] It is interesting to note that on one occasion the Caliph Hārūn al-Rashīd, while playing backgammon with Ibrāhīm al-Mawṣilī, lost the game and was compelled by the stipulations of the bet to remove his clothes.[151]

There was yet another indoor game called *laʿb bi'l-kaʿb*: draughts, or ossicles.[152] According to Lane, *kaʿb* means a play-bone, a little bone, more or less oblong in shape, from the foot of a sheep; it is thrown in play like a die.[153] No details of this game have been given in the available sources. It seems likely, however, that it was in the nature of other table games such as chess and backgammon.[154] It was a game which

145 *Table Games*, p. 240; Mez, p. 404

146 Cf. *Table Games*, pp. 239–40, 243–4 and the sources quoted there

147 *Murūj*, i, p. 157. At another place, however, Masʿūdī notes that it was Ardashīr b. Bābak who played this game for the first time (cf. *Murūj*, i, p. 158).

148 *Table Games*, p. 239; Rosenthal, *Gambling in Islam*, p. 42

149 Shābushtī, *Diyārāt*, p. 13; Mez, p. 404. See for a detailed discussion on Jurists' opinion on the game of *nard* and *shaṭranj*, Rosenthal, *Gambling in Islam*, pp. 88ff.

150 Ibn al-Jawzī, *Adhkiyāʾ*, p. 35

151 *Aghānī*[1], v, p. 39. Cf. for another story of *nard* competition involving the Caliph Amīn and the wazir Faḍl b. Rabīʿ, Rosenthal, *Gambling in Islam*, pp. 21–2, who quotes from Jahshiyārī's *Wuzarāʾ*.

152 Ibn Ṭayfūr, *Baghdād*, p. 55; Bayhaqī, *Maḥāsin*, p. 554

153 Lane, *Lexicon*, s.v. *kaʿb*. See also Rosenthal, *Gambling in Islam*, p. 41.

154 Shayzarī, *Nihāyat al-Rutba*, p. 103; Ibn al-Ukhuwwa, *Maʿālim al-Qurba*, p. 171; *kaʿb* might also be played with date-stones (cf. Jāḥiẓ,

appealed, it seems, mainly to children, although adults also took part in it.[155] From Shayzarī's *Nihāyat al-Rutba* it would seem that *kaʿb* was a game of chance.[156]

Shādghullī

Another game was known as *shādghullī*, about which the sources provide only fragments of information which are difficult to interpret.[157] The name *shādghullī* is said to derive from the Persian *shād* (enjoyment) and *gul* (roses).[158] On the actual playing of *shādghullī* the chronicles give no more than one or two brief anecdotes. It is recorded by Shābushtī that the Caliph Mutawakkil, on one occasion, is said to have had five million light dirhams (each weighing two grains) struck in the colours red, yellow and black, and to have ordered his courtiers and servants, numbering 700, to don new tunics and caps in contrasting colours. On a windy day, the Caliph gathered them together in a magnificent dome-shaped edifice having forty doors and built especially for the purpose. When all the courtiers encircled him, he ordered the coloured dirhams to be thrown into the wind, which caused them to scatter like the petals of roses, thus presenting a colourful and lively scene.[159] This was the game of *shādghullī* which the Caliph was playing with such elaborate preparation. Another anecdote in connection with *Shādghullī* is interesting. Abu'l-Qāsim al-Barīdī, on one particular occasion at Basra, is said to have sat drinking in front of a pile of roses valued at twenty thousand dirhams; into the roses he threw twenty thousand dirhams, equal in weight to half the same number of ordinary dirhams, and numerous fine pieces of *nadd*,[160] camphor and figures (*tamāthīl*) with which to play *shādghullī*. The attendants afterwards plundered the roses for the dirhams and the

Bukhalā', p. 137; *ʿUyūn*, iii, p. 261). The phrase *laʿb al-nawā*, to be found in Shābushtī's *Diyārāt* (p. 173), perhaps indicates the game of *kaʿb*.

[155] Ibid., *Nihāya*, p. 103; *Maʿālim*, p. 171; cf. also Badrī, *ʿĀmma*, p. 278

[156] *Nihāya*, pp. 103–4

[157] *Nishwār*, i, pp. 147, 234; ii, in *RAAD*, xvii, pp. 517, 522; Shābushtī, *Diyārāt*, p. 160; Ibn Zubayr, *Dhakhā'ir*, p. 122

[158] Aḥmad Taymūr, *Laʿb al-ʿArab*, p. 37

[159] *Diyārāt*, p. 160; *Dhakhā'ir*, p. 122

[160] For *nadd*, see Lane, s.v., where the word is defined thus: "A certain kind of perfume, well-known, with which one fumigates, or a compound of aloes-wood aromatized with musk and ambergris."

scent. The poet Abū Firās compared the game with a snowfall in the following verse:[161]

"The eye that sees the falling snows
Might think them petals of white rose,
Raining on men who play *shādghullī.*"

Samāja

Another game played by the caliphs and other high ranking officials at the court was *samāja*, something like masquerade.[162] The Caliph Mutawakkil is said to have participated in this game on the days of *Nawrūz*, and mixed with other masked actors freely.[163] *Samāja* is defined by Lane and others as a game which is foul, unseemly and ugly.[164] On the actual play of *samāja* our sources do not mention more than that the participants wore masks and plundered coins or other valuable objects thrown in the course of play by the caliph or other dignitaries.[165] It is reported that while the Caliph Mutawakkil was disporting with the actors of *samāja*, one of the actors came very close to him and began to look for a stray coin under the flaps of the royal coat. This provoked the displeasure of an old *nadīm* of the Caliph, who advised him not to allow any actor to approach so closely, warning that it offered too many opportunities for assassination. Henceforth the Caliph witnessed the performance from a height in a *majlis*.[166] Ṭabarī mentions the *ṣuwar* (figures, masks) of *samāja* found in the house of the Turkish general Afshīn when his house was searched at the orders of the Caliph Muʿtaṣim.[167]

An important feature of Abbasid society was the existence of social centres, "clubs", where people gathered together and played various games. The establishment of such clubs,

---

[161] *Nishwār*, i, p. 147; Eng. Tr. by Margoliouth, p. 161

[162] Ibid., i, p. 234

[163] *Diyārāt*, pp. 39–40; Ṭabarī, iii, p. 1318; *Imtāʿ*, i, p. 59; Ṣūlī, *Ashʿār awlād al-khulafāʾ*, p. 249

[164] *Lexicon*, s.v. *samāja*

[165] Cf. for example,*Diyārāt*, pp. 39–40

[166] Ibid., pp. 39–40; cf. also Mez, p. 424

[167] Ṭabarī, iii, p. 1318. According to Ibn Zubayr, the Caliph Muʿtaḍid on one *Nawrūz* occasion spent 13,000 dinars on the game of *samāja* (cf. *Dhakhāʾir*, p. 38).

according to *Aghānī*, dates back to the early Umayyad period, when a wealthy man established such a club-house in Mecca and provided it with facilities for the playing of chess, backgammon and dice.[168] The club-houses of Abbasid times were furnished with all the amenities of life; even pegs were fixed in the wall to receive the upper garments of visitors.[169] In addition to the club-houses accessible to dignitaries and belletrists, there were special rooms in the houses of well-to-do people; rooms reserved for indoor games and used only by the owner or by his guests. A merchant of Damascus, we are told, entertained his guests in his games-room with chess, backgammon, and also with books which he kept for this purpose.[170] An incident connected with Aḥmad b. Mudabbir, collector of taxes in Palestine under Muhtadī (255–6), shows that wealthy people also kept good chess-players in their households.[171] The hostelries (*ḥānāt*) conducted by Jews and by Christians may have served as establishments where people could play indoor games.

Ladies' games

The women of Abbasid society took an interest in indoor games such as chess and backgammon. Some of them also shared in outdoor games such as archery and horse-riding. Mahdī's daughter Yāqūta (the Ruby) is said to have been in the habit of riding out by the side of her father, dressed in male attire.[172]

Another game known as *fanzaj* was played especially by the Nabaṭī women of our society. It was a game of dancing, where ladies held hands and danced together, while singing

---

168 *Aghānī*[1], iv, p. 52. From Shābushtī's *Diyārāt*, it is known that the Christian monasteries to be found in Baghdad and other places were frequented by pleasure-loving Muslims where, in addition to wine-drinking and amusements, they also played indoor games. Cf. also Rosenthal, *Gambling in Islam*, pp. 23–4

169 Ibid., iv, p. 52; cf. also, *Table Games*, p. 243, n. 2; see also H. Zayyāt, *Mashriq*, 35(1937), *Muṭāla'a al-dafātir wa'l-kutub wa'l-lahw bi'l-al'āb fi'l-mujtama'āt qadīman*, pp. 499–500. Rosenthal, *op. cit.*, pp. 144–5

170 *Nishwār*, i, p. 195; Mez, pp. 402–3

171 *Murūj*, viii, p. 13

172 Ṭabarī, iii, pp. 543–44. De Goeje reads Yāqūta as Bānūqa. Muir's reading (*Caliphate*, p. 472) Yāqūta is more correct.

a chorus.[173] Jawāliqī identifies this game with *dastband*, a Persian word taken over into Arabic and meaning "the interlocking of hands" (in dancing). He describes it, furthermore, as a Magian (*majūsī*) game.[174]

Foot-racing is also mentioned among the sports of the slave-girls. The Caliph Mutawakkil is said to have been in the habit of organizing races amongst his slave-girls.[175]

Children's games

Among the favourite games played by children at this time can be numbered *Buqayrī, ʿAẓm waḍḍāḥ, Khaṭra, Dāra, Shahma, Luʿbat al-ḍabb, Dūbāraka, Laʿb bi'l-damī, Junnābī.*

Of the pastime called *Buqayrī* (cf. *buqara*, "to split open") Jāḥiẓ states that it was a game in which children made a heap of sand or dust. One of the players would hide an object in one of his hands, push both of his hands into the pile, asking his opponents to decide which of his hands contained the object.[176] A later author, Rāghib (died 505) describes *buqayrī* in simpler terms, declaring that the children made a heap of sand, dividing it then into two, an object being hidden in one of the halves and the opponents being asked to guess what the object was.[177]

ʿAẓm waḍḍāḥ or *ʿUẓaym waḍḍāḥ* was a game in which two groups of children took a white bone on a dark night and threw it away as far as possible and then ran in that direction to pick it up. The child who was the first to find it was victorious, and his group received the privilege of riding on the backs of the rival group from the place where the bone was found to the place from which it was thrown.[178]

Khaṭra (literally "danger") was a game in which children took some rags or scraps of material and twisted them together to form a whip. It was then given to a member of one group

173 *ʿIqd*, iii, p. 179; Jawāliqī, *Muʿarrab*, p. 237

174 Jawāliqī, *Muʿarrab*, p. 237

175 Ḥuṣrī, *Jamʿ al-Jawāhir*, p. 182

176 Jāḥiẓ, *Ḥayawān*, vi, p. 145; cf. also Aḥmad Taymūr, *Laʿb al-ʿArab*, pp. 12–13

177 *Muḥāḍarāt*, iv, p. 724; *Lisān*, s.v. *baqar*

178 *Muḥāḍarāt*, iv, p. 724; Jāḥiẓ, *Ḥayawān*, vi, p. 145; Ibn Manẓūr notes that children used to make the bone quite small; it was then called *ʿuẓaym*, the dimunitive form of *ʿaẓm* (cf. *Lisān*, s.v. *ʿAẓm*; see also Aḥmad Taymūr, *Laʿb al-ʿArab*, pp. 39–40).

of children who would proceed to "whip" the members of an opposing group. While the boy with the whip in his hand tried to lash the members of the other party, they tried to catch him. If the boy was caught, his party lost the game and had to carry on their backs the members of the rival group.[179] Jāḥiẓ, describing the game, says that the whip was thrown by one group to the other, to be caught by them. If they failed to catch it, they would throw it to the former group. If they did manage to catch it, they won the game and had the privilege of riding on their opponents.[180]

The game of *D̄ara*, said by Jāḥiẓ to be identical with the game called *Kharāj*,[181] is explained thus by Muḥammad Hārūn: "It is a well-known game, wherein a child hides something in his hand and asks his companions to find out what the object is."[182] Aḥmad Taymūr presents a different explanation of the game. He says that two children sat back-to-back, other children moving around (*dāra*) them. In course of their movement these children tried to beat the sitting boys, while they tried to seize those who beat them. If one of the moving children was grasped and held, he would sit in place of the child who caught him.[183]

Shahma was played on summer nights. Two groups of children fought each other over a particular boy. One group would attempt to snatch him away from the other group, which would try to protect him. The victorious group would enjoy the privilege of the riding on the backs of their defeated rivals.[184]

Laʿb al-ḍabb, the lizard game, so named because it required a picture of a lizard, was played by children, one of whom was asked to put his hand on a certain portion of the portrait, with his back turned towards it. If he could place his hand on the correct point, he could ask others to do the same. Should he fail, he lost the game and would be obliged to let all the participants ride on his back, one at a time.[185]

179 Ibid., *Muḥāḍarāt*, iv, p. 724; *Laʿb al-ʿArab*, pp. 23–4
180 Jāḥiẓ, *Ḥayawān*, vi, pp. 145–6
181 Ibid., vi, p. 146
182 Ibid., vi, p. 146, note 2
183 Aḥmad Taymūr, op. cit., p. 30
184 Jāḥiẓ, *Ḥayawān*, vi, p. 146
185 Ibid., vi, p. 146; *Muḥāḍarāt*, iv, p. 724; Aḥmad Taymūr, op. cit., pp. 37–8

Dūbāraka (mannikin), as the word indicates, is of Persian origin and meant "bride". On the night of Muʿtaḍidī (New Year's Day),[186] children used to make a doll the size of a girl, decorating it splendidly and arraying it with ornaments resembling the ones worn by a bride. The *dūbāraka* was then set on the roof of a house and the people amused themselves by beating drums, playing on flutes, and by lighting fires around it.[187]

Junābī or *Junnābī* was a game played with *junnābī* (a basket, according to the definition given by Aḥmad Taymūr).[188] The basket was hidden by one group of children and was sought by another. Usually the game was played by children,[189] although adults occasionally took part.[190]

Young girls played more often with *damī* (dolls) than with other toys. These dolls were made of clay fashioned in the shape of different animals or human beings.[191] On special occasions such as the *ʿĪd al-Fiṭr* or the *ʿĪd al-Aḍḥā*, *damī* were brought to Baghdad in such large quantities that the *muḥtasib* Abū Saʿīd al-Iṣṭakhrī (died 328) had to establish a special market there known as *sūq al-laʿb*.[192]

On special occasions, such as wedding ceremonies, a game known as *kuraj* was played by young girls. They took a wooden horse and covered it with a beautiful tunic, put a rope around its neck and pulled it about, playing and shouting.[193]

---

[186] For the origin of this day see Ṭabarī, iii, p. 2143; *EI*¹, s.v. *Nawrūz* (R. Levy)

[187] *Nishwār*, i, p. 217; Aḥmad Taymūr, op. cit., p. 30

[188] *Laʿb al-ʿArab*, p. 19

[189] *Lisān* and *Mukhaṣṣaṣ*, s.v. *janab*

[190] *Aghānī*², x, pp. 280–1; cf. also Aḥmad Taymūr, op. cit., p. 19

[191] Māwardī, *Aḥkām*, p. 251; Ghazālī, *Iḥyā'*, ii, p. 67; Abū Yaʿlā, *Aḥkām*, p. 278

[192] Ibn al-Ukhuwwa, *Maʿālim al-Qurba*, p. 56; Māwardī, *Aḥkām*, p. 251

[193] Ṭabarī, iii, p. 971; cf. also, Nawfal, *Ṣannājāt al-Ṭarab* p. 379. Jāḥiẓ notes that the children in the early Abbasid period played nutshell games mostly in the courtyard of the house. The children dug holes and threw nutshells into them (cf. Jāḥiẓ, *Bukhalā'*, p. 71; Eng. Tr. in "The life and works of Jāḥiẓ", p. 242). Nutshell games were used by thieves as one of their tricks: cf. *Nishwār*, i, p. 78. Rosenthal (*Gambling in Islam*, p. 65) mentions some other names of children's games played in different periods of Muslim history: *qula, zuḥlūqa, ṭuban, fiyāl, midḥāh, ḥājūra*. These games do not appear to have been popular among the children of the early Abbasid period.

Fig. 11. 'Id Celebration. A group of soldiers and high officials going to the prayer hall in procession.

Fig. 12. A Hajj Procession. A pilgrim caravan marching towards Mecca with flags and drums.

Chapter 7

Festivals and Festivities

Of the festivals observed under the Abbasids, some were of religious origin, kept by Muslims alone, others were confined to the Christians and Jews, and some were festivals celebrated by all, irrespective of religion. Some festivals, too, had a local and not a general importance.

Muslim religious festivals

The Month of Ramaḍān

The ninth month of the Muslim calendar is believed to be the month of the revelation of the Qur'ān, and hence special reverence and respect are shown to it.[1] This is the sacred month of fasting, which means abstention from eating, drinking and sexual intercourse during the hours between dawn and sunset.[2] In fact the beginning of the sacred month of Ramaḍān concerned profoundly, and still concerns, the life of every Muslim. As soon as its commencement was announced, people from all walks of life, even those who were inclined to neglect their daily prayers, thronged to the mosques for the *tarāwīḥ*, a special prayer offered in congregations during the month of Ramaḍān.[3] Ṭabarī notes that when Mutawakkil held the *tarāwīḥ* prayers in the Ja'fariyya

[1] See, for example, the accounts given by Maqdisī about the Ramaḍān observed in various countries (cf. pp. 100, 183, etc.). Cf. also Grunebaum, *Muhammadan Festivals*, p. 56; S. D. Goitein, *Studies in Islamic History and Institutions*, pp. 100–1; *EI*[1], s.v. *Ramaḍān* (M. Plessner)

[2] Grunebaum, *Festivals*, p. 56; cf. also *EI*[1], s.v.

[3] Ṭabarī, iii, p. 1452; Muq. pp. 100, 183; cf. also Grunebaum, *Festivals*, p. 54

mosque, no one prayed in Samarra; that is, when prayers were held in the Mosque of Abū Dulaf no one remained behind in the quarter of Al-Ḥayr to pray in the Great Mosque which Mutawakkil had built there.[4]

Maqdisī notes that the Ramaḍān festivities of Mecca were proverbial in the Muslim world.[5] In the tenth century AD Maqdisī found the people of Aden most enthusiastic in observing the sacred month of Ramaḍān. Two days before the commencement of the month, they decorated the roof-tops of their houses and beat drums (*dabādib*). When Ramaḍān started, the youths gathered together in the small hours of the morning and patrolled the city until dawn, reciting verses in praise of the month and the fast. The practice continued, it would seem, for the whole month. When the time of the *ʿĪd al-Fiṭr* was imminent, they collected money from the people and made more elaborate preparations for the *ʿĪd*.[6] People in other areas, such as Baghdad, also made elaborate preparations to welcome the month of Ramaḍān.[7]

The thirty days' (or twenty-nine days')[8] fasting of this month has always been regarded by the Muslims as a most important religious act, and is performed with much pomp and gaiety. The last ten days of the month of Ramaḍān were devoted to special religious ceremonies. The pious Muslims then retired to a mosque to perform the *iʿtikāf*, a religious custom of high merit in which a Muslim is obliged to sit in the mosque for at least twenty-four hours, devoting his time to prayers and other religious duties.[9] The thirty parts of the Qur'ān were generally recited in the *tarāwīḥ* prayers,[10] and the last day of its recitation, towards the end of Ramaḍān, was a day of much celebration. According to Maqdisī the beauty of the celebration of the "*khatm*" in the Aqṣā Mosque

[4] Ṭabarī iii, p. 1452

[5] Muq. p. 183

[6] Ibid., p. 100

[7] Baghdādī, *Bukhalā'*, pp. 90, 149

[8] Unlike the solar Christian calendar, the months of the Muslim lunar calendar are of either 29 or 30 days.

[9] *EI*[1], s.v. *Iʿtikāf* (Th. W. Juynboll). It was in these last ten days of Ramaḍān that the *lailat al-qadr* (The Night of the Divine Decree), which is decreed by God as "better than 1,000 months", is supposed to occur (cf. *EI*[1], s.vv. *Iʿtikāf* and *Ramaḍān*; also, Goitein, *Studies*, pp. 103–4).

[10] Muq. p. 100

surpassed all other places.[11] Though details of this celebration are not mentioned, it can be assumed that people on this night prepared some special types of food and spent the night in prayers and recitation of the Qur'ān.

It seems that the *muḥtasib*, in order to facilitate fasting, made arrangements to announce the time of the "*suḥūr*".[12] In some places, the mosque had public kitchens attached where food was served in the month of Ramaḍān.[13] Presumably the money for the food was supplied by the caliphs, or by philanthropists. From Tanūkhī's *Nishwār* it is known that people often exchanged gifts (*hadīya*) in the month of Ramaḍān.[14]

ʿĪd al-Fiṭr

The *ʿId al-Fiṭr*, or the feast of the breaking of the fast, occurs on the 1st of the month of Shawwāl, the tenth month of the Muslim calendar.[15] It is also called *ʿĪd al-Ṣaghīr*, or the Lesser Feast.[16] Once the new moon of Shawwāl was announced, the news was carried far and wide with much excitement. Since the *ʿĪd al-Fiṭr* marked the end of a period of exhausting devotion, it was celebrated with much greater enthusiasm than the *ʿĪd al-Aḍḥā*, known as the Great Festival.[17] Ṣābī in his *Rusūm dār al-Khilāfa* mentions the elaborate preparations made by the caliphs, wazirs and high ranking officials, and gives a description of the processions held by these people early in the morning on the *ʿĪd* day.[18] It was the custom of the wazirs and the military commanders to initiate splendid processions at dawn with relatives, friends, officials and

[11] Ibid., p. 183

[12] Cf. for the practice in Egypt, Kindī, *Wulāt*, 201. The *suḥūr* is the meal taken before dawn.

[13] Azdī, *Ta'rīkh al-Mawṣil*, p. 248. It seems that the food shops were not opened during the day. Licentious people are found in the sources disliking the month of Ramaḍān. Abu'l-Faraj al-Iṣfahānī is said to have hated Ramaḍān, because during it he could not quench his thirst for wine (cf. *Irshād*, v, p. 167).

[14] *Nishwār*, i, p. 99

[15] Bīrūnī, *Āthār*, p. 333; Eng. Tr. p. 331. For a detailed account of the origin of this festival see Qalqashandī, *Ṣubḥ*, ii, p. 406; *EI*², s.vv. *ʿĪd* and *ʿĪd al-Fiṭr* (E. Mittwoch)

[16] Grunebaum, *Festivals*, p. 63; *EI*², s.vv. *ʿĪd* and *ʿĪd al-Fiṭr*

[17] Ibid., *Festivals*, p. 63

[18] Ṣābī, *Rusūm*, pp. 9–11

servants. Dressed in gorgeous attire, they started their procession from the residence of the wazir or the military commander and paraded the city until they reached the *muṣallā*: the place of prayer, either the mosque or a spacious courtyard. It is said of Nāzūk, at the beginning of the 10th century AD, that on one of the *ʿĪd* mornings he brought out a remarkable procession consisting of more than 500 torch-bearers (*farrāsh bi-shumūʿ al-mawkabiyya*) and a large number of naphtha throwers (*aṣḥāb al-naft*), and marched through the city of Baghdad until they all reached the *muṣallā*. The people in the street greeted the military commander and the traffic came to a halt until his procession had passed.[19]

In the second half of the 10th century AD Maqdisī noted that the people of Mecca were very enthusiastic in celebrating the *ʿĪd* festival. They erected several ceremonial gates during the night of *Fiṭr*, decorated the market between the Safa and the Marwa, and welcomed the *ʿĪd* by beating drums throughout the night.[20] Maqdisī also noted that the *ʿĪd* celebration in Sicily was unparalleled in the Muslim world.[21]

Soon after sunrise on the day of the *ʿĪd al-Fiṭr*, the people, dressed in their best clothes,[22] assembled in the mosque, distributed the *ṣadaqa al-fiṭr*, alms marking the breaking of the fast, and performed two *rakʿas* of prayer, led by the caliph or another person appointed by him.[23] The caliph, clad in splendid attire, probably wearing the *burda* of the Prophet, attended the mosque with a large procession, while people standing on both sides of the road saluted him.[24]

Having performed the prayer, everyone present in the mosque congratulated, embraced and kissed each other. On this day friends meeting in the street or in their private houses did the same; indeed they often visited each other for this particular purpose.[25]

---

[19] Ibid., p. 10

[20] Muq. p. 100

[21] Ibid., p. 183

[22] *Murūj*, vii, p. 74; Bayhaqī, *Maḥāsin*, p. 211

[23] *EI*², s.v. *ʿĪd* and *ʿĪd al-Fiṭr* (E. Mittwoch); Grunebaum, *Festivals*, pp. 63–4

[24] Nishwār, viii, pp. 12, 91; cf. also Ṭabarī, iii, p. 1181

[25] Ibn al-Jawzī, *Muntaẓam*, v, pt. 2, p. 75, vi, p. 329; Ṣābī, *Rusūm*, pp. 10–11; *Thimār*, p. 187; Ḥuṣrī, *Jamʿ al-Jawāhir*, p. 106

The pomp of the *ʿĪd al-Fiṭr* was great. The royal palaces were brightly illuminated; the boats of the caliphs and of other men of high rank were displayed on the Tigris, beautifully decorated and lit with lamps. The city of Baghdad was adorned with brightly coloured materials until it "looked like a bride in all her beauty."[26] The people feasted in their homes and the merchants in their shops, the celebrations lasting, usually, for three days.[27] In Mecca, after the *ʿĪd* prayer young girls wearing splendid decorated clothes and holding fans in their hands visited the houses of the people and collected *ʿĪd* money from the elders.[28]

On the day of the feast two dining tables would be laid out in the royal palace, one after the dawn prayer, the other after the feast prayer.[29] On the first table only sweets were served, whereas the second table contained sumptuous dishes. From Ṣābī it is known that a considerable amount of money was set apart in the caliphal budget to entertain guests visiting the palace on the *ʿĪd* days.[30] Similarly a portion of the budget was also reserved for the payment of the standard bearers who led the caliphal procession to the *muṣallā* and back to the palace.[31]

Al-Ḥajj

In view of the hardship involved in making the pilgrimage to Mecca in the traditional style, the discomfort and strain of caravan travel through an inhospitable countryside in a difficult climate and, above all, the constant threat of Beduin

[26] *Muntaẓam*, x, pp. 35, 58, 157; *Kāmil* (Cairo, 1290), ix, p. 216; cf. also Badrī, *ʿĀmma*, p. 193

[27] *EI*², s.v. *ʿĪd* (E. Mittwoch)

[28] Muq. p. 100

[29] *Muntaẓam*, vi, p. 3; Ṣābī, *Rusūm*, p. 24; *Thimār*, p. 187

[30] *Rusūm*, p. 24

[31] Ibid., pp. 24–5. In the caliphal procession a large contingent of the caliph's private bodyguard and of other troops, attired in gorgeous pelisses, paraded on horseback in the streets of Baghdad. People standing on both sides of the road watched the march-past, while the caliphs and other dignitaries witnessed it from pavilions erected for the purpose. To ensure an unimpeded march-past of the troops, roads were closed to public riders (cf. Ṭabarī, iii, 1181; *Muntaẓam*, x, pp. 35, 38; Kāzarūnī, *Maqāma fi qawāʿid Baghdād fi'l-dawla al-ʿAbbāsiyya*, ed. k. ʿAwād and M. ʿAwād, Baghdad, 1962, p. 26).

attacks[32] (sometimes bought off by the government),[33] Muslims from the eastern lands of the Abbasid empire would gather together at Baghdad.[34] From the beginning of the month of Shawwāl, two months before the actual time of the *ḥajj*, people from Iraq itself and from regions much more distant, such as Khurāsān, would reach Baghdad. Such people, numbering several thousands, found shelter in tents pitched on the western side of Baghdad. Here the government supplied them with food and drinking water.[35] The period from the first arrival of the pilgrims till their departure on the *ḥajj* was an exciting time for the inhabitants of Baghdad. Every day new groups of pilgrims would enter the city, and the inhabitants of Baghdad, dressed in their best attire, gave them a warm welcome.[36]

The departure of the caravan was marked by elaborate celebrations. A large procession, with high-ranking officials at the front and the populace behind, accompanied the caravan to the outskirts of Baghdad and bade them farewell.[37] To protect the pilgrims from attack, a contingent of troops also accompanied them.[38] The caravan then proceeded towards Mecca under the leadership of an *Amīr al-Ḥajj*, a commander of the pilgrims,[39] who was appointed by the government in a ceremonial gathering attended by the caliph, the chief qāḍī and his deputies, and also by other dignitaries.[40] The *amīr* not only directed the journey, but supervised the

---

[32] Beduin attacks on the pilgrim caravan occurred frequently and many pilgrims lost their lives and property. At a later time the Qarāmiṭa also plundered the pilgrim caravans travelling to the *ḥajj* (cf. *Muntaẓam*, v, pt. 2, pp. 56, 65, vi, pp. 2, 33; Ṭabarī, iii, pp. 1941, 2027; ʿArīb, pp. 54, 118–19).

[33] The pilgrims were asked to pay a fixed toll for their safety (cf. Bowen, *Life and Times of ʿAlī b. ʿĪsā*, pp. 357–8). Apart from the Baghdad government, other princes too contributed towards the amount paid to the beduins (cf. Mez, p. 313). On one occasion, 9,000 dinars were paid to them; beduins of the escort party received four dinars each (cf. Mez, p. 313).

[34] *Muntaẓam*, vii, p. 276

[35] Ibid., vii, p. 276

[36] Kāzarūnī, op. cit., p. 24; cf. also Badrī, *ʿĀmma*, pp. 195–6

[37] *Muntaẓam*, vii, p. 263; Kāzarūnī, op. cit., p. 24

[38] Ṭabarī, iii, p. 1383; *Aghānī*[1], ix, p. 64

[39] *EI*[2], s.v. *Amīr al-Ḥadjdj* (J. Jomier)

[40] Ṭabarī, iii, pp. 1383–4; Kāzarūnī, op. cit., p. 24; cf. also Badrī, ʿĀmma, pp. 194–5

conduct of the pilgrims and led his own contingent of the *ḥajj* during the ceremonies.[41]

Arriving at Mina the pilgrims sacrificed camels, sheep or other domestic animals, one goat or one sheep for one man or one household, but as many as seven men might be partners in one cow or one camel. The flesh of the animal sacrificed was either eaten, stored or distributed among the poor; the skins were given to charity.[42] The people of Ḥijāz, according to Maqdisī, took no other *qadīd* except that which was procured from the sacrificed animals of Mina.[43]

The return of the pilgrims to Baghdad offered an occasion of festive celebration for the people in general. The caliph himself came out of the city to receive the pilgrims. In order to enter Baghdad the next day rested and refreshed for the festivity, the pilgrims sometimes passed the previous night in the suburb of Al-Yasīriyya.[44]

Relatives of the pilgrims offered their thanks to God for the safe return of their kinsmen, congratulated the pilgrims, and celebrated the occasion with great excitement.[45]

The procession of the caliphal caravan for the *ḥajj* was marked both by expense and by display. The *hawdaj* (litter) was profusely decorated with multi-coloured silk and materials woven with gold. The caliph, escorted by his bodyguard, appeared before the caravan, wearing the *burda*[46] (cloak) of the Prophet with the *qaḍīb* (staff) and the *khātam* (signet-ring) in his hands. A drum was beaten to inform the caravan that the moment of departure had come. The caliph, surrounded by members of his family, important dignitaries and troops with black standards, would now set out towards Mecca. On his way to Mecca the caliph showed his benevolence by distributing money and food to the people. This benevolence increased when the caliph reached Mecca, where he would entertain the inhabitants with lavish

[41] Grunebaum, *Festivals*, p. 37. The *Amīr al-Ḥajj* was assisted by a special staff; in addition to his normal duties (e.g., the supervision of the pilgrim caravan) he also took measures designed to ward off the harassing attacks of the Arab tribes (cf. *EI*², s.v. *Amīr al-Ḥadjdj*).

[42] *EI*², s.v. *Ḥadjdj*; Grunebaum, *Festivals*, pp. 33–4

[43] Muq. p. 96

[44] Mez, p. 314

[45] Kāzarūnī, op. cit., p. 24; Ḥuṣrī, *Jamʿ al-Jawāhir*, p. 110

[46] On the *burda*, see Chapter 2, *Costume*, above, p. 51

expenditure on food, iced drinks and gifts.[47] It is said that the Caliph Mahdī, in one of his famous *ḥajj* journeys, distributed 30,000,000 dirhams in cash amongst the people of Mecca and Medina. This sum was in addition to the various gifts and the ice that was brought especially from Mawṣil.[48] The pilgrimage made by Jamīla bint Nāṣir al-Dawla in the year 366 became proverbial in the history of the pilgrimage. She is said to have provided all the people present at the pilgrimage that year with *sawīq*[49] mixed with snow. In addition to many other things, she brought with her, loaded on camels, fresh green vegetables contained in earthenware crocks. She commissioned 500 mounts for those pilgrims who were limbless; bestowed 10,000 dinars on the Ka'ba, freed 300 slaves and 200 slave girls, gave handsome subsidies to those who had come to reside in Mecca, and provided 50,000 fine robes for the common population. It is also said that she had with her 400 litters each lined with satin, so that it was never known in which one she herself was.[50]

The social, cultural and economic effects of the pilgrimage in medieval Islam were of great importance.[51] In fact the *ḥajj* provided different people with different opportunities. If a man were a merchant, he might utilize it as a business trip; if he were a scholar, he might impart or gather knowledge and ideas; if he were a traveller, he might gain knowledge of the people and the land. Pilgrimage was, therefore, one of the important factors making for cultural unity and social mobility in the Islamic world.[52]

'Īd al-Aḍḥā

At the time of the sacrifice of animals in Mina, the whole

---

[47] *Aghānī*[1], iii, p. 94; Balkhī, *Kitāb al-Bad' wa'l-Ta'rīkh*, p. 96; *Muntaẓam*, vii, p. 84

[48] Balkhī, op. cit., p. 96

[49] On *sawīq*, see Chapter 3, *Food*, above, p. 134

[50] *Laṭā'if*, pp. 82–3 (Eng. Tr. p. 82); *Muntaẓam*, vii, 84

[51] *EI*[2], s.v. *Ḥadjdj* (B. Lewis)

[52] Ibid. The *Khaṭīb al-Baghdādī* gives exaggerated reports of *ḥajj* performed by students in order to learn Islamic sciences from the scholars attending the *ḥajj*. Cf. iii, 436, xiii, 286 (40 times); xii, 111 (60 times); viii, 45 (70 times). The Caliph Mahdī is reported to have requested Mālik b. Anas (d. 179) to teach his *Muwaṭṭā* to the students during the days of *ḥajj* (ibid., ix, 83).

Muslim world celebrated the great festival called *ʿĪd al-Akbar* or the Sacrificial Feast: the *ʿĪd al-Aḍḥā*, a title which is derived from *ḍuḥā* (the early part of the day) or from *ḍaḥḥā* ("he sacrificed an animal").[53] Like the *ʿĪd al-Fiṭr*, this festival was celebrated with great pomp; new clothes were put on, people bestowed presents on one another, and two *rakʿas* of congregational prayer were offered in the same manner as in the *ʿĪd al-Fiṭr*.[54]

The sacrifice of animals, which is a conspicuous feature of this festival, took place after the prayer. The caliphs themselves showed much interest in it and a number of animals were slaughtered in the precincts of the royal palace. Ṣābī notes that a portion of the caliphal budget was set apart for the purchase of animals (*aḍāḥī*).[55] It was the duty of the wazir to provide the animals at the Abbasid court for the members of the royal family, the troops, and various categories of palace servants.[56] The celebration of the *ʿĪd al-Aḍḥā* and the sacrifice of animals continued for three days, a period known as *ʿAyyām al-Tashrīq*.[57] The meat of the sacrificed animals was sent to friends and relatives and especially to the poor.[58] Maqdisī noted that the celebrations of the *ʿĪd al-Aḍḥā* in Sicily and the day of *ʿArafa* (the 9th day of Dhu'-Ḥijja) in Shīrāz were unparalleled in the Muslim world in the 10th century AD.[59]

Jumʿa

Jumʿa, Friday, was the Muslim weekly holy day. It is "essentially different from the Jewish Sabbath or the Christian Sunday" and is a day of obligatory public worship, held at noon.[60] The Friday ceremonial consists of an *ādhān*, which

[53] *EI*², s.v. *ʿĪd al-Aḍḥā*; Grunebaum, *Festivals*, p. 34

[54] Ibid., cf. also, Muq. p. 183; Kāzarūnī, op. cit., p. 26

[55] *Rusūm*, p. 24. The people of Basra fattened sheep for a year for the sacrificial feast and sold them at a price of 10 dinars each (cf. *Aghānī*¹, iii, p. 62).

[56] Bowen, *ʿAlī b. ʿĪsā*, p. 105

[57] *EI*², s.vv. *ʿĪd* and *ʿĪd al-Aḍḥā*; Grunebaum, 33–5; *Muntaẓam*, viii, 141

[58] Ibid.; Jāḥiẓ, *Bukhalā'*, p. 27

[59] Muq. p. 183

[60] S. D. Goitein, *Studies*, p. 11. For a detailed discussion on the origin of the institution of *Jumʿa* see, ibid., p. 111ff; idem, *MW* 49 (1959), pp. 183–95; idem, *EI*², s.v. *Djumʿa*

is proclaimed inside the mosque, and a *khuṭba*, said in two sections by the preacher in a standing position. During the pause in the midst of the *khuṭba*, the *khaṭīb* is required to sit down. After the *khuṭba* a *ṣalāt* consisting of two *rakʿas* is offered in congregation.[61]

In Baghdad, the *Jumʿa* prayer was offered with great ceremony and pomp. Maqdisī, writing in the 10th century AD, notes that the *Jumʿa* celebration in Baghdad was unprecedented in the Muslim world.[62] He also noted that in the east, especially in Nīshāpūr, there was held a special session in the morning where readers recited verses from the Qur'ān.[63] In summer iced water was also provided in these regions.[64] The Khaṭīb al-Baghdādī, narrating a story from the third century, notes that the Friday Mosque in Baghdad could not accommodate all the people and therefore roads had to be closed for traffic and the adjacent area was used for prayer. The gate-keepers (*bawwābūn*) at the *maqṣūra* did not allow a man to enter the *maqṣūra* until he donned the black *qabā'*,[65] a distinctive robe of the wazirs and high ranking officials of this period. Baghdādī adds that this was the custom in all the *maqṣūra* of the *Jāmiʿ* (Friday Mosque) in the early Abbasid period.[66]

As the *yawm al-Jumʿa* was a day of *ʿibāda* (worship), offices and schools were closed from the early Abbasid period.[67] A passage in Jahshiyārī's *Wuzarā'* clearly indicates that Friday

---

[61] *EI*², s.v. *Djumʿa* (S. D. Goitein); cf. also, Goldziher, *Muslim Studies*, ii, pp. 41–5 (Eng. Tr. pp. 49–52)

[62] Muq. p. 183

[63] Ibid., p. 328

[64] Ibid., p. 327

[65] On the *qabā'* see Chapter 2, *Costume*, above, p. 41

[66] *Ta'rīkh*, i, p. 48; cf. also, *Manāqib Baghdād*, p. 22

[67] Some *aṣḥāb* of the Imām Mālik b. Anas has disapproved of the practice of some Muslims who refrained from doing work on Friday in imitation of the Jewish and Christian weekly holidays (cf. Ṭarṭūsī, *K. al-Ḥawādith*, Tunis, 1959, p. 133, cited by S. D. Goitein, in *EI*², s.v. *Djumʿa*). During the time of the Imām Abū Ḥanīfa (d. 150), Saturday was the holiday for schools and judges. In the middle of the third century, judges observed holidays either on Monday or on Tuesday. But later, presumably from the time of the Caliph Muʿtaḍid, Tuesday was fixed as the day of rest for the judges because the government also observed a general holiday on Tuesday (cf. Ibn Māza (d. 536). *K. Sharḥ Adab al-Qāḍī*, Br. Mus. Ms. No. Or. 2407, fol. 18b).

was regarded as a holiday for the officials, to enable them to prepare for the *Jumʿa* prayer and other *ʿibādāt.*[68] In addition to Friday, the Caliph Mahdī fixed Thursday as a day of rest for all the government officials, but the Caliph Muʿtaṣim abolished the practice of two days' rest and ordered that offices should be closed only on Fridays.[69] This state of affairs remained unchanged until the Caliph Muʿtaḍid came to power in 279. Now again the custom of the days of the Caliph Mahdī was revived, with the exception that Thursday was replaced by Tuesday.[70] Friday was regarded as a holiday because "it was the day of prayer and because Muʿtaḍid loved that day, as his tutor used to free him on Friday from lessons. Whereas on Tuesday the officials would have time, in the middle of the week, to rest and to look after their personal affairs."[71] On Friday, however, he ordered the public *maẓālim* (*al-maẓālim al-ʿāmma*) to be held for the benefit of the common people.[72]

It was because of the public holiday that the poets and the people interested in poetry assembled together for the weekly *majlis al-shuʿarā'* (poets' gathering) on Fridays in the Jāmiʿ al-Manṣūr under the "Qubbat al-Shuʿarā'" (The Dome of the Poets).[73] In Jāḥiẓ's *Bukhalā'* a man is mentioned as passing his time in leisure on Fridays by visiting gardens with a packed lunch which he ate sitting by the side of a pool. Having eaten his meal he had a siesta in the garden, took a bath, and went to the *Jāmiʿ* for the *Jumʿa* prayer.[74]

Though Friday was a holiday for officials, markets and other places of business were not closed except perhaps for a brief period of *Jumʿa* prayer. We have reports showing that animals were usually slaughtered on Fridays[75] and people

[68] Jahshiyārī, *Wuzarā'*, p. 166; cf. also Shābushtī, *Diyārāt*, p. 119; see also, M. ʿAwād, *al-ʿUṭla al-usbūʿiyya fī'l-dawlat al-ʿAbbāṣiyya*, in *RAAD*, 18 (1939), p. 53

[69] Ibid., *Wuzarā*, p. 166

[70] Ṣābī, *Wuzarā'*, p. 27; see also p. 344

[71] Ibid., p. 27

[72] Ibid., p. 27; cf. also, Ibn Māza, *Sharḥ adab al-qāḍī*, Br. Mus. Ms. Or. 2407, fol. 18b; also, M. ʿAwad, op. cit., p. 54

[73] Khaṭīb, *Ta'rīkh*, viii, pp. 249–50; xii, pp. 95–6

[74] Jāḥiẓ, *Bukhalā'*, p. 20

[75] Ibid., p. 99; *ʿUyūn*, iii, p. 200

did their weekly shopping on this day.[76] During the later Abbasid era, presumably under the influence of the Jewish community, Muslims closed their shops on Saturday, suspended their business and passed the day in pleasure and enjoyment. This prompted the government in 488 to interfere and take measures against this.[77] The *muḥtasib* was ordered to ensure that shops were closed on Friday and opened on Saturday, and to punish those who, violating this rule, opened shops on Friday and closed on Saturdays. This was done to counteract the Jewish Sabbath institution.[78]

Local festivals

Nawrūz

Though of Persian origin, the festival of *Nawrūz*,[79] New Year's Day, was officially recognized by the early Abbasids. It was a spring festival.[80] It began with the first day of the Persian solar year, corresponding to the vernal equinox and the entry of the sun into the sign of Aries, and continued until the 6th day of the month.[81] The last day was known as the Great New Year's Day (*al-Nīrūz al-Akbar*).[82] On the first day, people rose early in the morning, went to the wells or streams, drew water in a vase and poured it over themselves.[83] They also sprinkled water over each other.[84] Reports differ as to the explanation of this washing and water-sprinkling. Some say that these practices were a good omen and a means to ward off harm; others declare that they served the purpose of removing from the air the corruption which produces

[76] Ibid., *Bukhalā'*, p. 110

[77] *Muntaẓam*, ix, p. 91; cf. also M. 'Awād, op. cit., p. 58

[78] Ibid., ix, p. 91

[79] In Arabic sources the word has been pronounced as *Nīrūz* (or *Nairūz*), which seems to be a misreading of the Persian word *Nawrūz* (cf. *Murūj*, vii, p. 277; Ṭabarī, iii, pp. 1148, 2143; *Nishwār*, viii, p. 145; *EI*[1], s.v. *Nawrūz*, by R. Levy).

[80] Jackson, *Persia*, p. 99; Iqbal, *Nawrūz*, in Oriental College Magazine, Lahore, 1969, vol. 45, No. 3, pp. 133–8

[81] Bīrūnī, *Āthār*, pp. 204, 216; *EI*[1], s.v. *Nawrūz*; Jackson, *Persia*, p. 99. Ibn Ḥawqal (1938 ed), p. 364

[82] *Āthār*, p. 217; Qalqashandī, *Ṣubḥ*, ii, p. 411

[83] *Ṣubḥ*, ii, p. 409; Grunebaum, *Festivals*, p. 54

[84] Ṭabarī, iii, p. 2163; *Muntaẓam*, v, pt. 2, p. 171; *Ṣubḥ*, ii, 409

Fig. 13. Journey by Ship. Illustration showing a double-decked ship sailing from Basra to Oman. The passengers are apparently Arabs, and the crew Indian.

Fig. 14. A Mansion. Illustration showing a two-storied building having projecting single balconies, high walls and highly-decorated exterior. Note the attendants and visitors.

epidemic diseases; while still other reports state that they were carried out only to cleanse bodies from the smoke which might have made them dirty, when attending to fires during the preceding winter.[85] All these explanations seem, however, to be improbable.

During the Abbasid period, and especially in the time of the Caliph Mutawakkil, the *Nawrūz* was celebrated with great pomp and rejoicing.[86] The Caliph, on the occasion of *Nawrūz*, is said to have struck five million dirhams, painted in various colours, and showered them upon his officials. Masked actors (*aṣḥāb al-samāja*) appeared before the Caliph, who flung coins to them and distributed roses fashioned from red amber.[87] Ibn Zubayr notes that, at one *Nawrūz*, the play of *samāja* was arranged for the Caliph Muʿtaḍid, which cost 13,000 dinars.[88] On the *Nawrūz* days a variety of sweet dishes (such as *ṣābūniyya* and *lawzīnaj*)[89] were cooked, and the people then distributed them to one another.

The *Nawrūz* festival was marked by an exchange of gifts.[90] According to Yaʿqūbī, ʿUmar II abolished the *Nawrūz* and *Mihrjān*[91] gifts, which were re-introduced by Yazīd II.[92] Under Mutawakkil, as the poet Buḥturī says, "the *Nawrūz* day has again become the same as was instituted by Ardashīr."[93] Not unlike the Persian kings, the Abbasid caliphs used to appear in their chambers, clad in gorgeous attire, in order to receive the presents personally. It is reported that the Caliph Mutawakkil used to sit in his chamber from morning to the time of the *ẓuhr* prayer, accepting the gifts offered to him by the high officials and other dignitaries.[94]

---

85 *Āthār*, p. 218 (Eng. Tr. p. 203); *Ṣubḥ*, ii, p. 409; Grunebaum, *Festivals*, 54–5; Iqbāl, op. cit., pp. 160–2, also 141–2

86 Nishwār, viii, pp. 145–6; *Murūj*, vii, p. 277; Mez, p. 426

87 *Diyārāt*, pp. 39–40; cf. also, Mez, p. 424; Grunebaum, p. 54

88 *Dhakhā'ir*, p. 38

89 On these sweet dishes see Chapter 3, *Food*, above, pp. 100, 99

90 Umar Khayyām, *Nawrūz Nāma*, p. 13

91 On *Mihrjān* see below, p. 289

92 Yaʿqūbī, ii, p. 366

93 Ṭabarī, iii, p. 1448; *Kāmil*, vii, p. 30. Hamza al-Iṣfahānī (d. 350) gives a table of *Nawrūz* from the year of the hijra down to his own times. He also wrote a treatise on the poems dealing with the feast days of *Nawrūz* and *Mihrjān* (cf. Goldziher, *Muslim Studies*, i, pp. 209–10; Eng. Tr. by C. R. Barber and S. M. Stern, pp. 192–3).

94 *Nishwār*, viii, p. 145

The caliphs, in fact, had the right to receive gifts from their subjects on this auspicious day.[95] Hence people of all ranks presented their gifts to the caliphs and also to the wazirs; high ranking officials and well-to-do people offered perfumes, jewels and pearls; merchants presented their precious goods such as carpets, clothes, or slave girls; poets offered their poems; and the common people brought gifts of flowers and fruit.[96] To visit the caliph at *Nawrūz* without a gift was held to be ignominious. The caliphs sometimes asked visitors about their gifts, these enquiries, as the sources reveal, often taking a particular form: "Where is your gift of the day?"[97]

The presentation of numerous gifts to the caliph made it useful to keep a record of all visitors who came to the palace with gifts,[98] who were offered in return sumptuous presents from the caliph.[99]

The common people, on this festive occasion, illuminated their houses with cotton pods (*ḥabb al-quṭn*) and clay censers (*al-majāmīr al-ṭīn*).[100] The royal houses, at the same time, would be illuminated with pods made of costly material, such as zahrī cloth[101] soaked in oil of balsam (*dahn al-balsān*), and other fragrant and expensive oils were burned in censers of stone (*al-majāmir al-birām*).[102]

During the six days of the *Nawrūz* festival, the people gathered in the streets and lit fires. The enthusiasm of the people in celebrating the *Nawrūz* was such that the attempt of the Caliph Muʿtaḍid, in 284, to prevent the unrestrained rejoicing in the streets during the summer weather proved unsuccessful; after only two days he was obliged to let the public resume their customary practices.[103] Ibn Ḥawqal

[95] *Nishwār*, viii, p. 145; *Tāj* (attributed to Jāḥiẓ), pp. 148–9

[96] Ibid., viii, p. 145; *Tāj*, 148–9; Khālidiyyān, *Tuḥaf*, pp. 32–3, 36, 41, 153, 155, 156; *Dhakhā'ir*, pp. 20, 38, 60; ʿIqd, vi; pp. 281, 289

[97] *Nishwār*, viii, p. 145; *Tuḥaf*, p. 156

[98] *Al-Maḥāsin wa'l-Aḍdād*, p. 197; *Tāj*, p. 149; cf. also, Munajjid, *Bain al-Khulafā'*, p. 64

[99] On one *Nawrūz* day the Caliph Mutawakkil is said to have given Buḥturī the sum of 1,000 + 500 dinars (cf. Ṣūlī, *Akhbār al-Buḥturī*, p. 96).

[100] *Nishwār*, i, p. 143

[101] The *zahrī* cloth is described by Tanūkhī as "exceedingly light" (cf. *Nishwār*, i, p. 143).

[102] Ibid., i, p. 143

[103] Ṭabarī, iii, p. 2163; *Muntaẓam*, v, pt. 2, p. 171; *EI*[1], s.v. *Nawrūz* (R. Levy)

notes that in the 10th century AD people in Jibal celebrated the *Nawrūz* festival for seven consecutive days with much enthusiasm and gaiety. They cooked a number of delicious dishes and donned elaborate costumes and spent a lot of money on the festivities. They also indulged in various sports, organised singing parties, and feasted even on the roofs of their buildings.[104]

Professor Tritton quotes a passage from an unpublished text of Ṣābī's *Kitāb al-Hafawāt* about the *Nawrūz* celebration of the *dhimmīs* in Baghdad in the fourth century. Ṣābī notes that some of the *dhimmīs* hired a special cook to work during the night to have the dishes fresh in the morning, and gave parties for relatives and friends, at which they served green melons, plums, peaches and dates. Women made a point of buying perfumes for the day, and tortoises were brought in to drive devils from the house. Eggs were dyed in various colours. To sprinkle perfume on a man and tread seven times on him was a means of driving away the evil eye, laziness and fever. Antimony or rue was used to improve the sight during the coming year; it was a good day for taking medicine. Colleges were closed and the students played; if a professor came in, he was not treated with respect and might be thrown into the fountain unless he paid a ransom in cash which the students spent on food. Ṣābī also adds that Muslims shared in jollifications on the occasion and even drank wine in public and ate cleaned lentils like the *dhimmīs* and joined them in throwing water on folk. Respectable people hit each other with water-skins or threw water about in their houses or gardens, while common folk did this in the streets.[105]

Mihrjān

Some months after the *Nawrūz*, the Abbasids celebrated another festival, Persian in origin and known as *Mihrjān*. The name *Mihrjān* is connected with the Persian month *Mihr-Māh*, during which this festival was celebrated.[106] The

---

[104] Ibn Ḥawqal (2nd ed. 1938), p. 364

[105] Tritton, *Sketches of Life under the Caliphs*, in *MW*, LXII (1972), p. 145, quoting from an unpublished MS. of Hilāl al-Ṣābī entitled *Kitāb al-Hafawāt.*

[106] *Āthār*, p. 222 (Eng. Tr. p. 207); *EI*[1], s.v. *Mihr*; Jackson, *Persia*, p. 371; Pūrdāwūd, *Mihr wa'l-Mihrjān*, in *Dirāsat al-Adabiyya*, Beirut, 1959, vols. 2–3, pp. 124–6

sixteenth day of each month was also called *mihr-rūz*. The *mihr-rūz* of *mihr-māh* was the occasion of the festival called *Mihrjān*.[107] The word *Mihrjān* means "love of the spirit".[108] Bīrūnī reports that *mihr* is the name of the sun, which was believed to have appeared to the world for the first time on this particular day.[109] This festival was marked by the wearing of holiday attire, by the offering of congratulations and good wishes, and also by much merry-making.

Just as the *Nawrūz* denoted the beginning of the spring, the *Mihrjān* indicated the beginning of winter: a time when people began to change their dress, to add extra coverings to their beds and to prepare themselves for the cold season.[110] The day was marked by great festivities, by singing and by sports.[111] As in the *Nawrūz*, the important feature of the festival, over and above the illuminations and the beating of drums, was an exchange of gifts.[112] On this day, too, the caliphs and wazirs used to sit in their chambers to receive presents, amongst them, at times, gifts of great value, such as an elephant of gold with diamonds for eyes.[113]

It is interesting to note that during this period, and perhaps for the first time in the Muslim world, people adopted the convention of sending cards of congratulation (*al-mukātaba fi'l-tahānī*) with the usual gifts offered on the days of *Mihrjān* and *Nawrūz*.[114] A certain Aḥmad b. Yūsuf is said to have introduced this practice during the reign of the Caliph Ma'mūn.[115] It is possible that these cards were on sale in the market. It is more likely, however, that people made them at home, and after perfuming and sealing them exchanged them with friends. Sentences or verses of benediction and congratulation formed the subject matter.[116]

---

107 *Āthār*, p. 222; *EI*[1], s.v. *Mihr*; Pūrdāwūd, op. cit., pp. 124–6

108 *Āthār*, p. 222; *EI*[1], s.v. *Mihr*

109 *Āthār*, p. 222

110 Ibid., p. 223; *Ṣubḥ*, ii, p. 412

111 *Murūj*, viii, p. 340

112 *Nishwār*, viii, p. 145; *Aghānī*[2], v, pp. 217–18; *Dhakhā'ir*, pp. 5, 28–9; Khālidiyyān, *Tuḥaf*, pp. 109–10, 180; *'Uyūn*, iii, p. 37; Nuwayrī, i, pp. 186–7; *Muḥāḍarāt* (Cairo, 1287), i, p. 261; Ghazūlī, *Maṭāli'*, ii, p. 136

113 *Nishwār*, viii, p. 145; *Aghānī*[2], v, pp. 217–18

114 Abū Hilāl al-'Askarī, *Diwān al-Ma'ānī* (Egypt, 1352) i, 95

115 Ibid., i, p. 95

116 Ibid., i, p. 95; Khālidiyyān, *Tuḥaf*, pp. 154–5

Sadaq

Sadaq (or *sadhaq*, *ṣadaq*), the "yule" feast, was an old Persian festival observed at the time of the Abbasids with much enthusiasm.[117] Since it was celebrated in winter with large bonfires, the festival was known as *lailat al-wuqūd*, "the night of the fires".[118] The *Sadaq* was held on the 5th or the 10th day of the Persian month Bahman. Ibn al-Athīr and Abu'l-Fidā' state that it coincided with Christmas.[119] At this festival the people of Baghdad flocked to the banks of the Tigris, lit fires on their boats and vied with each other in eating and drinking, in the brightness of their apparel, in music, in piping and in dancing. The barges of the caliphs, wazirs and high officials were decorated and illuminated. These high personages appeared in gorgeous attire and were drawn in the barges along the river, a splendid procession of boats, filled with courtiers and the common people, following in their wake. Some of the people spent the whole night there, rejoicing and playing round bonfires.[120]

On this night it was the custom to fumigate houses in order to ward off misfortune, and to keep fires well ablaze, to drive wild animals into them, and to send birds in flight through the flames, the people drinking and amusing themselves meanwhile around the fires.[121]

The celebration of the *Sadaq* festival[122] which the Daylamite Mardāwīj, the governor of the Eastern provinces, made in 323 with unusual splendour at great expense, became legendary. The prince, so we are told, collected faggots, set up large candles and stationed a number of naphtha throwers (*naffāṭīn*) and flame-throwers (*zarrāqāt*) in the wādī of Zarīn Rūdh, near Iṣfahān. Near each elevated place in the town, a "castle" made of tree trunks was built, the interior being filled with fluff (*mashāqqa*) and naphtha. To provide a splendid

---

[117] *Tajārib*, i, p. 310; *Āthār*, p. 226; cf. also Mez, p. 421

[118] *Tajārib*, i, p. 310. For the different legendary reports regarding the origin of the festival, see *Āthār*, pp. 266–7; *Ṣubḥ*, ii, p. 412

[119] *Kāmil*, viii, p. 222; *Mukhtaṣar fī akhbār al-bashar*, iii, p. 130

[120] *Muntaẓam*, ix, p. 57

[121] *Āthār*, p. 226 (Eng. Tr. p. 22); cf. also, Mez, p. 421. For these savage practices the celebration of this Persian feast is vehemently condemned by Ḥamadānī (cf. *Rasā'il*, Beirut, 1890, p. 279).

[122] Mez has mistakenly identified this festival with Christmas (see p. 421)

illumination Mardāwīj caused wax pillars and wax figures to be erected in his own palace-hall. Fire was lighted at one and the same time on the hills, in the desert, and in the "castles". Now a number of birds, to the beaks and feet of which nuts filled with fluff and naphtha were fastened and fired, were released into the darkness of the night, presenting a wonderful spectacle. Moreover, Mardāwīj arranged a great feast, for which 2,000 cattle are said to have been slaughtered, in addition to numerous birds and fowl.[123]

Other festive occasions

Among the occasions celebrated, especially at Baghdad, irrespective of religious allegiance, were the installation of a caliph or the birth of a child in the imperial house; also the time of circumcision, marriages, recuperation from illness and, in addition, the victories won by the Muslim armies over their foes.

The birth of a child in the imperial household was an event of importance, the ensuing festivities being more elaborate for a son than for a daughter. The caliph and the members of his family offered handsome gifts to rich and poor, to nobles and commoners alike. Poets and other dignitaries rushed to congratulate the caliph, receiving gifts and robes of honour in return. At Baghdad people illuminated their houses, merchants and craftsmen adorned their shops and buildings, and the common people marched through the streets with drums and trumpets. Sometimes ceremonial gates and arches were erected and the festivities continued for several days.[124] It is not known whether there were any spectacles or public entertainments in the caliphal palace on such occasions.

The circumcision of a royal prince was also marked by a great display of wealth and magnificence. The circumcision of Muʿtazz, the son of the Caliph Mutawakkil, took place with unprecedented pomp and expenditure, so that it has been recorded in Arabic literature as one of the unforgettable extravaganzas of the age.[125] In the great feast which followed

[123] *Tajārib*, i, pp. 310ff; *Kāmil*, viii, pp. 222–3; cf. also Mez, pp. 421–2

[124] *Muntaẓam*, viii, p. 254; ix, pp. 14, 38; Azdī, *Ta'rīkh al-Mawṣil*, pp. 243, 307; cf. also Badrī, *ʿĀmma*, pp. 213–14

[125] See, for example, *Laṭā'if*, pp. 122–3; Eng. Tr. by C. E. Bosworth, pp. 100–1; *Diyārāt*, pp. 150–3

the circumcision, the Caliph Mutawakkil showered upon the guests gold and silver coins, together with pieces of ambergris, amber, and musk, moulded into various shapes and figures. People present on this occasion seized coins in such numbers that they had to make several journeys to carry them to their slaves waiting outside the palace. When the entertainment came to an end, 1,000 robes of honour were distributed among the guests, with 1,000 mounts to depart on, each animal clad in gold and silver trappings. At the same time 1,000 slaves received their freedom.[126] The total expenditure on this occasion has been estimated at 86 million dirhams.[127]

It was the custom for the Abbasid caliphs, at the circumcision of their sons, to invite orphans and boys of destitute families into the palace, there to be circumcised with the royal prince, a practice which enabled the poor to share in the festivities. The caliphs, on such occasions, bestowed gifts on the parents of the boys and distributed alms (*ṣadaqāt*) among the poor. The Caliph Muqtadir is said to have had five of his sons circumcised at the same time and, with them, a group of orphans, whom he loaded with rich presents. The entire cost of this celebration is reported to have reached the sum of 600,000 dinars.[128]

On such festive occasions the people decorated Baghdad, erecting several ceremonial gates covered with costly material, and visiting the caliphal palace in their best attire. The celebration of the circumcision sometimes lasted for a week.[129]

An occasion of splendid ceremonies in the royal palace was the wedding of a caliph or other member of the Abbasid house.[130] The most famous wedding celebration during this period was that of the Caliph Ma'mūn to the eighteen-year-old Būrān, the daughter of his wazir Ḥasan b. Sahl, celebrated in 210 at "Fam al-Ṣilḥ" in Wāsit over a period of forty days. On the wedding night, when Ma'mūn and Būrān, for the first time, came face to face, a thousand pearls of unique size were showered from a gold tray upon the couple, who sat on

126 Ibid., *Laṭā'if*, pp. 122–3; *Diyārāt*, pp. 150–3; cf. also J. Zaydān, *Tamaddun*, v, p. 150

127 Mez, p. 428, quoting from Shābushtī's *Diyārāt*

128 Ibid., p. 428, quoting from Ibn al-Jawzī, fol. 12b

129 *Muntaẓam*, ix, p. 245

130 Cf., for example, *Dhakhā'ir*, pp. 98–101; *Laṭā'if*, pp. 120–2

a golden mat studded with pearls and sapphires. A candle of ambergris, weighing two hundred ratls, was lit in the bridal chamber and turned the night into day. Balls of musk, each containing the name of an estate, slave-girl, steed or other gift, fell on the crowd of guests, each recipient receiving the particular present which his ball of musk indicated. Robes of honour were conferred on all the guests, an event which brought to an end a festival unparalleled in its magnificence.[131]

An important festive occasion was the "Feast of the Cupping"[132] (*faṣad*) when, as at the *Nawrūz* and the *Mihrjān*, presents were given out and a special meal was served.[133] The Feast of the Cupping became a regular feature at the Abbasid court. The courtiers came in colourful dress, congratulated the caliph, wished him good health and presented him with gifts.[134] These presentations consisted of slave-girls, golden and silver utensils, perfumes, flowers and candles.[135] On one occasion, at the Feast of the Cupping the wazir Fatḥ b. Khāqān gave to the Caliph Mutawakkil a slave-girl, exquisite in beauty and accomplishments, who carried in her hands a wine-jar made of crystal and a golden wine-cup, along with a congratulatory letter wishing the Caliph good health.[136]

The day of the *bayʿa* of the caliphs was regarded as a day of festivity. People from all walks of life thronged to the royal palace (*dār khilāfa*) and offered their allegiance to the caliph in the form of congratulations.[137] The caliph arranged dinner parties for the high dignitaries and offered gifts and robes of honour to those who were high in his esteem. The dinner

---

[131] *Diyārāt*, pp. 157–9; *Laṭā'if*, pp. 120–2 (Eng. Tr. pp. 99–100); *Thimār*, s.v. *Daʿwat al-Islām*; Ṭabarī, iii, pp. 1081–5; *Dhakhā'ir*, pp. 98–101

[132] The feast celebrated the ceremonial bleeding, by the application of cups, of members of the caliphal family. The bleeding was believed to have a therapeutic effect.

[133] Jāḥiẓ, *al-Mahāsin wa'l-Aḍdād*, p. 184; Mez, p. 429; cf. also, Munajjid, *Bain al-Khulafā'*, p. 62

[134] *Al-Maḥāsin*, p. 184; *Aghānī*[1], v, p. 66; *Dhakhā'ir*, pp. 18–19, 197; Khālidiyyān, *Tuḥaf*, pp. 27, 28; Jahshiyārī, *Wuzarā'*, p. 250; Munajjid, *Bain al-Khulafā'*, p. 70

[135] Ibid., *Maḥāsin*, p. 184; *Dhakhā'ir*, pp. 18–19

[136] Ibn Abī ʿUṣaybiʿa, *ʿUyūn al-Anbā'*, p. 181

[137] Azdī, *Ta'rīkh al-Mawṣil*, p. 231; *Aghānī*[1], iii, p. 94

which the Caliph Mahdī gave on the day of his accession to the *khilāfat* (158) was remarkable indeed. It is said that he spent so lavishly on food and gifts that it was feared that the court treasury would be exhausted of its resources.[138]

The day of appointment of an heir apparent (*walī al-ʿahd*) was also an occasion of enjoyment, both for the royal family and for the common people. After the ceremonial formalities, attended mainly by the officials and the élite, a colourful procession went out of the royal palace.[139] The procession which took place after Muʿtazz, the son of Mutawakkil, was appointed heir apparent, is described by *Aghānī* as "unprecedented". It included a large contingent of Turkish troops, and also the high dignitaries with their servants, all attired in colourful dress. It paraded through the main streets of the city and crossed the river Tigris in decorated barges, until at last it reached the palace known as ʿArūs (of the Bride).[140] Free access was given to all who wanted to see and congratulate the heir apparent. Poets, to mark the occasion, now extolled the Caliph and the heir apparent and received rewards and robes of honour.[141] It is said that on this occasion, Ibrāhīm b. al-ʿAbbās al-Ṣūlī received 100,000 dirhams from the Caliph and a similar amount from the heir presumptive for the composition of his eulogy.[142]

The victorious return of the caliph or of a military commander from an expedition offered the populace a further occasion of rejoicing and pride. The whole of Baghdad was adorned with coloured materials. Beautiful pavilions (*qibāb*)

---

[138] *Aghānī*[1], iii, p. 94; *Murūj*, vi, p. 233. The wazirs also received congratulations on their appointments and entertained those visiting them with gifts. It is said that when Ibn al-Furāt became wazir, he offered all the visitors, who came to congratulate him, iced water and other drinks with ice. He also gave them candles and pieces of paper (cf. ʿArīb, p. 61; Ṣābī, *Wuzarā'*, p. 73). For a general discussion on the decoration of the caliphal palace and the appearance of the caliph on ceremonial occasions, see D. Sourdel, "Questions de cérémonial ʿAbbaside" in *REI*, 1960, pp. 121–48.

[139] *Aghānī*[1], ix, p. 32

[140] Loc. cit. The populace watched the procession, standing on both sides of the road, in a long row. On one occasion this row of people is said to have extended over a distance of four miles (cf. J. Zaydān, *Tamaddun*, v, p. 147).

[141] *Aghānī*[1], ix, p. 32

[142] Ibid. See, for some other references to poets' eulogies and awards, *Murūj*, vii; p. 194; Ṭabarī, iii, p. 1467; *Aghānī*, xi, p. 2

were erected for the caliph and his troops to march through.[143] At night there were brilliant illuminations. The ovation which the populace of Baghdad gave to the Caliph Muʿtaḍid on the occasion of his triumphal return from Takrīt in 283 was remarkable. The Caliph bestowed robes of honour and munificent rewards on the military commanders.[144] In the year 269, when the news that Muwaffaq had killed the ringleader of the Zanj reached the people of Baghdad, their joy knew no bounds. They celebrated the victory with great excitement by decorating the city and making processions.[145] In 223, when Afshīn defeated Bābak, the people of Baghdad celebrated the day with much jollification. The Caliph Muʿtaṣim bestowed on the commander robes of honour and offered one million dirhams and asked the poets to compose *qaṣā'id* in praise of Afshīn.[146]

Tahdhīq, the ceremony held to mark the occasion of the son of a caliph becoming proficient in the reading of the Qur'ān, was also a time of rejoicing. The *tahdhīq* celebration given for Muʿtazz was outstanding in pomp and magnificence. It is reported that thousands of pearls of different sizes, and thousands of dinars also, were bestowed on the guests.[147] In 167 the Caliph Mahdī is said to have distributed one thousand dirhams and to have liberated five hundred slaves, in order to honour the occasion of his son's *tahdhīq*.[148]

---

143 *Murūj*, viii, p. 198; *Muntaẓam*, v, pt. 2, p. 70
144 *Murūj*, viii, pp. 168–9
145 *Muntaẓam*, v, pt. 2, p. 70
146 Balkhī, *Kitab al-Badʾ wa'l-Ta'rīkh*, p. 118
147 *Dhakhā'ir*, pp. 119–20
148 Ibid., p. 112

Bibliography

(A) *Manuscripts*

AL-AZDĪ, AḤMAD B. ʿĀTIQ (d. 8th century) — *Kitāb al-Bayṭara* Br. Mus. Or. 1523

AL-BAGHDĀDĪ, AL-KARĪM AL-KĀTIB (637) — *Kitāb al-Ṭabīkh* Br. Mus. Or. 5099

IBN AL-ʿADĪM, KAMĀL AL-DĪN (660) — *Al-Wuṣlā ila'l-ḥabīb fī waṣf al-ṭayyibāt wa'l-ṭīb* Br. Mus. Or. 6388

IBN JAZLA (5th century) — *Minhāj al-bayān fīmā yastaʿmiluhū'l-insān* Br. Mus. Or. 5934

AL-JAZZĀR, JAMĀL AL-DĪN YAḤYĀ (679) — *Fawā'id al-Mawā'id* Br. Mus. Ms. Or. 6388

AL-KUSHĀJIM, MAḤMŪD B. ḤUSAIN (d. 360) — *Al-Bayzara* SOAS, No. 2091 (Copy of the Gotha MS)

AL-RASŪLĪ, ʿALĪ B. DĀWŪD B. YŪSUF B. ʿUMAR B. ʿALĪ B. RASŪL (8th century) — *Al-Aqwāl al-Kāfiya wa'l-fuṣūl al-shāfiyya fī ʿilm al-Bayṭara* Br. Mus. Or. 3830

AL-ṬABARĪ, ʿABD AL-RAḤMĀN B. AḤMAD — *Qiṣṣat qaws wa sahm* Br. Mus. No. Or. 3134

TAIBUGHĀ, AL-BAKLAMISHĪ AL-ŪNĀNĪ (8th century) — *Ghunyat al-Ṭullāb fī maʿrifat al-ramī wa'l-nushshāb* Br. Mus. Or. 1358

AL-WARRĀQ, NAṢR B. SAYYĀR (d. early 4th century) — *Al-Ṭabīkh wa iṣlāḥ al-aghdhiya al-ma'kūlāt* Bodleian Library, Oxford, Hunt, 187

Anonymous — *Risāla fīl-rimāya* SOAS, No. 46339

(B) *Published Literary Sources*

ABU'L-FARAJ AL-IṢFAHĀNĪ, ʿALĪ B. ḤUSAIN (d. 356) — *Kitāb al-Aghānī* Bulaq, 1284–5, 20 Vols. 21, Leyden; i–xiv, Dār al-Kutub Miṣriyya edition

ABU'L-FARAJ, GREGORY BARHEBRAEUS (d. 685) —
1. *Ta'rīkh Mukhtaṣar al-Duwal* Beirut 1890
2. *The Chronography* ed. and trans. from Syriac by E. A. Wallis Budge, London 1932

ABU'L-FIDĀ', ISMĀʿĪL B. ʿALĪ (d. 732) — *Al-Mukhtaṣar fī akhbār al-bashar* 4 vols. Istanbul, 1286/1870 (also 2 vols., Beirut)

ABŪ NUWĀS, ḤASAN B. HĀNĪ (d. about 195) — *Dīwān*, Egypt 1898

ABŪ SHUJĀʿ AL-RUDHRĀWARĪ (d. 487) — *Dhayl Tajārib al-umam* published by Amedroz and Margoliouth as vol. iii of the *Tajārib* and vol. vi of "Eclipse", Oxford 1921

ABŪ YAʿLA, MUḤAMMAD B. ḤUSAIN AL-FARRĀ' AL-ḤANBALĪ (d. 458) — *Al-Aḥkām al-sulṭāniya* Cairo 1357/1938

ABŪ YŪSUF, YA'QŪB B. IBRĀHĪM (d. 182)	*Kitāb al-Kharāj* Cairo 1352/1933
AL-ABSHĪHĪ, MUḤAMMAD B. AḤMAD	*Al-Mustaṭraf fī kull fann mustaẓraf* Cairo 1348/1929
'ARĪB B. SA'D (d. 369)	*Ṣilat Ta'rīkh al-Ṭabarī* ed. De Goeje, Leyden 1897
AL-AṢMA'Ī, 'ABD AL-MĀLIK B. QURAYB (213)	*Kitāb al-Khayl* ed. Haffner, Vienna 1875
AL-AZDĪ, AḤMAD B. MUṬAHHAR (d. 4th century)	*Ḥikāyāt Abi'l-Qāsim al-Baghdādī* Heidelberg 1902
AZDĪ ABŪ ZAKARIYYĀ (d. 334)	*Ta'rīkh al-Mawṣil* Cairo 1967
AL-BAGHDĀDĪ, MUḤAMMAD B. AL-KARĪM AL-KĀTIB AL-BAGHDĀDĪ (637)	*Kitāb al-Ṭabīkh* ed. Dawud Chelebi, Mosul 1353/1934; Eng. Tr. by A. J. Arberry, *A Baghdad Cookery Book*, Reprint from *IC*, 13 (1939), pp. 21–47, 189–214
AL-BAGHDĀDĪ, AL-KHAṬĪB (463)	1. *Ta'rīkh Baghdād* Cairo 1349/1931 2. *Al-Taṭfīl* Damascus 1346 3. *Al-Bukhalā'* 1384/1964
AL-BALĀDHURĪ, AḤMAD B. YAḤYĀ (d. 279)	*Futūḥ al-Buldān* Leyden 1866, Cairo 1956
AL-BAYHAQĪ, IBRĀHĪM B. MUḤAMMAD (d. 320)	*Al-Maḥāsin wa'l -Masāwī* Leipzig 1906–8
AL-BAYZĀR, ḤASAN B. AL-ḤUSAIN (d. 4th century)	*Al-Bayzara* ed. Kurd 'Alī, Damascus 1953; French Trans. by F. Viré, Leiden 1967
AL-BĪRŪNĪ, ABU'L-RAYḤĀN (d. 440)	*Al-Āthār al-Bāqiya 'an al-qurūn al-khāliya* Leipzig 1923; Eng. Tr. by Sachau, London 1879
AL-DAMĪRĪ, KAMĀL AL-DĪN MUḤAMMAD B. MŪSĀ (808)	*Ḥayāt al-Ḥayawān al-Kubrā* Cairo 1367/1956; Eng. Tr. by Lt. Colonel A. S. G. Jaykar, London, Bombay 1906–8
DENYS DE TELL-MAHRÉ (3rd century)	*Chronique de Denys de Tell-Mahré* ed. and trans. by J. B. Chabot, Paris 1895
AL-DIMASHQĪ, ABU'L-FAḌL (11th or 12th)	*Al-Ishāra fī maḥāsin al-Tijāra* Cairo 1900
AL-DĪNAWARĪ, ABŪ ḤANĪFA AḤMAD B. DĀWŪD (d. 282)	*Kitāb Akhbār al-Ṭiwāl* ed. Kratchkovsky, Leiden 1912
AL-FĪRŪZĀBĀDĪ, MAJD AL-DĪN MUḤAMMAD B. YA'QŪB (d. 817)	*Al-Qāmūs al-Muḥīṭ* Cairo 1332/1913
AL-GHAZĀLĪ, ABŪ ḤĀMID MUḤAMMAD B. MUḤAMMAD (d. 505)	*Iḥyā' Ulūm al-Dīn* 4 vols, Cairo 1358/1939
AL-GHAZŪLĪ (GHUZŪLĪ), 'ALĀ' AL-DĪN 'ALĪ B. 'ABDULLĀH (d. 815)	*Maṭāli' al-Budūr fī manāzil al-Surūr* Cairo 1299–1300

AL-ḤAMADĀNĪ, BADĪʿ AL-ZAMĀN (d. 398)	1. *Maqāmāt al-Ḥamadānī* 2nd ed. Beirut n.d.; Eng. Trans. by W. J. Prendergast, London, Madras 1915 2. *Rasā'il* Beirut 1890
AL-ḤAMADĀNĪ, AL-ḤASAN B. AḤMAD (d. 334)	*Ṣifat Jazīrat al-ʿArab* Leiden 1884
ḤAMDALLĀH AL-QAZWĪNĪ (d. 740)	1. *Nuzhat al-Qulūb* Trans. by Le Strange, *GMS* 1919 2. *ʿAjā'ib al-Makhlūqāt wa gharā'ib al-mawjūdāt* Cairo 1376/1956
ḤASHSHĀ' AḤMAD (13th century AD)	*Min al-Kitāb al-Manṣūrī fi'l-bayzara* ed. by A. Ḥafīẓ Manṣūr in *Mashriq*, 62 (1968), pp. 153–222
IBN ʿABD RABBIH, AḤMAD B. MUḤAMMAD (d. 328)	*Al-ʿIqd al-Farīd* Cairo 1948–50
IBN ABĪ ʿUṢAYBIʿA, ABU'L-ʿABBĀS AḤMAD B. AL-QĀSIM (d. 668)	*ʿUyūn al-Anbā' fī ṭabaqāt al-aṭibbā'* Selbstverlag 1884
IBN ABĪ YAʿLĀ, AL-FARRĀ' (d. 528)	*Ṭabaqāt al-Ḥanābila* Damascus 1950
IBN AL-ATHĪR, ʿIZZ AL-DĪN ʿALĪ B. MUḤAMMAD (d. 630)	*Al-Kāmil fi'l-Ta'rīkh* Leiden 1851–76 (also Cairo 1290)
IBN AL-BAYṬĀR, ʿABDALLĀH B. ḤUSAIN (d. 640)	1. *Al-Durrat al-Bahiyya fī manāfiʿ al-abdān al-insāniyya* Damascus n.d. 2. *Al-Jāmiʿ al-mufradāt* Cairo 1291
IBN DURAYD, MUḤAMMAD B. AL-ḤASAN (d. 321)	*Al-Ishtiqāq* Cairo 1958
IBN AL-FAQĪH AL-ḤAMADĀNĪ (d. 365)	*Al-Buldān* ed. De Goeje, Leiden 1303 (*B.G.A.V.*)
IBN ḤAWQAL, ABU'L-QĀSIM (d. 367)	1. *Ṣūrat al-Arḍ* 2nd ed. 2 pts ed., J. H. Kramers, Leiden 1938–9 2. *Al-Masālik wa'l-Mamālik* ed. De Goeje, Leiden 1872 (*BGA* II)
IBN HUDHAYL, ʿALĪ B. ʿABD AL-RAḤMĀN (8th century)	*Ḥilyat al-Fursān fī Shiʿār al-shujʿān* ed. L. Mercier, Paris 1922
IBN AL-ʿIMĀD, ABU'L-FATAḤ ʿABDU'L-ḤAY (1089)	*Shadharāt al-Dhahab fī akhbār man dhahab* Cairo 1350–1
IBN AL-JAWZĪ, ABU'L-FARAJ (d. 597)	1. *Al-Muntaẓam fī Ta'rīkh al-mulūk wa'l-umam* Hyderabad 1938–43 (v–x vols) 2. *Kitāb al-Adhkiyā'* Beirut 1965 3. *Talbīs Iblīs* Cairo 2nd ed. 4. *Akhbār al-Ḥumaqā wa'l-mughaffalīn* Damascus 1345/1926 5. *Akhbār al-Ẓirāf wa'l-mutamājinīn* Damascus 1347/1928 6. *Ṣifat al-Ṣafwa* Hyderabad 1936 7. *Ṣayd al-Khāṭir* Cairo 1927 8. *Dhamm al-Hawā* 1381/1962

9. *Manāqib Baghdād* (attr.) 1924

IBN JUBAYR, ABUL'L ḤUSAYN MUḤAMMAD B. AḤMAD AL-UNDULUSĪ (614)
Riḥla Ibn Jubayr, ed. De Goeje, Leiden 1907

IBN KHALLIKĀN, ABU'L-ʿABBĀS (d. 681)
Wafayāt al-Aʿyān ed. Wüstenfeld, 13 vols., 1835–45

IBN KHURDĀDHBIH, ʿUBAYD ALLĀH (d. c. 300)
Al-Masālik wa'l-Mamālik ed. De Goeje, Leiden 1889

IBN MANẒŪR, ABU'L-FAḌL (d. 711)
Lisān al-ʿArab Beirut 1955–6

IBN AL-MUʿTAZZ, IBN AL-MUTAWAKKIL (d. 296)
Dīwān Beirut 1961

IBN AL-NADĪM, MUḤAMMAD B. ISḤĀQ (d. 377)
Fihrist Istaqāma Press, Cairo; Eng. Tr. by Bayard Dodge, New York, London 1970

IBN MIHMANDĀR, YAZDAJARD AL-FĀRSĪ (3rd century)
Faḍā'il Baghdād ed. M. ʿAwād, Baghdad 1962

IBN QUTAYBA, ʿABDULLĀH B. MUSLIM (d. 276)
ʿUyūn al-Akhbār Cairo 1925–30

IBN QAYYIM AL-JAWZIYYA ABŪ ʿABD ALLĀH SHAMS AL-DĪN (d. 751)
1. *Aḥkām ahl al-dhimma* Damascus 1961
2. *Al-Furūsiyya* Cairo 1360/1941

IBN RUSTA ABŪ ʿALĪ AḤMAD (about 310)
Al-Aʿlāq al-Nafīsa Leiden 1892

IBN SAʿD, MUḤAMMAD (d. 230)
Kitāb al-Ṭabaqāt Leiden 1321–59

IBN SĪDA ʿALĪ B. ISMĀʿĪL (d. 458)
Al-Mukhaṣṣaṣ Bulāq 1321, reprinted from Beirut n.d.

IBN ṬAYFŪR AḤMAD B. ABĪ ṬĀHIR (d. 280)
Kitāb Baghdād Leipzig 1904 (also 1368/1949)

IBN AL-ṬIQṬIQA, MUḤAMMAD B. ʿALĪ B. ṬABĀṬABĀ (d. 709)
Al-Fakhrī fī ādāb al-sulṭāniyya Paris 1895; Eng. Tr. by C. E. J. P. Whitting, London 1947

IBN ZUBAYR, AL-QĀḌĪ AL-RASHĪD (5th century)
Al-Dhakhā'ir wa'l-Tuḥaf ed. M. Hamidullah, Kuwait 1959

IBN AL-UKHUWWA, MUḤAMMAD B. MUḤAMMAD (d. 729)
Maʿālim al-Qurba fī Aḥkām al-ḥisba ed. with abridged Tr. by R. Levy, Cambridge 1937

AL-IṢṬAKHRĪ, ABŪ ISḤĀQ (d. 346)
Kitāb al-Masālik wa'l-Mamālik ed. De Goeje, Leiden 1927

AL-JĀḤIẒ, ʿAMR B. BAḤR (d. 225)
1. *Al-Bayān wa'l-tabyīn* Cairo 1960–1
2. *Al-Ḥayawān* Cairo 1938–47
3. *Al-Bukhalā'* ed. T. Ḥājirī, 1958
4. *Al-Tabaṣṣur bi'l-tijāra* (attr.) Cairo 1935; also 1966
5. *Rasā'il al-Jāḥiẓ* (collection of 17 *risāla*) Cairo 1964
6. *Al-Maḥāsin wa'l-aḍdād* Cairo 1234/1818

7. *Kitāb al-Tarbīʿ waʾl-tadwīr* Damascus 1955
8. *Kitāb al-Tāj fī akhbār al-Mulūk,* (attr.) Cairo 1914

AL-JAHSHIYĀRĪ, MUḤAMMAD B. ʿABDŪS (d. 331) — *Al-Wuzarāʾ waʾl-kuttāb* Cairo 1938

AL-JAWĀLĪQĪ, MAWHŪB B. AḤMAD (d. 539) — *Al-Muʿarrab min al-kalām al-Aʿjamī* Cairo 1361/1942

AL-KHĀLIDIYYĀN, ABŪ BAKR B. MUḤAMMAD (380) and ABŪ ʿUTHMĀN SAʿĪD (d. 390) — *Al-Tuḥaf waʾl-hadāyā* Egypt (1956)

AL-KALBĪ, HISHĀM (d. 207) — *Ansāb al-Khayl*, ed. Zakī Pashā, Cairo 1946

AL-KHAWĀRIZMĪ, MUḤAMMAD AḤMAD (387) — *Mafātīḥ al-ʿUlūm* Maṭbaʿa al-Sharq 1930

AL-KHAFĀJĪ, SHIHĀB AL-DĪN AḤMAD (d. 1069) — *Shifāʾ al-Ghalīl fīmā fī kalām al-ʿArab min al-dakhīl* Cairo 1325/1907

KHUSRAW, NĀṢIR — *Safar-nāma*, ed. and trans. by C. Schefer, Paris 1881

AL-KINDĪ, MUḤAMMAD B. YŪSUF (d. 350) — *Kitāb al-Umarāʾ wa kitāb al-quḍāt* ed. R. Guest, London 1912

KUSHĀJIM, MAḤMŪD B. ḤUSAIN (360)
1. *Al-Maṣāyid waʾl-Maṭārid* Baghdad 1954
2. *Adab al-Nadīm* Bulāq 1298/1880

AL-KĀZARŪNĪ, ẒAHĪR AL-DĪN ʿALĪ B. MUḤAMMAD (d. 697)
1. *Maqāma fī qawāʾid Baghdād* Baghdad 1962
2. *Mukhtaṣar al-Taʾrīkh min awwal al-zamān ilā muntahā dawlat banī ʿAbbās* Baghdad 1970

AL-MAQDISĪ, MUṬAHHAR (d. 355)
1. *Al-Badʾ waʾl-Taʾrīkh* Paris 1899–1906

MĀRĪ B. SULAYMĀN — *Akhbār faṭāriqa kursīʾl-Mashriq* ed. Gesmondi, Rome 1899

AL-MASʿŪDĪ ABUʾL-ḤASAN (345 or 346)
1. *Murūj al-Dhahab* ed. de Meynard, Paris 1861–77
2. *Al-Tanbīh waʾl-Ishrāf* Leiden 1894

MATTĪ (IBN ʿAMR) — *Akhbār faṭāriqa kursī al-Mashriq* ed. Gesmondi, Rome 1896

AL-MĀWARDĪ, ʿALĪ B. MUḤAMMAD (d. 450) — *Al-Aḥkām al-Sulṭāniyya* Cairo 1298/1881; 1380/1960

MISKĀWAYH, AḤMAD B. MUḤAMMAD (d. 421)
1. *Tajārib al-umam* Oxford 1921
2. *Tahdhīb al-Akhlāq* 1326/1908

AL-MUQADDASĪ (MAQDISĪ), MUḤAMMAD B. AḤMAD (d. 375) — *Aḥsan al-Taqāsīm fī maʿrifat al-aqālīm* ed. De Goeje, Leiden 1906 (*BGA*, III)

MUḤAMMAD AL-MANGALĪ (d. after AD 1371) — *Uns al-Malāʾ bi waḥsh al-falāʾ* Paris 1880

AL-MAKKĪ, MUḤAMMAD B. ʿALĪ (d. 386) — *Qūt al-Qulūb* Cairo 1351

AL-NADĪM, ABŪ ISḤĀQ IBRĀHĪM AL-RAQĪQ (d. after 417)	*Quṭub al-surūr fī awṣāf al-khumūr* Damascus 1389/1969
AL-NUWAYRĪ, AḤMAD B. ʿABD AL-WAHHĀB (732)	*Nihāyat al-Arab fī funūn al-adab* Cairo 1923–1955
AL-QALQASHANDĪ, ABU'L ʿABBĀS AḤMAD (821)	*Ṣubḥ al-Aʿshā fī ṣanāʿat al-Inshā* Cairo 1919–1922
QIFṬĪ, JAMĀL AL-DĪN (d. 646)	*Ta'rīkh al-Ḥukamā'*, Leipzig 1903
AL-QĀRĪ, ABŪ MUḤAMMAD JAʿFAR B. AḤMAD (499)	*Maṣārīʿ al-ʿUshshāq* Beirut 1378/1958
AL-QĀḌĪ JURJĀNĪ, AḤMAD B. MUḤAMMAD (482)	*Al-Muntakhab min kināyāt al-udabā' wa'l-ishārāt al-bulaghā'* 1326/1908
AL-RĀGHIB, AL-ḤUSAIN B. MUḤAMMAD AL-IṢFAHĀNĪ (about 502)	*Muḥāḍarāt al-udabā' wa muḥāwarāt al-shuʿarā' wa'l-bulaghā'* Beirut 1961
AL-ṢĀBĪ, HILĀL B. MUḤASSIN (d. 448)	1. *Rusūm dār al-khilāfa* Baghdad 1383/1964 2. *Al-Wuzarā'* ed. A. S. A. Farrāj 1958
AL-SAQAṬĪ, MUHAMMAD B. AḤMAD (5th or 6th century)	*Fī Ādāb al-ḥisba* Paris 1931
AL-SARRĀJ, JAʿFAR B. AḤMAD	*Mashārīʿ al-ushshāq* Constantinople 1301
AL-SHĀBUSHTĪ, ʿALĪ B. MUḤAMMAD (d. 388)	*Al-Diyārāt* Baghdad 1966
AL-SAMʿĀNĪ, ABŪ SAʿD (d. 562)	*Al-Ansāb* Hyderabad 1962–6
AL-SHAYBĀNĪ, MUHAMMAD B. ḤASAN (189)	*Al-Makhārij fi'l-ḥiyal* ed. J. Schacht Leipzig 1930
AL-SHAYZARĪ, ʿABD AL-RAḤMĀN B. NAṢR (589)	*Nihāyat al-rutba fī ṭalab al-ḥisba* Cairo 1365/1946
AL-ṢŪLĪ, ABŪ BAKR (d. 335 or 336)	1. *Kitāb al-Awrāq* London 1934 2. *Ashʿār awlād al-khulafā'* London 1936 3. *Akhbār al-Rāḍī wa'l-Muttaqī* Cairo 1935 4. *Adab al-kuttāb* Cairo 1341/1923
AL-SUYŪṬĪ, ʿABD AL-RAḤMĀN (d. 911)	1. *Ta'rīkh al-Khulafā'* Cairo 1964 2. *Al-Mustaẓraf*
AL-ṬABARĪ, MUḤAMMAD B. JARĪR (d. 310)	*Ta'rīkh al-Rusul wa'l-mulūk* ed. De Goeje Leyden 1879–1901
AL-ṬĀLAQĀNĪ, QĀḌĪ ABU'L-ḤASAN (5th century)	*Risāla al-Amthāl al-Baghdādiyya allatī tajrī bain al-ʿāmma* ed. Massignon, Cairo n.d.
AL-TANŪKHĪ, MUḤASSIN B. ʿALĪ (d. 384)	1. *Al-Faraj baʿd al-shidda* Cairo 1375/1955; also, Cairo 1903 2. *Nishwār al-Muḥāḍara*, i, ed. D. S. Margoliouth, Cairo 1921; ii, published in *RAAD*, vols 12, 13, 17; viii, Damascus 1348/1930; Eng. Tr. by Margoliouth, London 1922
AL-TAWḤĪDĪ, ABŪ ḤAYYĀN (d. about 387)	*Al-Imtāʿ wa'l-Mu'ānasa* Cairo 1939–44
AL-THAʿĀLIBĪ, ʿABD AL-MĀLIK (d. 429)	1. *Yatīmat al-Dahr* Cairo 1947 2. *Laṭā'if al-Maʿārif* ed. Abyārī, Cairo 1960;

Eng. Tr. by C. E. Bosworth, Edinburgh 1968
3. *Thimār al-Qulūb* Cairo 1965
4. *Al-Tamthīl wa'l-Muḥāḍara* Cairo 1381/1961
5. *Khāṣṣ al-khāṣṣ* Cairo 1326/1909
6. *Fiqh al-Lugha* Cairo 1357/1938

WAKĪʿ, MUḤAMMAD B. KHALAF (d. 306) — *Akhbār al-Quḍāt* Cairo 1947

AL-WASHSHĀ', MUḤAMMAD B. ISḤĀQ (325) — *Al-Muwashshā* Beirut 1965

AL-YAʿQŪBĪ, AḤMAD B. WAḌĪḤ (d. 284)
1. *Ta'rīkh* ed. Houtsma, Leiden 1883
2. *Buldān* ed. De Goeje, Leiden 1891–2 (*BGA*, VII)
3. *Mushākalāt al-Nās fī zamānihim* Tehran 1323

YĀQŪT AL-RŪMĪ, AL-ḤAMAWĪ (626)
1. *Muʿjam al-Buldān* ed. F. Wüstenfeld, Leipzig 1866–70
2. *Irshād al-Arīb ila maʿrifat al-adīb* ed. Margoliouth, London 1907–26

ZUBAYDĪ, MUḤIBB AL-DĪN (1205) — *Tāj al-ʿArūs min Jawāhir al Qāmūs* Cairo 1306

USĀMA, IBN MUNQIDH (d. AD 1188) — *Kitāb al-Iʿtibār* Princeton, 1930; Eng. Tr. by P. K. Hitti 1929

ANONYMOUS, (The Falconer of the Fatimid Caliph ʿAzīz Bi'llāh AD 975–6) — *Al-Bayzara*, ed. Kurd ʿAlī, Damascus, 1953, French translation by F. Viré *Le traite de l'art de volerie*, Leiden 1967

(C) *Modern Books*

ʿABD AL-QĀDIR AL-JAZĀ'IRĪ — *Nukhbat ʿIqd al-Ajyād fi'l-ṣāfinat al-jiyād* Beirut 1326

ABU NAṢR, ʿUMAR — *Al-Hawā wa'l-shabāb fī ʿahd al-Rashīd* Beirut 1955

AḤMAD TAYMŪR, Pasha — *Laʿb al-ʿArab* Cairo 1367/1948

ASHTOR, ELIYAHU
1. *Histoire des prix et des salaires dans l'orient médiéval* Paris 1969
2. *A Social and Economic History of the Near East in the Middle Ages*, London 1976

BADRĪ, M. FAHD
1. *Al-ʿĀmma fi'l-qarn al-khāmis al-hijrī* Baghdad 1967
2. *Al-ʿImāma* Baghdad 1969

BEGG, M. A. J. — *The Social History of the Labouring Classes in ʿIraq under the ʿAbbasids* Ph.D. Cambridge 1971

BOWEN, H. — *The Life and Times of ʿAlī b. ʿĪsā* Cambridge 1928

BRITTON, N. P. — *A Study of Some Early Islamic Textiles in the Museum of Fine Arts* Boston 1938

AL-BUSTĀNĪ, BUṬRUS — *Muḥīt al-Muḥīt* Beirut 1870

BUTLER — *Islamic Pottery* London 1926

CRESWELL, K. A. C. — *Early Muslim Architecture* Oxford 1932–40

DICKSON, H. R. P. — *The Arab of the Desert*, London, fifth edition, 1972

DOZY, R. P. A. —
1. *Dictionnaire détaillé des noms des vêtements chez les Arabes* Amsterdam 1845
2. *Supplément aux dictionnaires arabes* Leiden 1927

DŪRĪ, A. A. K. —
1. *Ta'rīkh al-ʿIrāq al-Iqtisādī fi'l-qarn al-rābiʿ al-hijrī* Baghdad 1948
2. *Studies on the Economic Life of Mesopotamia in the 10th century* Ph.D. thesis, SOAS 1942

GOITEIN, S. D. —
1. *Studies in Islamic History and Institutions* Leiden 1966
2. *Mediterranean Society*, 2 vols, California 1966–71

GOLDZIHER, IGNAC — *Muslim Studies*, I–II; Eng. Tr. by C. R. Barber and S. M. Stern, London 1967–71

GRUNEBAUM, G. E. VON, — *Muhammadan Festivals* New York 1951

HAMEED, ABDUL AZIZ — *The Stucco Ornaments of Samarra*, Ph.D. thesis, SOAS 1962

HASAN, IBRAHIM HASAN — *Islam—a Religious, Political, Social and Economic study* Baghdad 1967

HINZ, W. — *Islamische Masse und Gewichte*, Leiden 1955

HITTI, P. K. — *History of the Arabs* (9th ed.) New York 1968

HOURANI, A. H. and S. M. — *The Islamic City*, Papers on Islamic History I, Stern, ed. Oxford 1970

IRAQ *Wizārat al-Maʿārif* — *Ḥafriyāt Sāmarrā* (*Excavations at Samarra*), *1936–39*, Arabic and English, Baghdad 1940

JALĪL ḌIYĀPŪR — *Pūshāk ba-āstāni Īrāniyān az Kuhan tarīn zamān tā payān shāhanshāhī sāsāniyān* Tehran 1343

KAHHĀLA, UMAR RIḌĀ — *Muʿjam al-Mu'allifīn* Damascus 1957–61

KÜHNEL, ERNEST —
1. *Catalogue of Dated Tiraz Fabrics Umayyad, Abbasid, Fatimid* 1952
2. *Islamic Arts*; Eng. Tr. by K. Watson, Germany 1970

LAMM, C. J. — *Cotton in Medieval Textiles of the Near East* Paris 1937

LANE, ARTHUR —
1. *Early Islamic Wares* London 1950
2. *Islamic Pottery from the 9th to the 14th centuries AD* in the collection of Eldred Hitchcock, with an introduction by A. Lane, London 1956

LANE, E. W. —
1. *Manners and Customs of the Modern Egyptians* London 1836
2. *Arabic-English Lexicon* London 1863–93

LATHAM, J. D. and W. F. PATERSON — *Saracen Archery—An English version and exposition of a Mamluk work on archery* London 1970

LEVY, R. — *The Social Structure of Islam* Cambridge 1957

LEWIS, B. — *The Arabs in History* London 1966

LE STRANGE — *The Lands of the Eastern Caliphate* reprinted London 1966

MAḤFŪẒ — *Shaṭranj* Cairo 1968

MAYER, L. A. — 1. *Mamluk Costume* Switzerland 1952
2. *Saracenic History: A Survey* Oxford 1933

MERCIER, L. — *La Chasse et les Sports chez les Arabes* Paris 1927

MEZ, A. — *The Renaissance of Islam*; Eng. Tr. by K. Bakhsh and Margoliouth, Patna 1937

MIAH, M. S. — *The Reign of al-Mutawakkil with special reference to religion, culture and government in the Islamic Empire*, Ph.D. thesis, SOAS 1962

MIRZĀ, TĪMŪR — *Bāz Nāma-e-Naṣirī*, English translation by D. C. Phillott, London 1968

MUIR, S. W. — *The Caliphate: Its Rise, Decline and Fall*, Beirut 1963, reprint of 1898 edition

MUNAJJID, ṢALĀH AL-DĪN — *Bain al-Khulafā' wa'l-Khula'ā'* Beirut 1957

MURRAY, H. J. R. — *A History of Chess* reprint, Oxford 1962

NAJM, W. T. — *Studies on the writings of al-Jāḥiẓ*, Ph.D. thesis, SOAS 1958

NAJI, N. J. — *Baṣra* (295–447/907–1055), Ph.D. thesis, SOAS 1970

PELLAT, CH. — *Life and works of Jāḥiẓ*; Eng. Tr. by D. M. Hawke, 1969

ROSENTHAL, F. — 1. *Four Essays on Art and Literature in Islam*, Leiden 1971
2. *Gambling in Islam*, Leiden 1975
3. *Humour in Early Islam*, Leiden 1956

ṢABBĀGH, M. N. — *Kitāb Musābaqāt al-barq wa'l-ghamām fī sā'āt al-ḥamām* Paris 1805

SĀMARRĀ'Ī — *Agriculture in Iraq in the 3rd/9th century*, Ph.D. thesis SOAS 1972

SARRÉ, F. — *Die keramik von Samarra* (*Die Augrabungen von Samarra, Band II*) Berlin 1925

SERJEANT, R. B. — 1. *Material for a History of Islamic Textiles up to the Mongol Conquest* Reprinted from *AI*, xi–xii, 1942–6
2. *South Arabian Hunt*, London 1976

SHABAN, M. A. — *Islamic History: A New Interpretation No. 2, AD 750–1055 (AH 132–448)*, Cambridge 1976

SHAWKATĪ, YĀR MUḤAMMAD KHĀN — *Ṣayd gāh-i-Shawkatī*, English translation by E. S. Harcourt in *Two Treatises on Falconry* Reprinted from the 1908 edition, London 1968

SOMOGYI, J. D. 1. *Muslim Table Games* Reprinted from *IQ* 1956–7, pp. 236–44
2. *The Arabic Chess MSS. in the John Rynalds Library* Reprinted from the *Bulletin J.R.L.* 41, 1959, pp. 430–45

TRITTON, A. S. *The Caliphs and their non-Muslim Subjects* London 1930

WENSINCK, A. J. and others *Concordance et Indices de la Tradition Musulmane* 7 vols., Leiden 1936–69

ZAKY, HASAN *Hunting as practised in Arab countries of the Middle Ages* Cairo 1937

ZAYDĀN, JURJĪ *Ta'rīkh al-Tamaddun al-Islāmī* Cairo 1904

(D) *Articles in Periodicals, Encyclopaedias etc.*

AL-ʿALI, S. A. 1. "Al-Albisat al-ʿArabiyya fī qarn al-awwal al-hijrī", *MMII* 1966
2. "The Foundation of Baghdad", in *The Islamic City* Oxford 1970, pp. 87–101
3. "A New version of Ibn al-Muṭarrif's list of revenues in the early times of Hārūn al-Rashīd", *JEHSO*, 1971, pp. 301–10

ASHTOR, E. 1. "Essai sur les prix et les salaires dans l'empire califen", *RSO*, 36, 1961, pp. 19–69
2. "Essai sur l'alimentation des diverses classes sociales dans l'orient médiéval", *AESC*, 23, iv–vi, 1968, pp. 1017–53
3. "The diet of salaried classes in the medieval Near East", *JAH*, iv, 1970, pp. 1–24

ʿAWĀD, MIKHĀ'ĪL 1. "Danniyyat al-qāḍī fi'l-ʿasr al-ʿAbbāsī", *Al-Risāla*, x, 1942, pp. 979–81; pp. 1006–7
2. "Al-ʿuṭlatu'l-usbūʿīyya fi'l-dawlat al-ʿAbbāsiyya", *RAAD*, 18, 1939, pp. 52–8

AYALON, DAVID 1. "Notes on the *Furūsiyya* exercises and games in the Mamluk Sultanate in *Scripta Hierosolymitana*", ix, *Studies in Islamic History and Civilization*, Jerusalem 1961, pp. 31–62
2. "Furūsiyya", EI^2

CANARD, M. 1. "Le riz dans le proche Orient aux premiers siècles de l'Islam", *Arabica* vi, 1959, pp. 113–31
2. "Byzantium and the Muslim world to the Middle of the 11th century", *The Cambridge Medieval History* new ed. 1966, iv, Pt. I

CRESWELL, K. A. C. "Architecture", EI^2

DOUILLET, G. "Furūsiyya", EI^2

DŪRĪ, A. A. "Baghdad", EI^2

EHRENKREUTZ, A. S. 1. "Studies in the monetary history of the Near East in the Middle Ages", *JESHO*, ii, 1959, pp. 128–161; vi, 1963, pp. 243–77
2. "The kurr system in medieval Iraq", *JESHO* v, 1962
3. "The taṣrīf and tasʿīr calculations in medieval Mesopotamian fiscal operations", *JESHO*, vii, 1964, pp. 46–56

GHANĪMA, R. "Ṣanāʿat al-ʿIrāq fī ʿahd al-ʿAbbāsiyīn", *MGT* Baghdad 1941, pp. 563–84

GHAZI, M. F. "Un groupe social 'les raffinés' (ẓurafā')", *SI*, xi, 1959, pp. 39–71

IQBAL, MUHAMMAD "Nawrūz", *Oriental College Magazine* Lahore 1969, serial no. 178, vol. 45, no. 3, pp. 132–63

JAWĀD, MUṢṬAFĀ "Al-Azyā' al-shaʿbīʿa, Majalla Turāth al-Shaʿbī", no. 8, 1964

JOMER, J. "Amīr al-Ḥadjdj", *EI*²

LICHTENSTAEDTER, I. "The distinctive dress of non-Muslims", *Historia Judaica*, xxx, 1943, pp. 35–52

LEWIS, BERNARD 1. "Government, Society and economic life under the ʿAbbasids and Fatimids", *Cambridge Medieval History* new ed. 1966, pp. 639–61
2. "Sources for the economic history of the Middle East", *Studies in the economic history of the Middle East* ed. M.A. Cook, London 1970
3. "Ḥadjdj", *EI*²

LEVY, R. 1. "Notes on costume from Arabic sources", *JRAS* 1935, pp. 319–38
2. "Nawrūz", *EI*¹

MASSE, H. "Čawgān", *EI*²

MITTWOCH, E. "ʿĪd, ʿĪd al-Fiṭr, ʿĪd al-Aḍḥā", *EI*²

PELLAL, Ch. "Khaysh", *EI*²

PHILLOTT, D. C. and AZOO, R. F. 1. "Chapters on hunting dogs and cheetahs, being an extract from the Kitāb al-Bayzara, a treatise on falconry by Ibn Kushājim, an Arab writer of the 10th Century", *JASB*, N.S. 3, 1907, pp. 47–50
2. "On hunting dogs, being an extract from the Kitāb al-Jamhara fī ʿilm al-bayzara", *JASB*, N.S. 3, 1907, pp. 599–600

PLESSNER, M. "Ramaḍān", *EI*¹

RAZIQ, A. A. "La Chasse au faucon d'après des céramiques du Musée du Caire", *Annales Islamologiques*, ix, 1970, pp. 109–21

RODINSON, M. 1. "Recherches sur les documents arabes relatifs à la cuisine", *REI*, 17, 1949, pp. 95–158
2. "Ghidhā'", *EI*²

ROGERS, J. M. "Sāmarrā: a Study in Medieval Town Planning" in *The Islamic City*, ed. by A. H. Hourani and S. M. Stern, Oxford 1970, pp. 119–55

SCANLON, G. T. "Housing and Sanitation: Some Aspects of Medieval Public Service" in *The Islamic City*, ed. by A. H. Hourani and S. M. Stern, Oxford 1970, pp. 179–93

SERJEANT, R. B. "A Zaidi manual of ḥisba of the 3rd century hijra", *RSO*, 28, 1953, pp. 1–34

SOURDEL, D. "Questions de cérémonial Abbaside", *REI*, 1960, pp. 121–48

SOURDEL-THOMINE, J. "Ḥammām", *EI*²

TRITTON, A. S.
1. "Islam and protected religions", *JRAS*, 1927, pp. 479–84
2. "Sketches of life under the caliphs", *MW*, 1964, pp. 104–11; 170–9; 1972, pp. 137–47

VIRÉ, F.
1. "Bayzara", *EI*²
2. "Fahd", *EI*²
3. "Ibn ʿIrs", *EI*²
4. "Faras", *EI*²
5. "Ḥamām", *EI*²
6. "Khayl", *EI*²

WALTER, B.
1. "Sirwāl", *EI*¹
2. "Turban", *EI*¹

WHITEHOUSE, DAVID *Excavations at Siraf, in Iran*, 1968–72

ZAYYĀT, Ḥ.
1. "Azyat al-Akmām", *Mashriq*, 1947, pp. 465–76
2. "Fann al-ṭabākha wa islāḥ al-aṭʿima fi'l-Islām", *Mashriq*, 1947, pp. 1–26
3. "Ādāb al-mā'ida fi'l-Islām", *Mashriq*, 37, 1939, pp. 162–9
4. "Lughat al-ḥaḍāra fi'l-Islām", *Mashriq*, 1969, pp. 423–542
5. "Thiyāb al-Washī", *Mashriq*, 1947, pp. 106–15
6. "Thiyāb al-Shurb", *Mashriq*, 1947, pp. 137–141
7. "Khubz al-aruzz", *Mashriq*, 1937, pp. 377–380
8. "Khubz al-abāzīr", *Mashriq*, 1937, pp. 380–381
9. "Kitāb al-Ṭabākha", *Mashriq*, 1937, pp. 370–6
10. "Muṭāliʿat al-dafātir wa'l-kutub wa'l-lahw bi'l-alʿāb fi'l-mujtamaʿ qadīman", *Mashriq*, 35, 1937, pp. 499–500

Index

India:
imports from: books, 74; chicken, 79, hawks, 216, 217; silk, 33; shoes, 50n; spices, 103–4; sugar, 100; buffaloes introduced from, 81; dates exported to, 145; gifts to princes, 54–5; dress in Sind, 35; cooks (slaves), 155
iqlīm (regions), 19
Iṣfahān:
fruit drinks from, 112; honey from, 102; houses in, 180, 194; saffron from, 104–5
isfidbāj (dish), 83–4
Ishāq b. Ibrāhīm (singer), 154
Ishāq al-Isrā'īlī, 80
Ismā'īl b. Ahmad, 206
izār (garment), 21, 34–5, 43; price of, 71

jarīb (weight), 138
Ja'far al-Barmakī, 248
Ja'far b. Yahyā (wazir), 36, 56
al-Ja'fariya, building of, 150
Jamīla bint Nāsir al-Dawla, 116, 282
al-Jawārihiyya (form of chess), 15, 266
Jews, hostelries kept by, 271
Jibāl, houses in, 180
Jibra'īl b. Bakhtishū (Hārūn's physician), 26, 62; and diet, 118; house cooled, 183; heated, 186
Jilān, hawks from, 216
jizya (poll tax), 188
jubba (garment), 10, 40; price of, 74
judge (*qāḍī*), 15, 20–1; costume, 43, 55; cost of, 72
Jum'a (weekly holy day), 283–4
jurāb, *jawrab* (socks), 50
Jurfan:
dress in, 65; vegetables in market of, 93
al-Jurjani, 'Abdallah Abu'l-Qasim (*muhaddith*), 93

Ka'ba (Holy Place in Mecca), 69
kabāb, 133
kabīr (dignitaries), dress of, 65
Kāfūr (Fatimid General), 128
kāmakh (a savoury), 106–7
Kaskar:
food production and prices in, 144; goat and fish from, 85
kālīb, see *kuttab*
khabīs (jelly dish), 100
Khālid al-Barmakī, 246
Khālid b. Yahyā, 133
kharāj (land tax), 101, 102–3, 104, 206
Khārijites, and archery, 223
khātam (signet ring), 281
"*Khatm*" ("sealing"), 276
khaṭīb (pl. *khutabā* preacher), 284; dress of, 64
Khaysh—canvas (for cooling houses), 120, 181–4
Khazz:
material from, 60; and *khazz*-silk, 57
khil'a (robe of honour), price of, 75
khirqa (garment), 58
khiṣyan (eunuchs), and pigeon-racing, 262
khuff (top boots), 48, 50; price of, 72
Khurāsān:
and Abbasid revolution, 59; cook, 155; dress, 65, of soldiers, 59–60 and n; edible earth, 113, fabrics, 55, 57; *hajj* pilgrims from, 280; material from, 66
khuṭba (sermon), 284
Khūzistān:
dress in, 35, 64; sugar from, 101; rice bread in, 90
Khwārazm:
cheese from, 98; fruit from, 110; melons in ice from, 115
al-Kindi, qāḍī, 20–1
Kirmān:
date cultivation in, 145–6; dress and textile industry in, 65; robes from Bamm in, 72; spices from, 104
kisā (garment), 43, 44; price of, 71–2
al-Kitābī, Nāhid b. Thauma (poet), 88
knife and spoon, 163
Kufa, products from:
boots, 74; fabric, 52; *khazz*-silk, 57; vegetables, 92, 93
Kūhī, materials, 57 and n
Kuhistān, sugar-cane from, 101
Kurds, market for produce of, 151
kurr (weight), 138
kuṭṭāb (sing. *katib*, secretaries), 17; costume of, 29, 40, 55

land, for building, cost of, 168–9
lawyers, costume of, 43
lawzīnaj (confection of almonds), 99–100
leeks (*kurrāth*), 84–5
lemons, history of, 109
lion:
buffaloes drive off, 81; hunting, 205, 211, 214, 215, 229; fight buffaloes, 241, 261; locusts, as food, 82, 133–4, 135; lynx-caracal, 210–11

Ma'bad (theologian), 170
madās (sandal), 49
madd (sing. *mudd*, weight), 146n
Madhār, pitchers from, 126
madīra (dish), 82–3
Mahdi, Caliph, 134, 190:
accession of, 294–5; built first hippodrome, 263; daughter, 'Illayya, 67; daughter Yāqūta, 271; and day of rest, 285; *hajj* of, 282; hunting, 204;

theologians, 170; against price control, 137; costume of, 64, 70; and hunting, 242
thieves, 49, 171; as spies, wages of, 148
thiyāb al-munādama (party dress), 56
Thousand and One Nights, 12
tikka (trouser-bands), 57
tiles, 180–1
ṭirāz (inscriptions on dress), 68–70; on *ridā*, 36
toilets, 188–90; cleaners of, 189–90
Transoxiana, dress in, 65
transport:
by canal boats, 187; of food, 150–1; truffles, price of, 146
tufayliyūn (parasites), 7
tujjar (merchants), dress of, 64
turbans, 3n, 30, 31, 38; price of, 72
Turkish soldiers, 52; as archers, 212–13; dress of, 59–60; horse riding, 249
Turks:
dress of, 41; play polo, 253
Turkistan, hawks from, 216, 217
Tus, cooking pots from, 121

'Ubayd Allāh (wazir), and polo, 253
udabā (men of learning), 37
ulamā (pl. *ulema*, men of learning), 37; give guidance on hunting, 241; and chess, 267n
'Umar II, Caliph, abolished *Nawrūz* gifts, 287
ushnān (saltwort), 129, 152, 161, 200

vegetables, 92–7; for *nuql*, 113; preservation of, 116; prices of, 146–7

wages:
builders, 168n; and prices, 136
wajīh (elite), 64
Wakī', Qādī, 20–1
washing:
of garments, 57; of hands, 129, 152, 158–9, 161–2; kitchen utensils, 130
washī (figured stuff), 52–5; price of, 74
Wāsit, products of:
carpets, 192; curtains, 195; pigeons, 237, 251
water:
drinking: carriers, 151, 186; jars for, 126–8; cooling, 127–8; with meals, 164
Wāthiq, Caliph, 94; diet and Christian physician of, 117–18; pigeon racing, 252
wazirs:
celebration of appointment, 295n; costume, 39, 55; cost, 72
weasels, for hunting, 214–16
weddings, 293–4; dish for, 132
weight-lifting, 259
weights:
jarīb, kurr, qafīz, ratl, 138; *madd* (sing. *mudd*), 146n; *mann*, 147
wells, 187
wheat:
growing, 87; price, 138; storage, 117; transport, 150–1
wīdhārī, garments from Samarqand, 72–73
wine, *see* alcohol
women:
dress of, 44, 45, 61, 62, 66–8; as flour-grinders, 87–8; games for, 271–2; middle-class wives as cooks, 155; at public baths, 196; sandals of, 49; spice-pounding by, 104
workmen; cost of living for, 148–9
wrestling, 259

Yahyā b. Masawayh, physician and dietician of Mu'tasim, 118
Ya'qūb b. Layth as-Saffar, 91; kitchen of, 120
Yazīd I, Caliph, and hunting, 204
Yazīd II, Caliph, re-introduced *Nawrūz* gifts, 287
al-Yazīdī, 132
Yemen:
products of: fabrics, 51n, 52, 55; hawks, 216; honey, sugar, 101–2; saluqi dogs, 212, 213, 235
houses of marble in, 180; people prefer beef to mutton, 81

Zaghūr, hounds from, 212
Zalabiya (almond tart), 100
Zanj:
hawks from, 216; rebellion, 136, 140, 296
Ziryāb, arbiter of fashion in Cordova, 96
Zubayda (consort of Hārūn);
dress, 53–4; shoes, 67; slave-girls, 42; underground aqueduct built by, 188
zoo, royal, 204, 205, 261, 262
zuhhād (ascetics) table manners of, 135, 161
zunnār (girdle), 61, 62
zurafā (elegant people):
dress of, 56–8; at meals, 160